D1356274

Weimar to Westminster

Weimar to Westminster

An Autobiography

Peter Rost

Dynasty
Press

ROS

Dynasty Press Ltd
36 Ravensdon Street
London SE11 4AR

www.dynastypress.co.uk

First published in this version by Dynasty Press Ltd, 2010.

ISBN: 978-0-9553507-5-7

Cover Artwork by Two Associates

Photography by David Chambers

Typeset by Strange Attractor Press

Printed and Bound in the United Kingdom

Acknowledgements:

My thanks to the many friends who urged me to record my story, believing with me that the world would be safe, as it was not likely to be published. In particular to Jeannie and Henry Hincks for nagging me until I promised to put pen to paper. To Dyfrig James for encouraging me to go on just when I was losing confidence; to Stephen Clarke for sorting out my dreadful punctuation; to Henk Termeulen for his tireless energy proof reading. To Daniela and Henning von Kapff for less than helpfully telling me to translate it into German; to John and Joan Reeves for advising me it was not commercial unless there is even more name dropping; to Julia Lady Arbuthnot for now refusing to call me 'Peter', but 'Otto Ludwig'. To Lady Colin Campbell for risking her reputation in recommending me to her publisher; to Dynasty for taking such a gamble with me; to Bob Jones for urging me not to give up and sharing memories with me. To Rex, our Irish Terrier, for not complaining too much that his daily rambles with me had to be shortened; to my bank manager for naively believing all this would reduce my obscene overdraft; to Matthew Parris, my former Parliamentary colleague, for advising me to find a 'vanity publisher'; to Richard Page, another former Parliamentary colleague, for telling me "not to bother". To Hilary, above all others, for patiently transcribing my handwriting scribbles, jogging my rusty memory, adding far more than I dare admit to my efforts and not complaining too much about my moody temperamental outbursts. She says she only did it knowing that nobody produces more than one autobiography.

To Judith, Bruno, Jessica and Julius, my children. Also to the many Parliamentary colleagues over my twenty two years that I found hard working, honest and dedicated, yet have recently been severely injured by a greedy, selfish and dishonest, very small minority.

Weimar to Westminster
Introduction

Nobody should attempt an autobiography after reaching their eightieth year when failing memory begins to confuse with fiction. This gives me only one more year . . .

My adopted country, from 1937 when aged seven, has been kind to me. The greatest honour was of course to have been elected to represent a part of that country in Parliament. This story shows how I have tried to repay that trust.

It has taken me many years to pluck up courage to scribble a few pages about my life. The literary world is crowded with ego-trips and it is only after frequent nagging and bullying by family and friends that I have been persuaded to try to put down the events of my life, coherently I hope, on paper!

Over recent years in retirement, I have time and again over the convivial lunches and dinners that make up life in Provence, been urged to record my story rather than just entertain friends with anecdotes of past events. I have resisted until now, partially through inertia and partially through believing that there is nothing particularly special in my life to justify exposure. But so many have said to me that this is untrue; that everybody has in them a biography, I have come almost to believe it.

There is another reason why I have finally overcome my reticence. As an M.P. from 1970 until I retired in 1992, I have been stunned by the exposure of the "Parliamentary Expenses and Allowances" fiasco that has so severely damaged the status of our democratic system. Surely retired Members who have been motivated by the urge to make a constructive contribution to society and not for their own financial or personal gain, deserve to be heard.

I claim my right to be one of those and so perhaps to help in a modest way in restoring public confidence in our system of government.

A few of my Parliamentary colleagues may indeed have been selfishly motivated by prospects of aggrandisement. But I know that the vast majority, with whom I spent twenty two years, were there because they had something worthwhile to contribute to the common good, the well-being of the nation and mankind. Their story and my small part of it, surely needs to be told.

My faith, confidence and belief in our democratic system of Government have to be part of my makeup. It stems from my birth in Germany in 1930 and my subsequent refugee status from Nazism in 1937 at the age of seven. The fear of dictatorship and what it did to me and my family makes the longing to live in a free society, appreciation of its strengths and the possibility of making a positive contribution to its health an imperative. There can be no more powerful motive for striving to play a role, however marginal, in that endeavour.

Peter Rost
August 2009

Chapter One
Heil Hitler!

My earliest memory, at the age of four, indicated the first signs of a devious nature. I hide my head in shame confessing what happened on the balcony of our Berlin apartment. I doubt if I am the only firstborn to show signs of jealousy when faced with the competition of a new arrival. It was my sister, then named Ilse but later anglicised to Margaret. The constant attentions of my parents proudly displaying the new addition to the family, was too painful to accept. The baby, newly delivered from the hospital, was put out on the terrace, well wrapped up in her pram.

A fit of uncontrollable envy overcame me. I grabbed the watering can, filled it and generously sprayed the pram and its contents with volumes of nice cold water from the tap. The arrival of my parents frightened by the noise interrupted the proceedings. Seeing the "scene of the crime" they asked me what I was up to. My reply was inspired and what you would expect from a "criminal" mind; I said that I simply wanted to help my new sister grow a bit faster. A brilliant excuse for an act of blatant violence. I say it was inspired because it produced hilarious laughter instead of the well justified anger that preceded my punishment. Consequently, I was only given a thorough soaking myself from the watering can. The incident may well explain my dislike, even today of showers, preferring baths, saunas or a dip in the swimming pool.

I was born in Berlin in September 1930 in the Weimar Republic until Hitler suspended it in 1933. I cannot claim to be the first Member of the British Parliament to be born in Germany of German parents; but I am told that I may claim to have been the first who started school at the age of six, with a programme that included compulsory activities in the Junior Hitler Youth Movement. Only in more recent years is this sinister part of my childhood something I wanted to publicise. I carefully omitted it from my declaration for my "Who's Who" entry, neither did I boast of it when seeking to be selected to fight for a Parliamentary constituency.

Such a revelation about my Berlin childhood might have proved a difficult hurdle on the road to Westminster; even more potentially damaging could have been the declaration that I was related (distantly I swear) to Karl Marx. My wife's keen genealogical research and questioning of relatives established that my paternal grandmother, Rosa Marx was a second cousin to the author of Das Kapital. My first reaction to this devastating news was disbelief. Surely Hilary's research, although backed up by my cousin, was flawed? If accurate, there must be some way of concealing this? I prepared a barely credible response to cope with the revelation. "Surely you have the wrong Marx family. Perhaps it is the Marks and Spencer's Marks?" At this stage a friend trying to be helpful suggested, "Even better, why not claim it was Groucho Marx?" Our friendship cooled after this contribution to my dilemma! It is little known that Karl Marx suffered from baldness (he is almost always wearing a hat in any photographs). This Marx gene for early baldness has been passed down through our family, affecting my father, my youngest son and my nephew, who were all suffering from acute hair loss in their twenties.

My mother, Elisabeth, came from a "pure Aryan" family according to Hitler's perverted racial theories. Her hair was blond, eyes blue and some of her family duly joined the Nazi party. Her sister, Tillo, was married to a moderately successful businessman, with a factory in Frankfurt am Maine, producing metal windows and doors for the building trade.

As the German economy began to boom as a result of re-armament orders, my uncle was offered large tempting contracts to convert from window frames to military hardware. Of course, so I was always told by way of apology, this profitable business could only be offered to paid up members of the Nazi party!

My father came from a Jewish family background. He was an atheist and I have no evidence that he ever entered a synagogue in adult life. But under Hitler's anti-Semitic laws, my parents' marriage had its legal status removed. So called mixed-marriages were forbidden and those so trapped became branded with the stigma of social outcasts in "respectable" society. An incident, in 1936 when I was six, highlights the dilemma caused. For some years I had the pleasure of spending my summer holidays with my mother's sister and my cousins, August, Günter and Hannelore. They had a splendid "mini mansion" set in the idyllic grounds in the forest outside Frankfurt.

When the time came for my annual stay to play with my cousins, my mother was informed by her sister that it was no longer "appropriate" for her family to be seen playing with and entertaining a "half-Jewish" boy. My parents were told that as nominal supporters of the Nazi party and dependant on the orders for arms, I could no longer be welcome. Naturally, it was impossible for me to understand why I was rejected. But this was one of the incidents, among others, that made my father realise that the Germany he was brought up in and loved was no longer a country safe for him to stay in.

My father, Frederick Rosenstiel, was a budding economic journalist, an editor with Germany's Frankfurter Zeitung, now re-founded as the Frankfurter Allgemeine Zeitung. We lived in Berlin because the newspaper's main office was there, although both my parents came from what is broadly called the Rhineland.

My father's family came from Wiesbaden, then a modestly small town on the Rhein. His mother's family, the Marxes, owned a large important department store in the town. The Marx family was highly respected and my grandmother, in spite of all the later deprivations, always regarded herself as of a superior standing to the rest. Steep slopes all covered with vineyards rose above and beside the river and town. Wine was the principal activity and my grandfather, Oskar, was a wine merchant and had a small vineyard. I have memories of walking through the vines with him while he talked about them. Presumably my taste for a full bodied, yeasty, fruity, aromatic "Rhein wein" is in my genes.

My mother's family lived in Offenbach, now an unrecognisable conurbation five miles from the centre of Frankfurt, but then a separate community. My maternal grandfather ran a traditional hardware store, of which we have so few left in the U.K. The French still have "quincailleries" in the villages, but they too are giving way to the super stores. The Merz family store sold all sorts of tools, animal feed and the goods required by what was still then a basically rural economy. I can still recall the musty smells wafting from the huge warehouse at the back, filled with sacks of fertilisers, chicken food and much else. The store was on the main road to Frankfurt and I watched fascinated the noisy rattling trams that passed by every few minutes.

Both my parents were from the solid middle class German bourgeoisie – what used to be described as the merchant classes, shopkeepers and wine chandlers. However, my father with a university degree in economics moved up a stage in Germany's social structure and so joined the professional classes. Moreover their life in Berlin, in a spacious apartment, in a well to do suburb, was cultured and refined. I recall the regular entertaining, with quite elegant dinner parties. The gold rimmed Rosenthal porcelain dinner service was set out on the table and the guest lists included a broad spectrum of Berlin's artistic elite, particularly from the musical and journalistic world.

On one such occasion, I was severely punished. My mother and her cook were preparing the evening meal and I was left to my own devices. A large bowl of preserved cherries had already been placed in the dining room on the side table, next to the starched white linen covered dining table set for the eight guests. I found my way in and clambering on a chair, I started devouring the desert with glee.

The disaster was not discovered until the guests had arrived and the dinner was underway. It was too late to prepare the missing sweet course. I was called in, having already spent some time in the bathroom with a severe stomach ache which was on the point of turning into a more rapid discharge of the dozens of stones that I had swallowed with the cherries.

My punishment would no doubt have been more serious if the guests had not succumbed to hilarious mirth and pleaded for leniency on my behalf. I am not sure which was worse, the painful belly or being laughed at by a roomful of grown-ups.

It was not only the Nazi regime that disapproved of "mixed marriages". Not at the time in Germany, but later on I felt the vibes that neither my mothers' nor my fathers' family approved of the marriage. I cannot recall any occasion when the two sides socialised together. German society was already evolving an "apartheid" attitude by the mid 1930s, actively encouraged by Hitler's propaganda machine. My mother in particular found the new attitudes difficult to cope with. She was an attractive woman and was embarrassed to find herself targeted by the regime. She received an official visit from a handsome blond haired SS officer, who explained that now her marriage was no longer officially recognised, she was free to marry a real Aryan German and start a new family for the Fatherland. I was a red-haired fair skinned child and my mother was assured that I would be accepted in the new order. My dark haired little sister was not mentioned. This visitation, in my father's absence was more terrifying than it sounds. In some blunt language my mother was warned that she needed to give serious thought to her position.

The brainwashing, anti-Semitic, pro Nazi doctrines were particularly pronounced in schools. Vivid memories remain of my two years at primary school in Berlin, before we emigrated in 1937. The mid-morning break, when youngsters in free democratic societies run around, talking and playing together with their friends , eating their snacks, was no longer the way in Germany. Instead we were obliged to march round and round the playground in single file, solitary figures eating our apple or whatever. A prefect in Hitler Youth uniform stood in the middle ensuring correct participation in the "exercise". Presumably, this system was designed to inculcate discipline and organised behaviour from the age of five. There was no opportunity to communicate or talk with the other children.

The discipline in the classroom would impress the staunchest hard line British teacher. Silence and perfect behaviour, of course, on the teacher's approach to the class. On entry, a military style stand to attention and a smart "Hitler salute" before sitting down again once the teacher had come to their desk. The wall behind the teacher was covered with an enormous map of Europe. Mid thirties Germany was in blood red; much of the rest of Europe was coloured pink – Poland, Austria, Czechoslovakia, parts of Denmark, disputed areas of France "stolen from the Fatherland" after the First World War – these were all German speaking territories with a Germanic culture, economic ties and lifestyles, " desperate to be reunited with the Fatherland". And Hitler, we were told, was determined to get them back.

Such brainwashing from the age of five, day after day, produced, not surprisingly, the fanatical fighting machine that nearly won its objectives in the war to come three or four years later. The classroom indoctrination about the life of Adolf Hitler, again on a daily basis, also raised the Fuhrer's image into a god-like figure, to be loved, respected and, above all, obeyed.

Equally influential to twisting the minds of vulnerable children, was the widespread management of youth organisations through the Hitler Youth movement. Those, like me in later years who participated in the junior Scouting activities, the "Cubs" and "Brownies" will know how enjoyable such organised groups were and how they helped to educate us; how participating in healthy outdoor activities with all the pleasurable company, helped the learning process of socialising in a disciplined framework.

Such was the junior Hitler Youth. Participation for the odd hour before and after school and at weekends was virtually compulsory. Opting out would have signalled a rebellious or non-cooperative nature and reflected badly on one's parents.

At the age of five and six, I cannot claim to have learned how to use a rifle; but we did play gentle military like games, were drilled to march correctly, joined in physical body building exercises and had competitive swimming sports. All great and innocent fun for youngsters, but designed to lead on to more serious Hitler Youth training.

No child at that age can have failed to be impressed, as I was, to be allowed to participate in one of those mass torchlight rallies in Berlin's Unter den Linden, which we have all seen from the pictures in the archives. Thousands of uniformed groups, with their parade banners and flags, rousing music from military bands and in the distance a huge stage, floodlit with a moustached figure ranting away, his inspiring voice blasted for a mile through loudspeakers preaching a hatred of the Jewish "vermin" that had infiltrated decent German society. Cheering marching crowds, hyped up and enthused, dedicating their lives to the betterment of the Fatherland, how could any youngsters fail to be carried away by the atmosphere of the occasion! I was young enough to be overawed but still too young for the full brainwashing and indoctrination process, which came later in the school years after I had left Germany.

Equally obscene was the continuous, well engineered, anti-Semitic and pro Aryan mind bending that was systematically aimed in the school curriculum at children too young to know better. It is no wonder that so much of the German nation, growing up to be teenagers and young adults and drawn into the fighting force, would condone the early military aggression which led up to the Second World War and the persecution, imprisonment and expulsion or murder of Jewish citizens.

My late father, as a journalist in Berlin worked with others who could see what was happening. In later years I asked him more than once, why he stayed until 1937. After all, my future may have been problematical, but his would certainly have been deportation to an extermination camp. His reply to me was that he just could not believe the German people with their culture and civilised way of life would ever allow it to happen. It was only when it became obvious that no organised resistance existed that could stop the brutal Nazi machine that he realised it was too late. Survival required a new start elsewhere.

An incident involving me finally resolved his procrastination to uproot us and go. For my sixth birthday I received a much wished for, tricycle. After school I rode this up and down our leafy suburban road in South Berlin. Our third floor apartment, with a large balcony overlooked the road. A boy living opposite, a year or two older than me came across and threw me off the bike and grabbed it saying, "I'm having this, you dirty Jew-boy".

His words meant nothing to me, but I cried until my father returned home from work. He immediately went over the road to ask for his lad to have his bike back. However, he was confronted by the boy's father who laughed in his face and told him to go and complain to the police. By 1936 the police would not have bothered with any complaint of theft, however blatant, from a Jewish family. I never saw my bike again.

Not many months later my parents and I emigrated to England. That latest incident of anti-Semitism must have made the decision to uproot their lives and my father's career somewhat easier. My father finally realised there was no safe future, nor much longer any secure employment for a Jewish journalist on Germany's leading daily paper even though the editor as we know from its published history was liberally minded, but no longer had any choice except to appear to conform to Nazi decrees. The paper was closed down by the Nazis in 1943 but rose, phoenix-like after the war.

Chapter Two
England

We arrived in London in the autumn of 1937, but without my four year old sister. Ilse as she was then, remained behind left in the care of my maternal grandmother, in Offenbach. It seemed wiser for my parents to settle themselves in with me first. In any case it had been thought sensible to send my dark haired, attractive little sister well away from Berlin and possible trouble, while we were making our arrangements to leave. My sister followed some months later, fetched by my mother. She has never forgotten the long train and boat journey, with crowds of refugees clutching bags and wearing labels. Her final departure from Germany was made all the more traumatic by the death of our maternal grandfather, who, having taken his granddaughter for a walk dropped dead in the garden from a heart attack witnessed only by the four year old.

My parents rented a flat in Golders' Green, a district of London rapidly becoming the landing base for refugees from Nazi Germany. Delicatessens were springing up everywhere; the Golders' Green synagogue became the "home from home" for the orthodox Jewish community.

Without having a word of English, I felt like a handicapped visitor to this foreign world. But my parents wisely entered me in to an excellent private preparatory school in Hampstead. On my first day I was taken on to the platform at assembly by the head master who introduced me to the school. I have no idea what was said, but afterwards the boys took great care of me, making sure I found my way about and had someone to play with. It took me a remarkably short time at Peterborough Lodge to learn the lingo. Very soon my English was better than my parents, who were fairly fluent from their schooldays in Germany. More importantly, I learned to play, and love, cricket and soon spoke English without an accent. This attribute became very important in later years, when I was envied by former refugee friends who queried why I should have no German accent, while they did. Yet I pass as a born English speaker. The answer, I have been told, is the critical "cut off point" which comes around the age of seven. It seems that only very few gifted linguists manage to speak without any trace of an accent after that age.

However, there was still an identity crisis to overcome. My first names were Otto Ludwig Peter. I was old enough to realise that my prospects of a future in England would be limited while being named after the two mad kings of Bavaria, or as my father insisted when challenged years later by my wife, my two very influential uncles. It was decided to anglicise my name, the "Ludwig" becoming Lewis, the "Peter" (by which name I was called already) remained and the "Otto" getting lost in the process, with much relief! Much later I legalised the change by deed poll and also abandoned my surname of Rosenstiel, changing it to the sort of "give-away" abbreviation adopted by many other European immigrants.

Readers will understand that today it would be no embarrassment to live in Britain with such a prominent German-Jewish surname. But in 1938, and even more so during the war, identifying yourself as an "alien" presented difficulties. Not everyone in England understood that far from being "Huns responsible for the carnage in Europe" and the hardships of war, we were victims of Nazism, not sympathisers!

My time at the Hampstead prep school was happy, but abruptly ended the next year when London's children were evacuated hurriedly in September 1939. I am ashamed to say my criminal tendencies resurfaced at school. The scene of the crime was in the football ground changing room. It seems that I was such an energetic player in my team that I had a bad fall colliding with an opposing boy and had to report to the nurse with a badly bleeding leg. However, my thoughts in the changing room turned dark. I had suffered severe losses playing marbles, the big thing of the moment at school, and my supply of marbles was severely depleted. It seemed likely that without some "new chips" my playing days and hopes of recovering my fortune were running out. Pocket money was very limited and I had no hopes of more.

There all around me on the pegs were more than twenty boys' trousers.

Each had pockets and most were weighed down with marbles, many originally mine. The temptation was irresistible. I carefully relieved each pocket of just one marble, no more. The cunning of the operation would be less likely to leave a trail of evidence.

The guilt hung over me for years and probably explains why I decided to become a more honest and reformed character!

Enough about my early criminal inclinations. My early experiences in my land of adoption made a profound impact which led me much later to follow a political trail. Life was not easy for a "bloody German" boy growing up in wartime Britain. It was not until after the war that bitterness against "these immigrants, what are they doing here?" died down. I could then see the stark contrast between the police state with its increasing terror, from which we had escaped, and the welcoming, relaxed liberal democracy that became my home. The generosity of the British administration and population was remarkable in the months leading up to the outbreak of war. All refugees were accepted as long as they could show means of support. Nor was it difficult to leave Germany but your assets had to be left behind or smuggled out. Those with foreign bank accounts, who had realised property or business in earlier years, could make a fresh start. But others, who left evacuation late, nearer the inevitable start of the war, were forced sellers of property and assets at very depressed prices. Many refugees had come out in September 1939 without any means of support; so those already in Britain helped the latecomers by offering phoney jobs and spare bedrooms, as cooks, caretakers and nannies. My parents did their bit; I had a succession of "nannies" for a few weeks each. Some were well known names in the arts and music world, like Irene Handl, Walter Goehr and Myra Hess, friends of my parents when they had enjoyed a life on the fringes of the intellectual world of pre-war Berlin.

Life for us in 1938 Britain was the lull before the storm. My parents had moved to a house in Hampstead Garden Suburb and my father's parents, Rosa and Oskar Rosenstiel had managed to join us from Germany. Thanks to my mother's non-Jewish ancestry they had been able to bring out many valuables denied to other Jews. Grandmother did not like being indebted in any way to my mother. She was the archetypal "Jewish Grandmother" and expected everything to be done her way. They did not "get on!"

My father's sister, Alicia, lived in Ulm near Munich in southern Germany.

Her son, Kurt, was already in England at Cambridge University before the war started and he became a regular visitor at our house, where my mother would act as a surrogate. He was Grandmother's favourite. A scientist, he had a brilliant mind but a flawed personality. He was much older than me and I only came to know him properly, well after the war when I was married and before he finally moved to Canada. Kurt enjoyed complexity. If there was a simple way of doing something he would inevitably reject it for some utterly complex solution. He could be very frustrating, but fascinating to talk to. As a chemist he worked during the war on the problems of fixing penicillin so that it could be used in battlefield conditions and after the war he took over a small chemical company, producing amongst other things, DDT sprays. Completely contrasting products, the one life-saving and the other later to be condemned as deadly! *to insects*

Even in his private life, Kurt could not avoid complications. He succeeded in having, almost simultaneously, three different families, producing four children and a step-daughter.

A study of my aunt "Alice", as she was known, explains some of her son's behaviour. It was family "gossip" that she would keep him shut up as a child in his room, for days on end. Her first husband, Kurt's father, died suddenly and in so called "mysterious circumstances". It was quietly assumed by my parents that she had either poisoned him or had deliberately not sought any medical help for him with an illness until too late. Her second husband, an 'Aryan,' Dr Stoess, worked at the largest hospital in Ulm.

However, the biggest mystery is how Alice Stoess managed to remain openly living in Ulm throughout the war. Unlike me, Kurt had been brought up as a practising Jew so there must have been a known connection between his mother and the local Jewish community. Her survival was explained away by saying that the doctors threatened to close down the hospital in Ulm if Alice was affected by the anti-Semitic rulings. Many more important Jews had failed to hold the Nazis at bay. More cynically my father would say that she "reinvented" herself. He joked that as a child he was ten years younger than her, but that suddenly found he was ten years "older". Causing much merriment she adopted the word "Von" in front of Rosenstiel, and widowed for the second time, she assumed the title of "countess" when travelling around the smart spots of Europe after the war. "Perhaps", my father would muse "her first husband was a little too Jewish to be associated with a member of an old established German 'Aryan' family."

My father who was offered a position with a small City merchant bank, as a qualified economic journalist, was settling in and earning a living, until suddenly and abruptly arrested when war was declared. He was carted off to an internment camp on the Isle of Man. He, and similar prisoners were released after a few weeks, when someone explained to the British authorities that these people, although German, were not on Hitler's side and were no security threat to the war effort. Needless to say, my father never showed any inclination later to return to the Isle of Man for a holiday.

Everybody recalls what they were doing when war was declared. While my father stayed working in London, my mother took my sister Ilse, later on entry to the Grammar School renamed Margaret, and I on holiday to Brean on the Bristol Channel coast, south of Weston super Mare. Then it was a tiny resort on the edge of sand dunes; a few bungalows and caravans with enormous sandy beaches. We were reminded daily that life was very likely about to change. All day long very noisy war planes flew from Bristol's airplane factory flying so low that we instinctively ducked. It was ominously scary.

Then came the historic Sunday morning radio broadcast. Prime Minister Chamberlain told us "no such message has been received" Nazi Panzers were not withdrawing from Poland and "in consequence we are now at war with Germany".

We started back to our London home to discover in horror that the "phony war" had begun. While frantic arrangements proceeded for an orderly evacuation of all children, we spent every night in the communal shelter that had already been prepared in anticipation.

But there was no bombing. After a few sleepless nights in a claustrophobic, crowded and smelly shelter with all our neighbours, we took our chance as did others and decided to spend our nights in our own shelter – the broom and store cupboard under the stairs!

Meanwhile most schools evacuated en masse, continuing as boarding schools in all sorts of country mansions. Other children were found accommodation with families in rural areas. My parents arranged for me to be billeted on a farmhouse at Amberly, near Arundel. It proved to be the unhappiest period of my childhood.

Life was austere and harsh, stern and strict. Silence at mealtimes. Tea, the evening meal, was a plate of bread and dripping; nothing else. It was the coldest winter for decades, with weeks of a severe freeze up on top of hard packed snow. We jogged the two miles from the house to the village school four times a day as we had to return for the daily lunch of stew and then back to school. The only thing that was in abundance was milk as it was a dairy farm. I was never very fond of milk, but after having to drink pints every day, morning and evening, I have a detestation of it and it's by-product, cream! My mother brought with her the German passion for yoghurt, barely known in Britain. During the war you had to make your own. Milk turned sour produces a smell that still gives me "goose-pimples" today!

Even the farmer's own children lived by the harsh regime. Apart from joining their parents, briefly, in their separate and comfortable sitting room, the only properly heated room in the freezing house, each evening, they each had their chores to do. The son of about my age cleaned all the shoes every evening, quite hard work on a farm.

When my parents managed to come and visit me one Sunday after the roads again became passable, they were shocked to find how much weight I had lost and how unwell and miserable I appeared. I begged them to take me away. They did not need asking!

Back in London, I was entered in a state school in Finchley; this was my fourth school and I was still only ten! There were to be another four; how I made it to university remains a mystery – but more of that later.

Soon after settling back into life in London and the new school, the real war started. There was heavy night bombing and a house in our road opposite us had a direct hit. We were shocked to see the wreckage in the morning. Another evacuation for the many London children, who had crept back, was sensible advice. This time I ended up near Malvern with my sister and mother. A tatty attic room in a large Victorian house became our home.

It was 1940 and I checked into my fifth school in the Malvern Hills. It was a terrible village school with only one class room. I learned my twelve times table and The Lord's Prayer, but little else. There were compensations; my father came out at the weekends and we walked the village of Malvern Hills, time and time again in all weathers. My love of the English countryside matured along with the sounds of Elgar's music, which is with me from then until now and which I am sure would not have had the same intense emotional impact on me had I not spent so many happy hours rambling around those hills.

As we all know the war went badly. Poland, the Netherlands and then France were overrun in weeks. My father was not alone in fearing that England would be next. He was not prepared to wait and concluded that it would be safer to move to America. He had been severely shaken by the events which had so disrupted a promising career. He was pessimistic about Britain's powers of resistance. Churchill's morale boosting leadership would not save us from being overrun. Roosevelt had not yet committed America and Pearl Harbour was still to come.

My father's plan was to move to New York, where he already had many friends and contacts and rebuild his journalistic career. The intention was for us to follow once he had settled in. He crossed the Atlantic and arriving in New York he quickly found his feet, becoming a Vice President of a medium sized but highly reputable merchant bank, Arnold and Bleichroder Inc., as their economic director. After the war he resumed his journalism from New York, writing a regular Wall Street column for the newly resurrected Frankfurter Allgemeine, as it was renamed in 1949. He also wrote regular articles on the US scene for London's leading financial weekly, the Investors' Chronicle – where I started my career after leaving University.

The rest of the family remained in London and the tide of war continued to flow in Hitler's favour. El Alamein and the invasion of Russia were still to come. The war in the Atlantic was going against us. The U-boat threat was regarded as too risky for us to join father in New York. By the time the war had turned in our favour and the Atlantic crossing was considered less risky, my parents' marriage had broken irrevocably. Soon after the war had finished, I was to have a step-mother in New York and a step-father in England.

Fate had now combined with events to shape my life. There were no more immediate prospects of moving to America. My mother decided that she needed to move nearer to London closer to her friends, rather than Malvern where she felt isolated, remote and friendless. My grandparents were living in our house in Hampstead Garden Suburb, which was deemed too dangerous for children. In any case my mother did not get on at all with grandmother, who showed her disapproval. It was a mutual dislike.

My mother had meanwhile crossed the boundary. When convinced that

Hitler was likely to arrive in Britain any moment, she had not only destroyed our swastika bearing birth certificates, stamped with "Juden", she took my sister and I out one morning and had us Christened at a nearby church, coming back with the precious baptismal certificates in their place. Grandmother was convinced that it was done to spite her! We moved instead to rural Hertfordshire, and of course, yet another school.

Chapter Three
Tring

The London blitz was at its worst. We had moved to the small market town of Tring, in the Chilterns about 35 miles away to the North West of London. On the awful well-recorded night of one bombing raid we could see the night sky alight from the blazing docklands, it gave the terrifying impression that the whole of London was ablaze. A few miles away, Hilary, who was to be my wife, was watching the same scene with her family. She recalls her father rushing to switch on the radio to see if the BBC was still broadcasting and the relief felt when the familiar voices came through. There must have been many faces anxiously pressed to the window watching the Armageddon like scene of flames, searchlights, planes, parachutes and tracer fire.

It was 1941 and accommodation was very scarce as we were surrounded by Londoners seeking refuge from the bombing. Anyway, not everybody wanted German refugees as lodgers. We found a remote semi-slum farmhouse, on the dried up branch of a former canal, two miles from Tring. It was run by a gentle and friendly elderly eccentric, but well educated and cultured recluse, whom we called "Nunck." The dilapidated house was divided into bedsits and an extraordinary motley collection of tenants, lived a sort of kibbutzy commune life. All shared the inadequate kitchen and there was some community cooking and dining. There was no mains water or electricity to the house, which could only be reached by a trek along the former tow path of the dry canal. The house had its own well and all the water for the house had to be pumped up and carried into the kitchen in buckets. Cooking was done on an old fashioned solid fuel range and the place was lit with oil lamps and candles. For us children it was a rural heaven; for my mother it was a very far cry from her neat Berlin apartment with her own cook.

"Nunck" was more like a pastor, a nature loving, vegetarian herbalist. He "adopted" me as a long lost son, aroused my interest in nature, gardening and herbalism, and encouraged and supervised my keeping of chickens. All useful skills as food rationing tightened and "outsiders" as we were did not get the odd perks available to the locals in the shops. Nunck allocated me a small allotment garden and started my fascination with planting seeds and watching them grow. A long way from my beginnings in a third floor flat in Berlin! More than once, "Nunck" took me with him to London, between the air raids, travelling on the cheap "Workmen's' train", at 6am. He showed me round the museums and in many ways widened my interests in life.

It was with little reluctance that my mother decided, as soon as some money from New York came to hand, that our primitive lifestyle was not the only way to survive. It was too far from the centre of Tring to get to school easily. There were no cars of course, except for those on special petrol allowances such as doctors and others directly involved in the war effort. Accommodation was found in an attic flat in the town – a little more convenient, but in my twelve year old opinion, much less stimulating.

I was assigned to the only private school in the town, apart from the Catholic girls' convent school, which my sister Margaret attended. She was later removed at the request of the nuns as being "too lively", due to her insistence on climbing all the trees in the grounds. She too was obviously missing the freedom to roam which we had at "Nunck's"! The alternative for me, at twelve, was a rather poor standard secondary and far from modern school, where academic achievement was not the highest priority. Nevertheless, it might well have served me better and saved my father "rip-off" fees, than Osmington, the private school to which I was sent, did in those days. This was my sixth school, with sixty-five pupils; apart from the headmaster, there were no qualified teachers. Most of the boys were the sons of the local shop-keepers or the surrounding farmers. Under present regulations the place would have been shut down long ago. But this was war time and private schools were a law unto themselves.

Although describing itself as a "Preparatory Establishment" hardly any of the pupils progressed into secondary education. Some stayed on over the statutory leaving age of fifteen, with no prospect of any educational qualifications. As long as parents continued to pay the fees, life went on.

Nobody at the school, to my knowledge, achieved a School Certificate. I seemed to have been the first, through teaching myself using the appropriate books which I acquired. The Head encouraged me, showing me copies of former Oxford School Certificate exam papers and urging me to get on with it. He was a graduate of Cambridge, but quite unable to teach. His History classes consisted exclusively of reading out aloud from a history book for three quarters of an hour. The books were totally unsuitable, designed for academic adults and much too difficult for any of the boys to understand. It was like trying to teach eleven to fourteen year olds, with not particularly high IQs the history of the Roman Empire by reciting Gibbon to them, without any explanations, questions or discussion.

Apart from his lack of academic teaching ability, he was a cultured man and with other qualities. He was a ruthless disciplinarian. The cane was used frequently, and, by all accounts, painfully. He insisted on gentlemanly manners from all those under his guidance, in and out of school. If a boy was reported in town not wearing his cap, or failing to raise it when meeting his mother or any other member of the female sex, it was the cane! Slovenly dress, dirty fingernails or forgetting a pocket handkerchief, warranted the same punishment, as surely as it did not wearing your school tie in the street. Bad language, noisy behaviour or neglected homework was also painfully rewarded.

Not surprisingly the school operated in an atmosphere of fear and terror. My formula for survival was such exemplary behaviour, sporting achievement and academic devotion, that I was promoted to head boy. That I hoped would exempt me from the torture chamber, which was the name given to the Head's study.

But not all was Dotheboys Hall. Once a week, the senior class was invited for a session in the Head's study. We were sat on the carpet and had played to us forty minutes of recordings of classical music. Despite coming from a cultured musical family, it was these enjoyable classes that awakened my love of music. It all started with Schubert's Unfinished Symphony and the like!

There were other plusses. I developed a love of sports and cross country running and was captain of cricket and football. English was taught by an unqualified teacher whose classes consisted of reciting Shakespeare's soliloquies which we had to learn as homework. It was a harsh discipline, which was probably needed, but it did inspire me with a love of classical literature. Unfortunately at the same time, the poor teaching was a "turn off". We were "told" to read classics, like Vanity Fair and Northanger Abbey, but with no preparation or explanation of what they were about, which might have made them comprehensible instead of a dreaded ordeal. It took me years to come to appreciate Jane Austen and even longer to face Thackeray again!

One of the staff, the maths teacher, had 'fidgety fingers'. I was too naive to find it improper that he singled me out for after-class private tuition. I would be seated in his chair while he stood at my side, with one hand inside my trousers. I discovered that another classmate, a particularly handsome boy, also received similar 'special' coaching. But without his help I would never have passed my School Certificate maths.

Osmington was the first of my eight schools where I stayed long enough to settle in and make any progress. I was fortunate that the Head saw some "potential" in me, which was evidently scarcely discovered in many of his other pupils. At that time Tring was served by several neighbouring Grammar schools and the prestigious Berkhamsted independent school, so that most of Osmington's clientele were 11+ failures or "late developers" avoiding the state system. The Head obviously selected me to enhance his reputation and open the prospects of new enrolments and financial survival. He must have been secretly relieved that I was one of those who failed the entrance exam to Berkhamsted. I stayed there for four years, until I was fifteen, as he had entered me for the Oxford School Certificate examinations.

When the time came I had to take the exams in Oxford, staying alone for some days at a hotel waiting for the eight subjects that I had chosen to come up. It can hardly be claimed that I had been well prepared for the ordeal, neither academically nor for the stressful setting in which I was being examined. Alone at fifteen in a place where I knew nobody and nobody knew me. It still amazes me, as it did to those at the school that I passed with several Credits.

My mother helped the war effort and earned some useful cash to add to my father's financial support from New York. She worked part time in a local munitions factory. As the employees were mostly housewives with children, a clever shift system was devised which suited the majority "one-parent" families of that time. All able-bodied men were naturally tied up with military service or other essential war effort. Women had to fill the factories and did so. Part time shifts caused the mothers least disruption while caring for children. Many factories worked on the same basis, with maximum productivity going twenty-four hours a day, with seven day weeks but divided into many short shifts.

The factory was owned by the Rothschild family, part of the merchant banking empire. How ironic that a refugee from Nazi Germany should be helping in a business owned by another much earlier refugee family, not only from Germany but from the same area – Frankfurt, which was my mother's birthplace! There were significant differences. The Rothschild's had become more anglicised and wealthy and established in British society than our family. One of the five Rothschild brothers, Lionel, had taken over the magnificent mansion in Tring, built for Nell Gwyn by Charles II. Known for his scientific interest in zoology, his collection of fleas, the largest in the world, rested with his other finds in a special natural history museum which he had built alongside the mansion. All the Tring children and others from the surrounding area must have spent hours, as I did, wandering through the collection on school holidays. We gazed at the stuffed Dodo; the stages of the development of a chick in an egg and of course the performing fleas seen through a magnifying glass. We all had our favourites!

While my mother was helping to manufacture munitions, presumably to be dropped over her sister living in Frankfurt, my German aunt's family were producing armaments for Hitler's war effort. Their steel building material factory was converted to military production; presumably to be used to bomb or invade us in England. My mother managed to retain some contact with her sister thanks to a mail service run by the Red Cross.

Not everyone is fortunate enough to be able to look nostalgically to a period in which they were blissfully happy. Such were the years for me towards the end of and just after the war. The terrible bombing was over and in the countryside we saw few of the dreaded robotic flying bombs nicknamed "Doodlebugs" which mostly had already flopped down before they reached so far north-west of London. Those that did penetrate sounded a bit like lawn mowers in the sky and we held our breaths hoping that their engines would not stop until they had gone safely past. The war was almost a game which the Allies were winning. We collected shrapnel, played soldiers, the junior home guard and were too young to appreciate fully the hardship, suffering and death that afflicted those closer to the action. By 1943 the war barely touched us in rural Hertfordshire. Wordsworth in his "Intimations of Immortality" expressed the feelings I had far better than I could. Between the ages of thirteen and sixteen I revelled for the first time in the company of close friendships; a small gang of friends and Graham Rankin in particular. After school Graham and I cycled for hours along the quiet country roads. In the warmer months we swam in the Grand Union Canal reservoirs just outside Tring, and in the winter months we skated on them. Life was not all swatting for my School Certificate exams!

We collected medicinal herbs for the war effort; I picked pounds of wild strawberries and there were rosehips to gather. As keen Boy Scouts we roughed it at camp in desolate Chiltern woods. Our scoutmaster, Jack Kingham, was an inspiration. Kind and gentle he taught us more than how to tie a reef knot; he included valued lessons in the "university of life". His business in Tring was a cycle repair shop but how he found time to make a living remains a mystery.

I became a troup leader and called my lot the "cuckoos". This was a misjudgement as it led to the inevitable teasing. But my choice was determined by my inability to make any other bird sounds, an essential requirement when communicating in enemy territory. Impersonating a cuckoo seemed easier.

The war did not quite pass us over. A heavy bomber returning severely damaged from a night raid over Germany, failed to make the nearby airfield and crashed into the wooded Chiltern Hills near us. It sounds morbid today, but we scavenged for the widely scattered wreckage after the authorities had checked for and removed any dead. As fourteen year old adventurous boys we searched and found unexploded munitions – unused bullets that would have been fired at enemy fighters. It was a popular but dangerous game, to dismantle the explosive material without firing the cartridge and this treasure trove was valuable barter-currency in and out of school "under the counter"!

At this time the allied bombing campaign was building up with massive 1000 strong raids. A large bomber airstrip was less than five miles from our Tring house. Every evening we would hear the deep-throated roar of the Lancasters revving up and taking off noisily; ready to join the convoys heading for some target deep in German territory, about to be blown to bits. In the early mornings, the same drone, a deep humming sound, as hundreds of American Flying Fortresses, took off on their way to a daytime target soon to be devastated.

At last came VE day. There cannot have been many of our age who resisted the temptation to join the mobs in London. With some friends and an adequate supply of food and drink, we travelled to Euston on the cheap 6am "Workmen's" train. We packed with thousands of others, the whole area between Trafalgar Square, Whitehall and Buckingham Palace. Pushing and shoving as only robust teenage boys can, we got as close to the Palace railings as we could. We sang, waved flags and every time the Royal Family appeared on the balcony we cheered. When Winston joined them, the crowds erupted! Time and time again, throughout the day, they came and went from the Palace balcony, like actors summoned for a dozen ovations.

By the evening we were exhausted – but it was still not time to go home. Spontaneous dancing took over. It was one of those few special days that one will never forget and will always feel honoured to have been a part of, not just as a passive spectator but as a player.

Soon it was the summer of 1946. The war over, I had returned from Oxford to await my exam results. Meanwhile the Head had sold the school, "lock stock and barrel", including the pupils, to a new owner. I, it appears, had been sold with everything else, as a teacher, aged 16! The Head had, ambitiously entered me for his former college, Magdalene, but instead of telling me that the only way his ambition for me could ever be achieved it was essential for me to carry on towards a Higher School Certificate, he persuaded me to go back to the school as a teacher under the new regime. Not realising what folly this would be, I accepted and so was "sold" with the school to come back in the autumn to teach, not only the juniors, but also my previous classmates. English literature, History, Geography and French were to be my subjects. What a joke! I was paid by the new Owner-Head, half a crown a week (12.5p), worth a little more in those days, but not much.

Apparently I was a good teacher; as a former Head Boy not only could I keep order, I was respected and obeyed, still carrying a little bit of a "hero worship" halo! Each night I studiously prepared my lessons for the next day and it all worked reasonably well. I purchased a trilby hat so that I could separate myself when I arrived on the first day to face my former classmates, who initially thought that I had failed my exams and was back to have another go. After recovering from their initial shock of disbelief, all went well.

Half way towards the end of the Christmas term, I entered the new Head's study and said that I ought to be paid more. He immediately doubled my salary to five shillings (25p) a week. Perhaps I should have asked for more!

It is only fair to my parents not to blame them for their ignorance about the English education system and so failing to give me any useful advice. My father was in New York and my mother knew little about the system. So I had to take control of the situation myself. Where should I go to get my University qualifications?

By this time we were living in two converted railway carriages, doubled up to resemble a bungalow. My step-father, with whom I had achieved a "modus vivendi", had left school at fourteen and was a former lorry driver. He could not understand why I never "had my nose out of a book" and I could not understand why he was never even seen with one. With lots of ambition, enterprise and hard work and certainly with the help of my mother who ran the office and kept the books, he was building up a private coach hire business. Starting with one second-hand vehicle, he later operated a fleet of four from a garage near to our home in Tring. He was a skilled handyman, mechanic, carpenter and builder; I learned a great deal from him, but he could give me no guidance on my academic needs.

For my mother it was a very long way from the sophisticated life as part of the artistic set that has been so well recorded as the pre-war Berlin scene. I draw the stark contrast with the early years of my life in Britain. Once my father had moved away across the Atlantic to New York, life with my mother and sister could not have been more dramatically different from its beginnings in Germany. I was transported into a very working class environment, no cultural stimulation or social life. When in my later teens I did start to make school friends, I was too ashamed to bring them to my home situated as it was on the fringe of Tring with other converted shanties.

It was only later, during my National Service and University life that I escaped from an uncouth home environment and began to learn a few social graces. I have no doubt, on reflection that my social and career development suffered from this late assimilation into the sort of society I knew I would need to live in.

It was after Christmas, half way through my second teaching term, before someone wisely told me that I would never make it to any University, let alone Oxford, unless I started working for a Higher Certificate. I decided to take the advice and resigned my job there and then.

Teaching, however unqualified, had taken one and a half terms out of the usual six terms Higher Certificate course. But the time was not entirely wasted as it strengthened my self-confidence and self-reliance and gave me a sense of maturity beyond my age. Now I had to find a school with a sixth form and catch up the lost academic time. Going back to school after having been "a teacher" required a certain adjustment, a change of mind-set and a bit of a climb down on the "road to adulthood"!

My sister Margaret was doing well at Hemel Hempstead Grammar school. Much to her surprise, I turned up there one morning and reported to the Head requesting admission to their VIth Form. I explained my background and hopes and declared a firm desire towards an arts rather than a science orientation. If a University place became possible, I would take an Arts degree.

I can only conclude that the Headmaster was not listening. He directed me to the Science laboratory where the sixth-formers were sitting at work benches, each pupil dissecting a frog. I was horrified, even somewhat sickened – clearly with my squeamish nature, I was not a budding surgeon. The dreadful smell from that laboratory is still with me. Later I learned it was formaldehyde. I also discovered that the Head, Mr Screeton was somewhat deaf which would explain my less than happy introduction to the school.

I walked out of the room in disgust and found the school library where I contemplated my next move. As lunch time approached I discovered the dining hall. Packed lunches and visits to the outside chippy were not encouraged. I joined the queue and was presented with the hot lunch. It was not only disgusting; it was also totally inadequate for a sixteen year old. Rationing in 1946 was of course still quite severe, but what was offered, could not be excused. It took me only minutes to decide that this would be no existence for me. I walked out of the school. It was the shortest time I had been in any of the eight establishments of my pre-university education; but it was defining.

My sister, twelve at the time, stuck it out to achieve her School Certificate. A braver soul than me, I thought in admiration. But what was I to do?

The answer came from an unexpected source. At that time I was an enthusiastic participant at Pendley Manor, a magnificent adult educational establishment promoting all sorts of amateur artistic events. It was owned and run by Dorian Williams, better known for his BBC equestrian and horse show broadcasts. The annual open-air Shakespeare Festival there had achieved widespread recognition. There were all sorts of other activities for arts enthusiasts and I had joined in ballroom and "square" dancing classes held for young people.

My first and only experience on the stage came when I was persuaded by Dorian Williams to take a part in Richard II. At sixteen I had no real ambition to "tread the boards" but Pendley with its enticing open-air theatre was a tempting setting for my debut. Whatever the Shakespearian play chosen over the years for the annual festival, Dorian Williams always played THE leading role, riding a fine horse where possible. All the rest of the cast were expected to walk. For Richard II a horse on stage seemed quite natural, but we had problems with other productions like the Merchant of Venice, Midsummer Night's Dream and Hamlet where his leading role did not look too appropriate on a trotting horse. That did not appear to matter and the producer had to accommodate a triumphant entry, head and shoulders above the rest of the players.

My minor role was as one of the King's entourage. There was only one line to learn, slotted in between two of Dorian's long eloquent speeches. It involved weeks of rehearsals and I was confident I knew my words perfectly, with a well honed delivery. I would certainly have refused the part, for my maiden stage performance, if it had meant learning pages of script. Despite my nervousness on the opening night, I was sure that I would manage my line to perfection.

The audience included my family and friends, with expectations raised that my stage performance would be a memorable occasion. It was! As the play proceeded, I awaited my cue, but Dorian muffed his lines and jumped between speeches, cutting out my contribution completely. I left the stage in my magnificent costume, looking and feeling like an idiot, having brought so many to see me perform!

However, Dorian redeemed himself by advising me to try Aylesbury Grammar School to find a VIth Form place. The problem was that although we lived only six miles from Aylesbury it was in the next County. I needed a special dispensation from Hertfordshire County Council to go "out county" for my education. Fortunately, although in Buckinghamshire, Aylesbury Grammar School was the nearest Grammar to my home and permission was granted. I turned up the next day, anxious not to waste any more time. The welcome was heart-warming and my confidence after my experiences at Hemel Hempstead was instantly restored. I was introduced by the Headmaster, Mr Furneau, into the VIth Form Arts class where my fellow pupils made me feel instantly at home. My subjects for a Higher Certificate were History, Geography and English Literature with French, German and Latin as subsidiaries.

The ethos of the school made it easy for me to come down to earth from teacher back to pupil. The sixth-formers were expected to be self disciplined. We could come and go, more like university students, and unlike Hemel Hempstead, no uniforms were required. I was treated as an adult. Working hard to catch up on the missing one and half terms I had lost, did not deter me from throwing myself into the extracurricular activities with enthusiasm. For the first time my eighth school made up for all the others. I joined in learning to play, what became my main sport, tennis, and started to play matches at weekends for the local Tring Tennis Club – in later years becoming the Chairman. I developed my cross-country running strength and my cricket blossomed at school. I also became the school chess champion, helping to win inter-school matches. More relevant to my later life, I developed valuable debating skills at Aylesbury, which would lead me on to bigger things.

Joining my first co-educational VIth Form helped to overcome my natural embarrassment and late developing interest in the opposite sex. There was a great deal of catching-up to be done.

My concluding school experience was by far the most fulfilling and fruitful. It helped to compensate for a great deal of what came before. I cannot praise the Headmaster and the staff enough. Outstanding Mr Deeming, their Deputy Head, gave me a love for English poetry and literature, a priceless legacy. It was at this time, thanks to some inspirational teaching, that my choice to read Geography at University was firmed up. I left in the summer of 1948 with good Higher Certificate qualifications. The school, its exceptional teaching and ethos did it, not me.

It has often occurred to me whether my fellow pupils, having had the luck or privilege of living all their lives in one town and going just to one school, could appreciate the advantageous start they had had to their lives. When compared to the disruptive home life and education which I had to surmount, it was clear that most of my class colleagues' had little idea of the handicap which boys like me had to overcome.

Chapter Four
Ablution Cleaning

I left Aylesbury with a decent Higher School Certificate in my pocket and felt the world was at my feet. But there was a gap to be filled before my National Service call up. It coincided with virtually the whole of the autumn school term. I explained the position to the new Headmaster of my old school, Osmington and was immediately offered my former teaching job back.

This time the pay was £1 per week. I was certainly not qualified but had experience enough to teach English, History and French. My more senior gravitas and manner made it far more enjoyable. Without my old classmates, I felt in full control and by all accounts, distinguished myself until the end of the term, at Christmas. I took the task seriously; not only did I set homework for my classes; I prepared the next day's lessons meticulously. The school and the Head got their money's worth and the episode was valuable for me. I even had vague thoughts of a career in teaching unless something more exciting and challenging turned up. But with National Service and University still ahead it did not worry me that I had as yet no clear idea of the direction of my life.

Meanwhile, I began to throw myself into the local life, apart from teaching. I missed the sport and camaraderie I had enjoyed at Aylesbury, so I joined Tring Tennis Club and in addition became quite a passable hockey player with weekly matches for the Tring Club. I still kept up my cricket and as a member of the Tring Cricket Club, I captained the Colts team.

More relevant to my future career, I joined the local branch of the Young Conservatives. The 1950's and 60's were the start of a boom era for the Y.C.s. All over the country at that time, strong groups were being formed in pretty well every Parliamentary Constituency. Parliaments and Conservative governments in the future would be filled by familiar politicians, who started the same way at this time. However, most of those I met at the Tring Y.C. branch, part of the Hemel Hempstead Constituency, had little if any political ambitions. It was the social life they were looking for. The Y.C. movement fully deserved its reputation as the best social club in town; it also became branded as the best marriage mart. But more of that later!

Little of Tring Y.C.s' weekly programme included politics. Occasionally the committee would bravely persuade a live M.P. to address a meeting. However, Y.C. dances, car rallies, dinners, picnics, treasure hunts, socials and tennis tournaments attracted a far larger attendance. Indecent amounts of beer, wine and cheese were consumed in the later years once rationing had ended. My first serious interest in the opposite sex also developed from the Y.C.s. The girls were plentiful, pretty and in some cases predatory. Some years earlier I had joined the Young Farmers' Club. Agriculture was one of my interests and there were some jolly "green welly" farm visits. But the social life was dull in comparison to the Y.C.s; nor were the girls as progressive. So I soon decided that although it was in my nature to prefer a rural rather than an urban life, farming was not for me. Gardening? Yes, including the muck shovelling required, but the thought of milking cows every morning at 4am was not my idea of a fulfilling life. I am sure the cows were grateful.

I was elected Chairman of the Tring Y.C. branch and so I soon met our local M.P., Lady Davidson. She was an enthusiastic supporter of the Y.C.s, fully realising the value of their assistance and potential as future adult activists in the Party. Her two sons, Andrew and Malcolm, joined our branch, to the delight of the girls whose membership increased amazingly and whose attendance at meetings became very regular indeed! I would often be telephoned on the day of a meeting by more than one ambitious girl: "Is Andrew coming tonight?" It was hard to hide my jealousy. But then I was only a "commoner" without the cachet of Honourable in front of my name and heir to a hereditary peerage. He was also fairly good looking!

There was a choice for me on leaving school at eighteen in 1948; either accept the offer from Birmingham University to read for an Honours Degree in Geography or first accept the "call-up" for my stint of National Service. I chose the latter; believing more benefit and enjoyment would come from the opportunities of a University, if I could participate with the extra maturity resulting from a delay.

It was to be the RAF, my preferred choice. The reason was not because I had any ambitions to fly, but – please don't laugh – those who knew the score and had been through the ordeal, had told me that life in the Army for National Service recruits was somewhat harsh. The uniforms were rough and "itchy"; the bedding did not include sheets; the food was inedible. The RAF on the other hand, was gentile, soft and civilised – a middle class elite "set"! Cotton shirts and collars, white sheets, no lugging around heavy rifles and back-packs. It sounded so much less daunting than the alternative.

Well I soon discovered the truth! Even the RAF's first eight weeks of "square bashing" was rough and tough. Not many of my fellows in our group were as fit as me. Many were "townies" coming from the slum areas of our industrialised cities, which were of much greater extent in those days. So the physical side of the training was no problem for me. My year and a half at Aylesbury was not only very sporty, I had also cycled daily the six miles there and back from my home to school, in all weathers. It cost less than the bus. Nor was my cycle the sort of light weight racer that youngsters enjoy today, this was a 1930s' heavy-weight, carthorse of a bike. Excellent for developing the calf and thigh muscles.

It was in the early days at the Wirral Peninsula training camp, that I decided to test the rules. My principal reason for electing to do my National Service before University was to give me an eighteen month sabbatical for studying in my free time. I hoped to enjoy a widespread reading programme to broaden my general knowledge in subjects which would not be covered in my selected university curriculum. So I soon found the camp library and set to.

Unfortunately, it quickly became clear the RAF "square bashing" sergeants had other ideas. "No wimps here, you will soon be far too tired to study when you have finished the day's harsh regime!"

Well they were right. Obviously if there was no reasonable time to study, before exhaustion and sleep took over, I had to find another solution. It came to me on one of our morning visits to the "ablutions", as the military call them delicately. I realised that one pathetic soul was responsible for cleaning up after the mobs had done their stuff. Having talked to him, he explained that it was not really his job in life, but that he had been forcibly delegated by the camp's non-commissioned officers, to clean the lavatories every morning and evening, as punishment for some misdemeanour.

So I volunteered to take over. He was delighted. Nobody discovered the change of personnel. One bout of dirty work each morning, another bout of smelly clean up in the evening; the rest of the day was mine, as I was not expected to join in the jolly activities on the mock battle field, obstacle course or rifle range. Clearly the RAF hierarchy had their priorities right. Clean washrooms are for more important than training a rookie.

It was a near idyllic existence. I had several weeks of six hours a day reading in the library before this happy state came to a sudden end. The RAF prides itself in fitting the right people in the right posts. As the careers officer ploughed through the CVs of all the new recruits, they found me. I was called out and sat down in the commanding officer's room. "What on earth are you doing cleaning the ablutions?" "Are you not waiting to go to university?" etc. Before I got far with my, I thought credible explanation, I was told to report immediately to the Commissioned Officers' Department for an interview.

I realised my slyly achieved study time was about to be abruptly ended. I was caught out and the RAF was determined to make better use of me. However, they presented me with a new problem. Would not a commission, if I made the grade, endanger my University plans? After all I had expectations of the usual National Service stint not a long-term career in the RAF.

Again, I escaped. The condition for accepting a commission was to sign up for a minimum of three years. However much I hoped to enjoy the "life-broadening" experience of National Service, three years of officer status was not part of my game plan. I reluctantly declined the tempting offer. A poor second-best RAF career was assigned to me. I was sent to Bawdsey Manor on the Suffolk coast, north of Felixstowe, to train as a "Fighter Plotter".

The job was not as bad as it sounds. It was the Cold War era. We had to learn how to operate the Nation's air defence system, its underground network of command centres, from where radar warnings of enemy aircraft required ordering our fighters from a number of bases to scramble and intercept. Neither our radar nor our airplane technology was remotely as good as today's. Jets were only just coming in; their fuel capacity was very limited in flying time. Night flying was hazardous, with fighters scrambled on the many exercises in which we participated. Trainee pilots on night exercises often called in to us panicking, with only "3 minutes of fuel left and where was the nearest airfield?"

All this involved mainly night shifts. Our daytime base and daytime sleep, was on the edge of Felixstowe. Most of our spare time, after a morning's sleep, was on its beautiful beaches, with long, lazy hot summer days. My study schedule suffered, but the company was congenial. I learned how to improve my Bridge (useful for later when stuck in Parliament waiting for late night votes!) and life was generally very relaxed.

One of our Bridge set was a well spoken Welshman, Taff Jones. He came from a hill farm in the Brecon Beacons, not the cosiest part of Wales. He never once told me, during our Bridge sessions how tough sheep farming was in his home territory. I was curious to find out. Fortunately he invited me to stay for a week when we were given some RAF leave. My ancient BSA motor-cycle carried us both.

Life was indeed austere and I learnt the hard way about the work involved in such primitive conditions. There was no electricity, just paraffin lights; there was no running water, just a nearby stream; there was no indoor bathroom, just an outside closet. It was a bleak March, more like the middle of winter to such softies from Southern England like me.

As if all that was not enough of a welcome for a guest, I also had to cope with the food. The farm was miles from anywhere, particularly far from any village or shops and there were no freezers and few fridges in 1949. Taff and his charming parents seemed to live off porridge, lamb chops and mutton stew. I did not see any fruit or vegetables. There was, however, the compensation of delicious home baked bread.

I stuck it out for a week, trying to keep cheerful, but it became more difficult as the days passed. When it was time to leave I was so constipated I could barely move. I rode off towards Cardiff and found a public loo. I must have sat there for at least an hour.

I do not mean to sound offensive. The hospitality was as friendly and as welcoming as circumstances would allow. The fault was entirely my inability to adapt to the life. Although I have found it less than tempting to revisit the Beacons even though their beauty is outstanding, I have enormous respect and admiration for those who make a living in such a harsh and remote area. It was of course 1949 and it cannot be possible that living conditions have not improved there over the years.

The time sped by and Demob was getting near. It was 1950 and some hard work at Birmingham University loomed ahead.

It is with some pride and a sense of achievement that I look back on my three weeks as an ablution cleaner. But the crafty way in which I promoted myself into the job worried me. Was I heading for a dodgy career of deception?

I was thankful that no real military engagement was involved. A slight adjustment in timing might have taken me into some active and dangerous theatre of war. My future wife's brother, Philip Mayo, only a few years younger than me, was sent during his National Service into the Malayan jungle under fire. As somewhat more cowardly, I admired the bravery involved. I do not think I would have enjoyed the experience myself though.

With National Service now over, I no longer resented the delay before starting University. The eighteen months sabbatical from "book work" was an important experience. I learned to mix with all sorts of people I would never have met in my previous life, to accept discipline and a modest and bearable amount of hardship. The emphasis on physical fitness was no problem to me and set me up for future years when my life turned more sedentary.

After the usual ceremonial Passing Out parade, I was released, proudly taking with me my RAF uniform and pleasant memories of congenial comrades. My Bridge playing had also improved.

Chapter Five
Birmingham

I would have preferred to try my luck at Oxford. But my eight schools did not quite add up to enough for me to make it. It is not intended as an insult to the "Red Bricks" to suggest that they lack the qualities to match up to what Oxbridge and Scotland's equivalents, can provide.

Birmingham has a great deal to offer those that are prepared to live the University life outside the lecture rooms. But let's face it, that life is provincial and the campus in the 1950s was full of young ambitious hard working students. Too many of them, however, were immature and too young to take full advantage of what the University environment could have given them.

Not that I would have fitted in easily with the other extreme, an Evelyn Waugh hedonistic Oxford as portrayed in Brideshead. *Revisited* Something in between would have suited me. My eldest son, Bruno probably enjoyed just that – a good prep school, a full span at Westminster School and then St Andrews University. But he had a father able and willing to afford to give him such an ideal start. I had had to sort out my own educational future as my parents had no understanding what the English educational scene was about.

Life at Birmingham was earnest. Most students had only one objective, to get a degree good enough to compete in the world of work. Having fun and widening one's horizons away from the narrow field of the curriculum was a risky luxury most were not prepared to follow. I was an exception, far less concerned about the quality of my degree than about finding what else I could achieve to help me through the life to come. Gaining only a second class honours degree in Geography was of no matter to me.

My tinkering with politics came from the opportunity to stand and be elected to the Students Guild, the governing assembly. I was re-elected in my second and third years. Monthly meetings took time out of studies but there were plenty of compensations – public speaking experience, discussing university management issues, financial control of the student union's budget and much else.

It was the era of forceful political controversy, with a militant left-wing student group within Birmingham as well as at other universities and internationally. That brought me into politics. One had to take sides, left or right, on important issues. Should our student union campaign for higher grants? Should we send delegations to communist student groups abroad and show "solidarity" on controversial political issues like unilateral nuclear disarmament? Were issues important to students, represented at Westminster?

In 1950 the left-wing was powerfully organised in our universities. It was not politically correct to proclaim Conservative views.

Watching the extreme left, their fanaticism and hearing their arguments helped to consolidate my right of centre views and strengthened my convictions. Having escaped from a Fascist dictatorship, I came to believe there is very little between extreme right and the extreme left regimes – they are both unacceptable. I concluded that only a truly democratic system could preserve us from either peril. I joined the University Conservative Party.

I also joined the debating society in the hope of improving my public speaking and looking for some intellectual stimulus. I was severely disappointed. Out of a campus of around 10,000, a programme of debates attracted only a handful of students. When a prominent national figure was advertised as a speaker, perhaps a hundred attended. Most meetings attracted less than twenty. This was no Oxford Union!

Disillusioned and feeling unfulfilled, I turned to journalism. A well run, edited and produced fortnightly student newspaper attracted my attention. I sought out the office and offered the student editor my help. He came from a newspaper family and knew his stuff. Very soon I was a "lead reporter" producing pieces on all sorts of topical subjects of interest to a wide student (and staff) readership.

There were few student halls of residence in the 1950. Most students had to find landladies with spare rooms in Birmingham. Many lodgings were seedy and overpriced. Worse still, such dispersed accommodation discouraged any adequate campus community life. Students streamed back to their digs after the last lecture and the Union became a morgue after five in the evening. The only exceptions were the "Saturday Night Hop" the only big, well attended, social occasion, and the Operatic Society. I was introduced to Gilbert and Sullivan.

Typical of what we students had to put up with, before the relatively luxurious dedicated halls of residence were built, was my first year's home. A nice enough widowed landlady, with an enormous Edwardian house, took in six students. Unfortunately for us, cats not students were her main concern. We all surrendered our ration books with their weekly allocation of 50 grams of cheese and 100 grams of meat etc. However, it soon became clear that her seven – yes, seven - cats received more than their share of our rations than we did. Some of us survived on packets of crisps at the nearby pub after the evening meal. The popular prank, not surprisingly was for one of us to remove one or other of her pets into some cupboard somewhere. As each cat was allocated its own dinner plate, this caused chaos, with cat hunts ordered by Mrs Watson, round each student room until the "lost" cat was found. It was all very mischievous and spiteful, but relieved some of the pent up anger that her cats seemed to be better served than her students.

I shared one of the rooms with a fellow geographer Peter Higgins. We had a super-sized double bed for the two of us and the room was barely heated by a gas appliance that leaked gas and had a meter that required constant filling. Peter suffered from asthma. The cold, damp winter of 1950 did not help. It was too often not just foggy, but smoggy – a severely polluted air filled with the residues of smoke-stack Birmingham. Not very good for asthma. The unpleasant air and the cold made it impossible to open the windows. To make matters even worse for poor Peter's asthma, I smoked a pipe. Not filled with normal tobacco, which we students could not afford, but with something called Heath and Heather's Herbal Mixture. I lost several close friends, who could no longer stand the stink. Nor do I suspect it helped asthma sufferers. By bedtime our room was filled with a lethal concoction of herbal mixture pipe smoke, filthy smog seeping in through the windows, even when closed, and a leaking ancient town-gas heater. I still wonder why Peter never complained and how he survived.

Peter was elected president of the Geography Society – in other words the "shop steward" of the one hundred or so geography students. Meanwhile, I was, as I mentioned before, their representative on the student's council. For two "illustrious" bedfellows, we certainly did not live in luxury.

Peter deserved and achieved a first class honours degree. He went on from Birmingham to a brilliant career with General Electric (GEC) reaching the boardroom as assistant to Arnold Weinstock, the Chief Executive.

As soon as I could, for my second year, I found some more congenial lodgings with the Bromwich family. While looking for new lodgings, my first question was always "Do you keep cats?" The Bromwich's passed the test with honours! The food was at last well satisfying and I had a room to myself. It was truly a "home from home" and Mrs Bromwich became a surrogate mother to me. We remained in contact, sending Christmas cards until her death many years later. She followed my career, my marriage and the births of my children and even visited Parliament to see me in action.

I achieved notoriety at Birmingham following my acquisition of an ancient London dark blue Taxi cab. This was the time when the new post-war models came in and the old 1930's Austin 12 charabanc, leather seated and sunroof version was being sold off for £50 a time. There was no starter so it was a crank-up job.

My vehicle, as did all those 1930's cabs, had enormous running boards at the sides, which made them ideal for my regular transport of a whole hockey team; seven inside and six out, standing three a side on the running boards. The eleven were assembled from various addresses and taken to the University playing fields.

There were also special occasions when groups of us would cram in for a visit to Stratford on Avon for a Shakespeare experience. We had some memorable evenings with leads played by many of the top actors of the day.

Having attracted attention around the place with my cab, I was surprised by an approach from the University Carnival Committee and asked to lead off the annual Carnival. Heavy sums were raised for charity from the long procession of decorated trucks and participants, bringing Birmingham's traffic to a halt. Proudly, in front of the long procession I drove the taxi, the roof open with a colleague squatting on the top dressed as King Farouk. (The last reigning king of Egypt until 1952) Why he was the honoured figure on my cab I have completely forgotten and it remains a mystery. Maybe someone can solve it?

There had been a previous occasion when I had succeeded in bringing the New Street traffic to a halt. I had chosen to take my driving test in the taxi. It was a freezing winter morning in the rush hour. The inspector had to sit beside me, but of course the early taxis had a large open luggage area and no seat next to the driver. I had placed an upturned orange box for him. He was not too pleased when confronted with this less than accommodating provision. It was very cold. His mood did not improve when we came up behind a milk float and did not have enough acceleration power to overtake. The traffic built up behind us. He got more and more irritated. Fortunately, the "emergency stop" was not included in the test those days! Needless to say, I did not pass my test. When I tried again later, it was in a more conventional vehicle and under more advantageous conditions, but not such an exciting experience.

No description of Birmingham at that time can be complete without a word of praise for Professor Kinvig. Perhaps only geographers would really have been aware of him, but he was truly a "giant" and was regarded as one of the founders of Geography as a serious academic discipline. He was the first to set up an Honours Degree course in human geography and he established the subject as "the study of mankind in relation to his environment".

One's first impression of him, as a new student was of a rather quiet, perhaps doddery man. But this soon was replaced by open admiration. His lectures were outstanding and memorable. As an example I recall a lecture on apartheid in South Africa. He told us that in his view, and this was only 1950, civilisation faced serious challenges. One was the coming clash between the West and the world of Islam, as represented by Muslim fundamentalism. The other threat, he foresaw was from man-made global warming.

What foresight! Only in more recent years have his prophetic insights come to be appreciated. It was his lectures that led me to make energy policy and environmental issues my principal concern in Parliament.

For my last summer vacation, I decided to pay my first visit to America. It was not only with the intention of seeing my father and step-mother, Laura. They had been visitors to Europe each year since the end of the war. My main object was to hitch-hike round the United States. I wanted to discover the "melting pot" and what was the "American dream". It meant an organised itinerary, to include John Steinbeck's dust-bowl trail as so vividly recorded in the "Grapes of Wrath".

After two most interesting weeks walking round New York, participating in the sophisticated, but somewhat artificial life of the Manhattan community, into which my father had become integrated, I decided to move on. Revealing my plans horrified my father. I might have been twenty years of age, but hiking alone to the West Coast and back was deemed "dangerous and irresponsible"! Nevertheless, I was generously granted a cash allowance which gave me $5 a day for six weeks.

I set off early one morning in mid July, with only a modest back pack, thumbing my way from Brooklyn Bridge heading towards Route 66. Getting lifts was not too difficult and generous hospitality was offered on most occasions, with even overnight accommodation. At Memphis we crossed the Mississippi and I was shocked at the visible signs of the Deep South's apartheid. Signs were everywhere "no blacks". Shops, hotels, residential areas and public transport openly "segregated".

One of many adventures came after Oklahoma City. It was a scorching day, around 40C and I was between lifts. An enormous truck pulled up and invited me in. After a few minutes he had a burst tyre. Replacing it was a dirty, sweaty business. He moved on, but after only ten more minutes another tyre burst. We went through the same unpleasant ordeal. We moved and then, you have guessed it, a third tyre burst. We struggled in the heat to change this tyre with his last remaining spare. He was ready to move on, but this time without me. "You Limey have brought me too much bad luck. Afraid we have to part company. Have a nice day Buddy!"

There I stood in 40 C of searing mid day heat. It took an age before my next lift could take me on to Albuquerque.

The Grand Canyon was my next target. Tourist facilities were nothing like as developed in 1951 as they are today. I planned to walk all the way down to the Colorado River, and set off at dawn taking only an orange with me, as I was sure there would be the usual burger stand at the bottom.

As a geographer, I should have known how deep it was, and how much hotter it was, 45 C, it would be down there. But I seemed to have missed this bit of information in my studies. Mule rides took you about one third of the way down the trail, but after that you were on your own. I reached the river at midday and slumped in it and drank a few litres of water, as I tried to recover.

There was not even a mirage of a burger bar, nor had I seen a human being all the way down! Of course the way back would be much harder. It was dusk before I made it, thoroughly exhausted. It might have been easier if I had not decided to collect a rock from each strata on the way back. My rucksack must have weighed 20kg but I got my samples.

At the top, I boasted about my feat to a National Park warden. "Did you know that nobody goes down there on their own? The place is full of hungry rattle snakes!"

Two days later I made it to Los Angeles, but not before another amusing encounter with a truck driver. "You's from England? Tell me, does Adolf Hitler still occupy your beautiful country?" I laughed, but realised he was offended. "Did you think that was funny?" Hopefully I was able to convince him that the war was over and Adolf was finished in his Berlin bunker.

Los Angeles was no place for cash starved back-packers then, and probably not today either. Several opportunities later for visits with Parliamentary delegations, staying in good hotels with chic restaurants and chauffeured transport, have given me a better impression of the place. So I moved on up the West Coast and found San Francisco more user-friendly.

On the trek back my planned route was northerly. Just one more incident, out of many, is worth recording. After Portland, I turned east along the massive Columbia River. It was my intention to camp down somewhere before dark. On this occasion I was finding it hard to get a lift. Becoming anxious and seeing a small van approaching, I stepped out in the road and stuck out my thumb, prominently and unfortunately just clipped the side of the van as it passed.

The driver did not stop. However, ten minutes later a police car arrived and without any explanation, hand-cuffed me and bundled me into their car and off to a police station next to one of the enormous hydro-electric damns that were being constructed. I tried to explain my British nationality that I was a student tourist and the rest. Stupidly, I had not brought my passport with me and it was left safely in the New York apartment rather than risk losing it. It was some time before my authenticity, no doubt my English accent helped, was accepted. It was then revealed that a young hiker had murdered a dam worker the previous day and the hunt was on. It turned out I was the lead suspect as the van driver had reported that I had shot at his van! It was not a very happy experience, but at least a police car took me, eventually, to the Washington State boundary, where I was dropped off in the middle of the night. Fortunately I found lifts from there to Salt Lake City and eventually to Las Vegas.

After two weeks in New York and the six weeks touring in less comfortable conditions, it was time to make for home. My flight back to London was easier than on the way out. My journey from London had been a National of Students Union charter. It turned out to be on an elderly propeller engined converted war-time bomber. To allow for refuelling, we had to start from Glasgow and take the short Atlantic route with hops first to Iceland and another refuelling stop in Newfoundland. Not one of today's six hour flights in comfort, but around twenty-four hours of noisy rattles.

I was ready for years two and three at Birmingham, knowing it would mean much harder work than the leisurely start. As the fear of final exams crept ever nearer, minds became more concentrated, all lectures were attended and we studied well into the night. There seemed less incentive for quite so many leisure and extra-curricular pursuits. Life definitely became more serious.

Chapter Six
Journalism

The job market for graduates in 1953 was buoyant. Science graduates with good specialist degrees found plenty of opportunities. Arts graduates were sought by industry looking for lateral thinking minds with ambition and ready to be programmed along the route to management. Oxbridge no longer had the monopoly as the reputation of the "Red brick" universities improved. Careers departments were already busy placing the new crop of graduates.

But I still had no idea where to look for my future. Industry did not appeal to me. The Civil Service or the media were possibilities but I was not keen enough to test them. Teaching was tempting; I had tried this and liked it. However, I was looking for something more exciting. Would there be any openings in journalism, I thought?

My father had often sent me his articles from New York for the Investors' Chronicle, regular commentaries on Wall Street and the American economy. He talked about the editor, Harold Wincott, a personal friend whom he would meet on his visits to London. Who better to ask about journalistic prospects than the "God-father" of financial journalism?

I plucked up the nerve to telephone his office and asked his secretary if her "boss" would accept a dinner invitation. In retrospect I would have loved to have been a "fly on the wall" when his secretary conveyed the message to him. Here was a brash young graduate cheeky enough to cold-call and take on one of the City grandees!

Harold Wincott is often proclaimed as the founder of modern financial journalism. He is credited with having converted a collection of shady hacks, giving tips, into a respectable profession. The paper he edited, under his guidance, became a quality publication, essential reading for serious investors and professional fund managers. The Investors' Chronicle, although part of the Financial Times group had independent editorial and production. Wincott became one of the City's favourite journalists with his witty weekly pieces for the Financial Times. He was respected for encouraging trainee journalists and had built up a team of around twenty young talented writers under his editorship.

Today's annual Wincott Memorial Lectures are a worthy testament to his achievements, after his untimely death in 1969 aged sixty-two.

When my telephone call was returned with an acceptance, I booked a table at one of Soho's smartest, fashionable and expensive restaurants. The food was good too. It was not a place frequented by penniless new graduates. On arrival I felt completely out of place, but it was my choice because my father had once taken me there and it was, as it happens, the only Soho restaurant I knew of!

I can truthfully say that in my naivety, there was no ulterior motive. The thought that I might have been fishing for a job really had not crossed my mind. It was simply an idea that as a "father figure" he might give me advice on my career, having by this time decided to try for journalism.

Harold Wincott duly turned up. He must surely have enjoyed the experience with tongue in cheek. Such a worldly man – he was virtually self-educated, no public school, no university – must have believed I was inviting myself into a job? I suspect he admired my self-confident effrontery. May be it recalled for him his own start in life, who knows?

We dined, with me doing most of the talking, about my journalism for the university newspaper, and plenty of worldly conversation, trying to impress by showing off my interest in wider affairs. He must surely have wondered when I would pop the question. I never discovered if my father had softened him up in advance, to prepare for my brash behaviour; but I rather suspect that he must already have decided before the dinner that he would offer me a job. Half way through the meal he felt, presumably, that he had played me along enough, making me do all the talking, frightened of coming to the point of my advance. Suddenly he spoke. He asked me if I wanted to join his editorial staff!

Wincott's policy with new boys was clearly to throw them in at the deep end. Without any experience of finance, stock markets or reading balance sheets, I was assigned to join the team that analysed each week's declared annual results and reports of publically quoted companies. Each company would receive a dignified review and the piece was expected to conclude with a recommendation to investors, hold the shares, sell them or buy.

Such a review required not only the ability to read a balance sheet, but also to take a view of the company's prospects within its field of operations. An assessment of the management and its past record was also relevant in judging the investment merits for readers.

Within weeks I had annual reports dumped on my desk as they arrived in the office. Without any appropriate experience or qualifications, I was expected to produce the required two or three hundred words, depending on the size and importance of the company. My handwritten copy would then be typed by the secretarial pool and, after my checking, would be sent to one of the deputy editors and then on directly to the printers in the daily batch of material. How technology has moved on since then!

It still shocks me to think that investors must have read and perhaps acted on my inexperienced scribbling. While my reviews naturally appeared well informed and in the style of my more experienced colleagues the important concluding judgement of the investment potential, came from a totally naive rooky. To be fair my learning curve was rapid. Even so I hope and assume today's Investors' Chronicle team are more qualified.

The deputy editor, Charles Anderson, had a brilliant analytical mind. He could look at a balance sheet and within minutes identify what directors might be trying to hide. Every report covers something the directors would rather the market did not know or that shareholders to discover. Why else do companies employ clever and highly paid accountants who can even deceive auditors? But few could deceive Charles Anderson, with his experience of dissecting balance sheets, exposing the truth in minutes and building up his review from that. I still had much to learn. At least readers – the larger investors and fund managers, got their moneys worth each week. So they did from the other senior member of the team, John Cobb. He explained a company's results not simply from an accountant's view but in the wider context of industry. His analyses were essential reading for the longer term strategic investors, as he could express an expert view on the prospects of the business against its global competition, technological status, management skills and capital investment programme.

Studying the regular contributions of my more senior colleagues helped me to develop some expertise. My wider background in economics and the subjects included in my university studies helped.

It was not all hard grind. As the leading investment paper, there were many invitations from companies and organisations seeking publicity. Our more senior staff had first pickings of the best junkets – the annual dinner of the Stock Exchange, the Association of Investment Analysts and many more. New boys had to attend and report on the less attractive events not held at the Dorchester or the Savoy. Many news conferences and annual company meetings, where one might be offered, at most a glass of wine, had to be covered.

I recall one of my very early perks, rejected by the more experienced staff. A young man sent us an invite to a news conference to launch his small private company's new product. I was sent along. His name was Jimmy Goldsmith and hardly anyone in the City had heard of him, yet! The event, although interesting, presented me with difficulties back at my desk. First of all he was not a public company with shareholders which might be of interest to our readers; secondly, his product was hardly likely to shake the investment world. So how could I write a piece in the paper, as he expected, when there was nothing relevant to our readers? He was launching his first product, what today would be described as a fruit smoothy. That was history in the making, for what followed was a multibillion empire of food and drink products.

Our routine was severely disrupted when there was a national printers' strike in the winter of 1954-1955. Not the first or the last, as the unions had a total hold over Fleet Street. The Wapping stand-off and showdown was still many years away. It had to come as the restrictive practices were ruining the industry. The national dailies all closed down, except for a few one-sheet emergency editions. They could not cope as we might today with the internet, electronic typesetting and fast printing. Only the weeklies had a chance to carry on, but very few made the effort that went into the Investors' Chronicle's management to print abroad.

A firm of printers were found at Delft in the Netherlands. Logistically, it was a difficult operation, but it succeeded. I was sent to Holland with the deputy editor, Charles Anderson and Margo Naylor, one of the paper's sharpest brains. Perhaps I was included in the threesome because of my French and German. It was just as well, the Dutch printers could hardly write or spell a word of English. Our task was no longer to write, but to proof read, edit and make-up the typed copy, which was sent to us every evening from the London office by special courier. We had then to put it all together and help the printers make some sense out of it. Overnight I became a sub-editor!

The final publication had to be dispatched overnight each Thursday, ready for the newsstand on Friday morning, as the bowler-hatted brigade marched into their City offices. How much easier such an operation would be today when all the nationals are printed and published overnight all over Europe, for the large ex-pat market. Undoubtedly our efforts were appreciated by our readers even if the Unions were not pleased.

Readership at this time was still small and select. Margaret Thatcher's wider share ownership revolution was still to come. There were few investment trusts and unit trusts were only just starting. The pension investment business was also much smaller than today. But signs of change were evident over my five years with the Investors' Chronicle and I was soon to play an active role in the exciting revolution on its way which developed into a more genuine capital-owning democracy.

The strike collapsed and we returned and resumed our routine, but a little wiser perhaps after some sightseeing of the nightlife in Amsterdam. As I settled into the work with great enthusiasm it began to be reflected in my small town community. Back at the ranch, friends and those who knew me as a boy started regarding me with special admiration. We were still in the early stages of the explosion of opportunities in higher education. Those who made it were tagged with some sort of genius status and often given a mention in the local newspaper. Very few Tring lads had made it to University, fewer were granted a career start as prestigious as being a journalist with a highly respected paper such as the Investors' Chronicle; and few of my acquaintances commuted daily to London. Work in the City, in those days, was for those from top-class family backgrounds with a public school education.

My status at the tennis club, amongst the Y.Cs and with my cricket companions, was elevated although at the time I could not see it nor understand why!

After four years my interest in the world of investment broadened and deepened. At the paper I was promoted as assistant to the editor of what was widely regarded as the main attraction for readers. In the front pages was the "tipping" section. Five or six shares were recommended each week, expertly selected for their prospects of capital gain. Some of the stocks featured resulted from tips or advice from outside the paper. Indeed we were flooded by advice from investment managers, brokers and private investors, only too eager to push shares in which they had already invested. Such tips we were aware had to be carefully vetted. There is an old established adage heeded by wise investors, "where there is a tip there is a tap". Other outside tips were more authentic, such as advanced inside hints of a takeover, attractive merger or favourable news likely to raise the share price.

The advice section had a high reputation in the investment world. It was the paper's strongest selling point. Shares featured almost always responded on the Friday morning of publication, as investors rushed in to buy. On occasions a sharp price movement started before the paper appeared on the bookstalls. Editorial staff were then under suspicion of advanced dealing on their own account. In today's regulatory regime, such insider dealing could be a criminal offence. There were no such constraints in the 1950s and the temptation was inviting.

I can remember on more than one occasion when an obvious leak producing a sharp price movement, in advance of publication, resulted in an internal enquiry by the editor. No editorial staff could be identified, but clearly such insider dealing damaged the reputation of the paper. After all readers paid to buy good advice. If the cream had already been removed and the recommended stocks had already moved up, why buy the paper? On more than one such occasion the problem was traced to the printers. They would have the copy a day earlier and we discovered that they had organised a small syndicate and were in league with a broker who could be relied on to act discreetly and presumably did quite well out of it too.

The investment advice section of the paper was particularly fascinating for me, as my interest in actual investment was awakened. Into my fifth year at the Investors' Chronicle I began to feel frustrated by my modest salary. The starting pay for a promising graduate in industry in 1953 was between £500 and £600 per annum. But the Financial Times Group was regarded as such a prestigious organisation to work for; they could get away with less. They hired my sort at £400pa. In 1958 even after four years the salary had only reached £1000.

Every week I could see some of the stocks I recommended to readers for one shilling (5p), quickly rising and making hundreds of pounds for even modest investors. More of my City contacts asked me why I had not considered moving directly into the stockbroker business where I would not be restricted in putting my newly gained expertise to work for more worthwhile gain. My tips were making money for others but it was quite improper to benefit myself.

My future was determined when I was approached by a small firm of stockbrokers – most partnerships were modest in those days – "would I consider joining as the investment researcher analyst?" Any clients I introduced to the firm would give me a share of the commission on top of the salary offered which was well ahead of my present pay. It was difficult to refuse and I realised that this was the exact direction in which I wanted to go.

With some reluctance, I invited myself into Wincott's office. It was not easy. He had been good to me; he was a friend of my father and he had had faith in me as a journalist. But I had to brace myself to explain that I wished to depart. He showed no sign of surprise. "I am sorry to see you go – but it happens to me all the time. I pick people like you, train them up and then they move on, hungry to make more money than the Financial Times Group is prepared to pay!" He gave me his best wishes for the future and I was relieved to find that I had retained his goodwill.

We remained on very good terms and some years later my wife and I were guests at his daughter's wedding, which took place on the last day of our own three week honeymoon tour of Europe.

Ever since I left, affectionate memories remain of my time at the Investors' Chronicle. As we moved towards wider share ownership, readership expanded. Financial journalism gained a more prestigious reputation with every respectable daily paper having a financial section.

If Harold Wincott had lived longer, he would have achieved much more to advance the era of a capital owning society. His reputation would have been acknowledged even more, as he certainly deserved. It was his inspiration that drew me to carry on the crusade towards a capital owning democracy and that finally led me into politics.

One of my special friends at University, also reading for an Honours degree in Human Geography, was Robert Jones. I was already well established for a year at the Investors' Chronicle before he finished his third year. I was aware of his interest in journalism and mentioned it to Harold Wincott, who invited him for interview and offered to take him on.

It did not take Bob long to become a distinguished contributor to the publication. While I developed a more specialist interest in the investment side, he became a skilled industrial correspondent. He would invite himself to visit a leading public company and produce an in-depth feature, almost weekly, analysing the company's products, management, research and marketing – what the company does and how it does it.

We shared an office and he would return from his visit rewarded not just with material for an excellent two-page exposé, but also piles of product souvenirs. On one occasion it was boxes full of "Penguin" biscuits which kept the whole editorial staff supplied with tea time goodies. Another time he returned with cartons full of boxed tissues, paper serviettes and toilet rolls. Less appetising.

In return for my help on to his first journalistic ladder, he did me a favour in return. He was a far too heavy smoker. I had retained the dreaded habit from student days, but consuming less than half a packet a day. Bob always seemed to run out of cigarettes half way through the morning. Day after day my packet found its way to his desk. In exasperation I realised that I was keeping him in cigs and decided it was a generosity I could not go on affording on our meagre salary. Drastic action was required, without offending him. One morning I arrived in the office with a pipe and pipe tobacco. Thereafter he had the painful experience of providing his own cigarettes.

I like to believe my health suffered less subsequently, as I never smoked another cigarette and in more recent years even found it not too difficult to give up the pipe.

Bob went on from the Investors' Chronicle with a distinguished career, writing industrial articles for The Times, the Economist and Forbes Magazine in New York. Later he became a lecturer for management students at the Manchester and London Business Schools, an Emeritus Fellow and until recent retirement, lectured in journalism at the City of London University.

Visiting us quite recently at our French home, I was horrified but not surprised, that he was still a chain smoker. However, he did manage, with frequent stops, to make the climb up the side of our local gorge to the village of St Cezaire, with Hilary and I and his wife Janet. The promise of an excellent meal at the restaurant at the top was no doubt a spur. I see from his internet blog "The Daily Novel" that he is still struggling with the nicotine demon over fifty years after our time together on the Investors' Chronicle, trying to quit the habit.

Not all of Wincott's protégés were as talented and dedicated as Bob. I recall one colleague who looked, spoke and behaved more like a barrow-boy from the East End, than a budding City gent. While we all tried to dress smartly in sombre suits, he often appeared in the morning in an open-necked shirt, looking as if he had been up half the night. He must have had more journalistic ability than was evident when walking into his office or his time on the editorial staff would have been even shorter than it was.

It was fascinating to discover what he was actually up to. He was running a one-man mail order business. How he found time to fulfil his journalistic commitments for the Investors' Chronicle remains a mystery to me to this day. Out of curiosity, I accepted his invitation on one occasion to accompany him during our lunch break. We scoured the wholesale warehouses behind Liverpool Street, until he found a product he could sell from a pictorial advertisement in a Sunday tabloid, usually promoted as "bankrupt stock". On our tour he found and negotiated the purchase of 5,000 binoculars, cheap and junky, light and small for sending through the post, probably manufactured in Hong Kong, which he could con the public to buy at twice his purchase price. The next hour or two would then be occupied arranging advertisements in suitable tabloid newspapers.

All of the callow young graduates liked him, for his roughish manner, brash style and keen sense of humour. He was a larger than life character, who did not operate according to the rules of sensible investment, which the Investors Chronicle preached to its readers. He speculated on the stock market, making money in bull markets, losing far more than he could afford when market prices fell. Towards the end of the 1950s, he was hit by a double whammy. The market turned down and his mail order business collapsed, when a new competitor undercut him on what had been his best money-maker – 3D spectacles.

His stockbrokers were pressing him to settle his speculative account, but he kept them waiting in the hope of securing a big loan from one of the most successful hoteliers of the time, Maxwell Joseph, who had bailed him out once before. His benefactor was always ready to see him, but this time he was only willing to offer encouragement. Each time he went he was full of hope, but finally he realised that he was not going to cough up any more money.

He came into the office one Friday to tell us that he had decided to emigrate to Australia and make his fortune there. Those of us who went to his leaving party the next day, found him his usual buoyant optimistic self. But his wife was in tears, saying goodbye to her friends and worrying about how they were going to make friends and earn their living in a country neither of them knew.

How he had managed to get accepted by Australian immigration and what happened to his unpaid debts, we never did discover, because none of us ever heard from him again.

Chapter Seven
The Investment World

My first investment was far from politically correct. I happened to glance at the Times business pages, not my regular reading during National Service, and noticed a report from a whaling company that was presenting its annual results. Another good year, so many more whales slaughtered and shareholders were to receive their annual 12% dividend on the Preference shares. The equity was held by the managers and directors, but the public could participate in a high yielding fixed interest stock. I checked the price of the Preference Stock and discovered they were trading at around £1, par value. That meant they would offer me a return of 12%. This sounded tempting.

I had saved up my meagre RAF pay and I used the £100 in hand, to take my first plunge into the capitalist jungle. I did not know any stockbroker then, which is not surprising, as it was not allowed for brokers to advertise or promote their business under the Stock Exchange "club" rules. However, I did know about a tiny merchant bank in the City, Anglo Continental, where my father had worked when he first came to Britain in 1937 until he moved to America. The managing director was an old family friend from Berlin times. Johnny Speyer acted as go-between for my father exchanging his dollars into Sterling for the monthly allowance my father had provided to my mother for our maintenance.

I asked the bank to purchase £100 of the Whaling stock for me, paid with my cheque and waited impatiently for my first half-yearly dividend.

It cannot have been the most profitable commission the bank earned that day, but it represented an exciting experience for me. I learned valuable lessons.

After a year or two, whales were harder to find; then came internationally agreed restrictions on culling what few were left. The shares started to drop. When the next year's dividend could not be paid, I lost half my precious investment. I had learnt a valuable lesson – If an investment looks too good to be true, it probably is!

Many more ups and downs had to be survived before I was clearly on the winning side. There was Suez, when I happened to be holding British Petroleum shares, which slumped in price as the Americans forced our humiliating withdrawal from Egypt. Then came the Australian oil and mining boom. My particular gamble was an exploration company that had the knack of drilling dry holes inland and off-shore.

My move from the Investors' Chronicle in 1958 to a brokerage firm was the start of twelve years on the Stock Exchange. Bragg Stockdale was a tiny set-up, two partners and a total staff of about eight people. I was the investment analyst asked to review clients' portfolios, recommend sales and replace them with those offering more promise in my opinion; this activity of course stimulated commission, but for the firm and not for me. Most of the clients were wealthy private investors, with many coming from the horse-racing world. Having a researcher from the Investors' Chronicle aboard no doubt added to the firm's prestige.

After some months my own clientele built up rapidly from the many contacts I had in my private life with my various interests. Personal recommendations from existing clients who were pleased with my advice was the only way of building up a business, as advertising of any sort was strictly forbidden by the Stock Exchange Council's arcane rules. Members were not allowed to offer their services, which might bring in the public "riff-raff" into the elite world of investors.

The work the firm had engaged me to do for the partners' clients took up most of my time, without benefit to me financially. I realised that my own clientele was building up enough for me to chance depending on it for a living. Indeed, I reasoned, if I was able to concentrate full time on building up my contacts from my varied social life, I might do very well. I moved to a larger partnership, Spence Veitch, where I was not salaried, but entirely free, dependant on commissions from the business I introduced.

By now, I was starting to take a more active interest in politics. As a Y.C I became chairman of the flourishing Tring branch. Later I became the Chairman of the Hemel Hempstead Constituency Young Conservatives, responsible for helping around ten local YC branches. This position also entitled me to represent the constituency on the East of England regional committee, with the opportunity to attend the annual National Conferences of the Conservative Party. My first conference was in 1955, which was Winston Churchill's last. We could all see that his days in office as Prime Minister were numbered and that his health and keen mental powers were fading. It was a particular privilege for a former refugee to meet him at one of the Party's social occasions. A much closer view than I had had of him on the Buckingham Palace balcony on D-Day!

My budding interest in politics came directly from my investment experiences. It was my overwhelming belief that capitalism, as represented by the Conservative Party, would only flourish, serve the nation's prosperity and beat back the tide of Labour's interpretation of socialism, if more of our citizens participated. So I became one of the proponents of the Investment Club idea in Britain. Small groups of people with only limited funds, get together for shared investment, able to buy shares together which they could not do individually, sharing the costs. The movement started in the U.S. where people were much more open to the idea of "the man in the street" owning shares, while in Britain it was then still regarded as an occupation of the wealthy.

With colleagues, expert investment analysts, we formed what I believe was the first club in the UK, the British Investors' Club. Our portfolio out-performed most professional management funds and we attracted around one hundred members. Most were modest private investors in the London area, many younger City people who had not yet made enough to hold a large portfolio on their own account, but who used it to build up their own investment capital and to have the benefit of our professional management without having to pay the fees and expenses. We held enjoyable monthly meetings at London's Brown's Hotel. The manager was keen to join our club so we ended by having the premises free of charge. The Club's committee was given full discretion to run the portfolio, but reported to the members, monthly, with details of purchases and sales and our reasons for making them.

After I was married, while still living in Chelsea, I formed another one of the first and longest running investment clubs, based initially on my wife's home in Hertfordshire. Her father, a bank manager with the Cox's and King's branch of Lloyds Bank, later took over as treasurer and kept the books, laboriously allocating the members' units each month in the days before calculators! The Mutual Share Ownership club would meet monthly, each member having subscribed enough for us to purchase one stock agreed by the membership. The Club thrived for nearly forty years before we finally liquidated it in 2000.

Many members built up quite sizeable sums with regular investments of as little as £2 per month, younger members finding deposits for a house and the older ones adding to their pensions. All learning from the experience, some went on to invest directly for themselves having been well schooled, I hope, by myself as a professional. The initial idea of the Club was for it to be for the Y.C.s, actively promoting the capitalist ethos, learning about the mechanics of investment, without having to risk too much, but by actions and not only words! Our committee consisted mainly of Y.C.s or former Y.C.s; a Chartered Accountant, Stephen Clarke, who stayed with it for all its forty year life. We also had a solicitor, two businessmen and of course my "senior" Conservative father-in-law. Soon we had also attracted the parents of Y.C.s who were anxious to join in the success of the Club. Apart from learning about investment, choosing, buying and selling shares, reading balance sheets and occasionally getting hot tips, when some junior in a firm would comment that sales were particularly strong, there was a vibrant social camaraderie. We would have celebrations and dinners even in the House of Commons after I was elected.

As the Club was structured like a Unit Trust, members could subscribe as much or as little each month as they wished. Some even put in lump sums occasionally. Units were credited monthly at the market price, to each member, according to how much was injected. The market price was carefully calculated at what we would have to pay to buy the portfolio on the first day of each month. A selling price was also fixed, based on what a member would get if selling the whole portfolio. As the management was unpaid and honorary, our only costs were normal brokerage commission and a small sum for postage.

The advantage of this open-ended fund was that members could withdraw all or part of their unit holding monthly or subscribe monthly whatever they wished. By the time in later years when the Club got established a few members subscribed up to £100 each month with most around £5 to £10.

Initially my Father-in-law, who kept the books, put in £5 per month and my brother-in-law, Philip Mayo sacrificed all of £2 per month. I remember joking with our Honorary Treasurer, Stephen Clarke at least nobody can think I married into the Mayo Family for money! Philip Mayo later became a millionaire as a director of National Freight when he helped arrange their buy-out.

The Club had its spectacular ups and downs. Our "downs" included the Australian Oil and Mineral boom. One of the "ups" was obtaining a nice stake in Dixons, when they first came to the market. I was a partner in the broking firm that launched Stanley Kalm's business on the Stock Exchange. They had six small photographic equipment stores in London, but enormous ambition as today's success as a leading retailer confirms. The shares soared over the years as did our Club's portfolio.

Our success was not just due to picking more winners than losers, it could be attributed to taking a really long-term view. We purchased stocks that we believed would grow over the decades rather than just weeks. I learnt hard lessons during my investment experience that real money, short of gambling, can only be made by taking a strategic long term view.

The committee had full discretion to buy and sell without consulting the members, but had to report their dealings at the monthly meeting. They had to give in great detail, what they had done and why. I had, as Chairman, convinced the membership that one could not manage a portfolio by looking at it only once a month.

One of our members, I recall, would never miss one of our monthly meetings. He took notes when we explained any changes we had made over the previous month. Years later he said he wished to withdraw from the Club as he had reached retirement. He shocked me by telling me that he had made "several hundred thousand pounds" by following my choices of purchases for the Club. He never offered me even a thank you, let alone any commission!

One of the Club's highlights was when the BBC Money Programme contacted us to ask if they could feature one of our meetings for a weekly programme. We consented without realising exactly what would be involved. We were asked to set up a mock meeting. It was the week of the 1987 Stock Exchange crash.

We obliged and a massive team of six BBC interviewers, technicians and producers descended on us. Many of the members were interviewed and for most it was their first appearance on TV. However, the Committee and I were a little annoyed at the whole performance on which the BBC insisted as it was certainly not a typical Club meeting.

Setting up the scene took the BBC two hours, while we had to wait. Then their sound technician messed up and they insisted on repeating the whole charade. To add insult to injury the four hours we had endured resulted in no more than three minutes of actual TV viewing in their Money Programme. I discovered why the BBC grabs so much license fee money, and wastes so much of it.

A National Association of Investment Clubs was set up; I was an active organiser, touring the country talking to a variety of groups, from women's institutes and rotary clubs to factory floors, explaining how to set up and run a successful club. I felt the need to do this because I believed that it was a practical route to enlarging the investing population, one of the aims of my political philosophy. This was particularly a way, I felt, of involving people in the business of capitalism and potentially a way of curbing growing union hostility. One of my proudest achievements was in forming an investment club with workers on the assembly line at Fords Motors. Their first investment was a few of Ford's shares. Soon afterwards they were forced to participate in a disastrous strike. Their shares slumped. Their members must have learnt a valuable lesson – the futility of strikes. for its shareholder

Of course, all this activity also helped to build my business. The more clubs I helped to start, the more business I had from those who engaged me as a broker. A club saving and investing say £100 a month was hardly a big deal in commission for the mainstream broking firms. Our club, the Mutual, started in that way, but in later years when the fund became more than £100,000 with each new purchase or switch involving £5000 – £10,000, it became more worthwhile.

Also I spread the word by offering a course of lectures designed for adult evening classes. At one time I had three six session courses, in Ealing, Hertford and Watford, running concurrently on the "Art of Saving and Investing". This work was supported by the Stock Exchange although no-one ever bothered to thank me for it. But perhaps the increased business which resulted was some consolation.

A national organisation was formed by those of us with a similar philosophy, the Wider Share Ownership Council. It was chaired by Lord Shawcross. I was an active member of the Council representing the investment club movement. As Hartley Shawcross, he had been elected as a Labour MP in 1945 and as a distinguished lawyer became Attorney General under Clement Attlee. He rose to fame, of course, as the prosecutor of the Nazis at Nuremburg. After a stint as President of the Board of Trade in 1951, he had finally retired from the Commons in 1958 and took his seat as a crossbencher in the House of Lords. Later he supported the Social Democratic Party. The Wider Share Ownership Movement could not have recruited a more eminent figure to lead the campaign across party lines.

Another staunch supporter of ours was Maurice Macmillan, the son of Harold Macmillan, the Prime Minister from 1957 until ill health forced his retirement in 1963. His forward looking views raised my hopes of more active incentives to promote a wider spread of investment. But we had to wait for Margaret Thatcher's 1980's revolution, with the privatisation of our nationalised industries to achieve a genuine capital owning democracy.

My frustration at the slow progress and lack of priority in the Macmillan Government's plans were not directed at Maurice. He was not included in his father's government of 1957 to 1963 and was not promoted until Edward Heath made him Chief Secretary to the Treasury in 1970. I was disappointed with the lack of momentum his father's "You've never had it so good" Government, was making to encourage the wider ownership of investment. More home ownership was not enough. I wanted to see real tax incentives for savers and investors. My opportunity to make the point came in 1962 when my wife and I were guests at a Lobby reception in the House of Commons. There had been a division bell as we were making our way to the reception. The principal guest was to be the Prime Minister, Harold Macmillan.

The lifts at the House of Commons are quite small, antiquated, intimate spaces with room for only four or five people. We entered the lift, followed by two other people, Harold Macmillan and an aide. The four of us started up slowly and then the lift came to a juddering halt. Here was my opportunity, a chance not to be missed or ever likely to be repeated. While my wife gazed studiously at the ceiling and the aide looked on in amazement, I weighed in.

"Prime Minister, you have your able son Maurice, with his brilliant mind who is actively promoting the Conservative ideal of more widespread ownership of capital. Why cannot you give him a job in your Government and show more support for our movement?" There was a small amount of throat clearing from the aide and as the lift started to move upwards again the Prime Minister conceded "Maurice does have some good ideas!" As we left the lift, he was heard to ask in a loud voice to one of his team waiting for him, with a jerk of the head in my direction, "Who is that man?" It did not occur to me until much later that Macmillan was probably more concerned about possible charges of nepotism than by any deliberate disregard of his son's abilities.

A most favourable development in the 1960s was the launch of the Unit Trust industry. Their enormous contribution to buttressing the popularisation of a capitalist economy cannot be overstated. Their early promoters were supporters of our political ideals and not just looking to earn a living. A prominent contribution, not properly acknowledged, was made by Sir Edward du Cann the M.P for Taunton. He launched one of the earliest Unit Trusts, attracting many thousands of first time investors with their small regular savings. This began before his distinguished political career as Economic Secretary to the Treasury in 1962 and then Minister to the Board of Trade in 1963. He became Chairman of the Conservative Party in 1965 and was later to play a prominent role in the promotion of Margaret Thatcher as Tory leader in 1975.

Edward du Cann made an important contribution to promoting wider ownership of shares as a Tory policy by setting up a practical working structure, unit trusts, for it to happen. As a Minister in the Macmillan Government he did his best to advance incentives for his strong belief in a capital owning democracy, but, as others he was ahead of the tide which only turned to a flood in the 1980s. His part in the forward movement should be more widely recognised as it was by those of us involved at the time.

Another prominent figure in our crusade was Edgar Palamountain, whose City career with the Municipal & General group of investment trusts played a promotional role for the wider ownership of shares. Small first time investors found an easy way of applying savings directly into equities, by little instalments. He was undoubtedly a contributor to advancing the message that investment through the Stock Exchange was not just for a minority of wealthy people.

My contact with him involved an incident when he was featured as the guest speaker at a large banquet organised by the National Association of Investment Clubs. I arrived, with my wife, duly attired in dinner jacket and black tie, fortunately well ahead of time. Edgar arrived in a bit of a panic. He had just looked into the boot of his car to discover that the bag with his formal dress, which he had thought his wife had put in there, was missing. He had come up directly from a day's sailing on the coast and was dressed in white slacks, open shirt, a V necked jumper and with plimsolls on his feet. I have reason to remember exactly what he was wearing. The organising committee eyed me up, and by general agreement it was decided that I was nearest in size to Edgar. We removed ourselves to a side room and duly changed clothes. As a leading organiser, how could I refuse?

My wife and I relinquished our places on the top table and discretely dumped ourselves further away at a less prominent place. I shall not forget the looks which were passed in my direction during the meal. One could imagine the thoughts of those who looked at me so plainly improperly dressed, daring to come to a formal dinner without even a tie, let alone a dinner jacket! Had they seen my feet they would have noticed the only part of my dress which was correct, my black shoes. As we took different shoe sizes Edgar was still wearing his plimsolls. To be fair to him when he did finally rise to speak, after I had spent a very uncomfortable dinner, he explained what had happened and I ended the evening regarded as a hero. I do not think, despite my high profile exposure, I gained any new clients for my investment business that night.

However, another occasion did assist in building up my business as a stockbroker. I decided that commuting from Tring daily was less attractive than living in London. My social life, tennis and other sporting activities could continue at the weekends, but a flat nearer to my work in the City was tempting. Searching the London papers I found a one-roomed apartment in a small block behind Paddington Station. Hardly the most fashionable area, but the rent was within my reach. At this time, the late 1950s, rent controls had not been lifted. One had to pay the existing tenant key money.

The room was tiny, with a bathroom but no proper kitchen facilities and only space for a single bed. But it would do. The existing tenant, to whom I would have to pay the key money, was an actor, Harry Towb. He was making his name in character parts on the stage and in early TV soaps such as the Army Game. I paid him his dues and he moved to larger accommodation in a

Regency terrace near Regents Park. Harry became a lifelong friend. When I married in 1961, Harry was my best man. He treated the wedding itself, in the old Norman church at Hemel Hempstead, as a superior theatrical production and at the wedding reception he excelled himself. We did not discover who had actually sent us telegrams until after we returned from our honeymoon since his rendition of them as coming from such unlikely people as the Pope, the President of the United States and obscure aunts we did not recognise, kept the audience in fits. He started the customary speech with the words "I first met Peter when I sold him a flat which I did not own at an exorbitant price; he got his own back by becoming my stockbroker!" Sadly, Harry has recently died, but his charming wife, Diana Hoddinott, lives on as Jim Hacker's wife in the TV drama, "Yes, Prime Minister".

A fascinating new interest resulted from my choice of "Rabbit hutch". Suddenly I was introduced to a whole clique of actors. As a reward for making money for Harry with the hard earned few hundred pounds that he could spare, I acquired a number of his colleagues who invited me to handle their investments. Although I enjoyed living in London, the miniscule apartment did not give itself to entertaining and as I contemplated marriage, I looked for somewhere a bit more spacious and moved on to a flat in the Kings Road Chelsea. The flat was next to the Six Bells and had two reasonably sized rooms, balcony overlooking the pub gardens, bathroom and a curiously triangular shaped kitchen. The scene in the Kings Road in the early 1960s was lively. Life in London was so very different to that of Hertfordshire. There was always something happening in the street and no-one seemed to sleep that much. The flat gave us the opportunity to start some modest entertaining of clients.

My collection of theatrical investors grew rapidly as one would introduce me to another. My senior partners must have been intrigued by the well known names which they saw on the buy and sell contract notes. There was Barry Foster of the Dutch detective, Van de Valk fame, Susan Hampshire, Bill Nagy and many others. At actors' parties we met some most interesting characters in informal settings; people like Harold Pinter and of course his wife, Lady Antonia Fraser. Many of those people we met were part of the vibrant fringe theatre of that era.

We would often spend evenings up the road at the Royal Court Theatre in Sloane Square where many of the new wave plays were introduced. No longer inhibited by having to catch the "last train" out to Hertfordshire we could enjoy the theatrical London life to the full. After the performance we would retire to the restaurant for supper, where we would be invited to join the 'actors' table' with many of the cast along with the chef proprietor, Clement Freud. The cuisine must have been good as the food writers said it was, but what one really remembered was that the whole scene was hysterically amusing. Round the table the actors each outdid the rest in a mounting tide of extrovert humour, with cabaret from Dudley Moore and others, interspersed with Clement Freud's sardonic wit and our friend Harry Towb's wonderful stories of his growing up in Ireland. We went home finally aching with laughter. Of course Clement Freud and I were to meet later in the House of Commons, in a much less artistic and fun packed environment.

My dabbles in the theatre were less profitable than my Stock Exchange business. It was however, tremendous fun. I became an "Angel", backing several productions, as one of a team, at £500 a time. They were all avant-garde plays by well known playwrights like Arnold Wesker, John Osborne and Harold Pinter and they were marvellous plays too, future classics. The trouble was few ever broke even. The London audiences were more interested in musicals and farcical lightweight comedies. But it was amusing and a wonderful experience.

I first backed "Fairy Tales of New York", a J P Donleavy masterpiece because Harry Towb, Bill Nagy and Susan Hampshire were in it. Night after night I would stand outside the theatre counting those going in. Not many performances had a full house. I think I could have reeled off the words of the play as well as the cast. It and many other of the plays deserved better.

The London scene of the time was vibrant with new talent and marvellous theatre. This was the era of "Beyond the Fringe", the "hit" of 1961. I had met Jonathon Miller a year or two earlier, before he hit fame. It was at a young friend's party in Hampstead. He was just out of Cambridge as a qualified doctor. When he walked into the room with my friend and started performing, mimicking and miming he had everyone entranced. "Who was he?" the guests asked. What was obvious was that he would be "somebody" very soon.

My business built up but the maximum a firm of partners would ever offer an associate, who was not a Member of the London Stock Exchange, was a third cut from the commission business introduced. I was naturally not on the firm's notepaper. Forward looking equity partners would encourage a promising newcomer to become a full member of the Stock Exchange; that allowed you to receive half of the commission you introduced. The senior partners encouraged me to apply to become a Member. Although the partnership would receive only 50% of my commission, instead of two thirds, it was worth their while, since they realised that my business would grow larger more quickly if prospective clients could see my name amongst the list of partners. So I became a Member of the London Stock Exchange and a half-commission partner. It did indeed help me to attract new clients, including some prized institutional business.

One of the main attractions of a stock-broking career at that time, was that one could and indeed had to combine office work with an active social life. Getting involved in many activities, organisations, clubs, politics and all the many interests in my life was the way to make contact with prospective clients. That indeed was the only way, through personal contact, as no advertising was permitted. The firm even found me an assistant, who could handle orders by phone when I was out and about, contacting prospective business. Soon a personal secretary was also needed and Fiona, tall and Nordic looking, with a soft dialect from the Shetlands, entered our lives. It was not long before my income was several times what I would have been earning as a financial journalist.

The buoyant optimism of the early 60's in the City was to change. It was while I was actively helping the spread of investment clubs that I visited the Houses of Parliament again, not this time as a dinner guest or curious tourist, but on legislative business. It was during Harold Wilson's administration in 1964, when the budget included a clause that would seriously undermine the existence of clubs. Tighter bureaucratic regulation and auditing was proposed for funds such as investment trusts, pension funds, unit trusts and other institutional funds run professionally by fee-earning managers, on behalf of the public ,mostly small savers and investors.

The proposed legislation would have been totally inappropriate for clubs which are groups of members agreeing to share their savings on a mutual investment basis, but with unpaid officers elected by the club's members, annually, administering the club. Investment decisions would be agreed by members democratically at regular meetings. The only costs incurred would be the brokerage commission, as most clubs would meet in member's homes or workplaces or even the back room of the local pub, and postage costs for sending out monthly statements to those unable to attend a meeting. Even audits were often arranged by a qualified accountant known to a member, prepared to volunteer their service.

Many clubs when learning of the Budget proposals were very concerned. It was my responsibility as an honorary officer of the National Association of Investment Clubs, to lobby against this damaging clause that would have put amateur clubs into a costly strait jacket.

I contacted Anthony Grant, the Conservative M.P., who was on the Opposition's Front Bench finance team. A meeting was arranged at Westminster. Tony Grant was an eager listener to our case and he drafted a suitable amendment to the Finance Bill which would exempt amateur investment clubs. Soon afterwards, when the amendment was expected to be reached, I was invited for my first visit to the Public Gallery of the House of Commons. To our relief, the Labour Government team, having had an excellent briefing by Tony Grant, accepted his amendment.

It was my first experience of how the legislative process works. It was beyond my hopes in 1964 that I would ever be more directly involved myself, but a seed was sown.

That came a year later and developed rapidly. Subsequent legislation from the Labour Government began to demoralise investors and the City. My broking business stagnated as penal taxation hit savers and investors. Markets went into recession. Business and company profits suffered. Labour's policies were starting to depress the market economy. I became more outspoken in private and in public, about what I saw reversing all my hopes and efforts to widen and deepen the ownership of wealth in Britain. More and more I was being told "why don't you stop talking and go and do something about it?"!

It was a wake-up call. Very soon I registered myself at Conservative Central Office, as interested in becoming a Parliamentary candidate. My C.V. was recorded; I was interviewed by a senior team of Tory M.Ps. My belief in and work for a capital-owning democracy and my understanding of the way in which the world of finance worked was not only noted – it must have assisted my progress towards Parliament. I was a little ahead of the main stream policy planning at the time, but this would soon change to a priority Conservative strategy. Having by that time moved into my parents' former home in

Hampstead Garden Suburb, where my wife became very active in the local Conservative party in Margaret Thatcher's Finchley constituency, may well have helped also.

Leading the panel to decide who was fit to be included on the Party's list of candidates from which constituencies could select, was a forward looking M.P., Geoffrey Johnson-Smith. In his view, I made the grade. Now all I had to do was to hawk myself around, looking for a constituency that would select me.

Then I realised that might not be easy, as there was keen competition and many talented people on the candidates' list. But I had advantages apart from my acknowledged work to promote a wider spread of capital ownership. One was not having a public school education, but coming from the Grammar School trail, like Ted Heath.

My other asset was my willingness to fight a hopelessly secure Labour seat, rather than expect to be handed a winnable one. So when the solid Labour constituency of Sunderland North looked for a candidate, I jumped in, where many others on the list were not willing to go.

Having Lady Davidson as one of my required sponsors, must also have counted. A prestigious matriarch of the Conservative Establishment, she also gave me sound advice. "Don't turn down a hopeless seat, the experience will set you up." She was right.

Chapter Eight
Sex, Politics and Espionage

Living our first year of marriage in the Kings Road allowed us to believe that we were part of the carefree "Swinging Sixties". In reality we only participated at the fringes. There were occasional visits to Carnaby Street but we were hardly among the big spenders there. Coffee bars, yes and we suffered overcrowded basements blasting out live jazz, rock or pop. Walking around night time Chelsea it was hard not to observe the gay club scene spilling out on to the pavements.

However, life was more earnest in the day time, when I trekked to my stockbroking office stuffily clad in a well tailored dark suit, a stiff collar, bowler hat and of course, black umbrella, even in a heat wave.

We had returned from our honeymoon to the Chelsea flat, in time for the annual Conservative Party Conference. The Investors' Chronicle obtained press passes for both Hilary and I on the basis that I would write them a short report. We took our places in the Press Gallery.

The Chinese were at the time starting to make a rapprochement to the West, and this was the first time a delegation had appeared as observers at the party conference. Hilary found herself in the press coffee room with the Chinese, all decked out in black "Mao" suits. To be sociable she asked them how they were enjoying being in England and the fine sunny weather. After some conferring amongst themselves their spokesman finally said "We have absolutely no comment to make." At this two other journalists at a neighbouring table started laughing and Hilary joined them.

The two journalists were Czechs and by the time I arrived for my coffee,

Hilary was talking to them like old friends. It was the first time I had direct contact with anyone from the Communist East and I was determined to find out all I could about life there. They in their turn knew nothing about the capitalist West, except from their propaganda. They were fascinated to learn that I was a stockbroker and I spent a great deal of time trying to convince them that owning shares was not just confined to the very rich and that ordinary people could buy them. They were not convinced and I arranged to take them on a tour of the Stock Exchange and to introduce them to some of my ordinary clients.

Part of the deal was that I would take them around the Stock Exchange and show them how the investment system worked and in return they would write a frank report back to their news agencies in Czechoslovakia. They would then let me know if their reports were printed without any censorship. They readily agreed to this as they said they were free to send back whatever they wanted, but that it was the editorial decision back home that decided what the Czech people could see.

Not only did I take them around the Stock Exchange, we got to know them well, inviting them to various parties at our flat in Chelsea, where they met our large circle of friends. We introduced them to several "small investors" including a former Czech businessman Denis Illovy, who had escaped from Czechoslovakia when the Communists took over.

I was at my desk in the City one day when the phone rang and a voice said "Peter, Charles here, long time no-see. How's Hilary? How about joining me for a drink to catch up on things?" I had no idea who was talking, but it was obviously someone I knew and who knew me. Perhaps I would remember when I met him? When I arrived in the bar, I was met by a man who I was sure I had never seen before but he introduced himself as Charles and started talking about some of my wife's relations whom I barely knew. I assumed he was a businessman I had met casually somewhere. But, we agreed a time and day for me to visit his office, which had an address in the heart of Whitehall.

When I arrived I thought I was about to be dragged into a real Le Carré plot. Eventually "Charles" admitted that we were strangers and that he worked for our intelligence services. It seemed that they had been watching our Czech journalist friends and reading the reports which they were sending back home. They were very impressed by my work on convincing them of the merits of capitalism and wanted us to keep up the social contact. He urged me to continue bringing them into our set, but to act discretely and tell no-one, except my wife, about this meeting.

The chilling part of the conversation was, however, when he told me that undoubtedly the Czech authorities would by now, be keeping us under surveillance and that we should assume that our telephone was tapped and that our flat was probably bugged. We should be careful with what we said, even in our car. I was given a number to call if I needed to and to let them know what the Czechs were doing. I was still in a rather shattered state when I found the opportunity to take Hilary on a walk out to the Tring reservoirs near my mother's home, to let her know what had happened, well away from any possible eavesdroppers. Hilary cleared up one mystery about how "Charles" knew so much about her family, her uncle was in MI6. I found it sinister that our intelligence services had obviously done their homework on us.

Eager to do our bit in the fight against Communism, we continued to entertain the Czechs and to introduce people to them. After a few months, however, we suddenly lost contact. I thought little about this, perhaps we had become an embarrassment. It was not until we met up with one of the Czechs at a further conference that Hilary asked him what had happened and where was his colleague. He was surprised we did not know that he was in the United States with his family having defected. The lone journalist told us sadly that he had had to send his wife and children back to Czechoslovakia, in order to retain his post. We realised that even talking to him was probably putting him under unfair scrutiny, so apart from the odd word when we met accidentally, we did not take up any more social contact.

Although it turned out well, I have always felt a little disappointed that no-one had bothered to acknowledge our efforts.

While Britain's younger generation revelled in the new permissive society, The City was still a pompously conservative, class-ridden village. Not far removed from the feudal system, everybody was expected to know their place and stick to it. No self-respecting broker would be at his desk much before 10am. The Stock Exchange dealing floor did not open until 9.30am. There were no computer screens, mobile phones, electronic instant dealing or herd of young traders flapping around from seven in the morning until late at night. A partner's lunch break would, more likely, stretch leisurely from 12.30 until three, when important clients were hosted in the firm's private dining room. Business shut down around 4.30pm or soon after. All some years away from today's crowded sandwich bars, where hectic dealers take twenty minutes away from their screens or snatch a takeaway and return to their desk with it. It is extraordinary that so much capital changed hands in such a short day.

This was not just a man's world — it was exclusively a gentleman's club. Women were confined to secretarial roles in the back office, the dingy basement or providing tea and servicing the elegant partners' table. It is hard to imagine that women were still excluded from Stock Exchange Membership in the 60s.

Dealing on the Stock Exchange was a monopoly shared amongst its Members. Banks and other financial institutions were excluded from becoming Members, until Parliamentary legislation ended the restrictive practices in 1986, the "Big Bang" as the City described it. Until then, ambitious, able youngsters found it difficult to join the "Establishment" Club. Most remained as junior clerks, not privileged enough, from the right family or school, to be admitted as Members and partners in firms. All dealings were transacted on the 'floor' of the Stock Exchange, based on instructions from brokers in their offices to their dealers on the 'floor'.

My rise to membership and partnership became possible only because I had a rare advantage. I was a qualified investment analyst, thanks to my five years with the Investors' Chronicle. So I knew something about picking winning investments which helped me build up a substantial clientele, a valuable asset to a stockbroking firm.

One flaw in my climb up the ladder had to be corrected. My coiffure was not chic enough, I was told by one of my senior partners. After all, as students we had crudely "sheep-sheered" each other's hair and during my national service, we suffered the regular two-minute 'short back and sides' ordeal. The 'letting it all hang down' fashion came later. In the sixties trendy hair styling was required, if you wanted to move up.

So the established partner, with whom I shared an office, introduced me to 'Cookie'. I was assured he would give me the 'makeover' required so that I could fit into the uniform essential for a budding 'city-gent.' Cookie's elegant salon was behind Sloane Square, and a fortnightly visit became a ritual for the next ten years. I was not to be allowed to let the side down any longer.

It was not only an exclusive men's salon, with appointments essential. It also seemed to cost a great deal more than other fashionable stylists in London. I soon discovered why. One of Cookie's clients and a friend, was Tony Armstrong-Jones, Lord Snowdon. His hair was regularly attended to at Kensington Palace. Hairdressers, like cab drivers, have a charming characteristic, they communicate fascinating gossip. I soon benefitted from a fortnightly resumé of the Snowdon's lifestyle. I was told that the marriage was already on the rocks although the media had not yet discovered or reported the sordid details. Cookie entertained me with regular unrepeatable stories of nightly escapes from Kensington Palace and enjoyment of 'sight-seeing' in the seedier regions of Chelsea.

I was too discrete to pass on such lurid gossip, however tempting, but the high cost of my fortnightly shampoo and snip was good value. On one occasion I arrived for my appointment and Cookie came out of the salon to apologise that he would have to keep me waiting because he was dealing with an 'important' client who had arrived unexpectedly. I sat down in the waiting area and read my newspaper. In a nearby chair was a woman also waiting, her face half obscured by a head scarf. I was surprised as this was an exclusively male salon and assumed that she was waiting for someone. The cleaning lady then appeared and offered me a cup of tea while I was waiting. She approached the woman with the same question; then I overheard "Do yer mind me asking ma'am, but 'as anyone ever told you, yer the spitting image of Princess Margaret?" "Yes" came the reply in a clear 'cut-glass' voice, "many times."

It was around this time, in 1963, that the Profumo scandal rocked Harold Macmillan's government. More than enough has been recorded about the affair, but I am obliged to add a marginal note, so far unreported, of an involvement in my own story. It was soon after Stephen Ward's death from an overdose of sleeping tablets on the last day of his trial which some claim was not suicide but murder by MI5. He was a successful osteopath, with many well known clients including the American, Averell Harriman, Winston Churchill, Duncan Sandys, Ava Gardner, Mary Martin and Mel Ferrer. He had a clinic in Cavendish Square near Harley Street. Over the years he had gained several other important patients, including Lord Astor, who allowed him the use of a cottage on his Cliveden estate. It was here that he introduced the call-girl, Christine Keeler, to Jack Profumo, the Secretary of State for War at the time. Unfortunately another of the call-girl's clients and one of Ward's set was a Russian diplomat, Ivanov, known to have been a spy. Others in the general melange included Daily Telegraph editor Colin Coote, MI5 head Roger Hollis and the Surveyor of the Queen's Pictures, Anthony Blunt, later identified as part of the Guy Burgess, Kim Philby and Donald Maclean spy ring.

When the investigatory Fleet Street journalists started sniffing around and getting a scent, stories of scandalous behaviour by 'high people in high places' began to leak out. One of my many journalist contacts from my time with the Financial Times Group contacted me to advise me of the Fleet Street rumours and what seemed shortly to explode in the public domain. He suggested that I should warn my M.P, Colonel James Allason, whom I knew well and was one of my sponsors for my application to get on to the list of Conservative candidates, that there was substance in the rumours. Allason was then Jack Profumo's Parliamentary Private Secretary – his 'bag carrier', as M.Ps disrespectfully described unpaid aids to Ministers. If Allason passed on my warning of pending trouble to Macmillan, I never discovered. But it was Profumo's ill advised dishonest statement to Parliament, denying any association with the call-girl that ruined his career.

Stephen Ward was a fine portrait painter and could well have made a living as an artist rather than an osteopath. He was commissioned to paint many well known people, including the Duke of Edinburgh and other members of the Royal Family. After his tragic death his unsold work was put up for a private sale in a London gallery. Before the public were invited in, Buckingham Palace had sent flunkies along to buy up any pictures of the Royal Family. There were certainly good reasons why the Palace wanted to disassociate itself from the scandalous revelations of the whole affair. Sex, politics and espionage were quite enough without any royal involvement.

Hilary and I were hardly collectors of fine art. A few tatty antiques and a large collection of antique maps was our budget limit, but along with a friend who had connections with the Royal Family I was able to attend the private viewing where many of the pictures were sold before it was opened to the public. I browsed around and found in a folder an exquisite unframed portrait of an adolescent, who I believed I recognised. "That is Prince Richard of Gloucester, done a year or two back" said my colleague.

I would have been tempted to buy it, even without such provenance, and now quickly paid the £50 demanded. We were pleasantly surprised and amazed that the royal lackeys had failed to identify it. So now we have a lovely portrait which still hangs on our drawing room wall at Norcott Court. What a splendid souvenir of the permissive sixties!

Chapter Nine
Two Lady Members

Certainly the most important event in my life since my birth was my wedding in September, 1961. We were one of the many couples at the time, who met through the Young Conservatives. We were both on the Hemel Hempstead Divisional YC committee, I was the chairman and Hilary Mayo was the hon. Secretary. The relationship only became serious for me at the Conservative Party conference in Scarborough in 1960. I was there on a Press ticket from the Investors' Chronicle – the magazine did not bother to send their own representative after I left them in 1958 and was happy for me to attend and give them a report – Hilary was there as one of the YC delegates from the Hemel Hempstead constituency. The second delegate was Christopher Grenside, a very active YC from Harpenden.

We YCs were booked into what was described as an hotel but which really an up market boarding house. I had however been invited to a wedding and was driving up to the conference from London and could not arrive until late, well after the other members of our delegation had settled in. I could not see how I could possibly arrive much before 2am and asked the others to make arrangements for me. This was the English seaside in the 1960s! The front door was locked at 10pm with a special dispensation for the night of the Conference Ball, when we could be a little later but all had to come together at a set time to save the hotel staff having to let people in at all hours. The idea of having a guest arrive at 2am horrified them; it was just not possible.

Christopher Grenside expressed the opinion that "Rost can sleep in his car!" Fortunately for me, Hilary was more sympathetic and expressed the view that driving from London to Scarborough, I really would need to have a proper bed for the night. She nobly offered to be up to let me in if the hotel would allow it. After much discussion, the proprietor reluctantly agreed to show her how the front door was locked, where the lights were and how the gas fire in the front parlour operated. Just before they retired to bed, she was presented with an alarm clock set for 2am on a tray.

There was no easy motorway then and I had a long night drive ahead of me. It was a black October night raining heavily and the street lamps were switched off everywhere at midnight. I found it hard enough to find my way to Scarborough, let alone the road and the actual hotel I was meant to be staying in. After sitting in the half dark, huddled over the gas fire, Hilary realised that there was little to show the outside of the place and she eventually found the switch for the external hotel lights and sign. At 3am I came past and suddenly in the darkness there was one hotel lit up in what seemed the whole of Scarborough. I would never have found it unless Hilary had waited up for me. You could say that it was a "magic spark" that lit up our romance.

Hilary showed me to my room, which I was sharing with Christopher. Having rashly told me about his comments, I made sure that I stepped on him firmly on my way over to my bed.

I was determined to invite Hilary out and offered her a lift back to Hertfordshire after the Conference, intending to stop for a romantic dinner en route. Unfortunately, Hilary caught the flu which was rampant at the time and spent the journey back wrapped in a blanket, sipping the odd glass of water. It did give me the opportunity, however, to invite her out later in London, for that "special" meal. My grandmother nearly stopped the romance before it had begun. I had been to see her in the house in Hampstead Garden Suburb, before I picked up Hilary from the tube station on the way to dinner. As I left, grandmother pushed into my hand a bag containing chocolates for me to eat. I did not examine them closely and when I picked up Hilary, I casually said "Oh there are some chocolates in the bag there". She opened the bag and took out a chocolate; it was decorated with a clear impression of my grandmother's teeth. She examined another, and another, they had all been "tried" and found too hard by grandmother. For some years Hilary thought that the chocolates were some part of a test which I had devised to check out prospective girl friends. It was not really a good start to a romantic evening.

I started skiing in Davos as a small boy on the famous Swiss Parsenn run, and after the war ended, I resumed my skiing usually joining my father and step-mother, Eleanor, for a holiday. Hilary had never skied as indeed was the case with most of the British population in the 1960s. It was not a common sport. In the spring, I took Hilary on her first skiing expedition to Davos. She was booked into the ski-school for her first lessons. I must admit to being a little impatient – I was getting bored skiing on my own, so I urged her to move up a class on the next day and again on the following day, until she was proficient enough to join me on the slopes. Doing the same rapid progress up the ski school class ladder was another determined "learner", Joe Dwek, who was later to transform Bodycote into a substantial multinational company and to gain a reputation for turning round ailing businesses. He joined us in trying out the easier runs. By the end of the fortnight, the two learners managed the Parsenn Run with me and it was only then that we discovered that Joe was actually on his honeymoon and that his new wife had not managed to progress further than class one! She cannot have seen much of her new husband during the daytime; I only hope that she had enjoyed the après ski life.

Driving back from the ski slopes in appalling weather we stopped for petrol at a service station near Bruges. It could not have been a less romantic spot. Dark, raining and rather seedy. Behind the service station was a small motel. We checked in and were soon snug under a duvet. I plucked up courage to ask Hilary to marry me. She accepted me on the spot and it was only later I realised that it was April the First. Fortunately she was not joking.

We married in the autumn '61 and moved into the Kings Road Flat. Soon Hilary found she was pregnant and having no doctor in Chelsea, she went to the Town Hall which was next door to consult the list. The doorman recommended his doctor, and Hilary duly signed up. At her second consultation she was asked if she suffered from "Morning Sickness". Fortunately she said no, but she was still given a prescription for the new wonder drug. "Morning sickness? Thing of the past," said the doctor. Hilary had the prescription made up, but fortunately she never needed to take the Thalidomide, because that was what it was! Just over seven months later our daughter Judith was born, healthy and perfect. By that time the first children affected by Thalidomide had already been born and we realised just what we had missed.

I acquired some fantastic in-laws. Hilary's mother Ena, had returned during the war to nursing and had somehow stayed on in the job of District Nurse as it was deemed never convenient for her to leave the temporary post, which became permanent with a pension. Her social work deserved a medal. As my business and political life developed, she as good as moved in during the day time looking after our growing family while we went off on various engagements. She was also an excellent cook and gardener.

Arthur Mayo, my new father in law, was a bank manager at the Lloyds Bank branch in Pall Mall, which had originally been Cox's and King's when he had started there in the 1920s. He remembered TS Elliot working there for a time, and discussing poetry with him. He was also at Berkhamsted School with Graham Greene and had many memories of him which he shared with us. Sadly Arthur had died before we made contact with Graham Greene in Antibes. In the Bank he had kept Montgomery's account for him during the war and discovered that he had a 'double' as he would come into the bank to discuss his account when he was "seen" reviewing the troops in North Africa – so much for the intelligence of our Intelligence Service.

Arthur was commuting daily to London from Hemel Hempstead. He went past his normal retirement age as he was asked to stay on to transfer the branch accounts on to the newly acquired computer; the first one in the bank. He found our flat in Chelsea attractive, particularly in winter with the heavy snowfall we had in 1961 to 62. He would often stay with us for the week and travel back home for the weekend. After two winters spent with us, he had central heating installed in his house, which at that time was quite a novelty. He often kept me up at night showing me that my skills at chess were not as good as I had thought they were.

It was Arthur who later, after we had moved from London, encouraged me to become a Mason. He had been through the Chair at the Gloriana Lodge and also the Lloyds Bank Lodge. He introduced me to sponsors for the Lodge at Berkhamsted. Soon after passing the initial rituals, I asked Arthur to join me as a guest at my new Lodge. When he arrived there was pandemonium. I had no idea that I had brought into our modest set up, a "high up" in Grand Lodge. Arriving fully attired in his magnificent regalia, the Master had to hurriedly rearrange the evening's ceremonies to accommodate the distinguished guest. Apparently, I discovered a representative from Grand Lodge does not just casually arrive, but has to be met with due ceremony. My prestige as a humble new mason rose considerably.

Arthur had more than one other distinction. He was born into a strong Liberal family. His grandfather had been an active Liberal and had been an Alderman of the City of London. His mother had also been active with the Liberal Party women's group and her sister had been at one time secretary to Emily Pankhurst. Needless to say Arthur started his political interest as a member of the local Liberal Party, where he held office. Soon disillusioned, he joined the Labour Party. As a young married man he lived in Welwyn Garden City, where Hilary was born, and knew many members of the Fabian Society. He moved back to Hemel Hempstead and became the secretary of the Labour Party there. He became a Councillor on the Hemel Hempstead Borough Council, where his main interest was in housing, particularly in raising the standards of the rented sector both public and private.

The front page of the Daily Mirror after the war with the famous "Whose finger on the trigger?" finally decided him. He was not taken in by the depiction of Russia as a benign and well organised state where the ordinary man did well, while the horrors of Communism were glossed over. State socialism he saw as a threat and he had been getting more and more concerned with the leftward movement of the Labour Party. He left the Party, to sit as an Independent. By the time of the 1951 election he had joined the Conservative Party where he remained the rest of his life. He became the first Conservative Mayor of the New Town of Hemel Hempstead. He always maintained that he had never changed his politics, but that the different parties had changed theirs. I think he was the only person to have held office in all three political parties in the same constituency! I was grateful that his change of party was not reversed, as I would have found a Labour father-in-law an embarrassment.

Soon after my marriage my grandmother's health was causing concern. She was living in the house in Brim Hill, Hampstead Garden Suburb, where she occupied the top storey with a companion, Alice Cohnberg. She was beginning to show signs of dementia, although she had periods of clarity. Her sight was going and she developed tunnel vision. Alice was also a German Jewish refugee. She had been working as a companion and help throughout the war. However, after the war she discovered that her sister and husband, who with their son Hans Ludwig had gone to Paris and had escaped from there to Lyons, had perished. They had been part of Claus Barbie's transport from Lyons to the death camps. Hans Ludwig had escaped and changed his name to Jean Louis. It was when Alice learned from his fiancée that her nephew, who had been in the Resistance throughout the rest of the war had been shot by the local French collaborators as the Americans arrived to liberate Villeneuve, that she had a breakdown.

Grandmother was told that Alice needed to be "directed firmly" to help in her cure. Grandmother did not need any second bidding; Alice was more of a slave than a companion. When I came to lunch with grandmother, I was always given enormous portions while Alice had some tiny scrap on her plate. I would always insist on not eating until Alice had a proper portion of the chicken, much to her embarrassment.

Alice's family had been fairly wealthy business owners, but grandmother dissuaded her from getting proper compensation after the war, no doubt afraid that she might up and leave. She had been employed by General Electric in Germany and much later, after she came to live with us, we did succeed in getting her a substantial pension from them, after grandmother's death.

The German government paid adequate compensation after the war to the refugees from the pre war Nazi regime and of course to the relatives of the concentration camp victims. My father received compensation for the disruption of his career with the Berlin Frankfurter Zeitung and also for having to leave their home. As I had been at school and was on a school roll, I received a modest token of money to compensate for the disruption in my education. My sister would grumble that not having started school in Germany, she received nothing.

During the War we had occasionally made it to London to visit my grandparents. Sadly my grandfather, Oscar Rosenstiel, only lived for a short time after it had ended. Unfortunately, although my grandparents had managed, with my mother's help to bring out most of their main household furnishings, they had stored their most valuable possessions in the London Depository, which had a direct hit. My grandfather had a non-Jewish partner in his wine business in Germany, so the firm survived the war and managed to keep going, even though the German economy was in ruins.

My grandparents were entitled to quite a considerable amount of restitution, combined with the amount that Grandfather's partner made over to him and the pensions which they had from the German Government.

Unfortunately Grandfather's death came before the financial payments were finally sorted out. My father was furious when he came on a visit from America to discover that Grandmother had ignored her husband's warning not to let her daughter have access to the funds, and that she had signed everything over to his sister Alice, who promised to pay her mother a modest pension in return.

It seems that Aunt Alice had also visited the bank deposit safe and had removed various items, including the rubies from Grandmother's wedding jewellery, which she took back with her to Germany. My father took possession of the key, but only relatively few valuables remained. As Alice Stoess had managed to remain in Germany throughout the war with all her possessions from two well off marriages, and to collect her parents' money plus a large part of the family valuables, she did quite well out of the whole affair.

Imprinted on my memories of Aunt Alice were her sporadic shopping visits to London, usually to buy expensive handbags. She would arrive to stay in the Ritz Hotel with two taxis to carry her suitcases. I have a horror ever since of travelling with bulky luggage and plead guilty to badgering Hilary when she travels with even a modest couple of suitcases. "You are as bad as my Aunt Alice," is even now my conversation stopper.

Hilary's encounters with my aunt were not all that smooth either. We would meet in her son Kurt's house in Lowndes Square, when Alice Stoess would complain endlessly about my father and would insist that Hilary had stolen all the family linen and was, in spite of Hilary's contradiction, Jewish, but in denial. Fortunately, Hilary has a good sense of humour and Alice's exploits became a family legend. Having had sufficient for our own needs, we never felt the urge to destroy family relations by trying to reclaim any of Aunt Alice's "ill-gotten" gains either.

My mother in law Ena had a former nursing friend who ran a very good nursing home in Hitchin. They were prepared to take grandmother and Alice Cohnberg together. Initially they shared a room, but the owner of the home soon summed up the situation and grandmother had a single room, while Alice was to live in the staff quarters, with some privacy and independence. After Grandmother's death, in her nineties, Alice Cohnberg came to live with us.

We moved into the house in Brim Hill taking over grandmother's "flat" on the top floor. The downstairs was let to the Frolics; a couple with a young son, to whom we gave notice to quit. We were stuck upstairs with all the furniture from our King's Road flat and my grandmother's furniture which included much of the stuff that my parents had brought from Berlin, large mahogany beds and wardrobes. And then to help matters, the Frolics sent up the furniture from their downstairs quarters as they bought their own furniture ready to move into their new house. They refused to use the garage as a temporary store, insisting on continuing to keep their car in it.

It was like living in some bizarre junk shop or furniture auction room. In those days telephones came fixed to the wall with a set amount of cord, something like four feet. Our telephone was perched on a pillar at the far side of a room, which had a three piece suite, a double bed, a table and a chest of drawers between it and the door; our "living room". My heavily pregnant wife dreaded the phone ringing as she had to climb over the mountain of furniture to get to it in time! It was not surprising that our first child, Judith, was born nearly a month prematurely, after a rush across London to the hospital in Chelsea where Hilary was booked in. Judith is still suspicious about her early birth, convinced she was a 'love child'. She could be right, but I would never admit it.

The first few weeks of Judith's life, until the Frolics finally moved out, were spent in a carrycot on wheels being moved from the landing, to kitchen, to bedroom, wherever there was space. When we did move downstairs, we found that the rooms had been decorated with pink and blue gloss paint, carefully working around the furniture and pictures on the walls. It was an extra-ordinary sight and gave rise to the family expression of "doing a Frolic" to describe a quick lick of paint somewhere. We were obviously not the smartest residence in Hampstead Garden Suburb.

We were now ensconced in Margaret Thatcher's Finchley constituency. Hilary became involved, when, during the campaign for the local council elections, we found a rash of Liberal posters in our road. She marched up the road until she found a house sporting a Conservative one, and demanded from them where she could get a blue poster for our window. She was soon on the local branch committee and we were having wine and cheese parties for our Member of Parliament in our home. During the election campaign, much to Margaret Thatcher's amusement, Hilary would pack Judith's pram with election literature, so that the baby was barely visible. Margaret would remind Judith of those years later, when she was quite "grown up". We began to learn the ropes of running an election campaign, raising money, operating a branch committee and the ins and outs of local politics.

There is one illustration, concerning my wife, which informs the way that Margaret Thatcher worked in those days. This was the time of the extremist Colin Jordan's Sunday Nazi-style rallies in Trafalgar Square, which were turning into riots, with large numbers of young Jews arriving wearing yellow stars ready to heckle and for a fight with the neo Nazi thugs. The police were finding it harder to keep order with each occasion, as more joined in. The Finchley constituency had a very large Jewish population, many of them like me, refugees from Nazi Germany, and many of the youngsters in the Trafalgar Square demonstrations came from the Suburb and were looking for a way to "fight back" what they saw as a Nazi take-over.

Margaret invited Hilary to lunch at the House of Commons and explained the problem to her. Hilary and a staunch Conservative local councillor, Alderman Miller, were detailed to approach the young members of the local synagogue and to persuade them to stay away from Jordan's rallies and not to give them the oxygen of publicity.

Alderman Miller was a much respected person in the Garden Suburb, having been instrumental in helping very many of the German refugees to get out of Germany and establish themselves there. With the aid of the local rabbi, the two of them tackled a fairly large audience of young men who were plainly angry and determined not to lie down under the insults being meted out to them. Hilary and Miller used all their powers of persuasion and finally got a promise from the young men that they would, for the next Sunday only, stay away from Trafalgar Square. If there was still trouble and publicity, then O.K. they could go back the following Sunday. Colin Jordan's rally the next Sunday was a disaster for him. With no opposition and no Press publicity, it fizzled out. This incident illustrated the way that Margaret worked; analyse the problem, decide what needed to be done; choose someone to do it and then leave them to get on with it!

By some strange way in which events in life connect up with each other, my father-in-law Arthur, had been on the Conservative Party Selection Committee in the Hemel Hempstead constituency when the time came to replace our long standing and much loved M.P., Lady Davidson. She had decided to stand down so that a candidate for the coming 1959 election could be selected. One of the candidates was a young and obviously highly talented, Margaret Thatcher.

Arthur relayed the story to me, that most of the committee was in no doubt about her being outstanding and well ahead of the other candidates. However, after such an amazing woman as Joan Davidson as M.P for so long, who was so well known in the constituency, with such a powerful personality, it was not fair to ask any woman to try to follow her act. So Margaret was rejected in favour of Col James Allason, a very capable and likeable, ex-military man, who certainly was supportive of the need to rebuild the Nation's defence capability, in the face of the nuclear disarmers. Arthur continued to watch Margaret's progress and was very relieved when that "marvellous young woman we rejected" was chosen to fight Finchley. He was thrilled that we had later become her constituents.

I have often speculated about how political history could have developed differently if Arthur and his Selection Committee had accepted Margaret. She would have lost the Hemel Hempstead seat in 1974 after an unfavourable boundary redistribution. Would she have found a safe seat elsewhere in time to become our Leader by 1975 and so our Prime Minister after the following 1979 election? Hilary and I worked energetically for James Allason and continued to do so after we moved to Finchley.

Much of our social life was still back in the Hemel Hempstead constituency, with my mother living in Tring and Hilary's parents in Hemel Hempstead. We returned there most weekends, to play tennis and hockey. The local Young Conservatives had elected me as their President. One such weekend is particularly memorable. It was November 22nd 1963 and we were to attend the main social function of the YC year, The President's Ball. It was a big fund-raising event held at Ashridge College. As the President and his wife we "presided" over the occasion. We dropped off our daughter Judith at my in-laws on the way only to hear the news from them of President Kennedy's assassination. It was my decision not to cancel the event, but so emotional was the shock to everyone that many similar events were cancelled. The atmosphere at our Ball was very subdued and not all those who had bought tickets turned up.

Before we were married, we had both taken part in the Annual Conservative Speaking Competition, competing in the first rounds in the Hemel Hempstead constituency. We were in teams of two, a Speaker and a Chairman. We did fairly well but nothing spectacular. I was rather annoyed with Hilary when I found that she had entered us into the Annual Competition in the Finchley constituency. Rather sulkily I told her that she would have to do the speaking this time and I would simply be the chairman. One was given the subject for the speech only a few days before the event and had to "mug it up" quickly to make a speech and answer at least three questions on it. Hilary always said that it was because she had no nerves, being absolutely sure she would not win, that we ended up winners in Finchley and had to go on to the next round. Again we won and went on to each stage finally losing out in the National semi finals. It was a certain Peter Walker who won the National Competition that year, then the scarcely known National Chairman of the Y.Cs. Later he started Slater Walker with Jim Slater, won a seat in Parliament and became Secretary of State for Energy in Margaret Thatcher's Cabinet. He entered the House of Lords in 1992.

Getting so far on in the Speaking Competition had a curious consequence, when Hilary was invited to act as one of the judges for the Hemel Hempstead Competition the following year. Along with a fellow ex-YC and member of our investment club, Stephen Clarke and a very conservative former army Major, chairing the panel, Hilary was set to judge the contestants. I made up one of the audience. After all the teams had finished the judging took place. Hilary and Stephen Clarke were both firmly in favour of one candidate and tried to convert the Major to their view. In the end he reluctantly bowed to their majority vote and Norman Tebbit, at that time a local resident and airline pilot, was announced the winner. I do not know how far he progressed through the other stages of the competition, but he certainly went a long way on the political scene!

We remained friends with Margaret and Norman and spent a memorable evening at a reception with them at the 1984 Brighton Conference, having a drink at the Conference Hotel bar when we decided it was time for bed as Norman needed a reasonably early night. We were staying elsewhere with friends, but we accompanied the two of them to the hotel lift, kissed them "goodnight" and saw them on their way. At breakfast the next morning we learnt with horror about the bomb blast in the Grand Hotel. We were probably the last people to see them before they were so appallingly injured.

We were spending more and more of our time at weekends travelling out to the countryside. Although we had made changes to the house in Brim Hill, modernising the kitchen and removing the traces of the Frolic's artwork from the living room walls, we still had a problem with where we really wanted to live. I never felt comfortable in a London suburb leaving every morning with my walk to the tube station suitably bowler hatted, with stiff starched collar and rolled umbrella, joining the dozens of other similarly attired City workers. At weekends it would be a rush to get out to Tring, where my mother and step-father had sold their coach business and had moved into an attractive house in a nearby village or to Hemel Hempstead, where my in-laws lived.

There was always something happening in our home area. Most of our contemporary friends lived there and although we made some new friends in the Finchley constituency, we never really put down roots. The problem with the Garden Suburb for us was that although it was a leafy and pleasant place, it was not the real country as we knew it. We decided to look for somewhere more rural.

Quite by chance at the tennis club in Tring where I was chairman, the captain, John Hawkes, who was the senior partner in a firm of estate agents, casually mentioned that the Davidsons' former home was still on the market. The enormous mansion, Norcott Court, which had been the main house in a largish farming estate, had been bought by a neighbour who had stripped it of the farm and buildings and had put the main house and garden back on the market for very nearly the same price as he had bought the lot for. He tried and failed to get planning permission for a clutch of executive homes on the site. The house languished for over five years, until the man saw some sense and reduced the price considerably. However, by this time the place was overgrown and the only easy means of access was by a neighbouring drive and a climb over a fence. Hilary and I had both known the elegant estate when the Davidson family had lived there and knew that it was a very light and airy place, but by this time there were only two windows visible on the front under the foliage. The house stood in the Green Belt in an area of outstanding natural beauty in the Chilterns.

We decided we wanted to live there. Getting John Hawkes to realise we were serious about it was another matter. He laughed. "What on earth do you want with that 30 roomed Victorian monstrosity?" "Live in it!" I replied.

Our offer of £8,500 was accepted. The house under all the creepers and undergrowth was in good structural order, very solidly built by an eccentric rich Victorian lawyer with no expense spared, on the site of an attractive Elizabethan manor house, which he sadly demolished. The same man John Loxley, in order to let in more light to the chancel of the Parish Church, had paid for some splendid Victorian gothic glass windows in place of the beautiful "Early English" ones. Modernisation and decoration would be our problem. The water had been turned off but not before the pipes had burst over the floors. The large Aga in the kitchen was a solid block of rust. The electricity had also been disconnected and as some of the wiring dated back to the early 1900s there was no prospect of having it turned back on until it was completely rewired.

It would be some months before Norcott Court would become habitable, and Hilary was pregnant with our second child. After her previous experience she refused to move from our now comfortable and warm house in Brim Hill, until the coming baby was at least six weeks old.

Our son, Bruno, was born in the house at Brim Hill as Hilary refused to have another child in hospital after her experiences giving birth to Judith in St Stephens, Chelsea, a former workhouse which they were starting to pull down and rebuild. Her ward was the size of a small aircraft hanger, with twenty beds spread down it partially separated by thin curtains. She was emotionally distressed by the sobs of the young mother in the neighbouring cubicle, who was an Irish girl from the unmarried mother's home run by nuns nearby. She had to spend the full fourteen days that was the rule in those days, looking after and breast-feeding her baby in hospital, preparing his layette, in order to hand him straight over for adoption on the hospital doorstep. She prayed out loud every night for a kind and loving family to be found for her son. When I went to visit Hilary for the brief visiting time allowed, she was on the point of breakdown. No wonder Hilary refused to have any more children in a hospital again!

It was with some trepidation that I came to be present for Bruno's birth, but it turned out to be a very relaxed, happy and unstressed affair. He was a very easy and calm baby, who considerately slept through the night almost as soon as he was born. We had none of the awful wakeful nights we had with his elder sister who never seemed to get over her early start in the hospital at Chelsea.

We finally moved into Norcott Court in the Easter of 1964. It was the coldest Easter for many years, after having been perfectly warm and sunny the previous weeks. We had hail and snow, and the house we were moving into had no hot water supply. The copper shortage had struck just when the plumbers were replacing the water system, and although all the pipes were in place, the hot water tank was missing. It eventually arrived on a hot June day, when we had to test the system with all the windows open and the house like a sauna. For now we borrowed electric fires from our neighbours and huddled over the open fires. Although we had been lighting fires in the house, the walls were still cold after five and a half years of neglect. The only hot water we had was from our prized twin-tub washing machine, which we kept in the bathroom and used as a boiler to heat water for the children's baths. John Bloom, who has never been given sufficient credit for his efforts, had made the washing machine affordable to all and we had bought our deluxe model to help cope with the rising nappy problem.

The house soon became a home to us although locally we were regarded as simply "borrowing" the place from the Davidsons. If we needed a delivery or people wanted to be given directions, it was always spoken of as the "Davidson's house". The Davidsons, Joan and before her, her husband John, had between them represented the Hemel Hempstead constituency for nearly forty years. I still remember attending the Conservative Party conference in 1964 after we had moved in to Norcott, and being amazed by the number of Conservative notables, Ministers, former Ministers and Members of the House of Lords who came up to us saying how pleased they were we had moved to Norcott Court and what happy memories they had of the place. It seemed as if half the Conservative Party knew about our move and had been guests in our house!

My Y.C activity in the constituency had brought me into contact with Lady Davidson as our M.P. Public meetings then were still well attended, and with few having TV, elections were still won and lost on the hustings. My first real political public speaking stint was on her behalf, in the 1955 General Election. I was a supporting speaker at her public meetings. I am never likely to forget my first such public meeting. It was in the Labour heartland of the new town area of Hemel Hempstead, being built on the rich agricultural fields about the town. The first houses were being filled with the ex-Londoners from the East End. Some from temporary housing in the bombed out areas, all of them seeking a new life and none of them familiar with the ways of the old country market town, which was Hemel Hempstead at that time. They were mainly manual, factory workers or came from the London docklands.

Such public meetings, my first as an election speaker, had the objective of building up for a climax, when the candidate, Lady Davidson, would arrive to address the meeting.

The first speaker was Lord Davidson. He no sooner got to his feet than he started being noisily barracked. John Davidson, formerly Chairman of the Conservative Party, was well known as having been Parliamentary Private Secretary (PPS) to Prime Minister Stanley Baldwin, before the war. He was hated by those who recalled the General Strike, because as a member of the Government before he earned his peerage, he was instrumental in the forward planning to keep the country moving and helping to circumvent the strikers.

The meeting started to get out of hand and after a minute or so it became obvious Davidson was not going to be allowed to be heard. He sat down to boos from the crowded hall. The atmosphere was not one that his wife, the candidate, would find favourable when she came to present herself, shortly. She was not due for another twenty minutes as she was doing the rounds at perhaps three other meetings in different villages, and it was my turn to rise. As a twenty five year old I had stood in front of student audiences, but as a political speaker on the "hustings" I was still "wet behind the ears" and filled with dread.

Much to my surprise and relief the audience calmed down. Perhaps out of pity for my youthful appearance. I did not dare to start on any overt political subject, so I started on my life story, how I was born in Berlin in Nazi Germany, and how coming as a refugee to Britain, I was grateful and would always value the democratic life here.... The militant group in the audience became silent. I had managed to keep going for fifteen minutes when Lady Davidson sailed in and made straight for the platform. Barely pausing, she thanked me, acknowledged the audience's applause and embarked on her speech. The tension in the air was gone, the trouble makers remained silent and the rest of the crowd listened enthusiastically.

Lady Davidson's constituency style was unique. After we had moved into "her" house, we came to hear of many instances of how she had dealt with the inevitable constituents' problems. Two of these come to mind as showing her way of getting action. In the nearby hamlet of Dudswell, she happened to be passing through one day, when a distraught resident stopped her in the road outside her house, where a group of workmen were starting to install a large red telephone box, right in front of the living room window of her cottage. Lady Davidson asked them why they were not putting it further along the road on a very suitable grass area beside a hedge. Their only response was that outside Nora's window was where it was on their plan and that is where it had to go! "It is nearly lunchtime" says Lady D "Stop work and go and take an hour's break." She went to the local head office in Hemel Hempstead and straight to the top man. Putting the plan, which she had "borrowed" from the workmen on his desk, she announced who she was and ordered him to move the offending box, immediately, to the less sensitive site. Without allowing any time for argument, she marched straight out of the office. It was so much easier to do what she asked, that she got her way. The telephone box still stands on its little grass patch by the hedge.

On another occasion one of her daughters drew her attention to a large family who were living in a converted railway carriage on some waste land off a nearby lane. 'Lady D' as she was known, went to see them. They were a delightful Irish Catholic family with seven children. The father worked locally but did not earn enough to rent a house large enough for his growing family. They had their names down on the Council's list, but there were no houses suitable for them. Lady D went straight to the local Council offices and to the Housing Officer. "Why are these people still living in these dreadful conditions, having been on the housing list for so long?" The answer came "We do not have any Council houses big enough for families of their size." "Why not?" asked Lady D "We have no land to build them on" came the reply. "Well what about the piece of land that their wretched converted railway carriage home is on?" There was no answer to this. Duly a pair of semi-detached five bedroomed council houses was built on the former waste land and the family moved into one of them.

When I was her constituency Y.C chairman, Lady Davidson as the local Member had invited me to her home (now mine) on several occasions. She was always informal and easy to talk to with a personality bubbling over with enthusiasm. She encouraged me to pursue politics and built up my confidence by praising me in public. She suggested I took public speaking classes organised by her political agent, a magnificent Scotsman, MacDonald Watson. Asking me to speak at her election meetings was an enormous boost. Speaking at the 1959 election was much easier as I was more practised and knowledgeable.

When the time came for me to apply to be added to the Parliamentary candidates' list, she agreed to be one of my sponsors. That carried far more weight with the hierarchy of the Conservative Party than I realised at the time. She had retired by then to the House of Lords, as a Life Peer, but she still was regarded as a doyen of the Party. Without her encouragement, it is doubtful that I would ever have made it into Parliament.

Her enthusiastic support for the Young Conservatives inspired many of my generation to take an interest and participate in our political democracy. She rarely refused an invitation to attend one of our events, or speak at our dinners. Her interest was well rewarded by an army of enthusiastic workers during and between General Elections.

Chapter Ten
Sunderland

Almost all ambitious Conservative prospective Parliamentary candidates are expected to prove their ability by fighting their first campaign in a solid Labour constituency. Some well connected, lucky or already established national figures may short circuit this by being offered a solid Tory seat, vacated by a veteran Member.

As I was now on the official list of approved candidates, Central Office advised me that Sunderland North were looking for somebody to fight the expected 1966 Election. The list contained several hundred hopefuls and a constituency looking for a candidate would select up to perhaps 50 names to sift through before deciding which to interview in greater depth to provide a genuine short list.

In solid Labour seats, like Sunderland, only a few people bother to offer themselves for interview. I was asked and accepted.

The competition I had to face when applying to Sunderland North was not too arduous. There were plenty such unwinnable seats in the wilds of the outer reaches of the North and Wales. Most candidates preferred to hunt for marginally winnable prospects, nearer to London. It was still a time when plenty of Tories regarded North of Watford as an uncivilised "no-go" area. For some it still is.

Perhaps it was my over eagerness and enthusiasm at the interview that got me selected to fight the seat. I even expressed belief that we could win, a statement however unrealistic, might have encouraged the selection committee. More likely it was my c.v. Too many Conservative candidates at the time were ex-public school professional lawyers coming from the "right side of the tracks".

It was possible for me to overcome the stigma of admitting that I was a budding stockbroker, by emphasising my crusade for a wider spread of wealth. My ten minute speech concentrated on hoping I could help more of the Tory Party to accept stronger policies to create a capital owning democracy.

My wife was quietly taken to one side by a couple of the ladies present after the selection meeting. They were concerned about her clothes. Hilary was very surprised as she had on a very smart suit in true Tory Blue! We were amazed to learn that in the North East at that time, red was the Tory colour, blue and green were the Liberals and the Socialists. Hilary had very little red clothing and I certainly did not sport any red ties in my wardrobe.

The first Parliamentary election campaign is a challenging ordeal. There was very little guidance. If there was an official Central Office text book, it never came my way. I had attended classes in how to cope with TV interviews. But as no TV political editors seemed in the least interested in what happened in seats which would not influence the National outcome, I did not get called to the studios and no TV crews were seen in our area. But the training did come in useful when I fought my next election in 1970, in a winnable seat.

I seemed out on my own, planning a campaign, preparing themes for daily speeches at meetings and learning how to do the door step canvassing that occupied most of the time of the three week campaign.

Unless a new candidate knew veterans who had been through it, there was very little help except from your constituency agent. Hilda Evans was one of the most experienced Conservative agents in the North East. Clearly I was not the first recruit that she had been asked by Central Office to train for future more winnable combats. Hilda had the whole of Sunderland under her charge. While Sunderland North was solid Labour, Sunderland South had for a brief time had a Conservative M.P, so obviously most of the effort was put into trying to win that seat back. She knew Sunderland intimately and while the Conservative voters from previous canvasses were indentified, these were mainly in the outlying areas such as Whitburn. There were not so many that it was not too exhausting to visit them and ensure they were still on our side.

Apart from the exceptional agent, my main support came from a group of enthusiastic YCs. It was not difficult to motivate them. They came out fighting. One of them had ambitions to become an agent and was a trainee with Hilda. As Hilda was mainly focussed on Sunderland South, John was seconded to our team in the North.

It was John who found us lodgings in Sunderland. His landlord had a house which he was converting into two flats, which had not yet been let. It was situated, picturesquely between the main road coming into Sunderland from the South and a branch railway line which went to the collieries along an embankment at the edge of the back yard. Both proved a fascination for my children, especially two year old Bruno, who coming from the middle of a farming area, spent his whole time in Sunderland trying to escape on to the railway line or into the middle of the main road, constantly pursued by our "mothers' help", Primrose. The top flat was finished if bizarrely, decorated with the then popular, three or four different wallpapers to each room, mostly floral. Hilary and I had our bedroom in the downstairs flat, which was not completed and which was still rather damp. We had one small gas fire in our bedroom which ate money and barely penetrated the cold. Having negotiated a lower rent for the place, we decided that the landlord was making up the shortfall through the gas meter! It was just as well that we were out campaigning from morning to night.

I wanted to "door-knock" the acres of council estates. These were large anonymous areas of housing, where one could only identify which estate was which by the initial letter of the roads. Hence if the road names began with an R, you must be in the Red House estate and so on. There were a few small patches of grass, all bearing the "no-ball games" sign, but no trees. Coming from the south we asked about the lack of trees and were told that they would all be vandalised, so they did not plant any.

None of the more senior active voluntary workers would come around the council estates with me. They were putting their efforts into the South and in any case I was told "Tories don't go there!" So I recruited the bravest of the Y.Cs, and my wife, and set about the endless depressing roads, looking for Tory votes. There were some there, but our side had no idea how to find them. More than once on the doorstep I was told "You are the first Tory candidate I have seen in this part of the world in all my seventy years!"

These concrete and brick deserts were regarded as solid Labour territory. Labour banners and stickers flourished in most front windows. Instead of passing such houses, as most canvassers would, at my prompting, our crew deliberately knocked them up. "I see you have a Labour sticker in the window!" Just occasionally we would get the reply, "All the neighbours are Labour, and as I am a Tory voter, I put the poster up so I don't get a brick through the window!" We gave up trying to persuade them to put up one of our posters; they did not dare put them up as the promise of smashed windows was no idle threat. Our landlord, with similar fears, had banned us from putting up any posters on our rented house. We, however, had no such reticence when it came to decorating our car with posters. It looked very jolly even though I found it hard to stomach so much red.

On the last Sunday of the campaign, Hilary and Primrose took the children out in the car so that I could concentrate on writing my final hustings election speech, ready for the local press. The scenery around Sunderland was beautiful and they had a good day touring around. On returning to Sunderland passing under a bridge, they received a brick through the windscreen which narrowly missed one of the children. The police were informed, but the perpetrators were never found, and we were regarded as rather foolish to expect anything else from sticking up a Tory poster!

Despite my appeal to all my friends from the South to come and help, apart from John Thompson, an old Fleet Street friend who took over as our "unofficial" publicity organiser, only one brave soul, Stephen Clarke, responded. He took the night sleeper from London and arrived in Sunderland at 7am. He found our house but no sign of life. He traced the Tory HQ but that was still closed. Not giving up, Stephen breakfasted and returned to our office at 9am to find it occupied by three of our dedicated voluntary lady helpers, stuffing my election letter into envelopes. Poor Stephen was put to work. I arrived soon afterwards to rescue him.

Unfortunately, he was unable to do much else to help. It was a Saturday. In Wearside politicians were not heard or ever seen on a Saturday. Only football happens there on a Saturday. Our crime was a similar offence to that committed in future election campaigns in the East Midlands – knocking on doors during Coronation Street.

It was obvious from the beginning that we were not expected to turn Labour out and win the seat. Sunderland South might possibly come back our way. The North, however, was solid Labour and would continue that way. If I was to make my mark and show what I could achieve as a candidate, my only strategy could be to attract as much attention as possible in the hope of persuading the few Tory voters who had not bothered to come to the polling booths previously, knowing it to be a hopeless cause, to come out and vote this time.

My opponent was the veteran Labour Minister, Fred Willey. We barely saw him during the election campaign. We met briefly when we all arrived at the Council offices to hand in our election papers. The mayor of Sunderland, who was taking his turn in the chair, was described as a former "sanitation operative". We discovered later that he had been in charge of cleaning the public lavatories for the Council, so we had something in common but I did not discuss techniques. The Chief Executive, carefully coached him in what he had to do, and we handed in our papers which had been scrutinised, for the mayoral signature. "You may now shake hands with Mr Rost!" the Chief Executive urged and we duly shook hands. Fred Willey's team came forward for the same ceremony, but this time the Mayor needed no urging, "Oh I know Mr Willey", he said as he shook him enthusiastically by the hand.

We were told by one of our Tory workers that when a new branch of the National Westminster bank was opened in the centre of Sunderland, the Mayor welcomed them with the classic words "It is so good of you people from Westminster to come all the way from London to open a bank here in Sunderland!"

Apart from his visit to put in his nomination papers, we were not aware of Fred Willey coming back into the constituency to do any campaigning at all. It was like fighting a shadow. He was not one of the Conservatives' most popular ministers in Harold Wilson's Government. He was made responsible for the Government's controversial land nationalisation plans and many land owners feared the worst.

His political career had been damaged by a stupid involvement as a director in a dubious failed business venture that lost many thousands of pounds for small naive investors. It was a pig farming business. Subscribers were told their investment would go into a share of the purchase of a sow. When the piglets were born the farm weaned and cared for them until they were ready for market. When they were sold, the punters received the profits, after costs. Unfortunately for investors the costs seemed to exceed the profits and the scheme collapsed after unfavourable media exposure. It appeared that the sows had been "sold" to investors many times over. The scandalous scheme became known as the"Pig in a Poke"! While Fred Willey had not been actually involved with the pigs, as a Minister for Agriculture he had lent his name to the scheme so giving it credibility and persuading investors that it was genuine.

The unfavourable publicity did not appear to have reached the Sunderland local papers. Perhaps they had been censored? Neither, it seemed, did the rank and file of the local Labour Party know of it.

One of my keenest helpers was John Thompson, an old Fleet Street friend and my daughter Judith's godfather. He was a leading journalist on the Daily Express, their Lobby correspondent and a leader writer. In our search for a subject to attract some attention to our campaign, John urged us to pursue Fred Willey's involvement in the pig business. We secured a young pig from an old friend of mine, Gordon Walters, an internationally renowned pig breeder in Tring. Incidentally it was Gordon who had recruited me into the YCs fifteen years earlier, so helping to start my political career. He had been a leading YC in the Tring area and felt it his responsibility to prepare me as his replacement.

My wife had her small van converted into a mobile pig carrier, complete with day and night quarters. We stocked up on pig feed and with the help of Primrose, who was a farmer's daughter well used to livestock, Hilary set off to drive to Sunderland, alone with the pig in the back of the vehicle.

John Thompson, in charge of publicity, insisted that the pig should be called "Ted" after Ted Heath. Unfortunately, we had been given a young female, so she became "Edwina". Some "sixth sense" caused us not to tell Hilda about the new aspect of our electioneering. Edwina was launched on the first day of the campaign. We set off to a suitable estate with a popular pub nearby, with Edwina in her "mobile" sty. John Thompson had arranged for the event to be well attended by the media. Photographers and film crews arrived in response to our press release. I walked around the area canvassing with Edwina meekly trotting on behind secured by her rope and harness. She was an amenable pig and had been hand reared. She smiled on her audience, most of whom had never been as near to a pig before.

When asked why our "mascot" was a pig, we would answer "You must ask Mr Willey that question. He will tell you all about pigs!" The headlines screamed in the Nationals, with pictures of Edwina "the Tory mascot in Fred Willey's seat". They had all been waiting for the chance to tell the story of Fred Willey's involvement with the pig scam and I had given them that platform.

Whether it damaged Willey's position is doubtful, but it did upset the Labour Party's complacency as we learned that he was recalled from London to Sunderland, during the election campaign to explain what it was all about. We understood that it was the first time during any election he had been in the constituency before Polling Day. He did not however, appear on the streets in Sunderland to take part in any electioneering. As the Labour votes were "weighed" rather than counted, it probably had little effect.

However, we encountered problems in continuing our campaign with Edwina, as some of our more mature helpers were, as I was firmly told by Hilda, not prepared to walk the streets and knock on doors, trailed by a pig. The reality was that Conservative Central Office did not appreciate our individual approach to campaigning, which was in their view a "distraction" from the main issues of the election. They had sent down their orders to Hilda and demanded that Edwina was "put out to grass."

She was found comfortable quarters with a local farmer, who refused our offers to let him keep her permanently. He may have regretted this later, as her brother eventually won the top pig prize at Smithfield, and after living with us for over a year Edwina, went on to a career with a local farmer breeding prize pedigree piglets. However, we did liven things up a little.

Shipbuilding was still the principal activity in Wearside in the 1960s. To make any impact I had to get into the yards and talk to the thousands of employees. I asked Hilda to book visits to all the yards suggesting invites to the canteens over the lunch period. She was bemused. No Conservative candidate had canvassed inside the yards. The Labour dominated shop stewards would give me a rough reception. The management would be embarrassed and would be reluctant to allow me in, in case I created havoc and riots, I was warned.

I insisted and reluctantly I was given the information, for me to ask for access to three of the leading yards. However, Hilary who had accompanied me to all my previous meetings was refused entrance on the grounds that she might hear some "bad language"! She protested but they remained adamant. They could just tolerate a Tory, but a woman was a step too far.

It was a far less frightening experience than I had feared. I was given a hearing and overheard comments such as "The lad has guts" for coming and talking "Tory stuff" at us.

Of course part of my intention was to start with a chat with the management in the board room. Business was no longer booming as in the immediate post-war era. A good look around left me with premonitions of problems ahead. What particularly bothered me was the rigid "class" structure that ruled the industry. Modern management styles, already beginning in other industries, were not much in evidence.

There appeared to be an "apartheid" system with total segregation between management, staff and workers. Separate car parks, canteens and work entrances. Much of what I saw reminded me more of the Victorian era of boss and employees too often in conflict rather than a more modern team spirit required for competition, productivity and survival. When I asked whether any sort of profit sharing schemes, pensions or equity participation for employees existed, the response was more often blank expressions of surprise.

I left fearful for the future of the continued world eminence of our shipbuilding industry.

Whether it was the state of our accommodation or a bug I had picked up canvassing, in the second week of the campaign, I began to feel very unwell. I had flue fairly badly, but I needed to keep going as I had several important commitments. Dr Burns, one of the Conservative Executive Committee, took over. I do not know what she gave me, but I duly took the medicine as prescribed. I managed to function in the daytime, but at night I took to my bed with a soaring temperature. Hilary spent her time pushing money into the gas meter to keep the pathetic fire going, in between lying watching the large pile of bedclothes beside her, steaming up the windows behind the flimsy curtains. Thanks to Doctor Burns, the campaign stayed on track.

Sunderland and the North East was a complete contrast to our home territory of the South East of England. After some time observing the way people behaved, and tuning our ears into the local accent, we began to make some sense of the scene. We were fascinated by the cottages, especially their front rooms, which were designed to be looked at from outside. The curtains faced the road with their backs to the rooms and each windowsill held some particular cherished piece of porcelain. Large dogs were the favourite subjects. It was Hilary who worked out that the "shivering sight" of the women in particular standing in the street chatting away; leaving their front doors wide open behind them, with the cold east winds blowing away, was because they did not heat their homes. They were as cold inside as outside. Only one room would be heated with a coal fire, where the family would live. The rest of the house was left as a permafrost zone.

I was surprised to find that in the North East with its prevailing easterly winds and cold climate, most homes had little or no insulation or double glazing. Even the larger houses and hotels were badly served. When I was first selected for Sunderland we had spent one uncomfortable night in a fairly large major hotel, shivering, while the ill fitting windows rattled in the wind and the rather tepid radiators discharged most of the heat outside. No doubt the abundance of coal had contributed to this situation. But living conditions were very Spartan. We were shown one architect designed house which was considered remarkable in the area, as it had been built with double glazing and insulation. Such a home was commonplace in our part of the country. The problems of fuel poverty and poor home insulation made a deep impression and stayed with me from Sunderland into my Parliamentary career.

The last week of the campaign was going well for us, but not nationally. Harold Wilson was still high in popularity and his position in the polls, ominous. Sunderland football club was at that time at the bottom of the First Division and faced the danger of relegation. By some happy chance the football colours were red and white, and red was the Tory colour in Sunderland. One of the last publicity stunts we tried was to construct banners and a red painted sandwich board, proclaiming in large letters "Keep Sunderland in the 1st Division! Vote Rost!" Accompanied by my excited four year old daughter, dressed in red waterproof with her favourite red wellies, and a small notice with "Vote for Daddy", we picketed the entrance to Roker Park, Sunderland's football ground on the Saturday afternoon. Our red rosettes merged well with the red and white ones of the crowds. Judith and I watched the game from the stands. Sunderland drew. I have forgotten whether that was enough to save relegation.

In the evenings, I organised a group of the more robust YCs for pub crawls. There was more than our fair share of pubs and many in the 1960s were not places for genteel Tories, let alone my wife who came along as well most times. But we were seen, recognised and respected for meeting the voters on their home patch – their locals. I remember an occasion when in a pub on one of the estates, we got talking to several local women about the problems of the day when one thoughtful woman came out with the fact that she had always voted Conservative. Her friends were amazed, but not hostile. "Well Betty, I've known you for over ten years and I never realised you were a Tory!"

On polling day we toured the polling stations. Each was picketed by shop stewards wearing enormous Labour rosettes. It was almost intimidating. The polls were fairly quiet during the day and our returns looked very good by four in the afternoon. However, as the evening came on we were amazed by the military efficiency of the Labour Party. The streets of the large council estates were toured by Labour adorned cars with loud speakers. The shop stewards stormed the streets with clip boards, standing at the ends of the roads ticking off the names of the men who poured out of their houses obediently, to be taken to cast their votes. The Labour avalanche swamped anything we might have achieved.

The result was better than I dared to hope. Labour's vote was up, but so was mine. Most importantly for the report back to Central Office was that we, in Sunderland North had achieved the lowest swing against us of all the constituencies in the North East. Sadly, for Hilda with all the effort they had put into it, Sunderland South had remained solidly Labour, further away than ever. I was full of praise for her and valued her friendship. She visited me in the Houses of Parliament when I finally made it, and invited me as a speaker in the North East from time to time.

We secured several good friendships which outlasted the campaign and I discovered what politics was all about at the sharp end. We saw a part of Britain we had not known before, the shipyards, the council estates and the pubs. My respect and admiration for the "Geordie" spirit has lasted ever since.

As with all first timers, Central Office was sent a report from our agent and the constituency chairman. It was not of course for my eyes, but it cannot have been bad as I was still on the candidates list and when the hunt for candidates resumed for the next Election, I found I had some more promising offers.

Chapter Eleven
Derbyshire

We were beginning to get settled into Norcott and to fall under its undoubted charm. Bruno coming there as a baby, was growing up to regard tractors and cows as the normal scene and both children grew adept at climbing trees and scrambling through the undergrowth. At the edge of the main lawn is an enormous lime tree, which is shown as well grown in paintings of the house made in the 1820s. It must have seen a succession of events and people. It became a pivotal part of our children's childhood and later my younger daughter, Jessica, chose to be married under its canopy.

Hilary researched the house and site with the local records office and along with the Court Rolls dating back to the 16th century. We found that Norcott had once been owned as part of the estate of John Hampden whose stand against "Ship Money" with John Pym and John Eliot, played such a major part in the start of the English Revolution. Hampden's statue stands at the entrance to the Commons alongside Churchill's.

For years the Norcott estate had been entailed through the Smart and Loxley families. Through descendants of the Loxleys, we found that during the Civil War, in spite of John Hampden's connection, the estate was in the hands of Royalists and Charles I used it as a base for some winter months. We were offered the ancient 17th century, twenty-seater dining table, which had been rescued from the old house by relatives, when it was "modernised" by the Victorian, John Loxley and he was consigning things, now regarded as precious, to the bonfire. It was in pieces in a barn, where it had been for about thirty years. We took days reassembling it, nearly coming to blows. It now stands in our dining room, once more back at Norcott where it belongs. Not surprisingly, the Loxleys would not part with the pewter dinner service which was left behind by King Charles when he ate off our table, but they did give us a copy of the house rules "For the Better Conduct of Norcott Court" penned by Charles I and published in London after the Restoration in 1660. With such admonitions as "Touch no State Matters" and "Make no Long Meals" it has amused our visitors. I do not think many people have house rules set by the King.

Twelve Rules for the Conduct of Norcott Court

Tell no lies

Voice no ill opinions

Lay no wagers

Make no long meals

Betray no secrets

Touch no state matters

Urge no health

Give no ill counsels

Help no enemies

Countenance no hatred

Covet no possessions

Break no peace

These twelve Good Rules, sincerely kept,
will give a quiet, peaceful and long life

This was copied from a printed sheet which was published in London in 1661 after the Restoration of Charles II. The rules which purport to have been made by Charles I were "found in the study at Norcott Court" after his stay there during the Civil War.

Due to a series of minorities the estate was leased out for several years. The Tuke family lived there in the 1920s when Anthony Tuke senior was Chairman of Barclays Bank. Tennis courts were constructed where the Bank had its annual tennis tournament. The badgers have now taken over the courts and any tennis playing would be dangerous today. Anthony Tuke's namesake grandson was born at Norcott, later to be Sir Anthony Tuke, and in his turn he too became Chairman of the Bank. He was a governor of Berkhamsted School for many years alongside my wife and apart from several photographs, he gave us accounts of the life in the house in the days when there were numerous servants rather than just the odd daily help and au pair.

It was, however, under Lord Davidson and his wife Joan, known as Mimi, that Norcott again resumed a place at the centre of National life. Stanley Baldwin regarded the place as his second home, particularly after the death of his wife. The Davidsons and the Baldwins holidayed together in France, along with Stanley Baldwin's cousin Rudyard Kipling and his wife. It was John Davidson who had suggested to Bonar Law that he took Stanley Baldwin as his PPS, which was the first step to his eventually becoming Prime Minister.[1]

R A Butler in his memoirs mentions conversations which he held with Stanley Baldwin in the open porch at Norcott and it seems that in his last years Baldwin was established there under Mimi's watchful eye, where he would hold court. R A Butler or Rab as he came to be known, was of course mostly famed for the 1944 Education Act which completely changed education in Britain. He held most of major offices of state except Prime Minister. Chancellor of the Exchequer under Churchill, Home Secretary with Macmillan and as Deputy Prime Minister and Foreign Secretary under Sir Alec Douglas-Home. I had certainly expected Rab to take over from Harold Macmillan when he stood down rather than Alec Douglas-Home, but at that time there was no leadership election process involving the whole party, simply "soundings" taken by the upper echelons.

During the Second World War, Norcott was conveniently placed in the Chilterns not too far from Chequers, to be an unobserved meeting place. Churchill used it when needing privacy for sensitive meetings and on occasions would stay overnight. We impress, particularly the foreign visitors to our house, by putting them in the bedroom where Churchill has slept. Somehow the fact that Stanley Baldwin also slept there and more often, does not have the same cachet.

Most of the farmland belonging to Norcott sold by the Davidson's had

---

1   Ref J.C.C Davidson's Memoirs and Papers 1910-1937 author Robert Rhodes James –
Weidenfeld & Nicolson

been kept by our neighbour living up the hill from us. We had bought a substantial part of the outbuildings and most of the 17th Century barn and coach house, with the Victorian house. But the rest of the buildings, the stabling for the horses, a staff cottage and a small part of the old barn, were not sold and remained empty for some time needing quite a lot of renovation. Just when we had decided that we could now manage to restore these rather run down buildings, they were bought by an eccentric, George Wilkinson.

George with his partner Judy moved in with their young son, Phillip. George designed and built sets for a small film company which mainly dealt, it appeared, with the building trade. George would bring back whatever materials he could salvage from the sets and used them for his cottage "makeover". The result was bizarre. The stables were converted into a living space with a magnificent fireplace, which lacked a chimney. The rooms were decorated in a strange mix of wall coverings and some of the rooms upstairs were accessed by doorways under four feet high. Unfortunately, George had learned very little from the building trade films which he helped to make and the result was in some cases, dangerous. One had to avoid the "live" water pipes in the bathroom and take "care" with some of the stairs. We used to warn our children when they went to play with Phillip, to mind the outward bound obstacle course.

The space over the stables he converted into a small dark flat, accessed by a rickety wooden staircase which he had reclaimed from his section of our large shared barn. He let this out to some Poles, but lived in constant fear of the Inland Revenue or the local Council finding out what he was doing. Matters came to a head when he asked Hilary to come and help him with his tenants. They evidently spoke French and German, but not very good English. Needless to say, George spoke no languages. He was worried that the authorities might catch up with the mysterious nightly comings and goings, with strange individuals visiting his tenants. This was the era of the Citizen Band (CB) radio, and many houses, including ours, had radio masts for the enthusiasts. We were puzzled why George's cottage had a particularly high mast especially when Phillip said his father did not use a radio.

Hilary had developed a nodding, minimal acquaintance with the Poles and was asked by George to find out what was going on and ask them to stop. He told her that his "tenants" spent hours at night on the radio, chatting away in

Polish. Very quickly, Hilary discovered that we had the English base of "Solidarity", the opposition to Poland's Communist Government, installed next door to us. The night time activities were arrangements for collecting political refugees from Heathrow, keeping them for a night or two before passing them on to other parts of their clandestine network.

George was terrified. Perhaps he had seen too many wartime spy films, but he was convinced that he was about to be visited by the British intelligence authorities, and be locked up – or worse pay out a fine!   It took all my persuasion to convince George that he was doing a marvellous service in supporting these Poles in their fight against the Communist Government. He feared he would be discovered by Communist agents, who might be aware that "Solidarity" was organising itself in Britain. Eventually, he reluctantly conceded that they were doing nothing illegal. However, as he had converted the stable flat without planning permission and was not declaring the rental income, or I suspect much else, to the Inland Revenue, he remained very nervous. It was intriguing to observe the preparations our Polish neighbours were making for the overthrow of the Communist regime. They were justly rewarded by the triumphant return to their homeland as a reborn free, democratic nation.

Although our much more modest stone built bergerie in the Pays de Fayence has been our principal home in recent years, we cannot face selling Norcott. Moving on from what has been the nucleus of our family life for nearly fifty years has proved too difficult to contemplate. Moreover, Norcott has been the focal point of our social and political existence. It represents an important witness to the Nation's modern political history. Letting it go would also seem to us like the premature end to the most significant chapters of our life, an end to a personal era. So we hang on returning nostalgically to what must be the largest 'pied à terre' in Hertfordshire.

By 1968 Harold Wilson's Government was beginning to fall apart, hit by a severe balance of payments crisis, austerity, the falling pound and rampant Trades Union strikes. Conservative Parties in the constituencies were actively seeking enough suitable candidates of the right calibre, to win the marginal Labour seats to give Ted Heath the Premiership.

I was invited to apply for Buckingham, a Labour marginal held by Robert Maxwell, the flamboyant Czech-born magnate, who later acquired the Mirror Group.

There were around 100 applicants and perhaps twenty or so were interviewed. I made it into the last five and braced myself for the constituency final selection meeting, at which one of us would be selected. The seat looked eminently suitable, near my Berkhamsted home and easily winnable if the national swing to the Conservatives was going to bring us into Government. However, Maxwell was a controversial extravert publicist, well ensconced and capable of using his undoubted wealth to fight back.

I failed to win the competition which saw William Benyon chosen to fight the seat. However, on my way out I was quietly cornered by the Chairman. "It was a very close thing, you know. We liked you but we did not dare to risk having you." The Executive feared the public personality based slanging match that would probably result, given Maxwell's belligerence, during a hard fought election. "Two refugees, one from Germany and the other a Czech, slogging it out in public, with no love lost between them, might be more than the electorate could tolerate." I am sure they were right! I knew more about Maxwell than he would wish to have exposed and my many media contacts would have tempted me to go for him.

Vacancies were coming up fast as constituency associations wanted to have their candidates in place quickly, to give them time to prepare for an election which seemed to be approaching us, as the Labour Government limped from crisis to crisis.

I was on the point of leaving for a holiday skiing with Hilary and our two children, when the phone rang in the house. For a moment I debated whether to answer it or not and fortunately decided to rush back in. It was the agent for South East Derbyshire asking me to come for an interview in fourteen days time. I was to be one of a dozen or so that had been selected for interview out of hundreds from the Central Office list. As we drove off, we were already working out how I was going to get back in time for the interview. I flew back early, leaving Hilary to drive back from Switzerland with two small children. I could so easily have missed that phone call!

Friends, who knew Derbyshire, told me how lucky I would be if I got the seat, with the Dales, the Peak District and the abundance of stately homes. But my research quickly revealed that the South East Derbyshire division was mainly the industrial area between Derby and Nottingham. The M1 ran straight through the middle and the largely working class railway and textile town of Long Eaton was at its heart. Suburbs of Derby were included as were worked out abandoned coal mines in the Erewash valley. There were some typical rural Derbyshire villages and the attractive old market town of Melbourne, but also the relics of the Industrial Revolution. What the constituency was not was the scenic part of Derbyshire, which was further north. Apart from a brief period between 1959 and 1964 the constituency had returned a Labour Member of Parliament since its inception in 1950. However, the Labour majority had been falling in recent elections. It was certainly not the mountain to climb that Sunderland had been!

The Selection Committee had whittled the list of applicants for the seat, down to about twenty, who were called for interview. This was a long process as they would only have two or three candidates at each meeting. After several sessions a short list of four was chosen. I was one of the four. I was told that the Committee was impressed that I had been prepared to cut short a family skiing holiday, to attend.

There was a revolution underway in the Party, promoted by our new leader Ted Heath. As a grammar school boy, coming from a humble lower middle class background, he was keen to broaden the range of new candidates closer to his background.

Fewer public school boys were on the candidates list and more were sought from other circumstances. A privileged education counted for less, while some experience in the "real world" of business and industry counted for more. A new look party hierarchy wanted to see less lawyers and fewer candidates whose main experience came from a spell in Central Office. But women, unless exceptionally talented, had a hard time. Not until our next leader, Margaret Thatcher, did the transformation become truly democratic.

Constituencies like to preserve their independence. A recommendation from Central Office could be the kiss of death for an ambitious candidate. Selecting their prospective M.P is a power and privilege enjoyed by party workers, justifying all the voluntary work they do for the Party. It is of course quite possible for a constituency to select a candidate not on the Central Office list. But most accept the benefit of prospects having been vetted and approved. Yet, recent political history is littered with examples of candidates pushed too hard by Central Office having been rejected.

Among the other hopeful candidates was George Gardiner, later "Sir"

George. While waiting for us in the anti room, Hilary and George's wife Juliet discovered that they had been at school together in Berkhamsted. I found out later that George, who was a talented Lobby correspondent, was rejected by the Selection meeting because of his remarkable facial similarity to the sitting Labour Member, Trevor Parks. Trevor was typical of a section of the Labour Party at that time in rejecting convention. He was probably the worst dressed Member in the House, frequently turning up in bedroom slippers, grubby baggy trousers and a shapeless knitted cardigan. He certainly never wore a suit and there was some doubt as to whether he actually owned a tie! I am sure that George, whom I knew through his journalism, would never have appeared in such a garb. There is no accounting for what small matters can influence decisions, and how much fate comes into play.

When my turn came for the final selection meeting, all the local Association "paid up" members could attend. Each of the four candidates, who had managed to make it, was given a chance to speak before facing a lengthy questioning session. Presumably my address went well. I emphasised my conservatism, my hopes for the country under Tory rule and what I hoped to do for my constituents. All that passed reasonably under my control, but it was the questioning afterwards that puzzled me. The first questions were fairly routine ones on where I stood on various points of policy such what about the rates of Corporation Tax? Too high, I replied. Then came the strange questions carefully phrased perhaps not quite as openly in these words but with the clear implications – "Do I sleep with my wife?" A little taken aback I replied "Of course perhaps too much, if you believe in the evidence of our children!" A second googly was bowled, again not quite so direct but implied, what were my drinking habits? My answer was a glass or two of beer or wine occasionally. But if we do not get rid of this Government soon I might have to turn to drink. More laughter greeted this. Then came the third curious question, what sort of car did I drive? No problem there, it was a modest British Leyland model.

The possession of an acceptable wife was an important part in the choice of candidate. However, the former practice of interviewing the wives or partners with their husbands, had been strictly forbidden. Nevertheless, Hilary had accompanied me on a tour of the constituency beforehand and we had been entertained for tea by the constituency chairman. No doubt she had been well inspected. The "two for the price of one" was not so overt but still around!

After our ordeal, all four of us were asked to wait outside while the meeting voted on us. The honours came to me. I made a short acceptance speech and Hilary was wheeled out on to the platform and asked if she would like to say a few words. She promised to give me full support and wisely asked about the women's groups in the constituency. By the end of the evening her diary was open and various speaking engagements were already filled in. Pictures of our two young children were passed around.

We all celebrated with some refreshments and the atmosphere relaxed. Hilary and I started on the long chore of trying to remember the names and faces of our new Party workers. We left Derbyshire that night happy that the hunt for a place in Parliament might be over. The real test of course was still to come.

It was much later, when we had got to know him well, that I cornered the agent about the proceedings. "What," I asked him, "were those odd questions about?" It turned out that in the brief time that South East Derbyshire had elected a Conservative M.P, for one Parliamentary session only, there had been problems. The M.P's marriage had broken down as his wife had not been able to cope with the position of being in the public eye. She had left him taking the children. He had then spent more time than he should in the bars at the House of Commons, where the alcohol flowed freely drowning his sorrows. The Party in Parliament had called in some of the constituency elders, who had travelled to London on more than one occasion to dig their Member out of the bar and pass him on to be propelled through the appropriate voting Lobby. His final act had been to drive his fast and flashy car while quite inebriated and cause an accident. Their carefully designed questions were to ensure that they did not have a repeat sequence of embarrassing events.

There is a footnote to this part of the story. Britain's first motorway, the M1 now cuts through the area, with Derby to the West and Nottingham to the East. When I had first been invited to take part in the selection process, I believed the area was unexplored territory for me. But on arrival in the centre of Long Eaton I realised that I knew the place, intimately. When I had nursed Sunderland in the run up to the 1966 election, I had travelled regularly by road from our Hertfordshire home. The M1 was still under construction and ended abruptly at the East Midlands Airport, south of Derby. Traffic then had a slow crawl for more than 10 miles before regaining the dual carriageway on the Nottingham ring road to the A1, on its way North to Sunderland.

The connecting route went straight through the centre of Long Eaton, with an almost permanent traffic jam. I had edged my way slowly through the High Street many times and knew every inch.

Each time I had passed this stretch I had cursed it for making my journey even longer, particularly when passing through late at night after two days of canvassing. It always seemed to be snowing, icy, foggy or raining as I drove through what looked to me like the drabbest town in England.

After being selected to contest S.E. Derbyshire in 1968, I changed my view. Without the traffic and getting to know the local people changed my dislike to a love of the area. We decided ahead of the coming election to show our confidence to the prospective voters that I intended to become their M.P., by buying a small house in the constituency. Although Melbourne or one of the other pretty villages on the fringes of the Constituency with their rural settings tempted us, we settled on Long Eaton. The small house we purchased was on the corner of the Tamworth Road, the very stretch I used to pass, breathing uncharacteristic expletives, on my way to Sunderland! We could not have shown stronger faith than to move into the heart of the working class area of the town and we were certainly given the impression that it helped to win the seat.

Chapter Twelve
Suspension

It was not many weeks after I had been adopted as the Parliamentary candidate in a winnable seat that I suffered a setback that almost ruined both my political and stockbroking careers.

I was consolidating my prospects of being elected at the next election, expected in 1970, by spending a great deal of my time in Derbyshire. Almost every week and certainly most weekends, I left my City office and took off in the car to the constituency. My business was handled in my absence by my assistant and my invaluable secretary, Fiona.

At the time I had many clients amongst the young hopefuls, eager to make their mark in the City. One of these had, I am not sure how, upset the hierarchy of the inner circle of the Stock Exchange and a decree had been sent out ordering that brokers were banned from dealing for him. There was a list of alleged malefactors circulated to all brokers with whom dealings were banned. Unknown to me another junior partner in my firm had been approached by Philip and had dealt for him. I had been away from the City at the time, nursing my constituency and would certainly not have allowed unapproved dealings as neither did my assistant on my behalf.

The firm needed to make a gesture and the junior partner in question was well connected with his father a senior partner on the Stock Exchange. I was chosen to "take the rap" on the grounds that I had introduced the banned client to the firm. Unfairly, it was stated that he was my client and any dealings he had with any other member of the firm were my responsibility. Had they shared the commission for any dealings with me I might have gone along with this, I protested. I was not prepared for the full force of their persuasive techniques and was not given time to think things through. I was asked for my resignation as a partner and to my eternal regret I gave in and resigned. Had I not done so, no-one could have connected me with the scandal which was nothing to do with me.

With the press already scenting a story, my resignation was all that was needed to divert attention from the other partners in the firm and for everyone to assume that in some way I was responsible for the rogue dealings. It was useless to protest my innocence.

Matters were even more upsetting for me when William Davis who we had counted among our close friends, wrote a scurrilous piece about us. He was the City Editor of the London Evening Standard at the time and his article would certainly have been read by people who worked in the City and the commuters to London. I had first met Bill when he was on the Financial Times and I was on the Investors Chronicle, both part of the same Group. We had entertained him at our home and he would stay overnight at our Berkhamsted home. I thought I knew him well. Although he knew perfectly well that we were not a wealthy well connected couple and that the Berkhamsted house was an ongoing "do it yourself" project – he had even helped clear the drive of undergrowth – he wrote a piece, which described me as a "wealthy stockbroker", "living in a mansion on the slopes of the Chilterns etc." The clear implication was that I was some sort of shady dealer, a dishonest wide boy living on ill gotten gains.

It was a disgraceful, unjustified piece of malicious journalism. Any decent journalist would have checked with the victim first, especially one who was a known friend. Though not a vengeful person, I was angry and hurt. If he had attempted to hear the full account, he could have written a different piece more sympathetic to me and perhaps exposed my accusers' unfairness. That would have been good journalism, righting an injustice.

Davis went on to the Guardian as their economics editor, but it was years later, when he was editor of Punch that an opportunity for revenge came quite by chance. Hilary and I were enjoying a skiing holiday in Davos. Swiss bistros and bars, like the French ones always leave piles of newspapers and magazines around for the customers to browse. We happened to flick through one, an obscure Swiss magazine, to find an article in German on William Davis. We were amazed to learn that Bill had a German background and that he had lived in Nazi Germany all through the war, only coming to Britain as a young adult. It was not the fact that he was German that bothered us but that he had never thought to mention it. All the time we had known him when he was fully aware of my background, he had carried on the pretence that he was British through and through. The piece in the magazine was a nasty exposure, implying that he was a Nazi sympathiser with much about his early life in Germany which had not appeared in the public domain in England. I do not know who the author was but he was obviously particularly exercised by the fact that such a person could be editor of such a quintessentially British publication as Punch.

Hilary and I were amazed. We knew what to do. Surreptitiously we abstracted the pages from the magazine. Back in Britain the article was sent to the one publication that would not be afraid to "have a go", Private Eye. A number of pieces about William Davis appeared and he was ever after dubbed "Kaiser Bill" along with some other less than polite names. I do not know what psychological disorder motivated him, but I felt I had done my duty and "evened the score"!

I was not alone in the broking firm of Spence Veitch in feeling unhappy at the way things were going. There were other brokers in the firm who expressed similar concerns. Already there was a great deal of disquiet at the way in which the Stock Exchange was run. The modern ideas of openness and transparency were anathema to the upper clique who were still operating as if in the Victorian era. Several of us banded together and left to form a new broking firm, Tustain and L'Estrange. It was a very happy set up. Larry L'Estrange even tried unsuccessfully to get elected to the Stock Exchange Council, but the establishment was too strong for him.

The firm was successful and we had attracted several younger brokers and even more established figures, who were trying to break away from the sterile and antiquated attitudes of those who were controlling the system. My business prospered.

Out of the blue and without any proper process of a charge or with an opportunity to explain or defend myself, I was called to the Stock Exchange Council and told that I was "suspended from the floor of the Stock Exchange!" No civilised system of justice was practised by the Stock Exchange Council, which operated and regulated itself like a private club behind closed doors, more like an offshoot of the Mafia.

Instead of calling me in to explain my side of the events which led them to this drastic action, I was given no proper right to defend myself. I might just as well have been a citizen arrested in some corrupt dictatorship, without a trial. All I could do was to set out in a paper in great detail what had happened and why. This represented some sort of appeal as the sentence had already been inflicted. My explanations were totally ignored.

The antiquated undemocratically operated Council, with its clubby rule book was totally out of order in a modern western society governed by fair practice. Under the Stock Exchange rules no member had any rights to challenge a ruling, however unjust. Members were specifically prohibited from going to law in the courts with a right to be legally represented, as one would have expected to be the case, with any properly run institution. My only course of action would have been to resign my membership and challenge the Council's action in a civil court. Although I had a very good case, this would have meant long periods during which I would not have been able to earn a living, as I would have been prevented from being employed by any firm. In other words, such action to clear my name would have involved my resigning as a partner in my firm and risking the force of the "old boy's network" from stopping me ever rejoining the "club". That I was not prepared to do. Instead I hoped that as the truth came out my reputation would be exonerated. Nor would such action have enhanced my prospects of winning the marginal constituency in the awaited election.

Unfortunately one or two newspapers enjoyed reporting what seemed to them to be a financial scandal. "Tory candidate suspended from the Stock Exchange!" The actual punishment for the alleged improper behaviour was not a suspension from being a Member of the Stock Exchange, but simply a six months suspension from entering the floor of the Stock Exchange. As a partner busy managing my clients' investments, I never went on to the Stock Exchange floor. We employed dealers to do that with instructions from the office by phone.

So the sentence did not prohibit me from continuing my business and throughout the period I continued in my office dealing with my clients as a partner and Member of the Stock Exchange. But because it was misinterpreted by the papers it did damage my business and that of my firm which was also implicated. Some clients, those who did not know me well, no longer wanted to deal with someone they considered little better then a crook.

However, when the initial "story" broke in the press, the unjustified charge nearly brought my burgeoning political career to a sudden end. My constituency officers were alarmed and shocked by the media's false interpretation and an emergency meeting was called. I travelled up to Derbyshire accompanied by Hilary which was a sensible move. She had become popular and was respected and her presence helped to calm the meeting down.

I tried to explain in detail what had happened. The charge, trial and punishment without even consulting me, was that I had dealt for an investor who had been banned from dealing on the Stock Exchange. That charge, even if true, would not stand up under today's reformed Stock Exchange regime. But in 1968 the Stock Exchange was still a monopoly and arbitrarily allowed to dictate who was permitted to invest. I was not even aware that I had taken instructions from anyone "banned". All brokers receive orders from banks and we deal on behalf of their clients. Many investors prefer to remain anonymous so they deal in a bank's nominees. A broker has no idea whatsoever of the identity of the bank's customers. A "banned" person would simply give his bank buy or sell instructions or use an associate's name that was not "banned".

How could I be found guilty of dealing for a reputable bank? Banks are most valued clients for brokers. In fact I was always only dealing in the shares of public companies quoted on the Stock Exchange.

I discovered that the "banned" investor was none other than Philip Barker, who had become a consultant for a public company whose shares were quoted on the Stock Exchange. I had received dealing orders from the properly appointed officers of the company. How that could be interpreted as dealing for a banned investor, remained unexplained. It is about as absurd as the Stock Exchange "Godfathers" charging me with dealing in the shares of Tesco or BP because they employed a banned consultant.

What was unforgiveable was that the SE Council refused even to consider my quite respectable explanation or that of my fellow partner Roger Tustain. Even more improper is that we had actually initiated our own punishment, when we went out of our way to inform the Stock Exchange that an investor they had banned was now a consultant with a public company, requesting their advice. Instead of advising us on a course of action and thanking us for our information, they charged, tried and punished us in our absence. Roger Tustain as the firm's senior partner was also suspended from the floor of the Exchange, which had a damaging effect on the thriving partnership he had built up. One cannot help wondering if this was the intention! This was still the ancient era when only old "blue chip" Stock Exchange firms were considered fit to be traders – not the new upstarts like us.

Fortunately I was blessed with some very intelligent and worldly wise constituency officers. My Chairman, Herbert Brewer a solicitor and his deputy, Annette Noskwith, whose husband was the owner of the famous women's lingerie business Charnos, trusted me. They accepted my explanation and a complete vote of confidence was passed in me. I continued my strenuous work to prepare for the 1970 election.

As my suspension was for only a short period and only technical, it did not affect my Membership and I was able to continue building up my business. But long term damage was done by this injustice. My Labour opponents in Derbyshire made the most of it, reminding voters that there was something "shady" about the Conservative candidate. Simple Labour propaganda about "City slickers" was bad enough without the implication of some scandal.

Even more damaging when I was elected and arrived at Westminster, there must have been a file on me prepared for the Conservative Whips Office, although no tangible evidence exists. It is well understood that all new members have information prepared and held by those who determine the political future of the new members. I can only imagine the comment in my file "not a safe pair of hands, dodgy past, not suitable for promotion" etc. I was tainted and my card marked. To make matters worse the Godfather of the young broker, who had actually dealt for the banned investor and for whom I had been sacrificed, was a prominent Conservative M.P, Selwyn Lloyd, who became Speaker. I am quite sure he did not get my side of the story.

The Stock Exchange Council at the time have a great deal to answer for. They almost ruined my business and surely damaged my political prospects. Their stupid and irresponsible actions hurt the public image of the Conservative Party at a delicate time in advance of an election that it was hoped would remove the Labour Government. After all, I was expected to win a marginal

Labour seat. They helped Labour's cause giving Harold Wilson ammunition which he used to discredit the "City spivs". Only Ted Heath helped Labour more when he described Lonrho as the "unacceptable face of capitalism".

It was with pleasure, some years later, in 1986, that I was able to support legislation that forced the Stock Exchange and other public institutions, to adopt modern democratic systems of self regulation, with the full right for aggrieved members to be able to have their defence to the findings of internal disciplinary actions heard outside the Stock Exchange, judged impartially in the Courts. To meet the "big bang" and the City's evolution, the Stock Exchange Council's monopoly was ended. Independent outside regulatory bodies were set up. Professional chief executives were to run the heart of the Nation's financial centre.

I wonder if there were any guilty consciences over how one of the Stock Exchange's honest members was victimised.

It is very difficult in today's world to look back and understand the rigid class structures which prevailed in the City of the 1960s before the Conservative Government's reforms. The attitudes of the older members of the Stock Exchange could truly be described as Dickensian. Many of the older established firms had hereditary successions going back for generations, only of course through the male lines; daughters were not permitted to inherit. The "Them" and "Us" culture prevailed throughout. Although the firms were dependent on the bright and clever young brokers and qualified analysts for their survival, they were not prepared on the whole to let them breach the higher reaches of the system. The senior partnerships were reserved for the favoured sons.

As with the gradually changing Conservative Party, the bright Grammar school boys were also penetrating the Stock Exchange and were not content in sitting back letting the less talented, but well connected amateurs take the credit from them. Many of the older brokers did not appear in the City until after ten in the morning and left early in the afternoon. They depended on their "Old Boy's networks", contacts made at shoots or on the hunting field. They had wealthy clients whom they wined and dined, but depended on the new blood in their firms to make the recommendations and to run their portfolios. The old guard belonged to another era which was passing. The "Them" and "Us" culture could not last. The Stock Exchange reaction was typical of an embattled institution whose time was running out. They retreated behind the barricades and resorted to issuing decrees and resisting all change. If the Government's radical reforms had not been implemented, the City would certainly have lost its standing as the world's leading securities market.

When change did come it came fast as the tide washed away their sand castles and the City moved triumphantly into the 20th century. The old ways vanished, which was just as well for Britain's survival as a prosperous economy and Europe's leading financial centre.

Chapter Thirteen
South East Derbyshire

From 1968 when I was adopted as the Parliamentary candidate, my life underwent a massive change. No longer was my leisure time my own. Everything was geared to getting to know the people in the constituency and learning about the disparate parts of it.

Each of the different villages around the main centre of Long Eaton and Sandiacre had their own individual face. Melbourne with its superb Norman Church and the ancient Melbourne Hall, the historic home of the Kerr's, Michael Ancram, Lord Lothian's family, with its formal gardens, was a proud and attractive small market town. Other villages such as Breaston betrayed their industrial past. The architecture varied between the harsh red industrial brick terraced housing and the softer lines of the old Derbyshire stone farmhouses.

Of all the contrasts the village of Stanton by Dale stood out; a small attractive isolated rural village perched on the edge of the escarpment which dropped down into the Erewash Valley, to the immense Stanton Ironworks, belching out fire and fumes in the valley. Alongside the Ironworks was a row of cottages with the telltale large front windows, built to give light to the weavers and lace makers, for which the Nottingham area became famous.

Spondon, close to Derby, was the home to British Celanese, now part of Courtaulds, and the village was a conglomerate of red brick houses built for the factory workers, interspersed with the odd stone built farm or rural dwelling left from an earlier age. After the selection meeting, Hilary and I were entertained by the then constituency Chairman, Arthur Dixon. He lived in a detached house in Spondon. He and his wife welcomed us with tea and cakes, telling us how pleased they were to have me as the candidate. All the time we were in the house, however, we smelt the pervasive scent of cats. Very nice people, we thought, but really that dreadful cat smell, how could they live there. It was some time later we realised that all of Spondon was suffused by the catty smell which came from British Celanese, along with a fine yellowy grey dust which was deposited liberally over the whole area. When the wind blew in certain directions it even reached our house in Long Eaton. It did not help Hilary's asthma. Fortunately, legislation has made the huge industrial complex much cleaner.

Around Spondon, by complete contrast, we came into open farmland and woods with no sign of the neighbouring heavy industry. Here was Locko Park, the home of Patrick Drury Lowe. He was the President of the Constituency Conservative Party. I had met him at my selection meeting, but I came to know him well over the years and he became a great friend. He was a most generous man and gave the local Conservatives almost a free run of his splendid house and grounds. We held many functions there and he was probably the largest fundraiser we had. He had inherited Locko Park in a very bad condition and had spent his time after his army career, restoring it. He was immensely proud of the house and enjoyed letting us see and use the place.

In Long Eaton textile, lace and small engineering factories were interspersed with the houses. The town grew into a typical industrial revolution mish-mash well before the concept of the modern industrial estate, when people had no transport and walked to work. When we first moved into the house in Long Eaton there were still one or two small firms that had sirens or whistles which sounded in the early mornings and again at "knocking off" time in the evenings, waking up the workers and their families. However, even in 1970 many of the old 19th century red brick mills were empty and falling into disuse. Gradually, over the twenty-two year period that I was the M.P the scene changed and many of the older factories were restored and divided into smaller units and the larger concerns moved to the outskirts. Although lace making, engineering and the 'rag trade' were still the main industries in Long Eaton, one of the largest manufacturers actually in the town was Pauls, which specialised in stainless steel and electrical products. I made it my business to get to know all the managers and owners of the various concerns. Early on I had asked Paul, the agent, to find party members who would invite me to small functions at their houses, where I could meet and get to know the leaders of industry in the area. This was most effective and in a relatively short time I came not only to know most of the influential people in the constituency, I also knew what concerns they had and their particular needs. When I came to prepare my election material I was able to target it precisely to the constituency.

The River Erewash, which was later to give its name to the reboundaried constituency, flowed through the town from Sandiacre in the north, passing the grounds of Trent College in the centre of town, to the River Trent at Sawley. Running nearby were the remains of the Erewash Canal which joined the Trent at Trent Lock and from there the Grand Union Canal system to London.

Trent College was a Victorian foundation, unusual for a public school in its specialisation in industrial technology. It was founded as a part boarding school by a Derbyshire industrialist, Francis Wright. It was intended to be one of a string of schools with a strong Christian emphasis, educating the future industrialists to a high level. It was the only school that actually got built. Trent College boasted the largest hall come theatre in the area, the May Hall, which was the scene of many constituency events. The Headmaster of Trent was Tony Maltby. He came on the scene at the same time as I did, a young and enthusiastic man with a young family, determined to drag Trent College out of its sleepy ways and to bring it to the fore educationally. We came to know him well as he had no compunction in using me as a "teaching resource", giving talks to the VIth Form, taking pupils around Westminster and urging me to take on his head boy as an "aide". Introducing me to Paul Thompson was an inspired move. He became an inseparable part of our election team and remains to this day, a great friend. Tony Maltby always included Hilary and I as guests at annual speech days. I was impressed with and admired his enlightened ethos.

To the south of the constituency the River Trent formed the boundary, running through Shardlow, past Shardlow Hall, also very kindly lent to the Party for various functions. The Trent wound its way with the flood plains on either side, by Aston and Weston on Trent eventually to the great mediaeval causeway bridge at Swarkeston. To the extreme south of the constituency was a large area of market gardening and horticulturalists, known affectionately as the "sprout men" which early on occupied me with their problems coping with lower cost imported vegetables.

The most important part industrially of the S.E. Derbyshire constituency, was of course the large Rolls Royce complex, which to the south of Derby was just edging into our area with Alvaston and Sinfin. During the war, German bombing raids sought out the Rolls Royce factory a few miles to the north of the market gardeners. It soon became apparent that the large glasshouse complexes of the vegetable growers had been mistaken by the bombers for Rolls Royce. As a decoy the glasshouses were deliberately sacrificed much to the pride of the owners. A successful raid on Rolls Royce could easily have changed the outcome of the war, as we might have lost the Battle of Britain.

Apart from the large number of constituents who worked for Rolls Royce, much of the smaller sub contractors in the machine tool industry in the area were dependant on Rolls, as were the retailers and service providers.

The constituency wrapped around Derby and to the north was also fairly rural, with Breadsall and Breadsall Priory surrounded by the more familiar "Derby Dales" countryside.

We had a year perhaps, two at the most to prepare for an election. Our agent, Paul Marquis, who at that time was based in Derby where we shared an office with the other Derby constituencies, set out a rigorous programme going round the constituency, visiting groups, hospitals, and firms getting me as well known as possible and picking up on the different problems. Life was easier once we had bought our house as we could stay there for weekends, making visits during the day and attending endless functions, like the wine and cheese parties in the evenings. Before then we had billets arranged with various Party workers, and became great friends with so many of them.

I had to show myself around the place and focussed my activities to ensure the maximum of media coverage. I had learnt a great deal from the Sunderland campaign on how to attract attention. No pigs this time, however, and certainly not speaking to half empty draughty halls at public meetings. Although we still had the public meetings during the actual election campaign, the days when these were the only focus of attention, were long over. People would not come out to meet the candidate that way any more. Organising, what I have to confess, were publicity stunts was far more effective.

Paul Marquis was very good at finding things for us to do. The derelict Erewash Canal was in danger of being filled in and used for housing. There was a small but effective pressure group determined to save the canal and to restore it for use for leisure boating. As our house in Berkhamsted was close to the Grand Union Canal, the idea was conceived for us to bring up a long boat from there all the way to Trent Lock, where the Erewash Canal started. There were a large number of the constituents who boated on the Trent and around so supporting the "Save Erewash Canal" campaign was a popular move. We hired a traditional long boat from a local Berkhamsted yard and set off. We had ten days to do the trip and back.

The permanent crew consisted of my wife and three teenage boys with reasonable muscle for winching up the lock gates. Paul Marquis, our agent, managed to be there most of the time as well but I am afraid that I cheated, spending my days in the office in London and joining the boat at arranged rendezvous where the canal and the road system allowed for the night and the weekends, being dropped off by my long suffering in-laws. I would be picked up again somewhere further ahead by arrangement, leaving the boat's crew to slog on up the canal. My children, Judith aged seven and Bruno, five, also joined the crew plus, of course, our Labrador cross collie dog.

Unfortunately, we discovered that the direct route between the Grand Union and the Trent was closed having some maintenance done. We had to go the long way round. In the limited time available there was no way to do this other than by breaking the rules and moving at night. Going through locks after dark was difficult, particularly as some were still manned by Waterways men in the lock cottages, so we studied the maps so that we could end the day on a long stretch of water as the sun went down and keep travelling.

Hilary probably bore the brunt of the expedition. Often she would be up at dawn to get underway, before cooking up breakfast for the crew. Feeding three teenage boys with hearty appetites on a small gas stove was not easy. Two of the boys were my secretary Fiona's children and the other the son of a friend who had "loaned" him to us. They became a very proficient crew, preparing the locks for us. Judith became an excellent look out for mud banks and low branches. I am sorry to say that five year old Bruno's main contribution was to leave the tap running in the sink, which emptied the water tank. We would waste time finding a lock with water on tap to refill it. He was not popular!

These were the days without mobile phones and telephone boxes were rare, so Paul Marquis and I kept the local media informed of our progress. Our agent had organised a massive reception party when we were due to arrive on the evening of the fourth day at Shardlow, grubby and exhausted. A popular canal-side pub provided an ideal setting. We were greeted by the media and the Erewash Preservation Society, with our boat duly draped with the "Save the Erewash Canal" posters. All the local Conservatives had turned out in force and it developed into a great party. However, there were one or two of our more senior lady supporters, who I think did not quite appreciate what had been happening and how we had arrived. One was heard remarking to the others that it was "disgraceful, our prospective M.P dressing and looking like a dirty bargee!"

I am ashamed to say that I did not help out very much on the way back from the Trent to Berkhamsted, again leaving the brunt of the work to Hilary. She always says that the highlight on the way back was when they approached a lock at the same time as a small pleasure boat and the man on it called to his wife to let our boat go first as we were obviously professional bargees with a "working boat!"

Hilary made herself known in the constituency and focussed on the day time events, the coffee mornings and lunches, which I could not get to midweek. She was asked to talk to the Melbourne Women's Association at their Christmas lunch. Mrs Kerr, Michael Ancram's mother, very kindly asked her to stay for the night at Melbourne Hall, before hand. Hilary had arrived for supper the evening before and after breakfast she prepared her speech, said her farewells to Mrs Kerr and packed her things in her car, ready to leave after the lunch. After she had spoken at the lunch she returned to The Hall and went back to her room for her handbag. Unfortunately, while she was there one of the Italian maids had liberally spread wax floor polish down the splendid wooden staircase. Hilary stepped on to the top step and slid inelegantly down the rest of the stairs on her back. Although speaking no Italian, she understood the maid's "Holy Mary Mother of God!" as she went down.

Hilary managed to get into her car and drive off – she was soundly told off by Mrs Kerr later for not having let her know what had happened. However, Hilary was concerned to get home as soon as possible and to see her doctor as she was eight months pregnant at the time! Although bruised, all was well and our third child, Jessica was born in the February, again at home with me present.

Chapter Fourteen
The 1970 Election

As the election time drew near, South East Derbyshire had a new Tory agent. June Evans was a young and enthusiastic Welsh woman filled with ideas on promoting the party and in particular the candidate.

In the run up to the election, I had focussed on trying to build up morale and confidence amongst our voluntary workers. We recruited many more as it became obvious that I genuinely believed we could overturn a 5000 Labour majority. Our younger people became particularly enthusiastic helpers. Whenever there was a free evening during the three week election campaign I organised a group of three or four dedicated beer drinkers to help me with the evening's activity, a pub crawl. To make sure my large consumption of beer would not be wasted, we arranged that my companions would go ahead into their local. When I casually walked in as though by coincidence, I would be greeted loudly by "Hello Peter, what are you doing here? Come and have a drink with us?" This technique not only attracted the maximum attention it also appeared quite spontaneous.

After a while some of the helpers would move off to prepare the next scene. Meanwhile other genuine locals in the bar were already talking to me and not feeling embarrassed to approach me. So we moved on round until closing time. I tried to ensure that, by arrangement, there would always be one well known local supporter in each pub, to help introduce me around. I also made sure that at the end of our crawl, a sober driver would take me home. Media cover about a candidate arrested for excess alcohol was not part of my plan.

Traditional electioneering consisted of mostly tramping the streets 'door-knocking'. While this worked in the villages, I realised that it was often a waste of time during the day in towns like Long Eaton. We were an area of high employment and with above average female employment. The East Midlands as a whole had little unemployment and we were exceptionally packed with small engineering firms, many with contracts for Rolls Royce. We were also the heart of the lace industry, which fed the factories making clothing and lingerie, mostly employing women.

Knocking on the doors of empty houses, even though one left a card proclaiming "I am sorry you were out when I called" to let them know I had been, was not the best way to meet voters. Canvassing after 6pm would find more, but I suspected did more harm than good. Having probably just come home from a long day at work was not the time to welcome someone trying to chat up a voter on the doorstep. Interrupting the evening meal was one thing, interrupting the favourite TV soap programmes was not going to win votes.

I radically restructured my programme, perhaps only doing two hours of door knocking, leaving our voluntary workers to find the votes. My strategy was to be where the maximum crowds could be found. I started before 7am, going out to each of half a dozen newsagents, different ones each morning. I would purchase a newspaper at each. There would always be a few voters on the way to work, buying the paper and their cigarettes. Even if not all recognised me, the shopkeepers did and we knew it would be passed around that I was there that day!

After breakfast there was a short time to read the piles of papers to see how the National Campaign was going, and to monitor the TV news reports. The agent would pick me up and the rest of the morning would be spent endlessly walking round the shopping centres and stores, buying something at each. The midday would see a quick pit-stop at our house in Long Eaton when I would unload my haul of groceries. There were no mobiles then so keeping in touch with base was always difficult on the move and it was important to make regular contact.

A longer lunchtime would be spent at one or two crowded local pubs, where we would have a snack lunch. No time was wasted in meeting voters and being seen. Market days were particularly fruitful. Wandering around the market stalls allowed me to chat up stallholders and their customers in a most informal manner. In 1970 most people still shopped in the markets.

Afternoons always included one or two factory visits, arranged by our very able agent. I always insisted on making a formal approach to the management making it clear that I only wanted to "stroll around" and not to interrupt any work. If a works manager wanted to escort me that helped because I would get a quick introduction and move on.

Of course by the time the election came I was already fairly well known in most of the work places, having invited myself on many fact finding visits over the previous year. Many of the business managers were active Party supporters whom I would have met at the seemingly endless wine and cheese parties or chicken dinner, fundraising events.

An important part of the actual election campaign was to research all the forthcoming events which were advertised on the local radio channels and newspapers. These would usefully cover weekends. Accompanied by Hilary and often our children, I would attend the sports grounds where things were happening; swimming school competitions, professional wrestling and bowling evenings. There was always a range of fund raising garden parties and fetes for various organisations or charities, flea markets, church bazaars and much else. It was a warm late spring and early summer, which made it all the more pleasant. Many of these activities allowed me to make maximum use of the week-ends.

Before the start of the campaign, I had recruited as my assistant Paul Thompson, Tony Maltby's head boy from Trent College. Paul came from a Derbyshire farming family, had just finished at school and was waiting to go up to Oxford where he had already been promised a place. He was interested in politics and keen to get some political experience on his C.V. before going on to university. He arrived every morning and stayed at my side all day, cheering me up through those occasional moods of depression when things were not going too well. He became almost part of the family. Life would have been harder and less enjoyable without his help over the three weeks. I could not have head hunted a better assistant. We had many good laughs together during the campaign.

Part of the unofficial campaign was the organisation of a "dirty tricks" brigade. They deliberately did not keep me informed of their activities as I would surely have had to have stopped some of them, such as tearing down the opposition's posters. To be fair this was done in recrimination at the tearing down of ours. As our posters were on boards which came courtesy of a local estate agent, Ron Craggs, taking the posters off them had given the impression that large parts of Long Eaton were up for sale! Our team were honing their skills for later elections, when they became quite a formidable force. There was another trick they played which I discovered later. They sometimes followed the opposing candidate's helpers, stuffing their election material in the letter boxes. Any which stuck out were carefully removed and substituted by some of ours.

The National Opinion Polls were indecisive. While they indicated a swing towards the Conservatives it was not enough to ensure Labour's defeat and was unevenly spread over the Country. A large swing against Labour in the Conservative heartlands would not unseat the Government. The predicted movement was not quite enough to overcome Labour's existing majority in South East Derbyshire. We struggled on anxiously. Bur my own feeling from the sort of reception we were getting, gave me hope.

What emerged as our strongest asset, was the Labour candidate up against me. Trevor Parks having stood down, the Labour Party needed to choose a new candidate for their seat. It was John Ryman, a prosperous and well known London barrister, who also happened to be Shirley Summerskill's husband. As very much establishment Labour it was suggested that she had something to do with his selection. But it was a miscalculation. He was quite the wrong candidate for Labour to put in a working class Midlands seat.

Our agent June Evans had insisted on concentrating our legally rationed spending on our literature on quality rather than quantity. My election address sported a colour picture, not a very common thing at the time, of me and my family in a rural spot with a typical Derbyshire stone wall in the background. We found later that many of our supporters had framed the picture for their living rooms! By contrast, John Ryman had produced an election address, fronted with large red print, and inside a black and white picture of himself and his wife, Dr Shirley Summerskill, sitting on a Regency style sofa. There was no contest – our children and dog won the competition. I heard more than once the grumble "why doesn't his wife use her husband's handle?"

He participated in the sport of hunting and was a member of a well known hunt. He was public school educated and some voters came to believe that I was the Labour candidate with my grammar school background and he the Tory! He might have made an impact in a more rural area, but not here.

Unlike myself, Ryman had not made himself known in the constituency and neither had he learned very much about his would be constituents. He planned to make a splash, by touring the streets in the area on horseback. Unfortunately, he had chosen to keep his horse in a field adjacent to the home of the local Conservative Association treasurer. The row over the fence between the local Labour Party and their candidate was soon relayed around. The horse remained in the field. No way were the trade's unionists prepared to canvas with a horse. I know how they felt after my Sunderland pig experiment.

Having been frustrated in showing off his horse riding skills, he had another hurdle to overcome. He had no home in the constituency, as I did. He arrived, infrequently, from his legal chambers in London in his very smart Jag or Rover, parked it at the best hotel in the area and borrowed a modest little runabout for his campaign. Of course all his workers knew about it and were not impressed.

Nor did he stay for much of the three weeks of the campaign. Hardly anybody saw him around and it was reported to us that much of the time he returned home to London. What we did discover was that the Trades Union activists were so disgusted at the candidate thrust upon them and his casual behaviour to hold the seat that they walked away in droves. We even recruited from former Labour supporters. His posters were removed from some of the Labour Clubs, the heart of any Labour constituency.

On the day of the count after polling day, one of the staff at the hotel who was a Party member, said that as he left the hotel he announced to the staff "I leave as Mr John Ryman. When I return here after the count, I shall be Mr John Ryman M.P.!" Without his assistance I might well not have made it and his boast might have been fulfilled.

Our campaign appeared to be going well. Confidence, enthusiasm and morale were building up. Most mornings I would have a friend helping who had surprised us by coming up from our home region, reporting for a days work. Hilary organised the HQ in our home refuelling the endless stream of helpers. My mother in law helped to keep the children occupied, although we had seconded the two elder ones to a school in Ockbrook along with Ron Craggs, the estate agent and his wife Mary Craggs' own children. My younger daughter Jessica, fourteen months old, nearly brought the whole campaign to a halt. She had had an infection of some sort and we had taken her to a local doctor. She suddenly produced a massive rash which was diagnosed initially as measles. We were wondering how we could put half our team into quarantine, and how many of our voters and workers she had infected. The baby had been quite an attraction. Fortunately, a second look found her simply to have had an allergic reaction to penicillin! With the panic over, Jessica went to stay for the rest of the campaign with my in-laws. We missed Ena's help.

Every night after our tour of the many hostelries some of my key workers would gather for a debriefing. I would be given useful titbits of news gathered by our army during the day. Most encouraging were the regular reports from canvassers about admissions from voters who claimed previously to be Labour who now intended to vote for us.

One of the difficulties I faced was being unable to keep up daily with the National campaign. Although I had been round each morning buying up all the major Nationals, I had little time to read them thoroughly. Most elections are now fought on TV, but candidates have to miss most of the debate and comment by the leading politicians. Even the evening news bulletins were missed as one was out at meetings or still campaigning. Apart from the early morning radio, I was out of touch preparing the days activities. Then my daily news conference when any local journalist could call and ask me questions. I collected interesting tit-bits from the previous day hoping that the media would find little stories they might use. One such typical incident was when canvassing in a not too friendly road, the door was opened and a rather large dog jumped straight at me and bit my leg. The owner was not particularly apologetic "He's Labour, you see!" I decided not to try and convert the beast and withdrew to seek some first aid.

Clever canvassing is a skilled business. You need three helpers who go ahead to knock up and as soon as a door is opened, the candidate sprints there before it is slammed in your face. Never waste your time trying to convert a staunch voter who confesses "Sorry I'm Labour"; they are not going to change in two minutes; nor waste time chatting to an obvious supporter keen to keep you on the doorstep. A good canvasser will assess if a voter is with you. If not, move on quickly. But if there is any doubt or hesitation the name and address would be marked down.

A list of prospects would then be sent to me for a personal follow up. Often actually meeting the candidate in person would do the trick. One problem I found when canvassing a good Tory area was that a committed supporter would try to invite me in with "do have a cup of tea you look as if you need it!" That would be true but fatal. In the twenty minutes I was chatting with a supporter, I could have called on a dozen uncommitted voters. So at the risk of offending we would have to move on.

The principal value of door to door work is that on Polling Day the team has an accurate list of names and addresses of supporters on the electoral roll. The committee rooms can be ticking off the voters' slips and they can then be reminded to vote if they have not yet appeared at the Polling Station.

In that first election in 1970, we held regular public meetings with guest speakers, but apart from one or two notable exceptions even then the audiences were starting to get thinner. In later election campaigns I came to resent them as a wasted effort because they actually hindered the work by drawing in our supporters to bolster up the audience, when they would otherwise be canvassing. In recent elections the public meetings have all but disappeared. TV has taken over the hustings.

Polling Day could not come soon enough. The three weeks of campaigning seemed like a lifetime and our crew was beginning to show signs of fatigue. Hilary lost some useful weight, but felt that there were other more comfortable ways of achieving this. Only counting the votes was more stressful than the preceding campaign.

In 1970 our Count was held over until the next day, when we proceeded to the Shire Hall in Derby. As the results came in overnight, we were still left in the tantalising position of knowing that we could go either way. Some of the swings in the neighbouring constituencies that had been called would see us in, others showed we would just not make it. Had John Ryman been following the news he would not have left his hotel that morning so certain of success and might have been a bit more cautious.

The Count was the tensest experience I had ever had. The result was inconclusive most of the way through. Only near the end could we see that Ryman's boxes of votes stopped being piled on the table and the Rost ones edged ahead. Hilary and I could not bear the tension and removed ourselves to a lobby and clung together. This was observed by the radio correspondent, unknown to us, who announced over the airwaves that it looked as if South East Derbyshire would be a Conservative gain as Peter Rost was kissing his wife!

I had overturned the Labour majority to one of 5000 for us. We had won a traditional Labour seat against national expectation and ahead of the regional swing. I felt so glad for the constituency workers who had invested so much in the effort to win the seat. To have lost really would have let them down. It was a triumph also for June to have won her first election as a new Tory agent. She remained as my agent throughout my career, eventually marrying one of our leading Conservative councillors, Robert Parkinson. My seat in Parliament in 1970, contributed to Ted Heath's slender majority of 30. A new and rather important phase of my life began as it did for the country.

Chapter Fifteen
Into a Deep Hole

The World does not need another ego-trip from a self opinionated ex-M.P. Enough of my former colleagues, far better known from Prime Ministers down, have published their memoirs covering the four years of Heath's Premiership. Most are lengthy, serious works of importance to the political history of the period, others are boringly pompous. Although a relatively unknown backbencher from 1970 until my escape in 1992, I was more than an observer on the fringe of events, and can immodestly claim to have contributed the odd footnote of interest.

The 1970 Parliament started optimistically enough having overturned an exhausted Labour Government. Unfortunately it also ended in tears, with Ted Heath's self inflicted downfall assisted by Arthur Scargill, the militant leader of the National Union of Mineworkers. It was an exciting period for a new Member. It encompassed our entry to the European Union and the unresolved issue of our crippling industrial relations leading to the question of "Who governs Britain?"

Being a new boy should not have been a problem, after surviving eight different schools. However Westminster is quite something else. It may seem a modest illustration but there was an initial difficulty for the new intake of female members. Few toilets in 1970 were identified as specifically for ladies or gentlemen. The Palace was fitted out for men only. From the 1970 election and increasing later, more women came into Parliament as all parties encouraged a better balance. The Palace had to become more accommodating for them, but seemed reluctant to do so. It was still a clubby male world.

There was no "instruction book" for newcomers. One had timidly to ask old established hands for even the simplest guidance. Where on the benches does one sit? Seats in the Chamber are not reserved except for the day's session. A Member may enter the Chamber before proceedings start and place a "reserved" card on a seat. But there are no separate seats, just long benches. So even a reserved place may leave you with little more than a six inch gap between Members placing themselves on either side. Most M.P's rears would not fit into six inches.

My first day in the Chamber taught me to be more careful and respectful. I found an unreserved place on the third row back behind the Front Bench. One can sit anywhere, but not on the front benches, reserved on one side for Government Ministers and opposite for the Opposition Front Bench. One has to be very careful on the benches immediately behind the Ministerial benches. These have to be reserved for the Parliamentary Private Secretaries, or PPS's, these are the Ministerial "bag carriers" or in Public School parlance "fags".

Apart from those customary placings, the rest of the Chamber is yours, but of course only on your own side not on the opposite benches. So I thought I was in the clear placing myself at the start of business on the third bench back on our side, in an unreserved place. In strutted a very grandee Member not decent enough to ask me to move, but angry that I had the nerve to occupy "his place", which had been his for twenty-five years, on a sort of long term tenancy. When he was about to establish his ownership by sitting on my lap, I hastily withdrew. I did not wish to anger him further by suggesting that he perhaps should reserve his seat with a card, like others did. Sir David Renton, representing Huntingdonshire was elected in May 1945. He was a QC and had been a Minister of State at the Home Office and much else and he went on to have a distinguished career in the Lords. I believe he forgave me later for my badly-mannered intrusion.

It proved an eventful first day. Having found a place nearby which seemed unoccupied either by reservation or tradition, I found myself sitting next to Jeffrey Archer. The brash extrovert but most friendly Member, who had won the by-election in Louth a year earlier, welcomed me. "My name is Jeffrey Archer. One day I will be Prime Minister!" I could not help liking his style. Some years later when he had become a successful author, he came to my constituency by invitation and at a crowded event signed and sold many of his books, donating most of the proceeds to my fighting fund. He raised huge sums all round the country for the Party.

The Party treated him with characteristic hypocrisy; a "goodie" while he was popular and raising money for the constituencies, but ostracised him when he was punished so excessively, unjustly. He deserved better and nothing has pleased me more then to see him re-established. The ruling grandees sponged on him until suddenly it was no longer politically expedient to know him. How nauseating.

The swearing in process in front of the Speaker's Chair was spread over three days in the mornings, before the main Sitting could begin. After swearing your Oath of Allegiance one was a fully fledged Member. But it was not possible to participate in debate until you had introduced yourself through the ordeal of making your Maiden Speech. Some new M.Ps who are well advised, wait several weeks for a suitable debating occasion. Others rush in before they have given themselves time to take in the surroundings and customs. I decided to wait and observe.

A friendly veteran colleague approached me in the cafeteria. I must have looked lost and overwhelmed by my new environment. He introduced himself, as David Mitchell[1] and kindly asked if I needed any help. I thanked him and wondered if he had any special advice for a 'New Boy'. "The most important priority for you is to find yourself a 'pair'. He explained that as there were about thirty more Conservatives than Labour, after the 1970 election, there would be a scramble and some Tories would have to go without. "If you want to carry on living any sort of life outside Westminster, you need to make a permanent arrangement.

My hunt started immediately. It had to be an Opposition 'New Boy' as more senior M.Ps already had fixed arrangements. After several unsuccessful approaches to Members who had wasted no time fixing themselves up, I discovered that David Lambie, the newly elected Labour Member for South Ayrshire was looking for a Conservative pair.

We were together until we both finally retired at the 1992 election. I can only describe the relationship with one's pair as very special. Because we are on opposite sides politically, we never discuss controversial issues. But a totally reliable trust has to be established; whatever the pressures from your Whips to

1 Sir David Mitchell, M.P for Basingstoke, Minister of State for Transport 1986-8

vote, you can never ever break an arrangement with your pair. So if he wanted to vote on a matter important to him, yet had agreed to pair with me on that day because I needed to be absent in my constituency, he would resist doing so, even if he was in the Chamber for a Division, or 'lend' his pair to a colleague wanting to be absent.

Likewise, he might wish to be away but I had agreed to cover for him by not voting, I would have to abstain or 'lend' my pair, just for the night, to a colleague unable to attend or find a pair himself. Of course for a three-line whip on an important issue, no pairing was allowed anyway, so we would both be voting.

Lambie was a teacher before Parliament and we had a good relationship. He was a passionate fisherman and quite regularly, on returning from his Scottish home on a Monday, he would bring me the best smoked salmon I can recall eating, which he had caught and smoked himself. In return, I would offer fresh fruit or vegetables, all organically grown, from our Hertfordshire garden, for him to take back to his family for the weekend. My main problem with having David for a pair was that he would want to be at Westminster on those many occasions when Scottish business was discussed. Those were the far too frequent, boring days when English Members could escape with their English pairs. People like myself, had to stay behind when Parliament was almost deserted.

The next problem was to find an office in the Palace. This was difficult as in 1970 there were very few. Most were reserved for senior Members, such as the Chairman of Committees and favourites of the Party Whips, who had patronage power over who would get an office and who would not. For most of us all that was offered initially was a cupboard locker in one of the Palace corridors. How like school! But there was also a cloakroom where each Member had a coat hanger and a space for a bag. Each personally named hanger had a large wide pink ribbon hanging from it. This was for the disposal of your ornamental sword, before moving into the Chamber. I used mine for an umbrella. How much more disrespectful can you get?

Not even at any of my numerous schools was I left so unguided. You could ask your Party Whips for advice or help, but they were more interested in observing your conduct, weighing up your intelligence, your ability and your ambition. They were, like the prefects of a school, not too willing to put themselves out as nursemaids. You soon discovered that you were on your own and left to feel your way and learn.

There were some offices, mainly used for secretaries, in an ancient building opposite Westminster above the tube station overlooking the river. This had been a former Club and the large rooms held several desks. My secretary, Fiona, managed to find herself a desk in a bay window overlooking the River Thames, with her two allocated filing cabinets. The secretaries had much more space than the Members at that time. This building of course was demolished and became the present Portcullis House, after I had left Westminster. More office accommodation came available later when Scotland Yard moved out of its splendid building on the embankment. Several fortunate Members had rooms there, which included not only a desk but also a sofa long enough to doze on during all night sittings when waiting for the Division. The secretaries were placed four to a room and had such useful equipment as photocopiers to hand, instead of having to dive down to the confusing maze in the basements under Westminster.

The move freed up more rooms for Members in the Palace itself. These were tucked away in odd corners, with views of the roof and stone pinnacles, most had multiple occupants. In such closed spaces, it was important that the occupants got along together, as phone conversations or dictations to secretaries were scarcely private. I recall some years later a colleague telling me that he had been offered larger office space but would have to share it with Edwina Currie, then fairly newly elected but making her mark already. It would not be fair to reveal his name. He declined.

I had been offered a desk in a narrow rather gloomy room where I would have been one of five Members. Although, without today's mobiles, it would have meant that I had a separate telephone number, it would have been an impossible place to work. Throughout my twenty two years I preferred to work in the House of Commons Library. Running much of the length of the building facing the Thames, the Library was superbly equipped with an array of reference books and all the newspapers and magazines. It was also staffed with a highly qualified team of librarians. Whatever project or speech you needed to prepare, they would help you with your research by providing you with background papers and all the references required. A book not in the Library was obtained for you from outside, including the British Library.

Research assistants employed by Members could obtain special passes allowing them to use the facilities when the House was adjourned.

The other main advantage of "squatting" in the Library was its proximity to the Chamber. It was easy to rush in if the TV monitor screened up the next speaker or business I wanted to follow.

I am probably being indiscreet when I reveal that one of the enormous rooms at the rear was furnished with the most luxurious leather armchairs. Only in London's ancient Gentlemen's Clubs would you find any similar comfort zones. The room was supposed to be silent; but the drone of snoring members could not be prevented.

The Party Whips tried to pace M.P's Maiden Speeches to perhaps two or three each day, slotted in to the main debates. As the first week of a new Parliament is spent debating the Queen's Speech – an outline of the Government's proposed legislative programme, there are plenty of opportunities without being restricted to particular issues under debate.

When a Member felt that the day's debate would be appropriate, the Whips would be advised as well as the Speaker and all sides of the House were prepared to give the new Member a respectable hearing. It is customary not to interrupt or heckle. There is also a pleasant custom that when you sit down the next Member called would be a veteran or even a Minister, briefed in advance, who would congratulate you and praise your efforts.

Maiden Speeches were supposed to be non-controversial and one was expected to be as polite as possible about your predecessor in the constituency. It was not so easy to do so, if you had knocked him out at the election and replaced him after a heated, less than cleanly-fought campaign.

Your speech, not to last for more than ten minutes, was expected to say something about your constituency, your hopes and political interests and ambitions in Parliament. After making the speech you were free to be called to take full part in the debates.

My father arrived in London from New York for his annual visit soon after my first weeks in Parliament. He was accompanied, as always, by my step-mother Eleanor and they stayed as usual at the Cumberland, where we had to guess what name they had registered under. Having changed his name to "Rost" for political reasons after the war in the McCarthy era, Dad frequently reverted to Rosenstiel as most of his old friends and colleagues knew him with this name. Asking for them at the reception desk in the Cumberland, we always got it wrong. I could not wait to invite them for lunch at Westminster. Without showing it too transparently, I could see that they were enormously proud and somewhat overawed by the situation. I am sure that my father never dreamt that he would be entertained by his own son in the prestigious dining room and to walk in to the Houses of Parliament with all its historic connections.

As an avid student of European history and particularly the post-war era, he understood more than most, what the "Mother of Parliaments" was about and for his son, a German refugee, to become an M.P. was regarded by him and his large circle of American-German friends as unbelievable. Like most sons separated from their fathers, I had been bombarded by advice by letter from New York. My father suffered the usual problem of failing to realise that I had grown up and at each changing stage in my career was worried that I was getting into deep water. I should not have given up the "safe" job of journalism with its regular salary for the uncertainty of stockbroking. After proving that I was successful at stockbroking, trying out a political career was most foolhardy as no one would let a German half-Jewish Refugee join the elite. On my having achieved this impossible position, he was both amazed and proud. He was right about one thing, however, I was about to take a cut in income. Politics in those days was not the way to make a fortune. Observing the more recent scene I cannot help noticing the contrast, not with envy but disgust.

I discovered for myself in my Parliamentary work with the members of the German Bundestag and contacts with a wide range of German citizens, what enormous respect and admiration existed amongst all German society for Britain and its democratic institutions.

The same applied to the vast majority of Americans, particularly those who joined the "melting pot" as refugees from Europe in more recent years. So I was aware of what my father must have felt and talked about with his wide circle of friends in New York. Indeed having spent three weeks with him and Eleanor in New York as a student before deciding to hitch hike around the US, even then I understood something about life in New York in what I can only describe as an upper middle class "ghetto". I learnt about the endless week-ends and bridge parties in the "kosher" hotels in the Catskills – the "ghetto's" lung and the charming Jewish character of the gossip about each other's family and life over coffee and homemade cheesecake.

Eleanor and I got on well, as she did with Hilary, on the many occasions she came to Europe with my father, often en route to Switzerland for the annual skiing holiday, where our growing family would join them if we could, to be spoilt by Granddad with chocolate cake. For both my father and Eleanor it was a second marriage, although Eleanor's husband had died prematurely leaving her with a young daughter, Janet. Her cousin was Henry Kissinger, also of course an immigrant to the U.S. from Germany in 1938, a distant connection but one which did her no harm in the slightly class conscious, snobbish New York "village".

My father and step-mother's tour of my new place of work reached its highlight when I was able to take them on to the famous terrace alongside the Thames and to see amongst the faces those of my more senior, well-known colleagues, recognised by my father.

Sadly, what was a happy occasion for them was tinged with sadness for me. My mother had died in 1967, after my first campaign in Sunderland and she never saw therefore, my election to Parliament in 1970. I had many unhappy moments knowing that I was never able to entertain her, as I had my father, and that she was never able to feel the pride, which she undoubtedly would, in my achievements. I doubt if she had any premonitions of where I was going, but if she did she was a very reserved person and never showed them.

Materially her life in England with my stepfather was as happy as one could expect in the circumstances. Stockey was kind and cared for her, but he was uneducated and lacked the understanding of the social background of my mother's German upbringing. He was in some ways too aware of his social inadequacies and tried to make up for them. He had made a success of the modest private-hire coach business which they ran and he had joined the local Masonic Lodge, which gave him some status in the Tring area. But lacking in any of the social graces, he was never able to rise above a very evident working-class background.

He enjoyed the visits to Germany, where my mother would stay with her sister and mother, who lived into her nineties. Although he spoke no German, he felt able to maintain his status through my mother. However, in Tring my mother was isolated, apart from a few of her German friends who were scattered around mainly in London. There was little entertaining. She would spend hours walking her fiercely protective king-sized poodle, Booby, in the woods at Tring Park only occasionally joined by a friend.

Stockey was protectively jealous of any social contacts my mother might wish to enjoy. Feeling unable to participate adequately and certain that they would consider him inferior, his only response was to isolate her from any life in which he could not hold his own. He would imagine slights and finally find an occasion to pick a quarrel with anyone who came too close. It was only when speaking German that my mother was free to say what she liked without guarding her words. My father-in-law's excellent German, which he liked to practiçe, allowed him to get to know her. Both were good musicians, Arthur was an organist and my mother played the piano well. But Stockey managed to upset relations with Hilary, although not completely and Hilary never felt able to chat freely with my mother when he was present. Booby's super protective attitude to my mother did not help when we brought the children to visit and she was unable to pick them up or even touch them until the dog was locked away.

In the years when I lived with them at my home in Tring until University, after which I had my own flat in London, I had a serious hang-up about bringing home any friends. I was ashamed of the shoddiness and lack of culture or the sort of entertaining, other teenage friends were able to enjoy and provide which I could not reciprocate. Looking back on it now, I sometimes wonder how or why I had as many friends as I did. It could not have been for the hospitality I offered, nor the spending power I did not have to treat them. My mother always did her best to make any friends I brought back for "tea", after a day's adventures, welcome. But for me it was always an embarrassment.

I particularly recall my 21st birthday, during the summer vacation when our home was still a slummy hut built out of two railway carriages. Contemporary friends had lavish parties and more lavish budgets. How could I compete? I was too ashamed and embarrassed to try. Those of my chums I wished to invite included the sister of Stirling Moss, the racing driver hero at his prime, who lived in Tring. Another of my friends was the daughter of the family that owned and started Champneys, the first British health farm. Frances Leif was one of my many girl friends.

My step-father Stockey, came to rescue my embarrassment and loss of prestige. He offered me one of his coaches from his prospering hire business, for an evening trip to Oxford for a theatre experience. I selected ten of my special friends and my reputation was salvaged, as at the time it was an unusual way of celebrating birthdays.

My sister, Margie, had different "adolescent" problems. Four years my junior, we seemed to live separate lives. Although we lived in the same house the age gap was too wide for us to have overlapping friends or any joint social life. I left for my National Service and University while she was still at school and moved to London before she was independent.

My sister also left home fairly early and married young. Ken her loving kind and caring husband, became a manager for the local bus garage, part of the national bus service, supervising the maintenance of the fleet, keeping it in good order. His skills with vehicle maintenance were often put to the test by his brother-in-law. He was an excellent mechanic and would have done well running his own business. They had three children, Hazel the youngest, unlike any of my own children, managed to have red hair like mine, unlike either of her parents. As the milkman at the time was also a redhead, Margie insisted that I visited to prove it was a family trait.

As time went on we both had families, and due in no small part to my wife Hilary, my sister and I got to know each other and have become closer than we ever were as children. My eldest daughter, Judith, resembles my sister in many ways and Margie's son David and my youngest Julius are as alike as brothers.

Sadly, Ken developed kidney failure and became less and less mobile due to joint problems. He was some years older than my sister and after a lengthy and uncomfortable illness, he died. Margie and he had tried to get out as much as possible and she had still kept up her connections with the Rambling Club. After his death she seems to have been permanently walking some footpath complex somewhere or other. She has now found another charming partner and they travel the world in between long walking holidays and appointments with the Morris Minor Club.

Of course my in-laws, Arthur and Ena, were thrilled to visit Parliament and see me installed, although my father-in-law insisted on reminding me that it was not his first visit to the place. As a young man he had the doubtful honour of knocking Lloyd George off a chair he was standing on to speak to an audience in a room at the House of Commons, when Arthur entered the room by the wrong door to attend the meeting.

My two elder children had attended the Opening of Parliament ceremonies. As the children of an M.P. they were allowed to wait in the Central Lobby while the processions went past. When Black Rod had gone down to the Commons, the children were brought forward by a kind policeman so that they could look straight into the Lords Chamber directly at the Queen on her throne with her crown and all her regalia. Judith was heard to exclaim "Oh I can see the Queen and her head is all full of lights!" Her primary school news book was well decorated with pictures. Later the children could see their Daddy joining in the procession between the two Houses.

My opportunity to enter into the debates came all too soon. My newly won constituency was plunged into crisis and it would have been uncaring and irresponsible not to have told the House about our troubles. Rolls Royce went into receivership. My leisurely initiation ended rather abruptly. I was dropped into a hole filled with problems. However, it allowed me to make my maiden speech and put my constituency prominently on the map.

Chapter Sixteen
Rolls Royce

All too soon after my initiation came the bombshell that Rolls Royce had gone into administrative receivership. The Group's headquarters and principal aero-engine plant were south of Derby, just straddling the boundary of my constituency. But my patch of outlying towns and villages was the home of a large share of the 20,000 or so workforce and most of the management. The regional economy was dependent on the area's largest employer and the spending power of employees, from hundreds of sub-contractors, to retailers, service and leisure businesses. The problem fell straight into my lap, with fears of massive redundancies. That was avoided as Ted Heath nationalised the company. Emergency legislation was rushed through Parliament, creating a new company to take over the assets of the old.

The story has perhaps not always been accurately told. I argued at the time that the company was not bankrupt as the media sensationally claimed. The problem was a severe liquidity crisis. Technical snags with the development of the RB211, the new generation of gas turbine engines, delayed sales to aerospace manufacturers like Lockheed already committed to buying the new engine.

Management had concealed the cash shortage until it was too late. By capitalising the huge development costs, instead of writing them off, accountants over- valued the assets. There was nothing improper in this; otherwise the auditors would have had to say so. It is common practice to credit the costs of developing new products, by adding them to the assets in your balance sheet. Such accountancy would only be questionable if not all such expenditure could be deemed to produce a return in future earnings.

Rolls Royce was fully justified in its confidence in the new generation of aero engines they were developing and orders were already on the books. The Group's troubles only arose because there were serious cost and time overruns. Rolls Royce was not the first or last high tech business brought to its knees by underestimating the time and cost of developing revolutionary new technology.

Rolls Royce's problems were not fully understood by the City nor some of the civil servants in the Department of Trade and Industry, who were advising Ministers. The Group was in a desperate competitive fight with the world's largest aero-engine manufacturers, both American, General Electric and Pratt and Whitney. General Electric particularly was well advanced in the development of the next generation of jets and Rolls Royce had to stay in the race, whatever the cost, to survive.

All new civil airlines now have these engines, with their much more powerful thrust in relation to their reduced weight and their much more efficient fuel consumption. If Rolls Royce had not survived General Electric would have had a world monopoly. Because the Group did survive and was able to finish development, Rolls Royce has now won near enough half the world's market for wide-bodied planes fitted with its engines. The Rolls Royce aero-engine business is highly profitable today and Derby with it.

It became clear to me as soon as the crisis developed that the Department of Trade and Industry in London was not up to date with its information on the development progress. When I immediately visited Rolls Royce, not of course for the first time, I was shown a demonstration on the engine's test bed. The thrust was being raised weekly and had almost reached its planned power at the time of the financial crisis. Meanwhile civil servants were still providing Ministers with less than accurate information.

My assessment of the situation was that Whitehall had lost confidence in the company's ability to finish the engineering development to achieve the required power. I knew that this was far too pessimistic a view as I had seen better figures than the officials who were briefing Ministers.

Another factor contributing to the panic nationalisation was the fear that the principal launch customer for the new engine, Lockheed, would sue Rolls Royce for late delivery. This would have been damaging but not fatal in my view, because the engine was on the point of being ready for manufacture.

However, Lockheed had sunk huge capital into developing a civil airliner, the Tri-Star, which was aimed at competing with Boeing and Europe's industry, the newly formed Aerospatiale Airbus.

Lockheed were desperate to get the engine quickly or they too might face financial collapse. I was not convinced Lockheed would try to drag Rolls Royce through the courts, as our Government told Parliament. Their senior directors were in London in constant contact with the development in Derby. They could see, as I did, that the engine was progressing fast after the initial delays. They understood that the engine was well behind schedule because Rolls Royce had first tried to use carbon fibre as the material for critical parts of the engine. This technology had to be abandoned as unsatisfactory.

I arranged to meet the Lockheed directors led by Dan Houghton, in the London Hilton. They were in considerable distress. "We have built the largest gliders in the World!" was the thrust of their message to me. It was clear that the last resort for them would be to ruin Rolls Royce by claiming enormous damages. All they wanted, all they needed to survive, was that launch engine. Nobody was listening and the nationalisation panic continued in Parliament. That, we were told, was the only way to save Rolls Royce from a horrendous legal action by Lockheed. Reluctantly the US Government undertook to guarantee Lockheed's bank loans at the request of the British Government which allowed the state takeover to proceed.

The legislation passed and Rolls Royce not only survived but flourished, becoming even more of a world leader. The RB211 was technically superior to its American competitors. It had better fuel economy, was quieter and had a better thrust to weight ratio. Under the leadership of Kenneth Keith, with his accountancy background, as the new Chairman, the management was strengthened by building up more financial expertise in the boardroom, instead of having an overemphasis on the engineering side. Kenneth Keith told the story of how he had shown the previous chairman, who had no financial expertise but an engineering background, what the problem was, with figures on the back of an envelope. He persuaded Stanley Hooker, the engineering designer, to come out of retirement and as Technical Director to lead a team of other retirees to fix the remaining problems on the engine.

I still question whether a better solution might not have been found which was less traumatic. In today's circumstances, if one of our most important strategic private sector defence companies were in financial difficulties, it would probably be solved with a Government guaranteed loan, which would allow fresh equity capital to be raised, or a taxpayer's purchase of a slice of the equity, as Government recently has salvaged the banking crisis, rather than outright nationalisation. However, the crucial role of Kenneth Keith as Chairman of a revived company would have been essential and would have had to have been a condition of any guarantee.

It was with relief and enjoyment that I was invited, in 1971, to the official launch of the Tri-Star with the RB211 at Rolls Royce's "home" airport at Castle Donnington, now East Midlands. My family came with me to see the planes. After the landing and the spectacular "silent", well much quieter, engine, we had the usual set speeches; my wife wandered off with my youngest child Jessica to occupy the youngster with a closer look at the plane, holding her up to see into the massive engine. A press photographer had followed her and the resulting picture of the child and plane went around the world.

By this time I was an active member of the Conservative Aviation Committee. Not as grand as it sounds, but an informal group of Members meeting weekly to discuss current issues and invite guest speakers from the industry. It was an invaluable opportunity to keep briefed. Our chairman, Cranley Onslow and deputy, Kenneth Warren, both had been involved in the industry prior to coming into Parliament. The Committee would be invited annually to the Farnborough Air Show, where our aerospace hosts ensured we were appropriately wined and dined. But almost as important as the lavish hospitality was the forum for keeping up to date and talking to key managers in the aerospace industry.

The Commons All-Party Aviation group made a visit to the United States at the invitation of their aviation industry and sponsored by Rolls Royce and British Airways which was considering the replacement of their fleet. Unusually, for such fact finding visits our wives and partners were invited as well for the week's study. We were flown first class, courtesy of British Airways and treated royally. The Conservative members of the group included Kenneth Warren and Norman Tebbit, who still had his pilot's licence and piloted the plane for a period on the way over causing a little anxiety amongst us passengers.

We arrived in Los Angeles for the first of our briefings with MacDonald Douglas. The Labour Members were led by Ian Mikardo accompanied by his wife Mary. Mik, as he was known, was renowned as the Commons' bookmaker, by his willingness to take bets on anything. He also collected ties and his wife was eager to pounce on any which might enlarge his collection. One of the Labour contingent suffered from sleep apnoea which did at times prove embarrassing as he would drop asleep during the briefings needing to be nudged awake. We were put up in a pleasant hotel in the Hollywood area and while we were engaged in some very serious briefings and factory visits, our wives were taken on splendid tours of the area. They encompassed the film studios and of course, Disneyland.

We were taken by Boeing's private plane to Seattle to see their outfit. The trip there was memorable as the pilot flew us up the St Andreas fault line and at the end of it gave us a quick tour around the top of Mount St Helens, describing it as an extinct volcano which had not erupted in centuries. Only a few years later, in 1980, it proved it was no longer "extinct" with its spectacular eruption, killing many people and wrecking houses and farmland.

Our visit to the American aero industry was a pleasant form of lobbying and of course a vital part of an M.P's life if we are to gain specialist knowledge which can inform debate. I see no reason why one should not also enjoy the accompanying junket especially to foreign parts, offered by good hosts.

There were some interesting colleagues still around when the new intake arrived in 1970. One was Sir Gerald Nabarro. I invited him to speak in Derbyshire. The largest Hall was booked and filled. With his trademark "handlebar" moustache, he was one of the most popular political characters of the time and a splendid orator. Just as the meeting was about to start with a packed audience waiting for the platform party to make its triumphant entrance, the Special Branch arrived with the news that there had been an IRA bomb threat.

After a hurried consultation, Gerald and I were evacuated from the building, while the constituency chairman Michael Wells and my wife, were detailed to go on to the platform and keep the audience of five hundred happy while the building was covertly searched. Few people in the hall realised what the hitch to the start of the proceedings was all about, while Michael and Hilary each said a few words about current topics, acutely aware of men searching the underside of the platform on which they were sitting. They were not too pleased with us afterwards, to have been written off as disposable prospective bomb fodder.

After the search the meeting was finally allowed to go ahead. Nabarro gave us good value as always. He was not just a flamboyant politician but an extrovert performer, more appropriate for Show Biz than politics. He did not deliver his address standing at a lectern, but paced around the platform and up and down the aisles of the auditorium.

Before the meeting Gerald had asked me, as I was warned he usually did, to name my oldest supporter in the audience. Also he wanted to know of anyone there with a distinguished public service record or a medal. He wanted the names of two or three other members of the audience deserving special recognition – such as a just married couple or my youngest YC supporter. Nab carefully worked these people into his speech. "The Conservatives value and support family life. I hope you are listening John and Mary. Congratulations on your wedding – did you enjoy your honeymoon?" "Agnes, I am particularly honoured to meet you" he would say walking down the aisle towards her "I am told by your M.P., Peter, you have just celebrated your 97th birthday . . . ." So he continued and of course carrying his audience with him as a professional performer.

I recall another Nab occasion at Westminster. It was the day of a mass student rally. Every college and university sent a large delegation complaining about inadequate student grants, to lobby their M.Ps individually. The spacious Central Lobby was packed and very noisy as each M.P. was summoned to try to find their local student constituents. It was bedlam. I came out from the Chamber to find my group from Derbyshire. Next to me in the rowdy Central Lobby was Nab. Above the hundreds of loud voices we heard him bellow to his group. He stared at one unfortunate long haired student shouting "and which are you, a boy or a girl?"

Another outstanding character of that era was George Brown. Belper and my South East Derbyshire constituency wrapped around Derby, and we had met at the Derby Council offices when along with our wives, we had handed in our nomination papers at the same time before the election and enjoyed a brief chat. Both Belper and my seat had been due to have minor changes by the Boundary Commission, which would have made a slight difference to me, but which would probably have made George Brown's seat much safer. The Labour Government chose not to enact these before the 1970 election. George Brown had been Foreign Secretary until 1968 and had challenged

Harold Wilson for the Leadership but he remained Deputy Leader until the election. His relationship with Harold Wilson was, not surprisingly, already strained by 1970, and Harold found a sure way of ridding himself of a rival. George inevitably lost the Belper seat and was promoted to the House of Lords out of the way.

I remember trying to entertain constituents in the House of Commons Dining Room, when conversation was drowned out by George's ever growing raucous voice, well fuelled by alcohol. However, my favourite meeting was when my wife and I were being entertained at the French Embassy for Bastille Day. The constituency boundary changes had been agreed and would become operational at the next election. From the other side of the rather elegant large drawing-room came Lord George Brown, holding out his hand to Hilary and shaking her hand said "You may not know me, but I remember you!" He then turned to me and said "Well, your Government's done the boundary changes that my 'something' Government refused to do for me."

But that was George, his behaviour might have been embarrassing but he was a likeable and popular figure all round. Parliament needs a few eccentrics and free spirits, to liven things up.

Chapter Seventeen
The Broom Cupboard

The most momentous event during my Parliamentary life was the vote in 1971 to join the European Union. Obtaining a narrow Parliamentary majority was Ted Heath's greatest achievement. As our negotiator in the 1960s when Harold Macmillan attempted to get us in, Ted was well prepared for some tough talking. He was not likely to have forgotten the humiliation when General de Gaulle, as France's President, vetoed our application after months of haggling.

Now de Gaulle had gone and all six founding nations wanted us in. Germany was particularly keen to help us agree acceptable terms. We were desired as a counter weight to the fear that France would dominate the decision taking process. The smaller partners wanted us to help strengthen the Union's voice in the world and to keep the balance between France and Germany, preventing any possible dominance of one over the rest.

As a pro-European, which is not surprising given my background, I had no problem with the pending vote in principle. Coming from the early years when my life had been severely disrupted, I believed some sacrifice of sovereignty was necessary if it ended forever, the senseless tragic history of conflict and war in Europe. As an economist and a geographer, it looked increasingly advantageous for us to build in Europe a counter force to the economic powers of America and the Far East, particularly the rising strength of China, India and Japan.

My main problem was the opposition amongst the voters, upon whom one relied to stay in Parliament. Unless I attempted and succeeded in explaining my reasons for strongly supporting Ted Heath's decision, my future looked threatened. So I arranged a series of public meetings in Derbyshire at which I was able to argue the advantages and respond to the critics. It was helpful that many of my influential and senior constituency officers were with me. They mostly represented local exporting industries and could see the advantages of free markets. The local media was also helpful, giving good exposure to my speeches and discussions at public meetings.

What was unhelpful was the organised hostility from Labour in Parliament and throughout the Country. Harold Wilson, who had earlier professed to be in support of our membership, changed his mind. Most of us believed it was raw, shameless opportunism, rousing opposition to the Conservative Government in an unprincipled campaign, contrary to his honest beliefs. Despite crude pressure by the Labour Whips, six Members voted with us. The rebellion was led by Roy Jenkins in a courageous move, typical of his political honesty. It led to a split in Labour's ranks and eventually to the formation of the Social Democratic Party. With the help of Labour's rebels, Ted Heath won the vote overcoming Tory opposition and the process towards our signature to the Treaty of Rome was underway.

In my view the whole debate should have been held across party political lines and was smothered in hypocrisy. Parliament should have asserted its independence on such a fundamental constitutional and historic decision. Members should have insisted on a free vote, instead of being bullied and pressured by the Party machines. Tony Benn had a point. He campaigned for a referendum. But that was not honestly conceived either. He only clamoured for one because he hoped the Nation would say "no". Britain formally joined the European Economic Community on January 1st 1973.

In the 1970s life at Westminster seemed to assume that all entrants had come from public schools and spent their time in a gentleman's club. Until modest recent reforms, sittings did not start until 2.30pm, allowing Members to continue their outside professions in the City or the Law Courts. Business organisers made sure there would be no voting until late in the afternoons and more likely not before 7pm in the evenings. Nobody pursuing an honest good money earning career should be expected in the House before then and certainly not inconvenienced by having to vote. Sittings frequently ended after midnight with important votes. That again was hardly a "user-friendly" existence for M.Ps with families.

How Hilary and I managed with eventually four children, remains a mystery. With no home near Parliament in London, I commuted daily and nightly to and from Berkhamsted, an hour and a half from door to door. Sometimes it was even the 4am Newspaper train home. I would try to creep into bed without waking Madam, but often the events at Westminster had been so compelling that I could not resist telling Hilary all about them. Hilary would get up in the morning, leaving me asleep, to take the older children to school. Hilary would say that we shared a bed, but rarely at the same time. The only plus point was that when the children were very little, pre-school, they would creep into bed in the mornings and "share" Daddy's breakfast bread and marmalade or camembert cheese.

It is only in recent years, with the increased number of women M.Ps with families, that more social hours were agreed, but not without resistance from the "old guard". Their attitude was, if you do not like the "clubby" atmosphere, don't join the club.

There were compensations for the long hours into the night when the prospect of important votes obliged you to hang around. It has never surprised me that too many long-serving Members developed alcohol problems. On sittings when the business was specialised, such as some obscure amendment to some important technical legislation, the chamber would be sparsely populated but the bars would be full.

There were a number of bars, each with its own clientele. The Kremlin, as it was called, attracted a noisy rabble of left-wing trades' unionists. But the beer was the best in the Palace. The Smoking Room bar was definitely the territory of the clubby Tory lawyers. Margaret Thatcher once ventured in escorted by her "mascot" Willy Whitelaw. Heads turned round and eyebrows were raised in disapproval. This was not the territory for women, not even if they were a "Prime Minister with balls."

Behind the lush leather armchairs on the Smoking Room was an annex called the Chess Room. It was in contrast to its next door neighbour's atmosphere, very quiet and dignified. On late nights with only a few M.Ps involved in some obscure legislation – usually related to Scotland, the Chess Room was seriously occupied. A league table hung on the wall with players' names. As in all respectable chess clubs, you challenged the name above you.

If you won you changed places. Of course a new boy like me had to start at the bottom.

After a couple of years I worked my way half-way up the list. There had obviously been many very late nights. The next name above me was John Stonehouse. He had been quite a distinguished Minister in Harold Wilson's Government until 1970, serving as the Minister for Technology and the Minister for Posts and Telecommunications where he introduced the two-tier postal system of First and Second class mail.

But he was not included in Harold Wilson's Shadow Cabinet after 1970. It was then that his troubles appeared to overwhelm him. Companies which he had set up got into financial difficulties, he "fiddled the books" and an investigation was started by the Department of Trade and Industry which he realised could lead to prosecution and possibly prison. Readers will recall that it was at this stage that he elaborately faked his own death by drowning , leaving a pile of clothes on a Miami beach, while in reality on his way to join his former secretary in Australia.

Our chess game was on the night before his disappearance from the House. Indeed I might well have been the last Member to speak to him. His scheme had been meticulously planned. It was no rash, spontaneous decision. Yet during the hour our game lasted, he showed no sign of unusual behaviour. There was no indication of any nervous anxiety or restlessness, even though he had decided it was going to be his last night at Westminster. I can only assume that my company, playing chess, without the chat that would disturb serious play, allowed him to hide away from the rooms in the Palace where he might have met his closer colleagues and give away hints of his intended "suicide" stunt. The game was a draw. The Division Bell rang, but his vote was not recorded. He had gone.

Chess was not the only activity that absorbed time late at night, when I was too tired to work on papers in the Library. We had a Bridge four. This had to be very discretely organised as gambling was strictly prohibited in the Palace. As a card game, even though we only played for pennies, Bridge was classed as gambling, and we were in fear of being sent to the Tower of London, if discovered.

My regular partner was Sally Oppenheim. She was a much better player than I but tolerated me because of an occasional intuitive flash of inspiration.

Being also an experienced housewife she discovered a House of Commons broom cupboard. This was right up in the rafters, well above the two Committee Room floors. The lifts did not go up that far, only some crumbling stone stairs. The room faced Big Ben and the shattering sound every 15 minutes kept us on our toes.

The room was only a broom cupboard but it was the largest I had ever seen, presumably because it had to accommodate the equipment for so many cleaners. We managed to stuff in a table and four chairs.

We hid ourselves there many times and were never discovered, taking with us a little nourishment. Our only problem was that we were out of the reach of the Division Bell, so we could only risk a night in the hideout when we were certain of the voting timetable. It sometimes misfired, when my absence at an unexpected vote had to be explained to the Whips. There was one unfortunate occasion when the Business of the House folded up earlier than expected and the midnight vote we were waiting for did not happen. We drifted down for it to find the House completely deserted. Everyone had gone home two hours earlier.

In September of 1971, Hilary and I joined my father and Eleanor for a few days in Bad Reichenhall in southern Germany. We were on our way to take part in the Twinning link which Long Eaton had with Langen in the Rhineland and took a detour to see the lakes and neighbouring Salzburg. On our last day there we decided to visit one of the salt mines which are abundant in the area. Initially my father decided not to join us, but having heard how interesting the tour was from some tourists, he hurried after us up the hill.

We were togged up in baggy overalls with tight fitting caps and sent hurtling down into the mine by a series of slides and a small railway. It was fascinating to see the huge caverns from which the salt had been removed, with their multi coloured walls rather like some modernistic cave painting. We stopped at a series of benches and sat to have our picture taken – looking like some group of prisoners in a work gang. All very pleasant.

On our last night, Hilary and I had dinner with Eleanor and my father and then made our way up to Langen for the Twinning ceremonies and a boat trip on the Rhine. We arrived back at Norcott to be met by my mother-in-law, Ena, to be told that my father had died the night after we had left. He had previously had a mild heart attack after playing a vigorous game of tennis in a humid thirty degree heat wave in New York and had been warned against any further sudden exertion. I immediately turned around and flew out to join my step-mother to help arrange matters. The situation was complicated because my father had died in Germany, in Bad Reichenhall, but the crematorium was in Austria, in Salzburg. Eleanor did not have any of my father's papers with her and she had to produce a copy of Dad's University degree as well as his birth certificate before the Austrian authorities would allow the cremation. Eventually the problems were sorted, but I could not wait any longer until his ashes were released and permission given for them to be flown home. My sister had to go and retrieve them and fly them back to the U.K. for the burial in my grandparent's grave. I have heard others complain of the Austrian bureaucracy.

The photo taken in the Salt mine arrived after my father's funeral. A strange reminder and last memorial. My cousin Kurt did the honours at the Golders' Green Jewish cemetery for my father as I was completely at sea. Arthur and Ena, my in-laws, attended the funeral along with several old friends and former colleagues of my father.

Within a month Arthur was taken ill with a ruptured appendix and died suddenly. Hilary and I were both left fatherless. What was even more curious was that my father had been born exactly one month before Hilary's father who had died exactly one month after him. The two of them had lived exactly the same number of days. Arthur had been in the same form at Berkhamsted School with Graham Greene whose early autobiography, "A Sort of Life" had been published that year. Hilary had written to Graham Greene asking him to sign a copy of the book for Arthur. The book had arrived inscribed with a glowing tribute to his former school mate the day before he was rushed to hospital.

Hilary had found she was pregnant just before her father died. Our fourth child and second son, Julius was born in May 1972 on Arthur's birthday. By this time business was very difficult in the House and I was unable to be home for the birth. My mother-in-law Ena rang the House of Commons to let me know about the birth. Unfortunately the person taking the message in the Sergeant at Arms' office conveyed the message "Your wife has given birth to a son" to Willie Ross a Scottish Labour Member, whose wife was in her seventies. Thinking it was some joke in bad taste, Willie Ross ignored it and it was not until Ena rang again much later to find out why I had not responded that I knew of the new edition to the family.

Chapter Eighteen
Who Governs Britain

Pundits believe a hardworking Member, with plenty of media exposure, will only add at most a thousand votes beyond the national swing. That bonus has to be earned and takes some years to be achieved. It can usually be accumulated in a new M.P's first Parliament.

My majority in the 1970 General Election was two thousand four hundred and so sounded secure enough, but that was deceptive. Many seats in the East Midlands were marginal, with bigger than average swings which exaggerated the National trend. South East Derbyshire with the 1966 Labour majority of five thousand five hundred votes was still regarded as a "safe" Labour seat. The Conservatives had managed to take it briefly in 1959, after many recounts, with a majority of twelve votes. It was in most people's eyes a Labour seat.

By 1973 Ted Heath's Government was running into several problems. Militant Trades Unions led by Marxist Arthur Scargill's National Union of Miners, were challenging the right of a democratically elected Government to govern. Due to the miners' strike Britain was subjected to a three day working week to conserve depleting coal reserves at our power stations. We were fortunate in our area to host the winter quarters of the National Showmen's Guild. They possessed a large number of fairground generators which they loaned out and moved around the local businesses, so keeping our local industry at work almost full time. On the whole we were managing well and the general opinion was that with only a little more time, we could have sat the dispute out.

Domestically of course it was a different picture. Hilary, like all other wives and mothers had to cope with finding alternative ways of providing the essential tea and coffee at breakfast time. The children, however, enjoyed it. "Oh it's another Happy Birthday day today" said an excited Jessica coming down to the candle lit table in the morning.

The Conservative Government's overall majority was only thirty-one, a precarious working number that could easily be overthrown at the next election. Public opinion indicated a lack of confidence in our Government to master the Nation's problems. Members with unsafe majorities, like mine, were well advised to work hard and win local support or risk losing their seats.

I concentrated on becoming well known as a caring Member who could get things done to assist people with their problems. The visitors to my regular advice "surgeries" lengthened, as word circulated that I had been able to solve most of the enormous range of personal problems. This work can be the most satisfying side of an M.P's activity. So much of the Parliamentary life, by comparison, can be deeply frustrating, as it is difficult even for Ministers to achieve what they would like. If you were an M.P. on the Opposition benches it could be even more difficult, not having such easy access to the relevant Ministers, because they were not "on your side".

Many of the problems brought to me by voters related to Local Government and so could be referred to elected councillors or even directly to the officials and officers. But even in these cases the intervention or just a nudge from the M.P. usually got results. No official, national or local wants to risk exposure in the media for incompetence or neglect.

After each advice session the local media would ask if any good newspaper material had emerged. Usually several cases could be mentioned, inviting the press to interview the voter directly to report the story. This not only helped me and the local Conservatives with publicity, it often resolved the problem more promptly. So when a complaint came to me from a voter that his neighbour refused to cut an over -hanging hedge or stop revving up his noisy car at 5am each morning, I was often able to help with this sort of problem and hundreds of others.

Simply by visiting in person, with a few friendly words would often do the trick. If not the voter could come back to me asking for tougher action. So we could set the local Press on the job and expose an unsociable neighbour. These sort of local complaints were hardly a matter for Parliament. But for those concerned, can assume more anger and stress than the bigger national issues.

When dealing with individual people with their entrenched opinions, not every problem was so easily sorted. Every M.P. has at least one, if not more, unsolvable case. Mine was the woman convinced that her chimney was being bugged by MI5, as was her car, while her house was being over flown by a spy plane. Reassurances from the Police, endorsed by me that no evidence could be found to support her contentions, did not persuade her. I never did discover from her why she should think that MI5 would be so interested in her.

I had another constituent who claimed that his house was being "persecuted." People would come in the night and scrape out the cement from between the bricks and cars would slow down passing the house, while their drivers stared in at it. It was useless to explain that the place needed re-pointing and that cement could crumble with age, or that boarding up his front windows with some rather garish material would cause anyone to slow down and gawp.

Of course there are many genuine examples of injustice or official incompetence. A dairy farmer was being harassed for alleged unpaid tax. Despite examining his books the Inland Revenue would not lay off. Their demands became more and more aggressive. His accountant could not calm them down. The problem was that his wife kept the books so neatly and tidily written, that the particular taxman sent to investigate refused to believe that the records were not faked and written up after the Revenue had started its enquiries. Because she kept the same pen for making the entries and used the same notebooks, they had, according to this man, obviously all been filled in at the same time and not over the weeks.

In spite of the fact that it was obvious that the small dairy round was not earning a fortune and their accountant's protestations, I was unable to reassure the Inland Revenue that my constituents were honest, hardworking citizens and that the figures they had given were genuine. They had no possible means of settling the ridiculously large sum claimed. Nearing retirement age, they tragically had to sell up.

This was my first example of the way in which the Taxmen operated, without any means of appeal other than to themselves to be decided by themselves. The mistake they had made was obvious to any fair minded person, but to have accepted this would have led to an admission that they were wrong, something they would not do.

Not all problems deserve to be solved. An apparently healthy looking middle aged man, living in a modern council house, demanded that I visit him to discuss his dilemma. Normally, every "surgery" day would end up with one or two house visits to people who needed me to see some particular situation or who were perhaps invalided. I always obliged.

When I arrived in mid afternoon, he was lounging in front of his deluxe TV in front of a roaring fire in almost tropical heat. The council had been asked to replace his banisters and decorate the hall, but had visited and decided that it was not a top priority as there was no danger. He evidently claimed to be partially disabled and said he had problems finding enough money to pay for his special diet, which, when Hilary asked his wife about this, seemed to be simply eating plenty of fresh vegetables and avoiding salt. He could not, he claimed, get any job and I must admit I got the impression he was not particularly seeking one.

Looking through the windows into the back garden which was an overgrown jungle, I had the nerve to ask him "Why don't you supplement your inadequate income by cultivating your garden and growing some vegetables?" After all, I went on to say that although I had a busy life I still managed to get out and do some gardening. "Oh I can't do that, I am unable to do any physical work". I indicated the son of the house, a strapping sixteen year old, who had just come in. "Why don't you get your son to do the hard work, I am sure it will do him good." After a moment's hesitation he came out with "I would love to do that, but of course we do not have any money to buy seeds!"

Every year for twenty two years, I spent some days before Christmas, touring the constituency from morning to night visiting all the hospitals, sheltered housing, nursing homes, special schools and elderly people's care homes. My visits would be unannounced but mostly expected. I tried to coincide with the inevitable Christmas parties at each institution and always started with a cup of tea with the matron or manager, giving them the opportunity to tell me of any problems.

My pre Christmas tour also included the Post Offices, Police and Fire stations and in the evenings the clubs which were so important in the area. Some were nominally Conservative Clubs and some were Working Men's Clubs, no matter, I was welcomed in all. Any special events, such as Christmas bazaars, sales for charity, carol services at churches and schools, were fitted in, as were some seasonal parties at the factories. In the evenings and at lunchtime we would find a selection of pubs to join in the merriment.

This experience, especially the visits to the care homes for the physically and mentally handicapped, had a penetrating impact on me, as I admired the extraordinary dedication of care staff and the enormous army of voluntary workers. Many of my important party supporters were involved in this unselfish effort, as indeed were some Labour councillors and their families.

I started my pre-Christmas stint with a car full of modest gifts, mostly House of Commons chocolates. These were presented to those I regarded as the particularly deserving carers. After several years, as I became better known as the M.P., return gifts would be presented to me on my rounds, to say nothing of endless plates of mince pies. My children would often come along with me, particularly to the places where there were elderly people, getting thoroughly spoiled and costing me a fortune at the bazaars where they did their Christmas shopping. One could not but be impressed emotionally by the community spirit that was so dedicated to helping the lives of the less fortunate.

When we eventually returned to our main home for our family Christmas festivities and the excitement of Father Christmas filling stockings, the thought of those less privileged, having to adjust to a much harsher life would be ever present. I realised what an honour it was for me to have the opportunity to help, as some sort of cross between a parson and a social worker. A sympathetic understanding had to be restrained, to prevent appearing to be patronising.

The power of Backbench M.Ps to help the lives of frustrated voters should not be underestimated. It is one of the most important attributes of our Parliamentary system and is lacking in many other nations, even those claiming to be mature democracies. Our last resort is to find an opportunity to raise a constituent's injustice on the floor of the Chamber. A Minister has to reply on behalf of the Government department involved. After such embarrassing exposure with the assistance of a virile, free and investigating media, remedies often emerge.

Having retired in more recent years to Provence, I have learnt a little of the French system as I did earlier on my frequent visits to Germany. When you ask a citizen from either country about their parliamentary representative, very few seem to know anything. Even fewer seem to have seen or would know how to contact the one person who should be readily available to sort out the many problems often created by the over bureaucratised society. We may not appreciate, but need to be thankful that, on the whole, our democratic system works. Aggrieved citizens have ready access to those elected, able and willing to help.

In desperation Ted Heath called an election in the spring of 1974, during the Miners' Strike. Our theme was to be "Who Rules the Country?" It was the only election since the Second World War not to produce an overall majority for any Party. Although the Conservatives polled the most votes, because of the way in which the constituencies were distributed, Labour finished up with a majority of seats. So Heath resigned and Harold Wilson regained the Premiership.

My secretary Fiona, who had been with me since my stockbroking days, was married to an airline pilot. Formerly with British Airways, Ivan had recently moved to fly with Gulf Air from the Middle East. He was anxious for Fiona to join him there, as he was away from their home near Oxford for well over six months of the year. Their children were in boarding school so there seemed to be no excuse for Fiona not to go out, except that she was a very independent person and resented the way in which women were treated. The idea of not being able to drive a car or to go out unaccompanied was anathema to her. She stayed with us for the February Election in 1974, but said that she would go out to the Gulf and try out the situation over the summer. She promised to come back to help for the inevitable second Election, given Harold Wilson's narrow majority, to be held in the autumn.

Knowing Fiona's attitude to surviving in a desert patriarchal society, I did not expect to be without her as a secretary for long. As I had already taken on an assistant with my stockbroking work as Fiona had her time wholly taken up with my Parliamentary work, I asked Hilary if she would take the job on temporarily, until Fiona returned, as I did not want to go through the palaver of advertising and interviewing a new secretary. Although she had no typing skills, Hilary had been accustomed to office work and reluctantly accepted the "temporary" post.

By the time that Harold Wilson called the second General Election in October 1974, which he won comfortably with a decent majority on his benches, we had lost all contact with Fiona. Apart from a brief visit in the spring to attend a family celebration with friends in the constituency, no-one saw or heard of her again. It was most strange and we often wondered what had happened to her. In the meantime, Hilary was getting to grips with my secretarial work and had taken over Fiona's desk overlooking the Thames. It was far too convenient, I must admit, to have my secretary available at all times – although she objected to taking messages in the middle of the night in no uncertain terms. In the course of her "secretarial" career, Hilary learned to touch type, to programme a computer, to access several word processing packages, do power point demonstrations and edit and produce a monthly newsletter, amongst other things. She can even read my handwriting.

For us in the marginal Conservative seats, it was a hard struggle in February and more so again in October. We held South East Derbyshire by one thousand votes. I was relieved, knowing that based on the National swing against us, my seat should have returned to Labour. I believe that it was the thousand personal votes we had built up, that saved me. On the doorstep, when suggesting to voters "this is all about who governs Britain – the Miners or the Government?" I received many unpleasant responses along the lines of "well your lot haven't been. Have you?"

There was no smart answer. We knew it was a fair question. The majority of voters thought so too and we were back on the Opposition benches. Ted carried on as our Leader. But a new star was emerging on our side. She was to shape history soon enough. For those of us to have been fortunate to witness the story from its beginnings, it was to turn out to be an exhilarating experience, without doubt the highlight of my twenty two years in Parliament.

My struggle to keep my parliamentary seat had involved me in an energetic programme of factory visits, shopping centres, hospitals, leisure centres, aged people's homes and, indeed, anywhere, any organisation where voters could be found. My policy was not so much to inflict myself on people who might be embarrassed to talk to me. I simply aimed at being seen and recognised everywhere, all the time. Pubs and sports centres were particularly attractive, since they allowed me to be seen in environments somewhat different from the shopping centres and sheltered homes. All this hectic activity took place well before the 1974 elections were called and between them. It made my canvassing so much easier in the campaigns themselves. More people knew and recognised me. Despite the unfavourable climate for our Government, I appeared to be well received on the doorsteps. My hard work was paying off.

By this time I had a large team of enthusiastic dedicated workers. They were encouraged by gaining the seat in 1970 and were determined not to let it go again, in spite of an unhelpful National background working against the Conservatives' efforts. Throughout the difficult February 1974 campaign I was again accompanied by Paul Thompson, who took time off from the Oxford Union to be my aid. We renewed the tactics so successful in 1970 and tried some new ones. The local leisure centre had a large indoor pool. It was crowded early in the mornings with an amazing number of mostly men keeping fit as alternative to jogging to work. I joined in making sure my presence was noted. It was not that I needed the exercise. A vigorous three week election campaign uses up quite enough calories. Hilary always relied on losing a substantial amount of weight at each election. She managed to knock off quite a few pounds in 1974 with two elections.

Early in the February campaign, I was hit by a flu bug that was doing the rounds. Anxious not to reveal that I had become incapacitated in case it hit morale on our side, I discretely visited a doctor friend, one of our supporters. He gave me a very powerful shot of something, I did not know what. He jokingly said that it would either kill of cure me. I staggered on, my temperature dropping just enough to keep going. I still wonder how many voters were infected by my recklessness.

One of our staunchest supporters was Ted Lawrence, an anglicised version of his original Polish name. His story had made national news in earlier years when he escaped from a Russian prison camp and walked half way across Europe to reach freedom. A fierce patriot and appalled at Harold Wilson's Government, he conceived the idea of walking from Derbyshire to Downing Street carrying an enormous wooden crucifix. He had a successful furniture factory in Long Eaton and he had made the crucifix in his workshops. I tried to lift the object but found it hard enough to carry more than a few yards let alone more than one hundred miles.

A greater patriot would be impossible to find, so determined to prevent Socialism, which he saw as the spearhead of Communism, taking over Britain. When I finally stood down from Parliament before the 1992 Election, our constituency officers asked us what we would like as a presentation. Hilary and I chose a couple of Ted Lawrence's easy chairs which he made as our leaving present. They are greatly treasured by us.

Ted was probably the most eccentric but only one of a large colony of Polish immigrants in my area. They integrated into the local community, soon building up their own businesses and were active workers for the Tory cause. Not one I met wanted anything more to do with a Socialist society. They had escaped from a totalitarian state and they refused to differentiate between what they had abandoned and what they recognised as the danger from the Left-wing of the Labour party. Many too had escaped earlier and had joined the Polish forces to fight Nazi Germany alongside the British army and air force.

The region between Nottingham and Derby was also the new home for several hundred Ukrainians. Their country was subjugated and their fierce nationalism suppressed by the old Soviet Union. Many escaped to Britain and became a valuable minority community. They too wanted nothing more to do with the socialism they had experienced. I was led to believe our region became the largest colony of Ukrainians in the UK. They must be thrilled that the Ukraine has at last won its independence. With such enthusiastic enemies of Socialism and such a fanatical army of helpers, it was not too surprising that we held on to our constituency in the two 1974 elections.

Half way through my first Parliament, I decided to leave stockbroking and resigned my stock exchange seat as a Member and left the partnership. The pressures of nursing what I knew was a marginal seat and the need to make some impact on the Westminster stage as well as giving my constituents the reassurance that being an M.P. was a full-time commitment, were paramount. It ended the mutterings from my opponents that I was only a part-timer more interested in making money than serving the voters. It was a sensible decision, since it had become in any case almost impossible to continue managing my clients' portfolios satisfactorily, even with an able assistant in the office. My attendance in the City office to supervise became less than the daily morning minimum needed to do things properly. I had a growing correspondence load to deal with and had to find time to serve on the Parliamentary Committees, which sat in the mornings and to research my Parliamentary work on the newly formed Energy Select Committee.

My broking clients gradually drifted off, knowing that I was no longer freely available at the end of the telephone or meeting them in my office to review their investments. It was obvious that I could not do justice to both jobs. It is interesting to speculate whether this would still have been the case with today's technology. The mobile phone and the internet access would have made life so much easier with the ability to remain in contact. I do not think that it is appreciated how cut off from the rest of the world, M.Ps were at Westminster in the 1970s. Without the regular televising of debates in the Chamber, we did not even know what was happening around Parliament, let alone maintaining contact with our homes and constituencies. Our secretaries were our pivotal contact points.

One of the most distressing and disturbing incidents in our lives came in June 1974. My eldest daughter, Judith, then aged twelve, was prone to teenage temper tantrums. These would usually burst like summer storms and would end with her returning to her usual sunny disposition as if nothing had happened. However, on this occasion she decided to storm out during breakfast after having been reprimanded by Hilary for "winding up" and distressing her little sister, Jessica.

Hilary set off with the other children for school, assuming that Judith was finding her own way there and cooling off on the journey. She could not have been more wrong as she discovered at the end of the school day that Judith had not been anywhere near school and had completely disappeared. I returned early from Parliament. The Police were called and the great search began. All Judith's friends' homes along with the school boarding houses and our own house were systematically searched. At Norcott each room had the door marked with a cross as it was searched, we still have the cross on our cellar door as a reminder of the trauma.

We spent the night on sofas, barely sleeping, listening and hoping to hear the sound of the front door being opened. The following day, as there had been no sign of Judith, the helicopters moved in along with a team of dogs with their handlers. The national Press and the B.B.C arrived in force and took up residence on our terrace. We live on the edge of Ashridge Forest, one of the largest National Trust areas in England, a very difficult terrain but the search began in earnest. We heard via the Press that a child had been found murdered nearby a week or two previously. Although the police did not mention this they were obviously very worried, trying to be optimistic for us.

During the morning, however, Hilary received the first of several phone calls from a man with a strong Irish accent. Each time he kept saying he was sorry, so very sorry and then putting the phone down.

Although this was before the Brighton bombing in 1984, which claimed the life of M.P. Ian Gow and nearly claimed the life of Margaret Thatcher, and the car bomb in 1979 which killed Airey Neave, Margaret Thatcher's Northern Ireland Secretary, as he was leaving the underground car park at Westminster, the IRA threat was a terrifying reality.

Much earlier, after my election in 1970, I was visited by special branch, as were all new M.P.s and warned of the threat. We were given guidance on avoiding risks and told we would be subjected to extra protection. Our house was included in the local constabulary's beat, with at least one visit up our drive each night. We were also advised to check our cars if they were left outside on the drive, a ritual which soon lapsed until after Airey Neave's death, when we became very security conscious, never getting in the car until a full check had been done.

It was not difficult to realise that the precautions in 1970 were a futile assurance for most of us, constantly exposed and impossible to protect securely. Any day the IRA could find that I lived in an isolated country house and travelled daily to Westminster on public transport or in my car and was publicly exposed when on constituency business in Derbyshire. How could I, or any back bencher, be protected except at enormous manpower costs? It was pretentious to believe I was a priority, having never participated in debates or spoken publicly about Northern Ireland.

The search was stepped up and enquiries made in the area for any suspicious strangers, particularly with Irish accents. Meanwhile Hilary and I spent the longest and hardest day of our lives, waiting for news.

Quite late in the evening, our daughter arrived back accompanied by two policewomen. She had been hiding under straw bales in an isolated barn belonging to a neighbouring farm and had finally been driven out by hunger and discomfort. Sheep nuts and ears of corn were not her usual diet. She had started back home with the naive idea that she could creep in the back door without being noticed, only to be met by the police as she crossed the neighbouring field and a welcoming party of the national Media, search dogs and a helicopter at the house.

The quiet Irishman who had telephoned, had simply been a caring individual, who must have had no idea of the reaction his concern had caused.

The incident had an amusing end, which certainly relieved the tension, when one of the team of search dog handlers got lost in Ashridge with his dog and did not turn up for several hours. He must have been at the receiving end of jokes by his colleagues. Judith also had a fairly hard time facing her school friends and even today this incident is a subject she prefers to avoid.

Giving up my broking career was a financial sacrifice. My income dropped overnight to about one tenth of my previous commission earnings. The Parliamentary salary when I entered the House was only around £3,000 per year. The gradual adjustment from a salary appropriate for a part-time gentlemen's job to an adequate payment sufficient to live on without recourse to dubious outside sources, was only just beginning. During the transition, I and my family had to live off the capital I had saved over the previous years.

The Tory Party is an unforgiving machine, always with its top priority the struggle for power. Losing one election can be forgiven, especially when, as in February 1974, events stack up against you. But to lose a second one eight months later was too much. Many constituents had lost their sitting Member. The rumbles for a change of Leader were becoming an irresistible force.

Ted's prospects of survival were not helped by a rising star whom he had promoted to his cabinet as Minster for Education and Science in 1970 and who then had joined the Opposition Treasury team, planning attacks on Denis Healey's crippling tax increases. Margaret Thatcher was starting to make an impact within the Parliamentary Party, although little known in the constituencies apart from having been in power when the free school milk was ended. Along with Keith Joseph, her mentor, she was promoting policies which she hoped would tackle Britain's "sick man of Europe" image, more successfully than Ted Heath. Too many Conservatives had lost faith in our ability to govern, and felt that Ted had not been strong enough and should have weathered out the storm provoked by the miner's strike rather than calling an election with such a confused message. He had failed to tackle inflation and rampant Trades Union power.

The challenge to his leadership came in February 1975. Margaret Thatcher at first backed Keith Joseph but when he failed to win the confidence of his fellow Conservative M.Ps, Margaret Thatcher put herself forward. She won in the first round of voting which was limited in those days to the Parliamentary Party. Of course most of us felt obliged to take soundings, but the views of the local Party activists could only be regarded as advisory.

Those of us confident that Margaret was our best choice had problems convincing our constituency officers. They may have heard of her – mainly through the Labour slogan "Maggie Thatcher Milk Snatcher!" – But they had no way of judging her leadership potential, far less about her ability to lead the nation. My chairman and executive were critical of me when I declared my preference. Typically I was told "How dare you vote out our Leader and replace him with a practically unknown woman". Ironically, when her turn to be forced to resign as Prime Minister and our leader in 1990 came, pushed out by a vote of Tory M.Ps, I was again criticised in my constituency, "How dare you vote out our glorious leader". I did not in fact support her successor, John Major, in the vote that time, but Michael Heseltine.

Ted Heath did not go without a fight. As a former Chief Whip, he knew how to handle the party machine. When a national paper revealed that I had declared my preference to my constituency executive for Margaret Thatcher, my new agent, June Parkinson, received a very early morning call from Central Office. A most senior officer of the party told her to try to put pressure on me to change my voting intention. She was reminded that she was financially supported as my agent by Central Party funds. Many less than rich Conservative constituency organisations were supported from a central fund, out of donations from richer areas and outside donors. This was not in fact the case with my constituency, but June checked with other agents nearby and found that they had experienced the same threat and did not feel confident in rejecting it.

June called me immediately before breakfast. I was angry at this threatening attempt to intervene in an M.P's democratic vote in the choice of a Leader. I reported the incident to the Press Association's Lobby correspondent, Chris Moncrieff, where it became prominently exposed in the London evening papers just before the M.Ps had their final vote. For me, it was a reminder of the way in which the far Left Socialist and Nazi regimes operated, from which I had escaped.

After Margaret won the election as Party leader, I was told from those closer to the events than I, that the incident and its publicity turned off some M.Ps who might have been inclined to support Ted Heath, annoyed with the attempt of Central Office to interfere.

Our new Leader now had more than three years to establish herself as a prospective Prime Minister, before the next election scheduled for May 1979, which she won. Sadly, Ted Heath started the longest sulk – thirty years – in political history. It did not do him justice and undermined his creditable achievements. Having observed Margaret and met her as a constituent in Finchley and later as a colleague in the House, I felt confident that she was the right choice. She made good use of the time until he big test, the 1979 Election. She "stomped" round the Country with enormous energy and enthusiasm.

More convincing noises started coming from her about the direction of Tory policy. My favourite theme of Wider Share Ownership began to be discussed more widely, in association with privatisation. A more radical approach to making Britain a more prosperous free-enterprise economy was also planned. Margaret established policy "think tanks" with her back benchers. Reports recommending policies for our Manifesto for the next election were thrashed out in detail. I worked with others in one such group, preparing a strategy to meet our energy needs from the proposed privatisation of the gas, electricity, coal and nuclear industries. One of my principle concerns was also beginning to reach the Party agenda – cleaner, more efficient energy, with less waste and pollution. I wanted to see more promotion of renewable energy and tackling the disgrace of so much fuel poverty among the lower income households. However, I was bleating about policies to deaf ears until much later. To illustrate how things were in those days, Hilary always recounts how people would ask her what her husband's main interest was in Parliament. She would reply "Energy" only to be asked, what on earth is that? "Energy" in those days was something you felt after a good night's sleep, certainly nothing to do with power generation.

It is my belief that the success of Margaret's Government stemmed from this widespread policy planning within the Parliamentary Party. She recognised the enormous range of specialist knowledge and experience on the back benches, encouraging Members' involvement with the Shadow Ministers she had appointed. Most policy ideas which became the thrust of later Government implementation originated from well qualified back-benchers and outside consultants from industry and "think tanks" we recruited to help us. Even my proposals for a sustainable, self-sufficient, cleaner and less wasteful Energy policy, slowly moved up the agenda.

My contribution to preparing policies for what we all felt sure would be a Conservative Government led by Margaret, also came through the Bow Group, a Conservative "think-tank". I chaired one of the policy groups to prepare a programme of privatising energy industries; coal, gas, electricity and nuclear. Our report on how to provide adequate environmentally clean, competitively priced energy, included many proposals adopted by Margaret's Energy Ministers. We recommended strategies to encourage the more efficient production and use of our energy, which have been accepted over subsequent years.

I confess there were hopes at this time that I might be included in the ministerial team taking government after the election win. I was immodest enough to believe I was better qualified than some of Margaret's energy ministers. Many outsiders in the energy world thought so too, as did more than one civil servant in the Department. But as I learnt throughout my life, ability is not all that counts!

Chapter Nineteen
Yes, Prime Minister

Prime Minister's Question Time is now a weekly half-hour "ya-boo" shouting match, hyped up by the adversarial structure of the Chamber. Government and Opposition benches face each other, as if preparing for a mediaeval battle.

No Speaker tries too hard to calm down the noisy House, nor some of the traditional puerile behaviour. It is, after all, a central highlight and an important feature of our Parliamentary system. Until recent reforms it used to be even more unruly, because only fifteen minutes was allocated, every Tuesday and Thursday. So the competition for members to get into the scrum was even more frantic.

Few democratic parliaments in the world allow such regular and red-blooded challenges to a nation's leader. Many more dictatorial systems provide no such robust opportunities. We entertain a continuous stream of visitors from every foreign parliament. They observe our Question Time from the Public Gallery with interest and puzzlement. How does a Prime Minister put up with such rude questioning and open criticism? Does it not demean a leader's status and undermine authority? Should you not treat your Prime Minister with more respect? Is it not undignified, they ask?

The truth is both sides need it and try to use the session to their advantage. Usually independent observers will say after the session that the score was even. But sometimes one side has an overwhelming victory, which can seriously damage the loser, either the Prime Minister or the Leader of the Opposition. The media will quickly expose the inadequacies of one or the other. It is the reason why both Government and Opposition take these ritual confrontations so seriously. They can make or break a Party Leader and have done. Harold Wilson was brilliant but Ted Heath struggled. Neither he, nor Margaret Thatcher, found it easy to convert an attack and throw it back with humour. Jim Callaghan, previously, and the new Leader of the Conservatives, David Cameron, now, apply humour and sarcasm with great effect.

Since Parliament invited the cameras in, the sessions of Prime Minister's Questions have assumed even more importance. The Media is not only able to show the displays live, but repeat them at peak times with comment. No M.P. would suggest millions of voters are glued to their TVs every Wednesday at noon, but the feedback consistently is that there are quite large viewing figures. Opinion seems equally divided between those who regarded it as entertaining, while others are disgusted at the noise and bad behaviour, and they say so to their constituency M.Ps.

What is not so widely known is how seriously the political parties prepare for the weekly show. A Prime Minister will spend most of the morning with a team of political advisers and civil servants preparing possible answers on every topic that might be raised. Most of this work will involve finding suitable replies to the most topical issues that are likely to come up. A Prime Minister will also use, or try to abuse, the weekly occasion to slip in what is more like a statement on a very topical issue rather than an answer to a question.

The Prime Minister will also prepare to defend his departmental ministers, if they are likely to be attacked for some current event which has found them criticised or wanting. The Prime Minister is responsible for all Government policy and therefore must be prepared to field attacks from all sides on any topic.

While the Prime Minister will be in a huddle with advisers, so will the Opposition parties prepare for effective onslaughts. Soon after entering Parliament I started taking a particular interest in participating from the back benches. After all, these battles are not just between the two Front Benches. They are opportunities for back benchers to raise any matter with the Prime Minister.

To "table" a Question which will be reached in the time allocated is a matter of luck. A ballot takes place in the Vote Office to determine their order on the paper two weeks before those Questions are debated. Later Questions can of course be tabled right up to Question Time, but they will be at the bottom of the Order Paper and will not be reached orally, receiving only a "dead-pan" written answer. Perhaps only the first six Questions that come out on top will be reached. The trick is to table an open Question which allows you to follow up on any topical issue. So the Order Paper will be filled with such Questions as "Will the Prime Minister list his engagements today?"

The questioner is not in the least interested in the Prime Minister's programme for that day, but when the Prime Minister answers, saying what he has in his diary, it allows an Opposition back bencher to raise any matter simply by asking something such as, *but would the Prime Minister also find time today to visit my constituency and see the lengthening queues of the unemployed at our job centre, as a result of the Government's mismanagement!* Or if the backbench questioner is a Government supporter, a friendly bouncer will come along the lines of, *will the Prime Minister meet my constituents so that they can thank him for the booming orders in our local steel plant,* or whatever.

Questions are not tabled to invite answers. They are put down to enable the tabler to deliver a well rehearsed supplementary. For my first period in Parliament from 1970 until Ted Heath's loss of power in the February Election in 1974, I joined the weekly ballot with hundreds of other M.Ps to get a Question near the top of the list. It happened rarely, but there are also possibilities to be called by the Speaker to put a supplementary to another Member's question. That happened to me occasionally, but the competition was severe. It was at this time that I was asked by our Party Whips to join a group I had not even known existed. It was a secretive handful of back-benchers meeting before each Prime Minister's Questions, to plan strategy of harassment or support. The group was led by Jack Weatherall, then the Deputy Chief Whip who later became a most distinguished Speaker.

Our group worked through the Questions on the Order Paper likely to be reached. If one of us had tabled one of these, we discussed the best line to take which would help the Prime Minister, Ted Heath. From his office came helpful suggestions of subjects he would like raised. We tried to oblige. If none of our team, which included Norman Tebbit and Nigel Lawson, when still a back-bencher, had an early Question, we agreed to try to catch the Speaker's eye for a supplementary.

When the Tories lost power in February 1974, we really got into our stride, planning Questions to embarrass Harold Wilson. Probably my greatest "bull's eye" was a little later into his period in Government, when everything started to go wrong – the devaluation of sterling, strikes, unemployment and much else.

67

Wilson seemed to prefer trips abroad, trying to strut on the world stage, as all Prime Ministers do when life is not so comfortable in Downing Street.

It was the occasion when I had drawn Question number one. The House was, as usual packed and Harold Wilson had just rushed back from some overseas visit. I opened up with "when the Prime Minister next finds time to visit this country . . . . ." The Chamber fell apart with loud laughter, even on the by now demoralised Labour benches. Harold's face suffused with red. All could see that he was angry; I thought he would have a stroke. He never recovered his balance that session.

It was a result of my active contributions to Prime Minister's Questions that I learned a stark lesson, the contrast between a rather introverted Ted Heath and the more extrovert Harold Wilson.

I managed during Heath's premiership to get an early Question to throw him a helpful line such as, *was he aware how well Rolls Royce were doing now, following his financial assistance*, when he was having a difficult Question session and was relieved at my support. After Question time I came into the long voting lobby, walking towards the Speaker's end, when Ted Heath came into the lobby from there. We started walking towards each other. I was thrilled; at last I thought he would recognise the help I gave him in the Chamber. As we came closer – there was no-one else around us, I waited for him to stop and speak to me; instead he walked straight past inches away from me, staring ahead, as if he had not seen me.

The contrast with Harold Wilson is worth recording. On the occasion when I scored against him and the laughter interrupted the business with Harold seething anger, I had a similar experience. After the Question time I had again come into the long corridor going towards the end by the Speaker's chair to find, this time, Harold Wilson coming towards me. I thought of ducking into the nearby cloakroom door, but he had already noticed me. I was wondering what his reaction would be, after all, I had quite severely damaged what was left of his prestige. When he reached me he stopped, slapped me on the shoulder with the words "Well done Peter. You really got me this time!"

After his surprise retirement as Prime Minister in 1976, Harold Wilson was interviewed at length on TV. One of the questions he was asked was, "Which Opposition M.Ps caused you most trouble?" He replied, Norman

Tebbit, Nigel Lawson and Peter Rost.

At least the first two went on to achieve fame later under Margaret Thatcher's premiership!

Question Time was not Margaret Thatcher's greatest strength. She often struggled, leaving her back-bench troops somewhat despondent that she had not scored enough hits. By contrast her set speeches allowed her to shine because she had time to prepare and receive assistance from a team of speech writers. Question Time is a tough test. It requires the gift of humour, wit and above all spontaneity – not her strengths.

In her memoirs she admits frankly "Little by little I came to feel more confident about these noisy ritual confrontations and as I did so, my performance became more effective. Sometimes I even enjoyed them."[1] Unfortunately many of us were, too often, under-impressed.

---

1 Quotation from *The Downing Street Years*, Harper Collins, 1992.

Chapter Twenty
Anyone for Tennis

When our legislators, before my time, imposed puritanical licensing laws on the Country, they conveniently forgot to make them apply to the Palace of Westminster. The bars remain open however long the House sits. During these all night sittings, that were frequent in my earlier days when Oppositions were able to filibuster legislation they did not like, the watering holes did good business.

No wonder so many M.Ps developed a drink problem. It has never been difficult for me to resist overdosing myself with alcohol, although too often one gets near the wine drinking limit in good company. What did concern me more, was the general unhealthy sedentary lifestyle. Looking at my colleagues, I was horrified how quickly so many politicians gave up the struggle to remain fit.

I recall an occasion during a debate about the nation's health when a grossly overweight colleague was pontificating about the need to supply adequate sports facilities in our schools to combat obesity and the health problems arising from it. Of course he was right, but I could not help thinking how much less under pressure our health service would be if more adults like him practised what they preach to the nation.

I was determined to do what was possible not to reduce my life expectancy or become a burden on our over stretched health service, if I could. It was a wake-up call when my suits began to shrink. The constant occasions when one was entertained or required to host guests soon amounted to an excess of food and drink leaving its mark on the waistline. That was at the Westminster end.

Life in the constituency was even more harmful to health with all those endless cheese and wine evenings, unhealthy "nibbles" and "rubber chicken" dinners.

I entered Parliament coming from an energetic physical life, with lots of sport through school, university and National Service. Later walking tours in my leisure time as well as the many hours a keen gardener has to spend looking after our four acres around our house, has kept me reasonably fit. Playing tennis several times a week at my Tring tennis club, with matches against other clubs, was my chief relaxation. But my new duties as an M.P. forced me to abandon this life of leisure. I felt it proper to stand down as Chairman of the tennis club and had to content myself with only the occasional game at weekends, when not actively engaged in the constituency. I did manage a small compromise. I became a sort of associate member of one of the clubs in the constituency and tried to snatch a game when I could.

My other previous leisure activities also suffered. During recesses it was possible to enjoy the odd long five hour ramble with our Labrador. But not regularly enough. In my pre-Parliamentary life, all this fresh air was the only way I could recharge my batteries. I often felt in sympathy with Wordsworth, Coleridge and the other romantic poets with their attachment to the natural world, but I soon found it difficult to give sufficient time to enjoy all my former activities.

The Palace of Westminster is vast, with several floors and constant movement from room to room is needed. I used the stairs rather than the lifts and I always walked up the Underground escalators if I could not walk in time and needed to take the train. But what I really missed were proper long country walks and my tennis.

John Hannam, the Member for Exeter, -later Sir John Hannam- came to my rescue. He captained the Parliamentary Tennis Club, a motley crew of members, some suitable to include in teams needed to play fixtures with other clubs, some most definitely not.

There were annual matches against such organisations as the Stock Exchange, Lloyds Underwriters, and The Law Society. The only team we never managed to beat was Westminster School. That says more about our poor standard than it did about Westminster School's young promising team, when we discovered that they did not field their best players. I am able to record, boastfully, that for these matches representing Parliament, I partnered John

Hannam, making the first pair. When it came to our second and third pairs for doubles matches, I am afraid there was a notable decline in standards.

We also played the Wimbledon Club, not the professionals, but its members and management team. One of the consolations for usually being beaten by them was that we were regularly offered tickets for the "big show" with seats in the "Royal box". Of course this perk only allowed us to sit in the rows well behind any royalty or their entourage that might be present.

There was however, one international match each year, against the French Parliament. A relic of bygone days, this took place in the Normandy seaside town of Deauville, when along with a golfing team, the tennis players opened the season. The atmosphere was redolent of the 1920s. We dressed for dinner in the evenings, put our shoes out each night to be returned polished in the mornings and room service was provided by a member of staff seated in each bedroom corridor, ready to be called to bring whatever we needed.

We were a mixture of Lords and Commons from all parties, but we played our part to perfection with visits to the casino, which part sponsored the event, and free use of the spa facilities, being jetted with sea water, rolled in mud baths, steamed in cabinets or wrapped in seaweed. Hilary and I got to know Maurice Edelman, the labour M.P. and author at this time. He lived near our Berkhamsted home in a flat at Hughenden Manor, Disraeli's country house, owned by the National Trust. Appropriately, he had written a biography of Disraeli and acted as a guide to the house. Maurice was the Chairman of the Anglo-French Parliamentary Group and spoke excellent French. Hilary had been at school at Berkhamsted with his daughters, before the time that the Labour Party had its "hang ups" about independent schools. He was one of our tennis players, another was Sally Oppenheim, my bridge partner. We did not see much of the golfers, although Bernard Weatherill, later to be the House of Commons Speaker, was their team leader, but we all got together for a gala dinner at the casino. As well as the French and British teams there were also some Belgian parliamentarians participating in the opening golf tournament of the Deauville season.

Hilary speaks French very well, having spent some time in France in the 1950s. Someone on the French side decided that she must be Belgian and she found herself separated from the rest of the group for the dinner; this happened at subsequent French events for some years until she discovered why. At

Deauville she found herself placed next door to a certain Valery Giscard d'Estaing, at that time the French Finance Minister, before he became President, and she spent the evening discussing the problems of inner city tower blocks and municipal housing. Most illuminating.

The dinner was an elegant affair as one would expect at one of France's leading hotels, and as French meals do, it continued until nearly midnight. When we were expecting to go to bed to get some sleep before the big match next day, we were escorted into the casino. Their hospitality was irresistible. We were even given a handful of chips in the interest of the "Entente Cordiale" and moved to the tables. We started playing and as a seasoned roulette player, I noticed that we seemed to be winning more often than usual. There was even the odd occasion when it appeared that the croupier had handed us back some chips that I had thought were lost or paid winnings in error. It was something that I had never seen in a French casino. I could only assume our hosts had pre-arranged matters to ensure our chips lasted a long time.

It was 3.00am before our hosts decided we could retire. Naively we believed that they would be suffering as much from lack of sleep as we did, on the courts the next morning. When we crawled on to the courts with our eyes barely open, even after lashings of black coffee, we were horrified to find a completely fresh unknown team of six young athletic Deputees, just arrived from Paris. We suffered a most humiliating defeat.

Sadly, there was only to be one more occasion for us to visit Deauville for tennis before the dream ended. The Deauville casino and Palm Beach Cannes were jointly owned and the mafia had moved in on the casino in Cannes. In one night they had "broken the bank" and the Deauville casino could not survive alone. The tennis continued between the French and Westminster Parliament, but it became a moveable occasion, one year meeting in France and the next in Britain.

The first year after the end of Deauville we were invited to Reims, to the palatial home of the "king of champagne", Taittinger. At the time one of the Taittinger brothers ran the business, while the other, Pierre Christian was a Minister in the French Government. Both could hit a ball with distinction and we would have found it difficult to win the match on level terms, but the French made sure that the court was heavily tilted in their favour.

We started our tennis week end with a flight on the Friday afternoon to

Reims airport. This was a small provincial airfield with a single building for passengers. Waiting for us in the reception was the mayor of Reims smartly dressed with his tricolour sash, with glasses of champagne and foie gras. Having been suitably greeted, we left slightly hazily for our hotel, where we found in our rooms the gift of an ice bucket containing a bottle of Taittinger Champagne. Resisting the temptation to try it immediately, we were collected for dinner, which of course had more champagne to accompany it. It was as one would expect, not only an elegant occasion but a very late night.

On the Saturday, we were taken round the champagne cellars and the miles of underground tunnels that stretch under the whole area, finishing of course with the inevitable champagne tasting. In the afternoon we were given a splendid tour of the countryside around Reims including a visit to the museum formed from one of the 1st World War trenches. By one of those strange quirks of fate, my paternal grandfather and Hilary's paternal grandfather both fought in the First World War, on opposing sides of course. They both faced each other at Reims, where Hilary's grandfather "bought" a piece of the marble base of the statue of Jeanne d'Arc from some of the starving occupants bartering for food. Hilary had brought the piece, bearing the name of Joan of Arc, with her and gave it to the museum. Unusually, we were not given any champagne to drink.

Saturday evening was the highlight of the tour when we had dinner in the Taittinger chateau. Five exquisite courses each accompanied by a different Taittinger champagne, in magnificent seventeenth century surroundings. It started with champagne cocktails and finished with pink champagne for the desert followed by a champagne brandy. I had no idea that there were so many different sorts of champagne. After some short but elegantly phrased speeches we staggered back to our hotel and bed to be ready for the next day's match.

We arose the next morning with hangovers, sleepy and feeling as if the last thing we needed to do was to appear on the tennis courts at 10am. However, we knew we had to play for England and made the effort.

After losing the early games we got into our stride and held our own. What we had overlooked was that our crafty French hosts had laid on a magnificent formal lunch halfway through the match. Having had the exclusive hospitality of the Taittingers, the other champagne producers were keen to get in on the act and show us that their products were equally good. An array of different champagnes greeted us for our meal. One scarcely noticed the food nor that our French hosts seemed to drink very little. But staggering back on to the courts after 3.00pm, we realised we had been cruelly ensnared. We were hardly able to hit a ball. Even the Captain, my partner John Hannam, who was a former county player for Devon, made a fool of himself. Naturally, the French won the day.

After this second humiliating defeat and show of gamesmanship by the French, we did not dare to reveal the true score to the media. I am afraid we "lied for England" and gave a less than accurate report to the Press. We were furious as much with ourselves for having been taken in as with our opponents, and determined to plan our revenge at our next encounter, which it had been decided would be hosted by us. We leant on our contacts at Wimbledon and were offered courts 1, 2 and 3 for our match. The Centre Court is of course kept only for the Wimbledon fortnight and its grass is carefully nurtured. It was only two weeks after the tournament and the courts were still "warm" from the world's best professionals.

The Wimbledon managers played the one-upmanship game with us and allowed us on to the courts the week before, so we could get used to the over-powering atmosphere and of course playing on grass. When the French arrived at the London hotel the night before the match, we had kept the location secret, simply saying that the courts were "near London". A mini coach picked us all up and drove us to Wimbledon. After changing at the lockers with the names of the stars, including French champions, we walked them on to the courts. As well as the players' changing rooms, the umpires and ball-boys were provided.

We were ready for the atmosphere. They were absolutely overwhelmed. For them it seemed the most exciting event ever in their tennis playing careers. For the first half of the match they could barely concentrate enough to hit the balls. We triumphed and could not resist gloating about it.

The following year the French took us to Versailles. I do not remember too much about the tennis playing but being entertained for dinner in the Trianon was something I will never forget.

There was a longer term beneficial result from all this athletic activity. Some close relationships with leading French politicians were established over the years. When in France we were always treated with respectful hospitality at the highest level – off the courts. There would always be small informal dinners or receptions with the Presidential Head of State or the Prime

Minister. Before he became President, Valery Giscard d'Estaing played for the French against us and Jacques Chirac entertained us when he was President.

Our political relationship with the French throughout our history has always seemed a "love hate" affair, but at least our tennis team managed to avoid embarrassing international incidents despite niggling temptations. No doubt our Foreign Office had anxious moments when we seemed to be provoked. There were many informal discussions which could only have helped soothe strained relationships at the summit level. Our spouses, always included on these weekends, helped to cement friendships.

Chapter Twenty-One
Top hats and Tea

Once a year, M.Ps are offered the opportunity to be included as guests to the Queen's Garden Party at Buckingham Palace. Always towards the end of the Summer session, before the long recess, it comes when tempers are starting to fray, even in the air conditioned Chamber as Governments rush to tidy up their Business programme. Everybody is anxious to get as far away from Westminster as possible.

The invitation card, bearing the Royal Coat of Arms, from the Lord Chamberlain with the request from Her Majesty for the "pleasure" of our company was appropriately gilt-edged and much larger than the normal cards. It made a very good show on the mantelpiece for those who were impressed by such things. What was even more pleasurable for me was that M.Ps spouses were included and our "unmarried" daughters over the age of 17. Our sons never got a look in. Nobody, it seems, has yet challenged the legality of such politically incorrect discrimination. Of course the whole procedure was a relic of the time when daughters of the upper ranks of society "came out" and were "presented" at Court for the season. These days "coming out" has quite a different meaning.

After several successive years, Hilary and I felt we knew the routine. Top hats and tails for me, some really boutique and designer dress and Ascot hats for the ladies. Hilary would always find something stunning to wear, but perhaps not from the most orthodox of sources. I recall one occasion when a Parliamentary colleague and his wife stopped us while viewing the Palace gardens. "What a fantastic dress Hilary. Where did you find it?" "In France, at our village weekly market, where we have our holiday "hide-out", Montauroux in the Pays de Fayence." She did not mention what she had paid for it. They were impressed. In fact the stall in the market is now to Hilary and her friends' distress, defunct. It was run by an elderly man who would buy up the ends of lines from the Paris fashion stores. He had some really interesting bargains at charity shop prices.

There was a very strong Tory wives group, much envied by the Labour wives who never seemed to be able to get anything going for themselves. The group would meet regularly for coffee and to go on visits together. They would use their connections or even their own members to find their way into all sorts of private areas, such as at Hatfield House, when Lord Cranbourne then the Member for South Dorset, hosted them around the house. On another occasion they were making and eating soup in the kitchen of Number Eleven Downing Street with Gillian Clarke, when her husband Ken was Chancellor of the Exchequer. I was always surprised, and impressed, with where they got to.

When the Conservative Government was in power and our Prime Minister was in charge at Number Ten, there was always a reception after the Garden Party for the participants. Ted Heath did this reluctantly and Hilary would say that she always felt he feared for the silver. He was not good at small talk and wives and daughters appeared to be overwhelming. Margaret Thatcher did it particularly well. She was a remarkable hostess. As we all trooped up the stairs of Number Ten into the interconnected reception rooms, Margaret stood at the entrance welcoming each couple.

With nearly a hundred Tory Parliamentary colleagues and their partners at each of the three Garden Parties and subsequent reception, it took a painfully long time before everybody got inside let alone their first drink. Margaret, remarkably, seemed to know the wives of most of the M.Ps and insisted on saying a few words to each as we arrived. I was particularly impressed when Margaret, who of course knew Hilary well from the time we were her constituents, remembered our daughter Judith's name and that of our son Bruno, enough to ask after them. The following year Judith came with us for her first Garden Party and visit to Number Ten. Margaret greeted her and regaled her with having pushed her in the pram, covered with election leaflets. It was obviously a scene which had impressed itself on the Prime Minister over the years.

Parents wedding - My parents, Ellie Merz and Fritz Rosenstiel, after their wedding, with my grandparents. Rosa Marx is second from the left, next to Oscar Rosenstiel.

right?

First day at school - After the first day at school, I am met with the traditional cones of presents and my little sister Ilse

Peter Nazi Flag - Peter with his flag after attending a Hitler rally as a member of the Junior Hitler Youth

Margie, Elly and Peter - Ellie with her children, Peter and Ilse now known as Margaret or Margie

Boy Scout - Back in uniform but this time an English patriot.

Now a Member of Parliament beside "Eventide" the ruined converted railway carriage that was home for many years

RAF Group – 'Square bashing' in the Wirral Peninsular Camp for National Service

Hockey Team - Tring Hockey Club team where I was a member until I entered Parliament

Skiing - Taking part in the ski race against the Swiss Parliament in Davos

Tennis cup – Chairman of the Tring Tennis Club I played most weekends in summer. I also played for the Parliamentary Tennis team.

Our Wedding photo - Our Wedding at St Mary's Church Hemel Hempstead. My parents are to the left and Hilary's parents on the right. Tucked behind are my parents' second partners, we were regarded as very modern. Harry Towb was my best man.

Peter Rost

CONSERVATIVE

1970 Election Address – The 1970 Election Address was in advance of its time by using colour photography instead of the usual black and white. It cost a large proportion of our allowed budget, but it made an enormous impact, with many people framing the picture of our family.

Norcott Court – Norcott Court our home for more than forty years.

Taxi with Farouk - My Taxi heading the Birmingham University Carnival with an unexplained 'Farouk' on the roof

Photo af airplane - The maiden flight of Tristar with the RB211 engine. Hilary carried Jessica over to see the plane when a press photographer called to her. This picture went around the world.

BP award – The Industry Parliamentary Trust presentation from the Chairman of BP, Sir Peter Walters. I had an assignment with BP looking at all aspects of their operation from the boardroom to the oil rigs. The Industry Parliamentary Trust acted as a two way bridge to educate M.P.s about Industry and industrialists about the workings of Parliament.

Peter in pub – Electioneering in the constituency pubs

Family Group – The family lines up for Hilary's 70th birthday. From left behind Hilary are Bruno, Julius, Peter, Jessica and Judith.

Montauroux House - Peter relaxing outside Maison Rost
in Montauroux, France

On one of these enjoyable receptions Hilary and I joined the long queue up the stairs, waiting to enter the Reception rooms and to be greeted. The long wall at the side of the stairs was lined with the photographs and engravings of past prime ministers, all in black and white until we came to the last one, at the top, of Harold Wilson, slightly larger than the rest and in colour.

As we climbed slowly upwards, there was a sudden rush as a male figure came storming down. It was Denis, Margaret's husband. Halfway down, tongue in cheek and true to character, he whispered in a loud enough voice deliberately for us all to hear "Oh God, not another of these boring Tory do's" Denis had become a caricature for the media and particularly "Private Eye", the widely read satirical magazine. They satirised him as an unabashed and extreme reactionary, only interested in golf and gin. But he hit back by brilliantly over-acting his characterisation.

Of course this was false and unfair. Denis was a successful and prominent businessman. In 1965 he sold his first enterprise to Castrol and was on the board until the company was taken over by Burmah Oil, when he joined their board. He was also a director of a number of other important publicly quoted companies.

Denis was wise enough to take a back seat once Margaret became Prime Minister. He was most of the time what a good consort should be, advisory but low key. However, as a robust right wing Tory, there were times when the media reported him making an indiscreet comment. It was as well for Margaret that there were rare embarrassments such as when he claimed that his wife had been "stitched up by the bloody BBC poofs and trots!"

No wonder the public loved him as they do an outspoken character. His way of dealing with the spoof character that "Private Eye" had made him was to meet it head on and out do the satirists at their own game, cleverly guarding his own privacy. Margaret in her autobiography conceded that despite the occasional irreverent indiscretions "I could never have been Prime Minister for more than eleven years without Denis by my side."

It was about this time that I attracted a few raised eyebrows amongst my more right wing colleagues. In 1971 the unpleasant Idi Amin had gained power in Uganda and started expelling the Ugandan Asians. Ted Heath offered them sanctuary and resettlement in Britain and even arranged air-lifts to bring them to Britain, around twenty-eight thousand people.

There was a certain amount of criticism within the Party and without from the anti-immigration supporters who had followed Enoch Powell. I had no hesitation in jumping into the controversy, after all I was a former refugee myself and Hilary and I were uneasy with the stance of the Monday Club, which was moving towards a more extreme right wing view. I offered Ted Heath some openly declared support inviting an Asian family into our home at Norcott and prominently announced this to the press. To the best of my knowledge we were the only M.P's family to do this and certainly the only one to tell the world about it. I hoped that this would counter some of the racist criticism which our Prime Minister and Government were subjected to. I am still waiting for a little note of 'thank you for your help' from Ted Heath. It must have got lost in the post. We were rather upset by the expressions of surprise from some of our colleagues on the "left" of the Conservative Party, notably Anne and Cecil Parkinson whom we had know from our Hemel Hempstead days. They appeared to assume that Hilary and I were acting completely out of character rather than from any real concern.

My constituency was not too upset. After all, the East Midlands was packed with the results of previous immigrations respected for their enterprise, although there were beginning to be murmurs about the City of Leicester, they were not acute at that time. We had plenty of space in our house and my own background made me sympathetic with the plight of the Asians.

The Patel family arrived from a holding centre in Hounslow, bearing large bags. It was an extended family, the elderly father did not come as he was too ill and in hospital, his wife spoke no English at all and was strictly religious and very uncomfortable in my presence. She had two daughters with her and her daughter-in-law and baby. Her son had already gone off on his own with his girlfriend, leaving his wife, Ranjan to the mercy of her in-laws. We only met him once.

Our first encounter with their different culture and language was when one of the girls, seeing our three storey house for the first time, said "What a beautiful bungalow!" We settled them in to the former staff flat at the top of our house where we tried to make them comfortable. Hilary was distressed to find that the grandmother had felt it necessary to throw away their meal because her "shadow" had passed over it. However, it soon became obvious that Ranjan and one of her sisters-in-law were anxious to cast off the restrictive life style and make their own way. After some weeks one of the girls had got a job with a bank and the other had been enrolled in a college to take some school exams. They moved out with their mother to a flat near to where their father was in hospital in the Harrow area. He died only a month or two later. We were left with Ranjan and her small daughter Pritti.

Ranjan moved in with us, out of the flat and actively embraced our way of life. She was a bright and intelligent person and was determined to put her previous life behind her. She had been forced into a marriage of convenience, when her husband's family, shocked at the way in which he had been behaving with another woman, decided he needed to be married. He had lived with Ranjan long enough to get her pregnant and had then moved out leaving her with his ultra-conformist family.

Although we kept in contact with the rest of the family for some time, we have remained friends with Ranjan over the years. She took advantage of a college course and in due time took her accountancy exams. She overcame the objections to being divorced and happily remarried another Ugandan Asian and had more children. After a brief interlude in Canada, they returned to the UK and have been happily running a small hotel ever since. In no way can this family be said to have been a burden on the British taxpayer, far from it.

It was much later, in the 1980s that I became involved with another refugee problem. Through my Select Committee on Energy work, I had come into contact with a Romanian Professor who was allowed by the Communist regime to come to the West for his research and for conferences. At the time few Romanians knew how to drive as it was forbidden to learn and to take a driving test unless one had access to a car. Usually only members of the Communist Party had access to a car. In effect this meant that only the establishment could drive. However, a student of the professor's at Bucharest University, did have a licence to drive, having an uncle with a car. Dan Radu therefore came as a driver along with a teacher of English, Nina Ions, who acted as an interpreter.

The professor was a guest at a reception in the House of Commons when he approached me and asked if I knew anywhere that his two aids could stay. I discovered that Dan and Nina were waiting outside with the hired car. Evidently the trio were short of cash and that although the professor had been offered accommodation with a colleague; the others were expecting to have to sleep in the car. I rang Hilary and having arranged for them to come back with me for the night, Dan found himself a tie and a jacket in his car and Nina hastily dressed herself up and the two joined in the House of Commons reception until it was time to leave.

For a couple of days, while the professor went about his business, Hilary looked after the two of them, taking them shopping in an English supermarket for the first time and generally feeling ashamed of our profligate ways in the West. The idea of having special tins of cat food appalled them, let alone some made with salmon, and our multiplicity of cheeses amazed them. As Nina said "In Romania we either have cheese or we don't have cheese. What sort of cheese is irrelevant." To Hilary's telling her how we cooked certain things she said "Mrs Rost, it is not that we Romanians do not know how to cook, it is what to cook that is our problem!" Nina knew quite a lot of what went on in the West because as an English teacher she had been allowed to visit the British Council in Bucharest and had open access to the English newspapers and uncensored films. She was of course assured that the opulent views of the West shown in the films were only propaganda and completely false. But as with most of her colleagues she knew this to be untrue. She was amazed at the naivety of the Romanian authorities in allowing open access for her and her colleagues and assumed it was because few of the hardliners understood any English.

The professor returned for them after a few days and they left for Romania with our addresses in England and France and invitations to visit us if they could.

Some time later after the borders had opened, we received letters from Romania asking if our new friends and their partners could come to stay with us for a holiday. Of course we said yes. The first to arrive were Dan and his new wife Clivia. They came by car, ostensibly on their honeymoon, but with every intention of staying in the West if they could. The car should have been entered in the Guinness Book of Records for packing the most into a modest vehicle. Every corner, including under the bonnet and around the engine, was stuffed with their belongings. They had asked for money instead of presents for their wedding, and gold and silver coins and US dollars instead of paper money. With spare tyres strapped to the roof and every sort of spare part for the car in case of breakdown, they had driven across Europe from Bucharest to our house in Provence. They arrived exhausted and appreciative of a proper bed after days of camping with their car.

After some days, Nina arrived with her husband Marion to make up the foursome. The big question was what occupation they were going to find. Both Dan and Marion had been top students at Bucharest University with degrees in physics and computer sciences. Marion soon found himself welcomed at Sophia Antipolis the top French Technology Park, near Antibes, where he was working with the University. His wife, however, found it more difficult to get work in France and it was some years later when Marion's job moved to Paris and after the birth of their daughter that she got some employment.

Dan and Clivia returned to stay with us in Norcott. Clivia, whose English was good, had been a theatre nurse in Bucharest and was soon on an NHS course to retrain to work in the U.K. However, Dan found it more difficult to find the work he was best suited for. One day Hilary took Clivia with her when she went to take some things down to our local rubbish dump or more properly called "household waste site". Clivia was amazed at what we were throwing away and soon introduced Dan to this Mecca. In no time he was collecting television sets, microwaves, radios and other items tossed aside. Painstakingly repairing them, often with only minor faults, they would be bubble wrapped and taken to a friend who was a pilot with the Romanian airline. They would be shipped back to Bucharest and collected by another friend who did any adaptations necessary for the local system and sold them on an eager market for "luxury" goods. Dan and Clivia's share of the proceeds went to help their families in Romania in the aftermath of the revolution.

In due course we found an agency which placed Dan with an international electronics and communications company which operated locally. He soon became a key worker for them and they were anxious to promote him. A problem now arose which if I had not been a Member of Parliament might have been disastrous. The Company wanted to send Dan to Canada and he applied for a residence permit. The Home Office responded by giving him notice to quit the country. By this time Clivia was working for the NHS and could stay, but her husband was not regarded as being essential. The reason was of course that Dan was still technically employed by the agency not the company he was working for. The agency had been enjoying a large fee for providing his services and had not been inclined to pass him on to be permanently employed. Dan could not prove therefore that he was doing essential work for his employer, as his "employer" was an agency. In spite of a glowing letter from the personnel manager of the company he was working for the Home Office remained adamant. I asked my colleague, Richard Page, in whose constituency we lived, for help. With two M.Ps, plus a letter from the Managing Director of the company, taking up his case, the Home Office finally relented. The irony of the situation was that Dan was involved at the time in keeping the B.B.C's transmitters working and in producing new equipment for them.

Dan and Clivia have gone from strength to strength since then. They are now full British Citizens. They bought a small house in Tring, which they furnished from the 'for sale' pages of the local paper and restoration of items from the "dump", before moving up the ladder to buy a four bedroomed house in a desirable part of Berkhamsted. They have three children now, all being educated at independent schools. Clivia runs her own business, a health and fitness centre, and Dan is in a very senior position in his company, responsible for their future product design. A very far cry from the day we first met in Parliament Square.

Chapter Twenty-Two
British-German Relations

When Ted Heath was elected Leader in 1965, replacing Sir Alec Douglas-Home, I was building up my Stock Exchange business and increasingly involved in my new role of husband and father. Our move from London into Norcott, our large country house, was also a challenging activity. Although I had become politically active as a Young Conservative, the thought of joining Ted's Parliament was only in its embryonic stage. The idea of trying to be elected to Parliament developed soon after, when I became increasingly angry and frustrated that Harold Wilson's Socialist Government was moving the Nation away from my ideal of a more democratic society participating in the capitalist system.

At this time Conservative leaders were not elected. Not even the Parliamentary Party had much of a say. Leaders mysteriously "emerged" out of a secretive sounding from a caucus of grandees. But our younger generation did not query the choice of leader. We never doubted that Heath's "appointment" was a breath of fresh air and many of us were inspired by his more professional leadership, in contrast to the old crowd. He represented a broader section of the community, grammar school rather than the elite minority.

Not surprisingly, it was his energetic pro-Europe stance that appealed to me. It was he who had tried to get us into the Common Market when he was Harold MacMillan's negotiator. Now he could try again in the more favourable circumstances of 1970, taking the lead as our Prime Minister.

It was an exciting time as a new boy in 1970, able to support a new-look leader. I soon decided I could help, perhaps, in a particular direction. Clearly our involvement in Europe required a total reconciliation with Germany. True enough, the war had ended twenty five years earlier. But large sections of the British public, with bitter memories of personal tragedy had not forgotten or forgiven. How could we play a constructive role in shaping a European Union, unless there was less prejudice, isolationism and more of a shift of attitude so that our former enemy was now regarded as our friend and ally.

I decided to play an active part in the Parliamentary British-German Group. After all, with my background living my first years in Nazi Germany, of German parents, who better to help the long process of rebuilding our relationship. I could hardly blame my parents. And yet the feeling remained that Germany's middle class professionals, business community and politicians could have prevented it, if they had acted earlier in unison. It would be wrong to suggest I had a guilty conscience about the land of my birth having created such bloodshed and all but wrecking centuries of civilisation in Europe. But I was aware that I could make a useful contribution to help ensure nothing ever like it happened again.

So why not help our Prime Minister's crusade to persuade the voters and our European founders of the Union, to let us join the club and particularly, regard Germany as a key partner to help us in. Sir Bernard Braine, the Member for South East Essex in the 1970s, founded and chaired the British German Parliamentary Group. He later became the "Father of the House", the longest serving Member. The Group was supported by over one hundred Members, at least nominally, as membership subscribers. At the German end, Peter Corterier, a leading SPD Member, organised their group.

I became Sir Bernard's deputy, together with Donald Anderson, the Labour M.P who later became an Opposition Spokesman for Foreign Affairs, and Nigel Foreman, the Conservative member for Carshalton. One of our principal duties was to help entertain the constant stream of German visitors. The Foreign Office organised such visits according to strict protocol. So the German Chancellor would have the full treatment, a banquet at Windsor Castle or Buckingham Palace and meetings at Number Ten. One or two of our group would be included and also invited to help entertain the entourage of lower ranking Germans that always accompany a leader.

There were big occasions. But there were also regular visits from German Ministers and delegations from their Parliament. Other important guests also had to be hosted, such as groups of their civil servants on a visit to exchange views and see how we operate our system.

Such less high profile guests were our responsibility. We would show them around the Palace of Westminster and organise receptions to provide the opportunity for them to meet other members of our Parliamentary Group.

Most of the official visits included a reception at the German Embassy in Belgrave Square. I would be a regular guest, appreciated by the Embassy as a link, with my German helping to talk to our visitors about the British scene. Wives would often be invited and there were plenty of more formal lunches and dinners at the Embassy. Naturally I had the opportunity to become quite friendly with a series of Ambassadors, and many of the Embassy staff, lower down the line. The skilful selection of Ambassadors, presumably by their Foreign Office, contributed enormously to a steadily warming relationship between our two countries. London was regarded as a key post, together with Bonn and Washington.

The first of these outstanding diplomats that served in my period was Karl-Gunther von Hase, a former German TV magnate. His love and understanding of Britain and belief in the European Union, made him a popular figure. He was related to Paul von Hase who was hanged for his role in the plot against Adolph Hitler. Other Ambassadors of equal quality were to follow.

I recall an embarrassing but now amusing incident at one of the early receptions of von Hase's that I attended. My wife and I arrived at the ambassador's private residence for the reception and were greeted by the Ambassador with a mischievous smile. He immediately said "Ah, I am so glad that you have actually come. We did enjoy your "thank you" note. I hope that you will enjoy the reception as much the second time"

I discovered that my secretary Fiona, who was taking a brief holiday, had decided to write the standard "thank you" letter on House of Commons' notepaper, at the same time as she formally accepted the invitation. Along with some other letters she had passed these on to the secretary of a colleague for posting at the appropriate time. Unfortunately the secretary had put the whole lot in the post without looking and my letter of thanks had arrived two days before the actual event. From then on, throughout von Hase's time in London, I was gently teased about this. Usually this would take the form of his introducing me to people at receptions with the words "Do let me introduce

Peter Rost to you, he does so **enjoy** our hospitality!"

A later, and most distinguished Ambassador, was Baron Dr Herman von Richthofen, who took up the post in 1989 and was still there when I stood down from Parliament in 1992. He remained as Ambassador for longer than the usual three year stint as it was on his watch that the Berlin Wall came tumbling down and the two Germanys, East and West, were reunited. His description of the event which he heard about at a reception in the company of Douglas Hurd, our Foreign Secretary, and their subsequent flight to Berlin, to be among the first to shake hands with the newly liberated East Germans in the old border zone, is a compelling story. He also highlighted Margaret Thatcher's reluctance to endorse the reunification plans, with her fear for the costs to Europe of taking on the weak East German economy.

However, I came to know him in a more personal way. Hilary, having mentioned casually to him at a reception, she knew some of the descendants of Frieda Weekley, who had eloped with D H Lawrence. Her maiden name was von Richthofen – was he related? she asked. It turned out that he was not only related but had been trying to find them, knowing that they were in the U.K.

Living in Nottingham, Frieda had been married to Ernest Weekley, who was a professor in modern languages at the university there. She eloped to Germany with Lawrence, who had been at one time Ernest Weekley's student and was then teaching in Ilkeston in my future constituency. She had three children, two girls and a boy had to be left behind. The eldest, Charles, had a son who in the mid 1960s was living with his wife and three children in a village near us at Norcott. We knew them well, as Judith ,our eldest ,attended the village school with the children. The year of the settlement of the Lady Chatterley's Lover case in the High Court, they had used the money to buy a car, which with its opening roof was used to ferry various children about to their different functions. The car was known as "Lady Chatterley's Lover" which caused some raised eyebrows in the Berkhamsted streets when the five and six year olds referred to it as such.

The resemblance of the Ambassador to the Weekley family was striking. Although they had moved away from the area, we knew their address and were able to pass it on to him. Richthofen was impressed and appreciative. Our standing in Belgrave Square moved up a notch.

In the 1970s, receptions and lunches at the German Embassy, provided an amazing throng of former German citizens, each with extraordinary histories. By far the most fascinating celebrity I got to know quite well, was Herbert Sulzbach. He had served in the German Army in the First World War and had then served in the British Army, becoming a Captain, in 1940. He would say he had served both Kaiser and King. Herbert was a tall and distinguished looking man, who spoke faultless English. He was born in Frankfurt am Main in 1894, the same area that my parents came from. His Jewish family was wealthy as his grandfather had founded a private bank, which later became the Deutsche Bank. In 1914 he had volunteered for the German army, in which he served with great credit earning the Iron Cross twice. The second one was presented to him personally by von Hindenburg.

Throughout his service in the German army, Herbert Sulzbach had kept a diary and in 1935 this was published. In 1973 the book was published in English as "With the German Guns: Four Years on the Western Front." I treasure my signed copy with its inscription from Herbert. In Germany, between the wars, Herbert's book was regarded as essential reading for all German officers and, apparently unaware that the author was Jewish, this continued to be the case under the Nazis in the Second World War.

In spite of his exemplary war record, Herbert was forced to flee to Britain, leaving as I did, in 1937. At the outbreak of war he was 45, still young enough to serve in the army, only this time, after the mandatory internment in the Isle of Man, it was in the British Army!

His great achievement was his contribution to the lasting post-war peace between our two nations. He dedicated himself as a British officer to the re-education of German prisoners of war. As a Captain he was put in charge of the rehabilitation of the inmates of Featherstone Park Camp in Northumberland. This was a prisoner of war camp which held only officers of the Wehrmacht and SS. As I can attest from my own experience of the German education system, these were convinced Nazis, thoroughly indoctrinated with anti Jewish propaganda and notions of Aryan racial superiority. Several thousand men passed through Herbert's hands and to his credit many of them later returned to Germany to take up posts in Government and the Law. Notably, one man became the judge at the trials of several of the Treblinka concentration camp guards in Düsseldorf.

He told the story of one Armistice Day at the end of the war, when he had explained to his prisoners the meaning of the two minute silence remembering the war dead. He expressed the view that if they really understood the message which he had been trying to give them, they would know what to do. For the first time when Eleven o'clock came, Herbert Sulzbach's German prisoners were on parade alongside the British officers and personnel at the camp, to keep the two minute silence.

His efforts resulted in the returning prisoners of war becoming the best envoys for peace and understanding between the two countries. He was decorated by King George VIth, perhaps the only soldier to be honoured by both Kaiser and King?

Herbert often embarrassed me in the company of prestigious guests at the German Embassy, by praising me for succeeding to become a British Member of Parliament. He said to me more than once that despite all his distinguished contributions to British-German relations, he had never had the privilege of a meal in Westminster as a guest of a Member of Parliament. Here was my opportunity. I was so impressed by his career, that I booked one of the private dining rooms in the House of Commons, twelve around a table and told him that Hilary and I would be his hosts, to treat him and his guests. He was to invite all his special friends and family. He was thrilled, it was a great occasion. His party included some very distinguished guests. I found myself seated next to Yehudi Menuhin's sister while Hilary discovered that Herbert's sister in law had been an actress in Berlin with Kurt Weill.

Adding to his many honours, Herbert was awarded the Paix de l'Europe medal for his promotion of cross-cultural understanding. It was always a pleasure to talk to him at the German Embassy and to show him around the Palace of Westminster. I also managed to explain to him the oddities of our Parliamentary system, which he respected enormously.

It was in 1974 that I had the idea of launching what I hoped might become a regular event, a mini British German conference. It began when I was invited to take part in the Annual Königswinter conference. Started in 1950, by Lilo Milchsack and her husband Hans, also survivors of the Nazi regime, in the small town near Bonn, the event had become somewhat unwieldy, with the huge attendance of opinion formers from both countries. Politicians mixed with the media and leaders from many institutions and organisations.

The conference I attended was in Edinburgh, with some two hundred delegates. It inspired me to plan a mini conference and get-together for only about ten or so parliamentarians on each side. No media or ministers, no outsiders and a number small enough to sit around a table. The idea was to keep the agenda informal, with a half day for each side to explain their own internal issues and problems, and then time to discuss issues of common concern.

No minutes were to be kept, although a report could be sent to the media if thought necessary. No resolutions, votes, agreements, just a very frank, informal hair letting-down, series of discussions. We approached the Foreign Office for a grant, so that a very modest budget could be financed. The Labour Government turned us down. So our Chairman, Sir Bernard Braine, approached the Anglo-German Foundation, a charitable institution aimed at promoting understanding between our two countries. They agreed to fund the event, enough to pay for the catering and accommodation and transport. So we were in business. I was thrilled, believing I could make quite an important contribution to mutual relations.

We decide to host the first conference at Windsor. Dates were agreed and a hotel booked. Shortly before the event, there was some sort of voting panic at the German end and they had to postpone. We cancelled the booking. A few days later their leader Peter Corterier, called back to say their crisis in the German Bundestag was over, and they could come after all. Bernard Braine contacted the hotel to find that our booking had been taken and trying to find a venue in the tourist season was proving impossible.

Bernard rang me to see whether I could find anywhere. As I was not at home he spoke to Hilary and told her the problem. Asking how many were involved and being told a maximum of thirty people, she immediately suggested that we hold the conference in our home at Norcott. After all, we had not so long previously held a day conference for seventy people, when Enoch Powell was a speaker. Bernard accepted and agreed with great relief.

When I arrived home, Hilary reported her offer to Bernard. I thought she must have lost her marbles. "But it's a whole weekend, not a one-day affair!" We were expected to cater and accommodate. Hilary spoke to Bernard to explain that perhaps Norcott was not quite the best location, but he would not be persuaded, he thought it was a splendid idea. Much better than an anonymous hotel and he had heard about Norcott's fascinating history.

After further thoughts, we realised we had let ourselves in for it. Firstly, we had to find rooms for at least ten German guests. We moved our children to Granny's for the weekend and ourselves out of our bedroom. We slept on a put–u–up sofa downstairs in our library for two nights. We booked rooms in nearby hotels. The British delegation had to find their own quarters, not too difficult as they had homes in London, not too far away.

Hilary was allocated a budget and took on a chef for the weekend, but the main "service" was provided by family and friends and we turned the house into a passable imitation of an hotel. My secretary, Fiona became a taxi service. It would have helped if all the Germans had arrived at Heathrow on the same flight. But she had three return journeys before they were all with us. Hilary hired a small mini–bus to take the delegates to and from their hotels and to cope with sight-seeing during the weekend, as well as making an early visit to Covent Garden to get the fresh vegetables for the chef and flowers to be arranged by our doctor's wife, Margaret Evans.

What was so remarkable was that the first British German Conference was a great success. The informality of a private family home helped. Knowing that Norcott was steeped in history also appealed to our guests – especially their leader, who had the room that two prime ministers, Winston Churchill and Stanley Baldwin had slept in. There was, however, one more problem. On the day after the first election in 1974, while waiting for the poll results, the announcement came of the loss to the Conservatives of the marginal Meriden constituency, so confirming a Labour majority in Parliament. There was an almighty crash in the kitchen. The house was certainly protesting, as part of the ceiling had come down and smashed much of our dinner service. It was a wedding present, the Rosenthal pattern we had chosen and we were distressed. Unfortunately, we needed the china for the dinner we had organised for the finish of the conference. We had to borrow other china to make up, it did not match and somewhat spoilt the effect of the table.

The principal guest at the dinner was our new Labour Foreign Secretary, Michael Stewart. Also we had the German Ambassador, von Hase with his very attractive, excellent English speaking wife. Michael Stewart made a keynote speech which was of great interest as we did not know what the new Labour Government's stance was on Germany and Europe. This was the first occasion for a serious analysis to be made. One of the other speakers was Philip Rosenthal, the SDP Member, who owned Europe's famous porcelain factory at Selb on the border with Eastern Germany. Needless to say, he commented on the fact that he had to eat his dinner from a Royal Worcester plate, while others he noted were allocated a Rosenthal one.

When my time came to answer the vote of thanks at the dinner, I told Philip Rosenthal of our disaster with the plates and noted that the pattern had been discontinued. With thirty places it had been impossible for us to produce sufficient of his plates for the meal. I could not resist, however, letting our guests know the real occupations of our admirable "staff" who had looked after them over the weekend. I introduced my mother-in-law, Ena and the mother of Hilary's brother's wife, Dorothy, who just happened to be a member of Lloyds Underwriters, who had served them at dinner. The admirable barman and receptionist was an experienced RAF pilot and Margaret our doctor's wife, and a solicitor friend, Joyce, had helped with the coffee breaks and lunches. It was a great ice-breaker, as the Germans, at least, seemed to have thought that Hilary and I lived in great style. I am not so sure that my British colleagues had been taken in.

However, the conference was a great success and formed the pattern for future annual events. The idea of meeting in a private house, away from the normal hotel conference suite venues, had allowed the delegates all to relax and really get to know one another. There was another interesting side to the weekend. We noticed that some of the Labour parliamentarians on our delegation had long sessions together on the lawn, during the breaks. Several of them not long afterwards were to form the Social Democrats.

At the end of the conference Philip Rosenthal had offered to host the next one in his home in Selb. Philip ran his porcelain business as a workers' co-operative, with genuine profit sharing. However, many in his party thought he was a crypto-capitalist, disguising himself as a member of the German Parliamentary Socialist party. That was an unfair criticism. He believed in spreading the wealth amongst those who created it and put it into practice in his family business.

Two or three weeks after the conference, we were surprised to find the first of several large crates delivered to our door full of Rosenthal plates. They kept coming until we had enough to provide covers for at least thirty people. Evidently, Philip had emptied the basement store of the discontinued "magnolia" pattern and sent it over to us. Philip Rosenthal's offer to host the following year's conference at his "schloss" in Selb was taken up. His castle was close to the factory which had been started by his father. The chateau was on a much grander scale than ours, but was still in the process of being restored, his father having bought it partly ruined. It was, rather like the Rosenthal porcelain styles, decorated in a mixture of the ultra-modern and the mediaeval.

The conference dinner was set in the enormous banqueting hall in a true mediaeval style. Only candlelight, a traditional German menu with sausages, sauerkraut and all the peasantry trimmings, were served on wooden platters. Each of us had a Rosenthal porcelain mug, which we were urged to take away with us as a memento, filled with German beer. For the wine drinkers amongst us, they did provide a more orthodox glass and German white wine. We loved the atmosphere, but we noted that one or two of the Germans in particular Philip's fellow SDP members, were overheard grumbling about the fact that he, as a multi-millionaire, was being hypocritical and should not have produced such peasant fare for his guests. However, for us he had judged it exactly.

My impression was that Philip enjoyed teasing his colleagues and the outside world, reminding us of his more humble background. He disliked the trappings of the smarter society his wealth and status obliged him to join. With his Scottish wife and bilingual children, he was a committed anglophile, with an Oxford University degree. On a visit to our Parliament to have lunch with me, he naturally took a particular interest in the china, with its House of Commons portcullis crest. There are at least a dozen dining rooms in the Palace, for receptions and private bookings of every sort and size. Several hundreds of members of the public are entertained there every day, sponsored by M.Ps but organised often by commercial interests, constituencies having an annual dinner and national institutions wishing to promote their lobby.

The substantial catering department is supervised by a committee of M.Ps. Every year or two, they are obliged to top up the tableware. There are breakages, but the annual losses are so large, they can only be explained by pilfering by guests looking for mementos. But even dinner plates went missing. Some visitors must have large handbags.

When Philip Rosenthal observed the British porcelain firms winning the regular replacement orders, he decided to intervene. In what I can only describe as a "tongue in cheek" move, he entered the bidding. His offer was so far below his British competitors, the House of Commons committee could not decently refuse to accept. If they had not done so they would have been accused of wasting taxpayers' money. Yet by accepting Rosenthal china, Parliament exposed the over-pricing cartel of the British factories, which had been going on for far too long. Moreover, it gave Philip enormous publicity, allowing him to promote Rosenthal's worldwide as "suppliers to the British Parliament." The humiliated British china firms made sure it did not happen again.

The following year, we returned the hospitality in my constituency at Melbourne Hall, situated in the village of Melbourne, south of Derby. The home of the Lothian family, the Hall was our conference centre. The heir to the Lothian's, Michael Ancram, was a colleague of mine at Westminster and his mother, Mrs Kerr, lived at Melbourne Hall. Our German guests were suitably impressed, hearing that it had been the home of the Lamb family and that William Lamb, Lord Melbourne, had been our Prime Minister. I was surprised that our German guests did not need to be told that Lord Melbourne's wife, the novelist Lady Caroline Lamb, had been one of Lord Byron's lovers. They were intrigued by the idea that they had met in the formal gardens around the house. The weekend included a tour of the Peak District and a visit to Chatsworth. It was the annual carnival in Long Eaton, my constituency centre, we showed the Germans how Derbyshire folk enjoyed themselves. The market was the main attraction for them, as having enjoyed the Stilton cheese we provided at the conference dinner, they emptied the town of all traces of it.

The annual British-German Parliamentary Group conference tradition of alternating between Britain and Germany continued. We entertained the Germans on the Isle of Barra, one of the Western Isles in the Outer Hebrides. The airstrip is the sandy beach in low tide. All loved the magnificent scenery and talking sessions suffered from a certain amount of absenteeism as many of us were tramping the hills. It did prevent one problem we had encountered with previous conferences, the German habit of arriving and leaving at different times with varying forms of transport. Our guests had only one complaint; there was no Marks and Spencer on the island.

Over the years we had conferences in Hannover, Bonn and most appropriately, Coburg, the home of the Saxe Coburgs – the name Prince Albert brought to the British Royal family with his marriage to Queen Victoria, until it was anglicised to Windsor during the 1914-18 war. Most memorable was the conference in Berlin which took place in the Reichstag, which had yet to be redesigned, and was still in its post-war condition, hastily done up after the Reichstag fire. During our visit to Selb, I had had my first view of the East German border and the wall, when we visited a nearby small village which had literally been divided in two as the small stream in the middle had been the dividing line between Upper and Lower Saxony. We were shocked by the massive watch towers which overshadowed the place and even more when we realised that we had guns trained on us all the time, as we toured the part of the village left in the West.

Berlin was of course another matter. Entirely surrounded by the Wall it was an amazing experience. I had made one brief visit there earlier, for a conference, but this time as I had been for the Selb conference, I was accompanied by Hilary and we had more leisure to look around. The Wall ran alongside the rear of the Reichstag and the crosses marking the places where people had died trying to cross the border, were reminders of the horror of the totalitarian Soviet style Socialist Government, in the East. We decided that a visit to Western Berlin with its Wall, should be compulsory for British youngsters, to give them an understanding of the meaning of freedom. I indulged myself with a nostalgic trip on the S-Bahn. This used to be a special treat for me as a child and we went out to Sud-Ende, to find my old home. Unfortunately, the old elegant apartment blocks had been pulled down or bombed and more modern ones put in their place, but I was pleased at least to find that I could still remember my old address and some of the buildings around the station.

It was soon afterwards that I had a unique opportunity to look behind the Wall, on a visit to East Germany to see East Berlin under Communist occupation. I was selected to represent our Parliament with a small party of Parliamentary colleagues, to accept an invitation from the East German government, for a week in the German Democratic Republic.

My Parliamentary work for British-German relations also involved me in broadcasts on German radio and TV. Reporting on the British scene in German was difficult for me. For my first six years, I had naturally spoken only German, but it was simple children' conversation. Later on, my mother had felt it was not advisable to speak German and so never had the opportunity to learn the sort of language required to comment on the political scene. Words like "inflation", "unemployment", "gross national product", "social security" and many more were not in my vocabulary. I had to prepare interviews and discussions in advance with a dictionary. So I organised German speaking classes at Westminster. The Goethe Institute provided tutors and every Tuesday lunchtime, a small gathering of Members of Parliament attended in a basement room at Westminster. We progressed eventually to two classes, for novices and one for more advanced speakers.

All my time and effort in helping the British and Germans to understand each other, ended on a happy note. In 1979 I was awarded the Verdienst Kreutz (the Grand Cross, German Order of Merit), a great honour that had also been accorded to several of our colleagues, including Ted Heath and Sir Bernard Braine. I was indeed in some distinguished company, especially as the presentation was made by the President of the Federal Republic and Head of State, Richard von Weizsächer. Yet another strange coincidence has emerged since our retirement to France. Our Montauroux neighbours include a distinguished Geman couple, Daniella and Hans-Henning von Kapff. Naturally we have come to know them well. They look after our chickens when we spend a few days in the U.K. He is a cousin of von Weizsächer.

There is an amusing footnote. Foreign medals are not by long tradition, appropriate to be worn in Britain by UK citizens at ceremonial or public occasions, when British Citizens show off their awards. However, special dispensation can be granted on behalf of the Queen, by Buckingham Palace. I am now able to wear my decoration when occasions and invitations state "decorations may be worn".

Chapter Twenty-Three
Riding the Moguls

As a keen skier, when arriving at Westminster it did not take me long to discover the House of Lords and Commons Ski Club. There were sporadic competitions against the French Parliament. We faced them at Val d'Isere. They usually outclassed us which was not surprising. The French ski champion, Jean-Claud Killy was a native of the resort. I still recall how I found myself by accident riding with him up to the top of the highest run in a two-person gondola. He was the "fore-runner", an honour that would be bestowed on a distinguished professional, to give us amateurs some encouragement. It had the opposite effect on me.

Our main fixture was the annual meeting with the Swiss. This was not just a longer established event, dating from a challenge in 1956 by a British M.P to a member of the Swiss Parliament, but a serious race, on a giant slalom course. It always took place in Davos, the gateway to what most regard as one of the World's top ski areas. Davos, next door to Klosters, favoured much by the Royal Family over the years, including Prince Charles and his sons, has some stupendous long runs, connecting the two villages.

It was co-incidental that Davos was so familiar to me, as that was where I had learned to ski and had revisited many times long before Parliament. After our marriage and before entering Parliament, Hilary and I had brought our children there for their first attempts with the snow, with Grandpa.

Grandpa, my father, too, had started skiing there in the early 1900s, when the resort was still more known for its T.B. and Asthma sanatoriums than a ski resort. Featured in Thomas Mann's "The Magic Mountain", which describes well the life of the T.B. sufferers, it was the home of Robert Louis Stephenson for some time when he too had serious chest problems. The late Arthur Conan Doyle was also a visitor and is recorded as having arguments with the local farmers when their cows insisted on eating the flags from the golf course he had set up in the valley.

When my father started there, only one cable railway existed which only ran a short way up. It had been built to reach the Schatzalp sanatorium and to access the top of the mountain and the best slopes, you wore "skins" on the wooden skis and walked. It took a four hour struggle up for one run down. That was your day. This was how my father and his companion Tony Morisani, regarded as the founder of modern Davos, did it. It was he who invested in the Parsenn Bahn which opened up the largest skiing area and built and owned the three smartest hotels. The British and Swiss teams stayed in one of them year after year. I recall from my earlier years in Davos, before Parliament, I used to see Morisani still setting off up the mountain each morning. He must have been in his eighties then. Shunning the easy lifts perhaps explains why he lived to a ripe old age.

Our team was open-ended. All Lords and M.Ps were eligible regardless of ability. But only an agreed number from each side were counted, for an aggregated score. Our side had some notable people and many of them could even ski. Winston Churchill (the grandson of . .) was one of our best. Ian Orr-Ewing, Lord Lyell, Michael Ancram, Cecil Parkinson and John Hannam usually made it into the top dozen. I and others came in around the half way mark and so were included in the team score. There was always a long tail, best not mentioned. But we all enjoyed ourselves immensely.

Our problem was that to make the Swiss Parliament your chances were dim unless you had been some sort of ski champion. So after each Swiss election we were overwhelmed by a new batch of young Swiss ex ski-heroes. Our answer was to bend the rules. Over the twenty years I participated, we extended several times the number of skiers we could count for the team. In the 1970s, it was, I recall, the first dozen. Unfortunately, after one Swiss election only two of the first twelve were British. So it became the first twenty and we won, being a little stronger than the Swiss in the middle ranks. But the happy state of affairs only lasted until the next election, when a new Swiss intake changed the balance again. We had to extend the eligible number to the first thirty. Of course, our hosts were gracious enough to consent to this manipulation.

The "Followers", husbands, wives and children, had their own race. Our children entered enthusiastically, three of them managing to win at different times. Bruno and the Churchill's son, Randolph, were both fiercely competitive and Bruno was particularly pleased to beat him one year. The social après ski side was, of course, important. We always ended the week with a grand dinner. One year hosted by us and the next by the Swiss. Lord Limerick living up to his name would always regale us with some of his amusing "limericks", made up for the occasion. Patrick was also an excellent skier as was his son Edmund, one of the competitive young "Followers".

Unfortunately, with one or two exceptions the British did not speak much German and in any case Swiss-German is difficult. They were inclined to stick together in an English speaking group and I found that I was often alone with Hilary socialising with the Swiss. I would speak German while Hilary would speak French. We were glad when Sarah Keays joined us, with her excellent language skills, and helped us with the burden of integrating with our hosts. At the time everyone assumed that she and Cecil Parkinson would be married as soon as he had his expected divorce. They were certainly very much together. However, Hilary in particular was very sceptical. We had both known Ann Parkinson since our time together in the Young Conservatives in the Hemel Hempstead constituency and Hilary was very surprised to hear from others in our party that she had agreed to a divorce.

There was a week's so-called training before the race. This was just an excuse for some enjoyable sociable skiing. We tried to sort ourselves out according to our standard and each group was provided with a Swiss Ski-school instructor. So most of us improved our technique. Although I had been skiing for years I had not benefited from ski lessons since I was a child, so I and some of my colleagues needed the instruction.

The British group was intended to be all-party. But few Labour M.Ps wanted to be seen indulging in skiing by the media, that kept a close eye on our antics. They believed it would damage their image back home to be seen in an elite resort, mixing with the aristocrats. Labour peers were less particular, feeling more secure as they did not need to be re-elected. Our team included a number of well-known politicians, and among the peers, some very distinguished figures. One such was Lord Shackleton, the former Labour M.P and the son of Ernest Shackleton the Antarctic Explorer, who started his career with Scott on the Discovery. Lord Shackleton was also an explorer and traveller. He had great fun with my children, telling them stories about head hunters in Borneo, graphically explaining how to shrink heads and various other horrific tales. The children were particularly impressed with his connection through his father of "Scott of the Antarctic" and could not hear enough from him.

One of our earlier skiing trips was notable for a nasty accident to Toby Jessel, the M.P for Twickenham. We were skiing down one of the hardest runs in a severe snow blizzard. It was also a very cold January, around minus ten at 2,000 metres. We followed our expert Swiss guide in a snake-like procession. I could only just see my colleague three metres in front. Suddenly he vanished. It was Jessel who had missed the piste and plunged down a crevasse.

Of course I stopped, as did Lord Hunt, who was immediately behind me. Toby was only about three metres down, but stuck. No way could he get himself out and up and was in danger of falling much further. John Hunt, the famous leader of our successful Everest Expedition in 1953, when Edmund Hillary and Sherpa Tenzing made it to the top for the first time, was of course a seasoned climber. As a distinguished member of the British Ski team, we teased him about his attire. He always looked when skiing as if he was still climbing Everest. Wearing an ancient rucksack, in 1920's thick woollen trousers, he did not fit in well with the rest of the party wearing smart fashionable, brightly coloured anoraks or one-piece ski-suits. He was asked more than once, what was in that bulky looking back-pack. Well this was the occasion when I found out. John Hunt opened up his pack, found his pitons, hammered them into the ice, got out his rope and threw it down the crack. Toby half climbed and was half hauled out, having broken his shoulder.

Of course at that time there were no mobile phones and the front of the party had long since belted down the run. One of our group behind skied on down to raise the alarm. Hunt next brought out his thermal blanket and wrapped up the injured Toby. Next out came the brandy flask. We knew that it could be at least half an hour before the rescue sledge could come from the top. Although a good skier, the person sent for help, would have to get down to base and telephone for the emergency team, which always waited at the top of the runs, with what skiers called the "blood wagon". In the severe weather conditions, having to wait for assistance, unaided by Lord Hunt's rucksack, who knows what the outcome might have been?

Of course our annual visits were a great social event, finishing up with a grand prize giving dinner with lots of speeches, as you would expect from such a large assembly of Parliamentarians. Good friendships were made over the years and a much better understanding between our two Parliaments. This type of association has achieved more than the occasional summit between leaders and ministers. Many from both sides over the years, reached higher political rank and brought with them memories which have maintained a strong bond between our two nations. Our Scottish friends may want to know that we did our best to persuade the Swiss to allow us to return hospitality by organising our annual meeting in the Scottish Cairngorms ski resort. I regret they were never tempted to accept.

There was another, slightly more serious side to the annual event. Lower down the mountains, at Chur, was a "Friends of Britain Association" and each year one of us was expected to be their guest speaker. This was not the most popular assignment amongst the British Parliamentarians as it involved some German speaking, and took a whole evening with an hour's journey each way, when colleagues preferred to "chill out" in their hotels. I was co-opted for one of these and volunteered. They were an appreciative crowd, mainly of ex-pat Brits but also of Swiss business people, all eager to have an update on the British political scene. I had been warned before we left England about the event and we brought with us "essential" provisions of crumpets and marmite and, of course, stilton.

Chapter Twenty-Four
Chunneling

A proposal linking Britain with France was first made in 1802 and some primitive digging started. A more serious tunnelling project came in Queen Victoria's reign, in 1882. But the Government was afraid a link would undermine our defence. After all, had not all our enemies come from the other side of the Channel and would it not be easier with a land link?

It was not until the early 1970s that a more realistic plan emerged. This was scuppered by the British Government, unwilling to share the costs with the French Government. Enthusiasts continued to dream about a land link, but Margaret Thatcher, our Prime Minister from 1979, made it quite clear that no public money would be available. While the French Government was willing to become a partner, they were told that our share of the cost would have to come from private investors.

That made it difficult to move plans forward but there were determined private sector companies keen to provide the finance. An Anglo-French consortium was set up in 1985. Proposals were invited and detailed engineering schemes were presented. One serious alternative to the twin rail tunnel finally selected was an enormous bridge, with just a section in the centre of the Channel underground to allow shipping through unimpeded. Artificial islands would be required.

Another rejected scheme was an underground road tunnel, as exists in the Alps and elsewhere; but not as long. This was wisely rejected, as it would not take rail traffic. Far-sighted planners anticipated the development of advanced high speed railways through Europe, such as today's two and a quarter hour

Eurostar link between the centres of London and Paris. It was also hoped that more rail freight traffic could be carried through Europe.

The reason why the Thatcher Government insisted the project would have to be financed without public money from us was the opposition from the Ferry companies, particularly P & O. A state subsidised tunnel would represent unfair competition. P & O was a substantial subscriber to Conservative Party funds.

This obstacle held up the start of the project. It was not easy to raise the required cash, and took all the resources of the City of London and Paris. Shares were offered for public subscription with the attraction of generous travel rights. Investors willing to subscribe for at least 1500 shares, costing £5,250, were offered travel at a nominal £1 per passage as often as they wanted, with no restriction on the times of day or the year, as long as space was available. For this size of investment the rights lasted for the whole lifetime of the shareholder.

I subscribed for the full rights. I also applied from France, as by this time having a second home in Provence, the travel rights would be valuable, and I was afraid the offer would be oversubscribed and I might not get the full ration. The cash came in but the offer was not oversubscribed and I could now look forward to the construction.

A Parliamentary Eurotunnel committee was formed, with a group of enthusiasts like me. We were regularly briefed as the work progressed from 1985, with site visits. The refusal of our Government to participate in the financing angered me. After all, this was Europe's biggest infra-structure project ever. Taxpayers finance motorways, airports, nuclear power plants and railways, but not something that would symbolise more than anything else, our commitment to becoming a full partner in the European venture. At the very least we could have helped ease the strain to finance the construction, by guaranteeing the loan capital. Or taxpayers could have underwritten the share offer, giving the Government a stake, if private investors had not taken up all the shares. A modest indication of support would have made it easier and less expensive to finance the project.

But we were in the middle of the Thatcher Government's programme of privatisation – selling off our vast state industries. Any proposal to participate in a new state investment, however strategically, symbolically or potentially of economic value, was not on the agenda. The French were not pleased. There would be obstacles enough, without making it so difficult to raise the required amount.

When the construction overran the budget and then overran the timetable, additional funding was required. This added an extra burden of debt and servicing that debt. The market price of the shares slumped to around 10% of what we founders had paid. But I did not mind. I was expecting eventually to start benefiting from the free rides for our family on our "chilling-out" visits to our French home.

Indeed, I followed progress week by week, eagerly noting how many meters the tunnel construction advanced daily. When progress was fast, it could be several hundred meters in a week, and I celebrated. But suddenly there was a period when my regular automated phone report indicated trouble. Progress almost ceased. I made enquiries and discovered that one of the massive drilling machines had struck underground water. There were also occasional halts to progress for servicing these huge machines. It was a nerve-racking time and I followed it so closely, it felt as if I was part of the team. I think my family also thought I was taking the whole affair too personally, judging by the sarcastic comments.

What was not widely understood was that the tunnelling was only a small part of the total operation. Once completed, with a ceremony under the middle of the Channel, when the British drillers met the French, there was great excitement. But that was only the beginning. Cementing the tunnel, fitting it out for safe, fast rail traffic, the elaborate safety systems and the large quantity of specially designed vehicles for private cars and trucks, and much more, took about as long and cost as much as the drilling itself. There are of course two tunnels with a service tunnel between them. The engineering was amazing, as was the technology. Guided by lasers, the tunnels met from each end with just centimetres out of alignment.

The Tunnel was completed in 1994 and the official opening was a grand affair and took place at each end of the Tunnel, at Folkestone and Calais. Her Majesty the Queen drove out of the shuttle from the Tunnel, in her Rolls Royce, accompanied by the French President, François Mitterrand. Special Magnums of Champagne were bottled for the occasion and consumed by several hundred V.I.Ps at the massive reception. We managed to rescue some of the empties from the skip to keep as lasting souvenirs. One rather amusing side to the celebrations was that Hilary has a rather attractive red suit which she wore for the occasion, only to find that all the service personnel were similarly attired. Much to the amusement of our table, she could not get up from it without being accosted and asked to give directions or answer some other problem. In the end she gave up explaining that she was a guest herself and directed people to the toilets or the bar. For some time afterwards, when meeting any of our fellow table guests at other functions, she would be jokingly asked "Can you direct me to the toilet?"

It was not only the lack of Government support on the British side which angered me. There was the shameful refusal to construct a fast rail link from London to the Tunnel, to connect with the modern French TGV network to Paris and beyond. When eventually built and opened only recently, it cut the time for the London to Paris journey by a half hour, to little more than two hours. Airlines can no longer compete and Eurostar is taking an increasing proportion of the traffic. The finances would not have been so strained if a fast rail link had been built from the Tunnel to London to coincide with its opening, as the whole project would have reached profitability years earlier.

Despite the spectacular success, logistically, the project is only recently breaking even, as traffic rises. A first nominal dividend was paid in 2009 to long-suffering loyal shareholders. But not before a drastic financial reconstruction, writing down the debts, watering down the equity by converting a chunk of the debt into shares. Meanwhile, there are still xenophobic M.Ps who regard the land link as unwelcome. The opposition originally was quite intense. The old argument of defence and security was resurrected. "And what about rabid dogs coming through from France", we were asked. The defence fear is surely absurd. Are we to believe that alien forces would fight their way through Europe to Calais, as if NATO does not exist? Who are the potential enemies and why bother trying to invade us through a tunnel when our skies are open to missiles and all else, while our 3,000 miles of coastline is an open invitation? The reality is these reactionary chauvinists, fear the land link would lead to closer ties in all sorts of other undesirable ways, and so undermine our independence. They are the remnants of what was a vocal pressure group opposed to our membership of the European Union.

My original investment is still only worth a fraction of the issue price, but at least the tunnel is built, running and attracting increasing traffic, including nearly one hundred journeys for me. I believe it is helping to cement the Entente Cordiale, which is surely more important than the enjoyable experience I have had as part owner of a fantastic enterprise. Even more important over the longer term, it will divert more road traffic on to rail. The benefits as a counter to global warming have yet to be realised, as high speed rail networks spread through Europe. They might eventually even be built in Britain, but don't count on it in our lifetimes.

No history of the "Chunnel" project can be complete without the recognition of the contribution made by Sir David Mitchell M.P. This has been shamefully under-reported. Appointed by Margaret Thatcher as Under-Secretary of State for Transport in June 1986, he undertook the immensely detailed work, under Nicholas Ridley M.P, the Transport Minister, involved in getting the legislation through Parliament in the face of plenty of filibustering. He supervised the progress of the construction, was closely involved in the negotiations with the French Government and ironed out endless problems between conflicting interests.

By no means least, he took responsibility for quelling the opposition to the project that came from many quarters. Rowdy meetings from Kent citizens, essential compulsory acquisition of land and property, environmental lobbies, dockers, ferry companies and much else, became his burden. Local M.Ps harassed him in Parliament. I have no doubt that without David's patience, persistence and determination to see the project through all its difficulties, it might never have happened.

Chapter Twenty-Five
"A Poxy Little Runt"

Only twice can I remember having a "spat" with any of Margaret Thatcher's ministers. The first scene of my misbehaviour was the Division Lobby. It would be wrong to assume this was a private sort of place where things done and said remained hidden from the public domain. There is nothing more gossip leaky than a packed Lobby of M.Ps.

The cause of my displeasure was Alan Clark, the son of Kenneth, Lord Clark, the distinguished art historian, most widely known for his magnificent book and T.V series, Civilisation. Alan Clark was one of Margaret Thatcher's favourite "boys" and by his own account in his infamous diaries, he adored her. She appointed him as a junior Employment Minister in 1983, a job well beyond his ability. Later he did slightly better as a Trade Minister and then Defence.

Our little tiff occurred on the night of his first business on behalf of the Government, one of those obscure amendments to employment legislation, debated briefly after the main Business finished at 10pm. Clark admits with creditable honesty that he had not prepared himself for the explanatory speech on the matter in hand. He had spent the earlier part of the evening at a wine tasting dinner, and his speech, prepared for him by his departmental officials, was technical and incomprehensible to him, and most of the House. He had made no attempt to brief himself, was clearly the worse for too much alcohol, and did not hide it. Nor did he try to conceal that he was reading a brief he did not understand. He lost his place and gabbled on, to the increasing rowdiness of Members, with Points of Order and notably Clair Short, the Labour M.P, accusing him of being "incapable" a euphemism for "drunk" – not a proper Parliamentary word.

In particular, Labour women Members and Trades Unionists regarded the Order under discussion, equal employment rights for women, as a serious matter. Our Minister was blatantly treating it frivolously and with disdain. His obviously uncaring and disinterested conduct from our Front Bench quickly resulted in total chaos. I had never seen such genuine anger, as compared to the contrived bogus rows that often formed part of the debating style. He was a "Tory Toff", scoffing at the rights of ordinary workers. In my view, as an observer on our silent and embarrassed benches, it was harmful to the caring image of Margaret Thatcher's Government.

Relief to his incompetent handling came when the time was up, and the Vote was called. From here I quote Alan Clark's own diary, published in 1993 after I had left the House. "One more brief kerfuffle and the Division was called. Nobody spoke to me much in the Aye Lobby, although little garden gnome Peter Rost sidled up and said 'After a performance like that, I almost considered voting against.' Poxy little runt, what's he ever done?"

Well his diary report was accurate, and it all leaked out. I suspect most agreed with me, that he deserved a little kick. After his response to me, somewhat ruder than my criticism of him, the Daily Telegraph published a letter from me, prominently, "What have I ever done? Well at least I did not dishonour my distinguished father." Honours were even and all is now forgiven and almost forgotten. I was flattered that he recorded it in his diaries and as good as conceded that his behaviour that night fell below the standards we expect from one of Margaret Thatcher's Tory ministers.

My only other squabble with a colleague came about after the 1983 General Election. The Boundary Commission, as is their duty every decade or so, had revised the East Midland constituencies. Rising population persuaded them to make quite radical changes affecting the whole area.

Derby continued, divided into North and South both larger, swallowing parts of my constituency. My largest loss, however, was to the new South Derbyshire, which along with several Tory voting villages took Melbourne which had been a key area for me, along with Amber Valley to the north taking some of my rural villages. Amber Valley was won in 1983 by Phillip Oppenheim, the son of Sally one of my bridge partners. Erewash, as my new constituency was called, comprised the old core of Long Eaton and Sandiacre, but also took in Ilkeston. West Derbyshire, slightly to the north-west of Derby remained fairly unchanged and had been won by Matthew Parris in 1979. To the south, the new constituency of South Derbyshire was won by Edwina Currie.

When she arrived triumphantly at Westminster in 1983, several colleagues crept up to me saying it was all my fault that I had let her in. What male chauvinism, I thought and quite unkind. Edwina was a friendly, jolly neighbour and we got on well enough. She struck me as a Margaret Thatcher "clone" – a bit more pushy, but ambitious, highly talented and motivated, but not loved all round in a male dominated parliamentary environment.

What was left of my former constituency was merged with Ilkeston, which had been a Labour seat for years with Ray Fletcher as the member. Ray, who was married to a flamboyant former German Countess, had been an enthusiastic member of the British-German Parliamentary Group and was a very likeable man. However, the former mining areas of the old Ilkeston constituency of Cotmanhay and Heanor, did not come along with the package. Most opinion thought that the new Erewash seat was unwinnable for us. As a sitting member, I would have been unchallenged if I had chosen to go along with the southern part of my old constituency or to the other new seat of Amber Valley, rather than take on the Erewash seat. I decided to stay and fight it out. I believed that Ilkeston was not as solid Labour as it was portrayed.

The election was my seasoned agent, June Parkinson's greatest challenge. As usual she was well ahead in the tactical battle. We had the extra help of a young trainee agent, who along, yet again with Paul Thompson, supported me throughout the campaign. However, we started the battle for Ilkeston long before the election was called. June, along with the local councillors for the area, identified likely conservatives who would form the basis of new branches. We held meetings in the area and I did my best to find suitable speakers, although I could not as a fellow M.P go into another constituency in public, I could attend privately.

We dug out plenty of Tories on our extensive canvassing. Many times we were told, they just did not regard it worth voting previously, living in a former Labour mining town. But when we encouraged them to believe the seat was winnable, they came out with enthusiasm. In any case the National trend was working strongly in our favour. Another advantage I had, was that our local radio and newspaper s had made me well known and identified when I started touring the shopping areas, factories, sports grounds, old people's homes and the rest. After all I had been the Member for South East Derbyshire since 1970, in the neighbouring towns such as Long Eaton.

I held the new seat comfortably, but only after a lively energetic campaign. Our organised pub crawls got us seen in the rougher Ilkeston pubs where few Tories had ventured before. I was told that the town had the highest proportion of pubs per citizen in the whole of Britain. Judging by the number we found, it could well be true.

June Parkinson, my excellent agent had, as usual organised as many high-profile stunts as we could devise, particularly with our "battle bus", a large van decorated with posters and accompanied by some nubile Young Conservatives handing out leaflets. The vehicle had the habit of turning up in a prominent position when any of the Labour heavyweights, like Denis Healey for example, chose to be in the constituency.

One particularly successful ploy was organised by my wife, Hilary. She happened to notice that the annual Ilkeston pram race was scheduled for the Sunday before polling day and entered us as a team. The team had to consist of one person in the "pram" with up to three supporters. The race, around the back streets of Ilkeston, took in eight or nine pubs, at each of which a quantity of beer had to be consumed by the team. As the pram pushers needed to stay relatively sober, the occupant of the pram took in most of the liquid refreshment.

Obviously I could not compete openly as a candidate in the coming election, so we decided on a more historical motif, and I dressed as Disraeli, complete with stove pipe hat and goatee beard, sporting an enormous blue rosette. I occupied the "pram". Hilary had difficulty in finding suitable costumes at the hire shop for the two main pushers, Paul Thompson and John Cousins, but finally decided on two "Andy Pandy" costumes – Blue and white with, of course, blue rosettes. Hilary's costume was the best though. Clad in a blue dress, with cardigan and giant pearls, she had found a full head mask of Margaret Thatcher.

We set off on the track near the front, but although we were not quite last, we fell back. I did my best with the beer, but the real triumph was our audacity to bring "Margaret Thatcher" walking through the residential area of "Labour" Ilkeston, waving to the watching crowds. They loved it. We finished up, needless to say, in yet another pub, where news got around to the local Labour Party that we were "canvassing" in Ilkeston. They turned up in force. Stupidly they tried to get us disqualified and their complaints did not play well with the locals. They just marked themselves out as lacking in a sense of humour.

Soon after the election came my little tiff with Edwina, the new Derbyshire South M.P. Repton School, which happened to be in her territory, had a long established rule in their constitution, that one of their Governors should be a Derbyshire M.P. By tradition the most senior M.P. was usually asked to fill the post.

In 1983 Matthew Parris was the Governor, having taken over from Spencer le Marchant the former Member for High Peak. Spencer was not well and had arranged the handover to Matthew before the election, at which he had stood down. Properly, all the Derbyshire M.Ps should have been asked about the appointment, as certainly Matthew was not the most senior. However the Labour Members were not interested in the post. Tony Wedgwood Benn as the most senior and ex-public school himself, preferred to have that "blot" in his past forgotten. A governorship of a prestigious public school did not slot in to his proletarian image.

My first inkling that Edwina was not happy with the situation came when she wrote a letter complaining that she had been "humiliated". When she had been to a function at the school she found Matthew Parris sitting on the platform as a governor while she had to sit with the parents, in her own constituency. She felt that the post should certainly have been hers and that Matthew had no right to be there.

The situation was explained to Edwina, and although she was not completely satisfied she accepted it. However, the problem reared its head again, when Matthew decided to stand down from Parliament in 1986 and therefore gave up the post of Parliamentary Governor for Repton. As I was the most senior Member, the Governors approached me. I accepted with pleasure, but only after I had received assurances that they wanted me and not their local M.P Edwina, who was obviously anxious for the post. We should comply with tradition, they argued, I was senior. "We are a national institution – it is not just a local constituency school". I still suspect that they could have "bent the rules" but were frightened of Edwina. I had also checked with the other long standing M.Ps in the area, such as Margaret Beckett, that they were in agreement.

When Edwina discovered that she had not been invited all hell broke loose. She challenged me and I tried to explain, I had no interest in trespassing on what she regarded as her domain. They had asked me, according to their constitution. What bothered her was that on the school's big occasions once more she, the local M.P., would be in the audience while I sat on the platform.

She stormed into the Chief Whip's office and accused me of trying to muscle in on her territory. Presumably she did not explain to the Whips, why. It is a long standing convention that a Member does not go into another M.P's constituency to an open event, without an invitation. This is of course intended to cover public events, not private school occasions. So I was called in to explain myself. Once the situation was made clear of course they accepted my story, and that was the end of the matter except that our relationship cooled somewhat, for some time afterwards.

However, Edwina did eventually become a governor at Repton School, after I had stood down in 1992. Although she, Greg Knight and Phillip Oppenheim had been elected to Parliament on the same day in 1983, it was Edwina who had taken the oath first and was therefore the senior Derbyshire M.P. I understand that Repton has now, as have many independent schools, modernised its governing body and no longer insists on having a Derbyshire Member of Parliament on the board. This no doubt is a relief avoiding further scenes with pompous parliamentary prima donnas.

Chapter Twenty-Six
Alternative Medicine

My life-long almost obsessive love of the countryside, nature and the pursuit of organic fruit and vegetable production was inevitably bound to lead me to an interest in natural or alternative medicine. It became all a more serious business when I discovered that one of my constituents was the head of Weleda's UK operation. Part of the large Swiss based international organisation, Weleda are Europe's largest producers of herbal and homeopathic medicine. Martin Viner ran the operation from a large complex of laboratories in Ilkeston, which became part of my constituency of Erewash after the reboundarying. Nearby was the largest herbal garden I was ever likely to see, where many of the raw materials were produced.

Herbalists and homeopaths believe that nature works holistically. Plants with medicinal use benefit from being sown, grown and harvested in tune with the lunar and solar cycles. To many it all sounds cranky. But I am modest enough not to condemn or ridicule something I do not fully understand. What I can say is that I was amazed and impressed by the quality of Martin Viner's produce from his large vegetable garden.

I have grown vegetables since a boy and despite trying and applying all the right treatment to the soil, water and fertilizer with loving care, I never produced cabbages the size of footballs, nor tomatoes the size of oranges. Such seemed to be the result of his biodynamic gardening. Of course it is not size that matters. Produce needs to be harvested at the right time, even at night, to ensure it contains the full nutrition and flavour, which is most efficacious for the human body. Again, a lot of nonsense say many, but not those millions who claim to have benefitted health-wise from natural and herbal treatments, where the so called orthodox pharmaceutical products failed.

When we moved to our holiday cottage in Provence, I was surprised to find that far from being regarded as a pursuit of a weird minority, biodynamic methods were accepted as the norm by the local horticulturalists there. The vegetables they produce for the market stalls and even the supermarkets are superb. I try to follow, but often fail.

One reason why homeopathic and other natural medical treatments are discounted as quackery by so many is that they have never tried or been cured by the holistic approach to ill health. So often we have become accustomed to regard some condition in isolation to the rest of our body. The pharmaceutical industry has almost brainwashed us into expecting a "pill for every ill". We demand an artificially produced medicine to give an instant cure without considering the side effects or in some cases dangerous addictions. The other reason sceptics reject natural medicines is because they often work slowly and do not always produce the instant results of the magic pill.

My many hours with Martin Viner and at Weleda, not only in Ilkeston but also in their home territory of Switzerland and Germany, convinced me that society had a right to hear the case for alternative therapies and the holistic approach to medicine, rather than have them discredited out of hand. I felt that the unquestioning acceptance of all orthodox medicine, which is assumed by the mainstream in this country, led by the pharmaceutical industry, needed to be challenged. So I helped to set up an all-Party Parliamentary Group, the Natural Medicines Committee. Bill Cash, the Member for Stafford, was my joint chairman and we were supported by a surprisingly large number of our colleagues from all sides of the House. David Tredinnick, the Member for Bosworth, was a particularly active and committed leader of the committee. Meeting weekly, these sessions were always open to the public, that is outsiders, who wanted to learn more. A guest speaker was invited to each meeting, representing a section of the field of alternative medicine and interesting discussion followed each presentation.

Word got around and over the months we had to move to larger committee rooms at Westminster to accommodate sometimes up to a hundred Members and outsiders. We invited speakers representing the whole range from acupuncturists, producers, practitioners and those dealing with Colour therapy, traditional Chinese medicine, scientifically qualified disciples and many more.

We obviously struck a rich vein of alternative medical practice which, unlike the case in most other parts of Europe had been ignored in this country. Our group not only operated as a forum for information and education and debate. We also developed a lobby to improve and widen the acceptance of alternative therapies within the NHS. There have always been general practitioners practising orthodox and alternative medicine jointly, so of course we have had a homeopathic hospital in London and in other centres for many years. But many M.Ps who were sympathetic to people being offered an alternative, found resistance in many of their own regional NHS areas. We had meetings with our Health Ministers and discovered enough support to persuade the Department of Health to send strong guidelines to Regional Health Authorities, so they should allow patients to have alternative forms of treatment within the NHS, if it was appropriate and demanded.

Over the years a more supportive approach widened the availability with university medical schools offering curriculums. We were not surprised that the powerful pharmaceutical companies tried to suppress any idea that alternative therapies could work or should be taken seriously. After all, if around two million people are dangerously addicted to sedatives like valium for example, why not allow patients to take a simple herbal medicine, which is as efficacious but without the strong addictive qualities and much less expensive! Obviously there are serious conditions for which only the mainstream orthodox medicine is suited, but the "sledgehammer" approach of dispensing without looking for alternative treatment for many minor complaints has had the effect of rendering many of these drugs useless, when they really are needed. The oversubscribing of antibiotics in the past illustrates this point.

My own experience need be of interest only to me and proves nothing. However an old injury giving me persistent back pain after hard gardening or carrying heavy objects was never cured despite physiotherapy and pain killing pills. My daughter Jessica, a keener earlier follower of alternative therapies than even I, recommended an acupuncturist. One course of treatment and I was miraculously cured, or so it seemed. It has never reoccurred.

As it became clear that there was far greater interest in our Parliamentary Committee's activities which I had helped to lead, I felt it necessary to widen my knowledge of the subject. There is always the problem of treating some of the fringe practitioners with caution, even though they may have big followings. But we thought it only fair to give all who felt they had something to contribute a platform in Parliament.

Meanwhile I took the opportunity of some visits abroad and saw how seriously it was all regarded elsewhere. In France there are thousands of "Pharmacies" who call themselves herbalists and homeopaths, alongside the pharmaceutical industries' products. The consumer has a more even handed choice. I am glad to say that following our efforts things are now changing in Britain where more chemists are now stocking homeopathic and herbal medicines on their shelves. No doubt there is a demand for them.

In countries like Germany and Switzerland we see the same co-ordination, not competition. I visited the Rudolph Steiner headquarters and hospitals run on holistic principles, using orthodox medicine, homeopathy and other treatments in combination. The treatment in them comprised the total hospital environment; the architecture, the decoration and the food were regarded as important as the actual medical regime. Each hospital had a room set aside for music, even concerts, and exercise with simple dance movement. There were additional treatments such as colour therapy and aromatherapy with the food in the pleasant communal dining room, where staff and ambulant patients ate together, all produced organically and fresh. I was convinced that we should not ignore or worse, oppose, what we do not find convenient or cannot always explain with medical science.

It became obvious to me and our supporting Parliamentary colleagues, that the alternative practitioners needed a more effective voice. Their organisations found it difficult to unite under one strong association, an industry-wide promotional body, as has every other powerful voice in our democratic society. So we encouraged the many different factions, some of which were destructively squabbling with each other, to form one overriding body, a National Association. They needed to have set standards for their practitioners and to police these. So that the unrecognised "fringe" could be weeded out, we also supported Government proposals to establish a registration system, so raising the status of approved practitioners.

My modest contribution to all this was not just fascinating and instructive but also rewarding. Looking at the scene today, compared to the 1970s, the natural therapists have gained much higher credibility and recognition. You only need to look at our medical schools to see how much more seriously the established medical mafia now has to regard what previously too many preferred to ignore or ridicule.

I was about to invite Prince Charles to address our committee, after one of his many supportive speeches. However, the 1992 General Election was called. All Parliamentary business was suspended and as I was not standing for re-election, the Committee's business was no longer my affair, but it is encouraging to see that our work continues in Parliament.

Chapter Twenty-Seven
Combined Heat and Power

A few miles south of Nottingham situated on a tributary of the River Trent, is a landmark that can be seen for miles around. It is one of our largest coal-fired power stations, Ratcliffe on Soar. Six enormous circular concrete cooling towers bellow out huge plumes of steamy warm air, creating artificial clouds that obstruct the sun.

A coal fire power station burns coal to produce super heated steam which drives the massive turbines that create electricity which is fed into the National Grid. In a modern power station the unavoidable smoke and carbon can be filtered to reduce pollution. But the cooling towers are needed to disperse the huge amounts of heat created from driving the turbines, in the same way in which a car's radiator keeps the engine from overheating and an old fashioned steam engine rejects waste heat.

Even the most modern steam technology applied to an electricity plant, is only able to achieve a 40% thermal efficiency. Many older power plants only convert a third of their fuel into electricity. The rest, up to 70% of the fuel value, has to come out as heat, from the turbine cooling system. In other words we can only produce electricity from the conventional steam driven turbine by also producing more heat than electricity. In most of the rest of Europe, much of this heat from power stations is not thrown away in cooling towers, to add to global warming. It is piped into buildings, in district heating networks.

What very soon developed as my principal political issue, after entering Parliament, resulted from a study of this enormous and unnecessary waste of energy. Not only my constituency but throughout the whole country, millions of citizens suffered from having to live in poorly insulated homes, therefore needing to pay far more for heat than they should. Moreover, this heat could have been provided from what is still being rejected by electricity production. Most of my voters lived within a few miles of one or other coal fired power station, discarding two-thirds of its energy as waste heat. Within sight of this waste, darkening the sky, were many housing estates where people suffered from inadequate heating. Little has changed since the 1970s.

Yet, in the Netherlands, Finland, Sweden, Denmark, France and Germany, as well as in Eastern Europe, a large proportion of heating is provided by district heating systems, insulated pipes running underground from power stations into homes, public buildings, hospitals, leisure centres, hotels and commercial buildings and horticultural glass houses. So, why not in Britain? What went wrong? I was determined to expose the scandalous answer. Politicians have mismanaged our energy policy and we are now paying an increasingly unnecessary price for our folly.

If we want to understand the reason, we need only to look at the contrast between our generously endowed energy sources, compared with mainland Europe. Britain is virtually built on coal. We discovered masses of oil and gas within our sea boundaries. We were the first nation to harness nuclear power. The rest of Europe, with marginal exceptions, had far less raw energy within their territories. Some coal, yes. And the Dutch had their own North Sea Oil and Gas. But they decided to conserve not squander it. So Dutch oil and gas were used for power stations designed for obtaining electricity and useful hot water for district heating. Some of this useful hot water has helped them build a flourishing horticultural industry – acres under glass, producing all-year round vegetables, salads and fruit for export to Britain! Most cities, including their suburbs, are served with district heating networks. Why were we not doing the same, with only one or two tiny exceptions?

I have visited many other countries, where citizens and the economy benefit from combining the production of electricity and by using the cooling heat, providing up to 80% thermal efficiency from the fuel – half as electricity and half as useful heat. So what happened here, while much of the rest of Europe developed a far more efficient energy policy? On my many visits to European countries, I never found the scandalous fuel poverty which our wasteful system has inflicted on our lower income citizens.

The explanation is that we were so abundantly endowed, there seemed little urgency for politicians to demand more efficient production and use of energy. We became complacent. Now that we have almost exhausted our oil and gas, all but closed down our coal industry and not built a new nuclear plant for twenty five years, our profligacy and short-sighted development of any energy policy is coming home to roost. Because we have so mismanaged our affairs, our economy is handicapped by much higher energy costs than many of our competitors. Industries requiring heavy energy use, for example steel making, cement, railways, chemicals and construction, are suffering.

What is equally evident from the incompetence and ineptness of past governments is that we have allowed our nation to drift into dependence on energy imports. The truth is this mismanagement and lack of foresight has left us dangerously insecure. Russia could shut off supplies of gas and oil or the precious pipelines can be interrupted. We are now dependent on France to build our new generation of nuclear power stations. Oil and gas has to be imported from Norway, North Africa and the unstable Middle East. Our present electricity demands can only be met by importing French nuclear electricity via cables under the Channel.

Despite this obvious vulnerability, high costs to the competitiveness of our industry and the unnecessary suffering of a large proportion of our people from shivering in their homes, we are only now beginning to tackle the problems. Tinkering with wind power will only divert attention from the real issues. We need to tackle drastically the enormous waste of energy in the way we produce and use it. We need a strategy to restore our security through self-sufficiency. We need a serious and urgent move to develop more renewable, nuclear and waste fuel into energy.

It is thirty years ago now since I, with colleagues on the Energy Select Committee, studied the potential and feasibility of a barrage across the Severn Estuary. That alone would produce 10% of our electricity needs. Our report was rejected by Government because it would have required some financial help. The costs of producing power from it were fully examined and estimated at around 4p per unit. Allowing for inflation, the barrage would now, thirty years later, provide the lowest cost electricity available to the Grid. It was, however, regarded by the Government as uneconomical, because at that time our electricity was costing us only around 3p per unit to produce. What folly!

Now the project is being rediscovered. No doubt there will be another long enquiry into the engineering costs and benefits. After perhaps another ten years of debate it might go ahead, in 2025 – but don't count on it.

The truth is, we do not have a coherent "energy policy". There is no longer term strategic planning. Yet the priority of adequate secure and environmentally acceptable energy at a competitive price should be at the top of a Government's agenda. There is no longer an Energy Select Committee. There is not even a separate Energy Department with a Secretary of State at the Cabinet table. It seems we will drift on without the sort of credible strategy that, for example, we see in France. Without much indigenous energy, a long term plan was devised to create self-sufficiency and competitively priced electricity. Around 80% of France's electricity is supplied by more than fifty nuclear power plants. The rest comes from hydro. Electricity even helps their balance of payments as large amounts are exported to us and elsewhere.

The nuclear pressurised water reactor design rights were purchased from Westinghouse in the U.S.A. After a detailed study of costs and benefits, environmental issues and long term needs, France went ahead on assembly lines, like a car factory, to produce and commission around five reactors per year. To reduce costs they are built in clusters on each site, with identical design, so benefitting from the economy of scale.

How does this compare with us? Having designed and built the world's first nuclear reactors, the early Magnox plants, we have spent much of the past thirty years arguing what new designs should be built, debating if we could afford to build, arguing whether we needed them and how they would be financed. Now the French will do it for us for half the cost and in half the time.

The folly of our shambolic energy policy does not only stem from complacency because we have been so generously endowed. A main handicap, bringing us to today's mess, was our state owned gas and electricity industry. Until privatisation under Margaret Thatcher's Government in the 1980s, we were handicapped by a monopoly Central Electricity Generating Board, a monopoly distribution grid and a state owned retailer. The electricity industry wanted us to use electric heating and subsidised the supply and installation in our homes. As only a third of the fuel used in producing electricity is converted in power stations as a saleable product, electricity for heating is an inefficient use of power.

Meanwhile we had a monopoly nationalised gas industry. The natural gas from the North Sea was over- exploited at very low prices, as if there was no tomorrow. Only stupid householders or those too far from a gas supply, refused to have gas connected to their homes for cooking, hot water and heating. Trapped between two monopoly state owned suppliers, electricity and gas, fighting each other for market share, no wonder district heating, as supplied by combined heat and power stations, did not stand a chance. And no wonder we have ended up with worse wastage of energy and fuel poverty than our European neighbours.

Our Governments stood by and watched our self-sufficiency end and the proportion of our imported energy rise, at much higher prices than we could have provided domestically. Meanwhile we allowed our nuclear power construction industry to wither, demoralised and financially damaged by endless indecision and procrastination, but no orders to build.

Our Energy Select Committee produced a number of well researched reports, setting out our proposals for an energy policy that would reach some of the strategic objectives we believed were necessary. But Governments were not ready to listen, let alone act. A sensible policy, for using the heat from our power stations instead of heating the atmosphere or the local river, required incentives. Otherwise companies prepared to extend heating networks could not make the sums add up, while our State Gas and Electricity suppliers offered heating at artificially low prices. The competition was not on a level playing field. Governments were slow to raise building standards, so that more of the heat is wasted than in the rest of Europe. Even today, after considerable toughening up, our new buildings are obliged only to meet insulation standards well below the rest of Europe.

When fuel prices did begin to rise, the problems facing my less well off constituents made me determined to campaign seriously to remedy the scandal of large sections of our population having to shiver in poorly insulated homes. Our electorate were having to purchase energy at higher costs than needed, if the energy were produced and consumed less wastefully.

I was invited by Sir Derek Ezra (later Lord Ezra), former Chairman of British Coal, to help a pressure group called WARMER. We wanted more initiatives to promote more home insulation and more use of waste heat from power stations for heating buildings. "Warmer" also campaigned to use our municipal, industrial and domestic waste as fuel in combustion for electricity and heat production. Nearly all our waste, much of it a useful fuel, was and is still dumped in enormous refuse pits or shipped abroad where it was used as a fuel for others to use. Very few waste–into–energy plants existed, such as at Edmonton in London and in Nottingham. Only in more recent years are we making some slow progress.

There was and still is public resistance, due to ignorance and the use of outdated technology. People did not want a refuse burning plant near their homes. I cannot blame them, when those plants that did exist were not environmentally acceptable. Only more recently, have companies applied the clean burning systems that have operated in the rest of Europe for decades without pollution, even in city centres.

I urged Governments many times over many years to provide a carrot and stick policy to motivate investment in improved energy efficiency. I argued many times for a tax on landfill. Finally it was introduced and has been steadily increased, so that it now saves local authorities money to send rubbish to specially designed power stations, rather than to landfill sites.

Similar incentives should be provided, I argued, throughout the area of energy use. More fuel efficient cars would have been built decades ago, and purchased eagerly by users, if road tax had been adjusted to reward the cleaner cars and punish the "gas–guzzlers". Why has it taken so long? The same principle could be applied to civil aviation. Less polluting airliners should be rewarded in the tax system; other less cleaner engines should be taxed more heavily.

It is encouraging seeing the Government at last giving more priority to policies that stimulate more efficient production of and use of energy throughout the economy. But much still could be done. For instance, we still waste more than half the fuel that goes into our power stations to produce electricity. The problem is that most of our power stations have been built in remote areas, away from the towns where the cooling waste could be economically pumped into buildings. On the many fact-finding visits over the years, I have seen and admired a much more developed system of smaller power stations, close to urban areas. Clean burning, they create no opposition from residents. No wonder, because they offer heating water on tariffs that cannot be matched from electricity or gas central heating. I was not surprised that it is difficult to find homes in the rest of Europe that are not cosily heated in winter at an affordable cost.

As my interest in energy policy developed, and became more critical and audible, I was invited to join the Combined Heat and Power Association, earlier known as the District Heating Association. In more recent years, I was honoured to be invited to become a Vice-President. I was never paid a penny for my work with the CHPA. All the publicity I gave the Association was voluntary, because I believed in it. I attended and spoke at endless conferences and so often and so regularly in Parliament that nobody seemed to accept I was committed because I believed fanatically in the importance of my campaigning, not because I was being paid as a lobbyist. A higher compliment was offered to me by Selwyn Gummer, when Secretary of State for the Environment. At a large energy conference he praised me as an influential voice in directing energy policy to promote more efficiency and so reduce the nation's contribution to global warming.

Meanwhile, much of my Parliamentary effort was concentrated in the work of the Energy Select Committee. I encouraged visits abroad to overcome the depressing negative attitude that if it "wasn't invented here, it was not worth looking at!" After more than twenty years of campaigning, broadcasts, media articles, speeches in the House, endless energy conferences and lots of publicity, particularly from our Energy Committee reports, modest progress is discernable. At last Government is offering a lead in promoting change, getting our energy utilities and companies motivated, and rousing public opinion to respond.

One of the areas of progress is particularly encouraging to me. Small scale combined heat and power plants are becoming widespread, as their cost-effectiveness is proved. Hotels, hospitals, leisure centres, housing estates, public buildings and universities are installing their own mini-power plants, to provide electricity and central heating water. The development of the gas turbine for power generation and availability of natural gas has assisted this form of micro-generation. Such plants of course achieve a thermal efficiency of around 80%, since the cooling water is as valuable as the electricity and is, therefore, not wasted, as it is produced on site.

Even the Palace of Westminster and Whitehall, now have their own power and heating network, as does Windsor Castle, thanks to the environmental conscience of Prince Charles. Those involved in the Combined Heat and Power business know, and have acknowledged my contribution, persistent and wide promotion on all sorts of platforms in and outside Westminster, over a long period of time.

As the technology has developed, micro power plants are becoming economic. Individual larger houses and small groups of sheltered housing, which would have a greater demand for heating because of older residents, is the next growth area. That is because electricity suppliers now have an incentive to encourage their customers to generate their own electricity and sell the surplus back to the Grid. It is also now happening because of rising fuel prices, which therefore rewards a more efficient use of fuel.

I succeeded in amending a Bill into Parliament in the early 1980s, The Energy Act, which obliged utilities to offer a fair price for electricity generated outside their own systems. As I am not a Parliamentary draftsman, those specialised lawyers who prepare Bills, the appropriate wording was produced for me by the Combined Heat and Power association. Its new skilful and energetic chairman at this time was William Orchard, senior partner of Orchard Partners, the energy consultancy. Orchard was the first chairman of the CHPA to make the organisation a more effective lobby, which was much needed. He reorganised the Association on a more businesslike basis, with its first Executive Director, David Green. He was a superb lobbyist, well known and respected in Whitehall.

From then on the CHPA became a professionally organised body. The leading electricity producers joined, as they were obliged to work with rather than try to exclude, smaller independent electricity producers. The CHPA was also now attracting a wider share of new players. Renewable energy companies became members as did suppliers and consultants beginning to see more business opportunities for combined heat and power investment.

My Energy Bill was supported by the Government and passed into law. It ended the shameful monopoly abuse of the free market. The Utilities had for too long discouraged the competition from private generators, by offering only a nominal price, much less than they were charging the customers, for the same power at the same time. In other words, utilities were buying power from one customer and selling it on to another at, perhaps, three or four times the price. The Energy Act ended this anti-competitive behaviour, and opened up the market for micro-generation. Not just the surpluses from small combined heat and power plants, but those from solar, wind generators, small scale hydro power and other renewable energy, are now offered a market price, which is encouraging new investment in environmentally produced energy.

When towards the end of my Parliamentary life in 1992, I walked round the streets of my constituency, I still met too many examples of hardship from families unable to live comfortably in homes they could not afford to heat adequately. Costly energy was still leaking like a sieve from the roof, walls, windows and draughty doors. But at least I had done my best and indeed achieved more than I realised at the time.

The Civil Service and State machine moves slowly. Major shifts in attitudes take time, much time. My contribution, which was my principal and most absorbing concern in my political life, has I believe helped to change energy policy towards what I regard as the right direction. The next challenge, only now beginning to be debated, is how we can reconcile the worldwide increasing demand for energy, with the risk that global warming will overwhelm us. I believe we have the technology that can more than meet that challenge. But will our political leaders make it happen?

Chapter Twenty-Eight
Nuclear Power, Brown Bread and Sandals

As time went by my energy interests became by far my main activity during my time in Parliament. There were endless speeches to empty Chambers. There were many hours spent helping shape reports from the Energy Select Committee, mostly ignored by Parliament. There were many "fact finding" visits all over the world, but as it was "abroad", nobody much cared. A succession of Conservative Energy Ministers invited me to discuss my specialist knowledge with them. Naturally I was arrogant enough to believe I should have been promoted as one of them, knowing a great deal more about the issues and having strong views on what Government policy should be than those appointed. But of course Ministers are not appointed only for their specialist interest in the department they go to.

However, on reflection, my voluntary lobbying and my major contribution as a leading member of the Select Committee, probably achieved as much, or more, to influence opinion and decision makers. Having close contacts with our endless succession of Energy Ministers convinced me how frustrating the job was, finding it difficult to do what one wanted, without carrying the Cabinet with you.

In particular my persistent criticisms about our poor standards of building insulation and our wasted heat from power stations attracted increasing recognition, not only in Parliament and Government. A flattering occasion during an energy policy debate resulted from one of my many contributions, advising tougher building regulations and more incentives to promote a more efficient use of our energy. The prominent Labour Member, Dennis Skinner the outspoken ex Derbyshire miner, spoke after me and referred to me as "the Member for Insulation." In all the twenty-two years we overlapped in Parliament, I had never heard him say anything polite about any Tory. So I was flattered.

The constant shuffling of Ministers was one of the reasons why there was no coherent energy strategy. The department was treated for far too long as the poor relation of Government, where new ministers were schooled, ready for moving on to 'more important' Government posts. After all, it is only now that Energy supply, its cost, security, efficiency and environmental impact is moving nearer the top of the political agenda. For most of my time there was little interest. It was regarded as the least "sexy" subject in Parliament and Government.

My many opportunities to see what was going on elsewhere in the energy world took me to the Athabasca Tar Sands in Canada, the tidal barrage in Brittany, France, wind and solar power to Denmark, district heating and micro-generation all over the world and much else. I was able to visit Europe's only fast-breeder reactor near Lyons, in France. A prototype that worked, but had safety and cost problems which are not yet overcome to justify replacing the world's existing generation of Thermal Nuclear Power plants.

Some of these fact finding visits were with the Energy Committee, others organised for me by the Combined Heat and Power Association. As the joint chairman of the all-party Parliamentary Renewable Energy Committee, I was also able to study the progress of wind power to its present technology and reduced cost, solar power in Japan and elsewhere, wave energy installations in Norway and other technologies worldwide, helped me to present a balanced view of where we should be going. Early on I had seen what was happening to develop clean ways to burn our coal, as well as every technology using waste material for energy production; methane from sewage and landfill. All helped me build up enough knowledge to talk intelligently in Parliament.

The status of nuclear power and its potential was also an important issue for me. Having visited nuclear power plants in Japan, America, France and the rest of Europe, I was convinced that we needed to get our act together, choose a preferred design and get on with construction, instead of spending so many more years arguing about it.

I made contact with Westinghouse, who held the patented licence for what

I accepted was our best option, the Pressurised Water Reactor (PWR) system. Colonel Ronnie Challoner, of Challoner Associates, acted for their public relations. As their most important client, Challoner worked hard to help Members interested in our nuclear future, understand the issues. From his consultancy business, based in London, he took me to PWR plants in America and Spain, where I had briefings in the technology, safety, cost and environmental impact.

I also visited Japan and France, to see why they had chosen the PWR design as the preferred option. Having visited not just the construction sites in France, but also the factories producing the components for relatively easy assembly, it was obvious that if Britain wanted competitively priced electricity, we needed to stop squabbling and start building. Not one plant at a time every five years, but, as the French, a substantial programme of several a year, to obtain the benefits of economy of scale in construction design and cost.

This was not to be. Resistance to what was regarded as foreign technology replacing British designs won the day. We started commissioning a painfully slow to build and ridiculously expensive, gas cooled reactor design. They worked; indeed they still are, safely, but now coming to the end of their economic life. The whole industry was state-owned, bureaucratic and inefficient.

Margaret Thatcher realised that nothing much would change until a new chairman was appointed to run the CEGB, not just prepared but determined to buy nuclear plants. Previous leaders could not make up their minds. Despite winning the support of Mrs Thatcher, who had scientific qualifications and understood the issues, the Westinghouse route was rejected. We were not prepared even to pay royalties for the licence. Meanwhile, France was commissioning four or five a year, on nuclear islands, all of an identical design, at half the price and in half the time we were constructing our little family of Gas-Cooled Reactors. Our design worked well enough, and had attractive safety features. But they had to be built on site, rather than assembled from factory components. It proved a lengthy and costly process.

In 1982, our Energy Secretary, Nigel Lawson, wisely appointed Walter Marshall to run the nationalised CEGB. As the then Chairman of the UK Atomic Energy Authority and previously Chief Scientist at the Department of Energy, he understood the need to proceed with a cost-effective development of nuclear power and he strongly favoured the Westinghouse model, widely applied in most of the rest of the World. However, he failed to overcome powerful lobbies and the Treasury's reluctance to finance a major programme. Despite support from Margaret Thatcher, then Prime Minister, only one PWR, at Sizewell, has ever been built in the UK, so far.

No wonder our nuclear industry is almost dead, and the efficient and well organised French industry now has to show us what we could have done decades earlier. Just another shameful example of muddle, incompetence and lack of commitment, which has seriously damaged Britain's competitiveness. Our energy costs today are much higher than those of our trading rivals. Evidence of what happens when there is no strategic planning.

My outspoken views and criticisms, gave me the opportunity for media interviews and broadcasts, and many articles in newspapers and magazines. I was elected as an Honorary Associate Member of The Institute of Energy and received many invitations to speak at conferences covering a wide energy policy agenda. However, few were listening in the corridors of power, where it mattered. I discovered that I had established more of a reputation in the real energy world, than recognition at Westminster, where attention was focussed more on immediate issues, such as the second miners' strike in 1984 or the priority of developing our oil and gas reserves.

Undoubtedly my credibility in Parliament on my energy campaigns, such as combined heat and power, higher energy efficiency, renewable energy and environmental concerns, suffered because I had acquired several outside consultancies. What was not understood was that these commercial contracts resulted from my perceived value as an adviser, not as a lobbyist. There is an important distinction. An advisory consultant guides an outsider how to present their case to Parliament and Government, opening doors and explaining how to approach the powers that be. A lobbyist, on the other hand, openly acts as an advocate, promoting the client's commercial interest.

As an example, I became an unpaid adviser to Combined Heat and Power (CHP) interests, not to make money but because I believed fanatically its development to be in the best interests of Britain, its people and economy. Many M.Ps, paid for promoting commercial interests, do so for the cash. My activities, even when paid, came as a result of my genuine interest to promote and having proved so, long before approached with a request to advise.

Moreover, I always declared any commercial interest I might have had, when speaking, writing or working on the Energy Select Committee.

My experience should have enhanced my credibility as an authoritative voice on matters requiring knowledge gained from outside, which many M.Ps lacked. Pontificating, as many M.Ps do on important issues, without adequate study of the problems, harms the status of Parliamentary Select Committee reports. I worked hard to brief myself, from expert sources close to the issues, before attempting to deliberate, criticise, judge or make recommendations to Parliament or Government, on important matters of energy policy.

In 1989 we finally tackled the privatisation of the electricity Industry. I was strongly in support, having advocated it years earlier, to break the state monopoly. I was appointed to the Standing Committee, about to start examining the legislation, line by line, in great detail.

Completely out of the blue, The Guardian Newspaper printed a piece accusing me of being in the pay of the Danish District Heating Association. This was completely untrue. I was not even an advisor to them. I was accused of being unpatriotic, by trying to advance foreign commercial interests to the disadvantage of our own industry. That too was nonsense. The reality was that the district heating industry was international. The Danes were world leaders, having extensive heating networks in most of their towns and cities. Their people did not need to freeze in under-heated homes. Nor did their power stations throw away more than half their fuel as unwanted steam, up cooling towers as in Britain.

British companies and local authorities in Britain were beginning to get the message. The members of the Combined Heat and Power Association were starting to get orders for the specialist insulated pipes and gas turbine power plants, metering and all the other components required for an efficient heat network. Some of the equipment was not available from British companies because we had, until now, limited demand and investment compared to the rest of Europe. So Danish companies, establishing themselves in the U.K., in anticipation of a growing market, were getting orders. Consequently, the nearest my actions came to the Guardian's damaging allegations was that, because I was a vigorous campaigner for using our waste heat from electricity production, to heat homes rather than throw it into the atmosphere, I might be helping Danish suppliers. It was certainly my hope that the privatisation of our electricity industry would encourage privatised companies to sell their waste heat, rather than cause global warming with it. This indeed is what has started to happen in recent years.

Any suggestion that I was personally benefitting from my campaigns to reduce fuel poverty and waste, was nonsense, totally untrue and hurtful. The Guardian was running an investigative campaign against M.Ps who profited from consultancies by asking questions in the House. This culminated of course in the infamous "cash for questions" debate. The libellous piece in the Guardian was not written by any of the number of journalists who were well aware of my energy interests and had reported them, including my criticisms of Government policy. They understood the issues I had been raising, which were often in tune with the Guardian's own and knew me as someone who was certainly not involved in any dubious practices.

Senior editorial staff had clearly been made to realise too late that they had attacked the wrong person. The Guardian telephoned my home and as I was out, spoke to Hilary. They were anxious to make amends but she was incandescent, and having prefaced her remarks with the fact that no doubt they would ignore anything she said, or the truth of the matter that I was solely interested in the welfare of the British people and certainly had not made any money out of my District Heating interests. The next day the Guardian ran a prominent piece about me, quoting Hilary in full and praising my efforts to save energy waste; a virtual apology. It was probably the most glowing recommendation the Guardian has ever printed on behalf of a Conservative M.P.

Had this been the end of the matter, then I would have let it rest with a chuckle at the expense of the Guardian. However, it was not. Unfortunately, two Labour Members mentioned the original Guardian accusations in the House, so that it was on the record, and no-one sought to clarify the position with me.

An all Party Committee appoints members to serve on Standing Committees, those that examine the legislation in detail. In reality the Party Whips influence the choice, quite improperly. Overnight, my name was withdrawn from the Electricity Privatisation Committee just before it was due to start its work. It was alleged, incorrectly, that my participation would not be impartial, but be influenced by my paid energy consultancies. The fact that I was one of very few M.Ps with enough knowledge and understanding of the issues to make a valuable contribution was irrelevant.

I had no option but to consult Parliamentary colleagues who had been libelled by the media and was advised to engage Peter Carter-Ruck, acknowledged as Britain's sharpest and most successful libel lawyers. After examining the case in great detail, they took me on and we started proceedings against the Guardian.

What happened next made legal history. I had powerful supporting witnesses, such as Lord Ezra, explaining why the allegations were untrue and because they had been repeated on the floor of the House, had clearly damaged my Parliamentary reputation. My removal from the Electricity Privatisation Bill Committee was an example. Even the Danish District Heating Association was ready to give evidence that the Guardian's allegations were false.

I found myself in the middle of a High Court legal argument, not about my defence to the Guardian libel, but about whether I should be allowed to defend myself properly. The relationship between the sovereignty of Parliament and the independence of the courts became the intriguing debate between the two sides. It was unreal. We were in one of the older, little used, courtrooms, lined with enormous tomes and utterly dusty. The lawyers had brought in trucks with quantities of leather-bound books, from which they cited cases back in distant history.

It appeared that Parliamentary papers, even published papers like Hansards, could not be quoted in the courts, without a specific Act of Parliament. So my case was prejudiced as I could not show that the Guardian had been quoted in Parliament or that the article had caused me to be removed from the Committee, and my reputation had been damaged. My lawyers argued that this was an injustice. Any other citizen was entitled to produce any documents in their defence, but not an M.P!

The argument raged on. My lawyers cited Habeas Corpus to claim I had a right to defend myself. After two or three days, including an appearance by the Solicitor General, the actual case at issue had not even been raised. Just the principle of whether or not I could obtain a fair hearing had been explored and the Guardian graciously conceded. The evidence was overwhelming, even if I could not produce it in court! They agreed to pay my costs, which for the nation's top libel lawyers was enormous. I, in exchange, agreed not to ask for damages, provided a prominent apology was printed in the Guardian. It was.

This was not just a happy outcome, without ill-will, but established important constitutional case-history, making it easier in future for M.Ps to seek justice, by applying Parliamentary papers where appropriate, as can any other citizen.

However, the injury was done. Not even the written apology after the High Court case repaired my reputation where it mattered, amongst the Parliamentary Establishment. "No smoke without fire" prevailed and I was unfairly tainted. It not only led to my removal from the Committee about to examine the Government's Electricity Privatisation Bill. There was an even more damaging consequence. I was denied my expected promotion to chair the Select Committee on Energy. Sir Ian Lloyd, the Conservative member for Havant, had chaired the Committee for ten years. He was a senior figure, fair, impartial and knowledgeable. He managed the Committee's business with distinction. An advocate of nuclear power, but critical as I was, about the Government's botched up policies, his other principal interest was Science and Technology. He established the Parliamentary Information Technology Committee and the Parliamentary Office of Science and Technology. He deserved, but was never invited to a Ministerial appointment.

Ian had notified his intention to retire from Parliament at the next election, expected in 1992, as had I. However, he volunteered to stand down as Chairman in 1990, so that I could have the opportunity of taking over for the final year of the Parliament. He assumed, as I did, that as the next most senior member of the committee, I would be elected, having his backing. I knew members from both our side and Labour, regarded me as the best choice. I had won the support of the Labour members, by my open criticism of the Conservative Energy Minister, and my refusal to tow the party line when I did not think such support was justified. All on the Committee recognised my expertise in depth, the contribution I had made over the years to the Committee's work and the strong support I had given the Chairman. Indeed, occasionally in Ian's absence, I had taken the Chair, being regarded as his deputy.

Select Committees are appointed by Parliament. Ministers and Party managers are not supposed to interfere in any way, in the selection of members, nor in the choice of topics they investigate. A committee of senior back-benchers supervise the appointment of Members to the Select Committees. However, Parliament has all but surrendered its control of the Executive. Our democratic system has become undermined by the pusillanimous submission of M.Ps to the patronage power of the Party machines and the Whips, whose only interest is in the management of the Government's business regardless of principle. So, quite scandalously, if you want to serve on a Select Committee you seek the support of the Whips.

When the Conservative Whips' office discovered that Ian was standing down as Chairman of the Energy select Committee and that I was clearly the favourite to be elected by its members to take over, a panic strategy of "skulduggery" was rapidly organised. A Conservative Member of the Committee, loyal to me, was" pressurised" to resign, so that a "stooge" could be appointed, who would organise a campaign to prevent my election. Michael Brown, the M.P. for Brigg and Cleethorpes, was persuaded to do the dirty deed. To be fair I do not know what story the Whips had spun about me. Members of the Committee were lobbied or had their arms twisted, possibly with threats or promises, to vote, not for me, but for a junior member, Dr Michael Clark. He was elected by the Committee. I knew nothing about the carefully planned campaign until the vote. Ian Lloyd told me afterwards how embarrassed he was, but although the Chairman it was by that time, "out of his hands".

Entirely coincidentally, perhaps, Michael Brown was promoted later to the Whips' office. Several outsiders, prominent figures from the Energy world, said to me, "They got you at last"! It is the price you pay for speaking frankly and critically on issues, not just following the Party line. Michael Brown lost his seat in the 1997 Election, but established a new career as a political journalist and broadcaster. In my view he has distinguished himself more after Parliament than he did on the Energy Select Committee.

Resisting the urge to resign in a sulk, I stayed on the Committee. A year later, the whole Committee was abolished, when a Governmental reorganisation transferred the independent Department of Energy into an enlarged Department of Trade and Industry. I felt vindicated.

Again, some of my friends from the energy world joked, that the only way the Government could shut me up, was to have the whole Committee killed off. I did not regard it as funny. We were a powerful voice, advocating in our well researched reports, Government changes in energy policy that might have avoided the shambles we have today. Instead we have no more independence, relying on imported energy from unstable parts of the world, higher energy prices, inadequate environmental concerns, enormous energy wastage, no new nuclear plants, little progress on renewable, nearly exhausted oil and gas reserves and a coal industry all but shut down. What a record!

My energy interests continued, with fact finding tours all over the world, visits to the Middle East to study the Oil Industry, many tours of European cities to see how heat networks have reduced the costs of heating buildings and also reduced the costs of electricity generation, and much more. I certainly proved that what is not invented or happening in Britain is not necessarily useless.

I became a "graduate" of the Industry and Parliamentary Trust. This is a twinning organisation with twenty or so of Britain's leading companies, offering "scholarships" to M.Ps. I accepted a course with B.P. It involved giving up around thirty days of my time, fitting in, where available, over a year, between my Parliamentary work. The experience involved an inside view of every side of the operation of a large multi-national corporation. My first day started at the top, a fly-on-wall in the Boardroom, when Sir Peter Walters was Chairman.

After the initial start, each of the Directors provided a day or two for me to study in each department. So my course included several days in Aberdeen, with visits to off-shore oil rigs and much else, allowing me to see from the inside, how management works, from the Boardroom downwards. We took in every side of the oil and gas industries' technology and engineering and BP's ancillary energy interests, such as solar voltaic.

At the end of the course one becomes a fellow of the trust, but not before the twinning side of the organisation comes into play. In return for giving me so much of their management time, I was expected, and willingly did, entertain several teams of their management, to working seminars in the House of Commons, showing them how our Parliamentary system works, or doesn't, from the heart of our democracy. I still recall how shocked some of BP's bright young managers were at some of the archaic procedures and activities they witnessed from the Strangers' Gallery, as observers of our Committees and the strange traditions, somewhat out of time with the way one of our leading oil companies operates. My part of the deal also included showing a team around my constituency, observing one of my advice centres and other routine activities, meeting my electorate.

I discovered that the Trust is an inspired organisation, helping a mutual understanding of two completely different worlds, but interdependent on each other. It is only a pity that so few M.Ps get the opportunity to participate. Our system of Government would be greatly improved if more M.Ps learnt and understood more about the outside world of industry and business that create the wealth of the Nation.

I conclude on a more optimistic note. When I stood down at the 1992 General Election, I felt disheartened that my more than twenty years crusade had made little impact. No coherent energy policy was yet on the Government's agenda.

The world price of oil was depressed. Gas was plentiful, so why bother to produce and use our energy less wastefully. Most of my Parliamentary colleagues thought, when I campaigned for "Energy efficiency", that I meant little more than double glazing. When I argued for combined heat and power production, with district heating and co-generation, I had to explain in detail what I was talking about. When I tried to promote more renewables, I was told they were too costly. As for a strategy to combat global warming, that was not even on the agenda. It was still a theoretical argument between scientists.

I recognise now that over the years, Parliamentarians who have pursued campaigns have required persistence and patience. No Government Minister, when pressed, will ever concede publicly anything that did not originate from that Minister's programme. Why admit you are not up to it and lose face? Backbenchers can nag, but ministers will not submit to pressure until their civil servant advisers suggest that the backbencher's campaign makes some sense and should be adopted – but without admitting that the minister did not think of it first.

The political scene today is transformed, and most of what I advocated so vehemently is now firmly established near the top of the agenda so it reassures me that my effort was not wasted and that my principal activity in my parliamentary life has achieved something after all. It is now clear that, while I have not been acknowledged for my contributions to a fundamental and important shift in Government policy, my dedication and persistence influenced a sluggish administrative machine to change priorities.

Chapter Twenty-Nine
Worker Shareholders

Margaret Thatcher's greatest achievement was the ambitious privatisation programme of the 1980s. It transformed the British economy, allowing private enterprise to flourish and restart creating more wealth and prosperity after the depressing 1970s, when Britain came close to being the "sick man of Europe."

When I talk to the younger generation about the 1980s' revolution, they are amazed how much of our economy was previously state owned. What is even more remarkable is how much we managed to return to the private sector, despite the hostility whipped up by the Labour Opposition in Parliament, attempting to protect vested interests. The Electricity Industry, British Gas, British Shipbuilding, British Telecom, Cable and Wireless, Britoil (our North Sea Oil company), British Rail with its hotels, British Ports, British Coal, British Steel, British Airways, British Leyland the makers of Rover, The National Bus Company and more, were all privatised during or shortly after Mrs Thatcher's period of Government.

When we examined the inefficient, wasteful, unenterprising and loss making way in which most of those businesses were run, it was no wonder that our economy was dragged down and taxpayers burdened by their losses and subsidies.

It all started off in a tentative experimental and modest way with National Freight, early in 1982. My brother-in-law Philip Mayo was on the main board as the Director of Legal Services, and as keen on promoting wider share ownership as I. He is credited with the proposal of a worker buyout. Under the chairmanship of Peter Thompson they prepared the company for a management and worker buyout, a proposal which was readily accepted by Norman Fowler, our Transport Secretary.

National Freight was an easy guinea pig. Management wanted to be privatised. They operated in a competitive market, where all other companies were private sector businesses. They were well managed and profitable, and smaller than any of our nationalised monsters.

Philip Mayo, with his legal background, was not as interested as I was in a national political career, but he was for many years a local district councillor. He did, however, strongly share my views that we should advance to a genuine capital owning democracy. Before moving to privatise National Freight, he was heavily involved in the housing association sector where he introduced the concept of shared ownership, for those who had not enough capital to buy outright. He was the chairman of the Dacorum Borough's Housing Committee and was instrumental in setting up the mechanisms for the sale of much of the housing in Hemel Hempstead's new town area, introducing again the concept of shared ownership in alliance with several housing associations. Working with the local M.P, James Allason, Philip's ideas became the template for the sale of council housing, nationwide, for Margaret Thatcher's Government. So, while I was promoting investment clubs, he was creating home owners.

It is one of those strange coincidences which we all experience in life, that neighbours of ours now in France are the James family. Dyfrig James is a high powered director of Lafarge, the French based international cement and building materials group. He is responsible for their Northern and Central European aggregates and concrete operations. Previously, at the time of the management buyout of National Freight, he was a Director of one of its companies. He reminded me that my account of the company's privatisation, under my brother-in-law's guidance, is not a complete story. Over 100,000 employees became shareholders at a stroke – the biggest jump in Margaret Thatcher's privatisation campaign in the early days.

Many of the truck drivers were reluctant to subscribe, even at a bargain price, so everyone was given a token share. They soon regretted rejecting the "once in a lifetime" opportunity to risk some of their own cash to buy a decent sized stake, and must have envied the thousands of their colleagues that did.

The National Freight buyout offered shares at a very attractive price to all employees, with bank loans available for employees, such as the truck drivers, unable to raise the capital. To keep things simple, the initial shares were priced at £1. It was very successful, although initially it involved a great deal of hard work for the management, travelling around the country to persuade the workers to invest money in the company. Moreover for most of the employees it was their first ever Stock Exchange investment. Philip would always quote feeling very apprehensive about one truck driver who, he found, had mortgaged his house and put all his savings into buying as many shares as he could, into what was after all a very speculative investment. After not many years, this man has become a millionaire, fortunately, but he could have lost everything.

Before his premature death, aged 59, Philip was recruited by the British Council and the Foreign Office on a voluntary basis, to advise Governments in Eastern Europe on the privatisation of their state owned enterprises. He had been very successful financially with National Freight and felt that he needed to give something back to society. He was particularly thrilled with "his" first privatisation in Poland, which entered the new Polish Exchange as company Number One. His contribution to assisting former Communist economies transform themselves into today's free market successes, has never been properly acknowledged.

It was hugely encouraging for me. I had a paper published ten years earlier by the Monday Club, indicating how I believed many of our state industries could be sold off, attractive to savers who had never become investors. Now it was beginning to happen, and there were plenty of supporters in Margaret Thatcher's Government keen to move it forward, particularly Nigel Lawson.

The earlier privatisations were selected because they were easier. British Rail hotels, the bus business, Rolls Royce, B.P and others, were not monopolies or utilities essential to our lives. They were also, on the whole, profitable, so not too hard to sell off. The more difficult State enterprises came later. But, one by one, they were returned to shareholders who were encouraged to become investors for the first time, by attractive bargain sale prices.

My particular concern was that the public, not only City institutions should benefit, and that the privatisations should be organised, principally to spread the ownership of shares and not primarily to raise money for the Treasury. I was publicly critical at some of our earlier efforts, which appeared to line the pockets of the merchant banks too generously. As a former stockbroker, I could also see that many smart dealers abused the system, by making multiple applications, knowing the shares would be over-subscribed and would start dealing on the

Stock Exchange above their issue price. There were some professional short term speculators, who borrowed many thousands of pounds from the banks, as a cheque was required with each application. These cheats used a list of perhaps one hundred false names and post-box addresses. I knew of City dealers who made thousands of pounds from each privatisation by selling their successful multiple applications immediately, waiting for the next bonanza.

Stricter control could have stopped this. When the French started to follow our example with their privatisations, much later, they found a way of preventing such abuse. The application forms had to be handed in to your own bank branch. The bank would then finance the purchase, if you had made proper arrangements with your branch, to obtain the shares on your behalf. This avoided multiple applications and made it less easy to cheat, unless you had many bank accounts! Moreover, the French ensured a fairer allocation. Everybody, rich and poor were only able to receive a set amount of shares up to a modest limit. Such simple measures stopped the abuses. No doubt they learned from our mistakes, but we should have done more in this direction.

There was another flaw in our arrangements which the issuing merchant banks could have prevented. But it was contrary to their interest to do so! The price at which each privatisation was issued was fixed by the issuing banks and those who advised Government. It was supposed to be attractive enough for investors to scent a bargain, but not too cheap to upset the Treasury, anxious to collect as much as possible.

Fixing such a price was always going to be difficult, since general market sentiment can change quickly, day by day, according to unforeseen events. So the banks advised the Government to have the issues underwritten, that is, guaranteed, in case investors did not come forward for all the shares offered. Such underwriting, to cover risks and ensure the Government got its money, were very costly, and highly profitable to the banks because they managed to fix the selling prices low enough to ensure the underwriting was unlikely to be called.

I believed there was a better way, without costly underwriting, which would have guaranteed small investors a profit, but still given taxpayers a fair deal. What could have happened is an auction by Government of a small percentage of the sale, with the City institutions bidding against each other. The highest bidders would get their shares and dealings would start on the Stock Exchange.

A public offer for sale could then follow, at a tempting discount to the winning auction price. This system would have ensured the big investors did not get their privatised shares too cheaply, but a market would have been set by them. It would have guaranteed the taxpayer a fair deal and other public investors, rationed, with no-one getting more than a fixed number. But at a nice discount to the established market price.

As the institutional investors, pension funds, insurance companies and investment trusts were offered only a small percentage, initially, to establish a market price, they would want to enter the market when dealing began in the remaining stock, offered to the public. The big investors would want to build up their holdings, so ensuring the general public would see a paper profit on their applications.

My proposals were attacked by those who argued, suppose a privatisation was not underwritten and not fully subscribed. Would not the Government have failed to sell its shares? My answer was simple – Why should it matter if not all the State's shares were mopped up in the initial offer. The rest of the shares could have stayed with the Government "on tap", as demand developed. Many Government "Gilt Edged" loans are sold this way, "on tap" as investors want to buy when market conditions improve. In due course the issue is fully sold, as would surely have happened with any privatisations not fully taken up initially.

I would have imposed a further condition, which would have put the spivs out of business. It would not have been beyond the wit of the City for brokers handling the deluge of sales in the early days of dealing, as short term investors cashed in their profits, to be obliged to collect a tax on sales in, say, the first six months. After all, brokers have to act as taxpayers already, collecting Stamp Duty for the Treasury on all Stock Exchange dealings. This would have discouraged short term new issue dealers, making sure more of the privatisations were placed with longer term investors. It would have built up a larger number of real new investors and so ensured the establishment of a stronger capital owning democracy.

My interest in the privatisations was not only to see more people sharing in the nation's assets. I was particularly anxious to see our main energy utilities, electricity and gas, sold to the private sector. My concerns were that both these state monopolies were frustrating the energy policies I believed were needed. It was essential for our economic prosperity that we had secure, adequate, efficient and competitive sources of supply. That was not likely to happen under the existing State utilities.

British Gas was abusing its monopoly, offering to convert all-comers to our North Sea supplies, at unrealistically low prices, so that every business and householder wanted a connection. This distorted the energy supply. The resource was squandered, sold at prices that encouraged waste instead of providing incentives to use it more efficiently. Now that our reserves are running down, the day of reckoning is with us. We have to import increasing proportions of our gas needs, at much higher world prices, and from long distances sources like North Africa, Russia and the Middle East. These can hardly be described as sources as free from political risks as our own North Sea.

When our Energy Secretary, Peter Walker, was ready to slot the Gas Industry into the privatisation programme, an agitated Sir Dennis Rooke, the British Gas Chairman, invited me to lunch at his HQ. As a senior member of the Energy Select Committee, he hoped to make use of my influence. With a touch of anger, he said to me "I built up the Gas Industry. It now supplies most of our heating and industrial requirements. Why should it now be sold off?" There was an unreasonable attitude of "it is my fiefdom". I suggested to him that it was a national resource of great strategic value and should not be underpriced and should be used efficiently. He could not expect to isolate us from the World energy market. Rather than sell it to UK consumers below World prices would it not serve the British economy better if we sold it at market prices, even if that meant exporting some?

David Howell, when our previous Energy Secretary, had courageously imposed price increases on Gas, at 10% a year for three years, to reduce the imbalance between oil which was taxed, so distorting the market. Dennis Rooke did not approve, but it was a correct thing to do; I was one of the few M.Ps to say so in the House of Commons. There is a powerful argument that gas is a premium fuel and so more of it should be used for electricity production, together with district heating.

The Dutch, although they had discovered large reserves in their sector of the North Sea, decided to use much of their gas in combined heat and power plants, close to urban areas. This provided electricity and space heating in buildings, with a combined fuel efficiency of 80%. Was this not a more efficient way to burn our Gas? This is precisely what has been happening since privatisation. Market forces in the private sector, have shown that higher profits can result from this increased efficiency and reduced pollution.

Another important benefit from Gas privatisation, which is helping us towards a more rational energy policy, is that the monopoly of the gas grid has been opened up to all. North Sea Gas producers are no longer at the mercy of the State monopoly as their only buyer. Gas landed on- shore can now be sold directly to large consumers, and there is more market price related competition. Even more important, British Gas discovered they can make more money by converting their gas into electricity and selling it in competition to the electricity utilities, and then also selling their hot water for heating, again competing with the electricity companies, who try to sell us electricity for space heating.

This more rational use of a premium fuel would not have come about without breaking the monopoly. Now, if gas supplies from the North Sea or elsewhere, are not offered a market price by British Gas, they will sell it on the open market and British customers would have to do without. That is the free market in operation; and it works.

The privatisation of our state owned electricity industry was far more difficult. The principal problem was who wanted to buy our aging and inefficient nuclear plants. More than half the world's nuclear plants, in many other countries, were in the private sector. But they were economical Pressurised Water Reactors (PWRs). Foreign utilities learnt from our mistakes and selected a less complicated, expensive to build and run, design, rather than the hotch-potch of indecision that is the penalty for pioneering a challenging new technology.

Cecil Parkinson was appointed by Margaret Thatcher in the June 1987 reshuffle, as our Energy Secretary. He had to grapple with the problems which came to light in deciding the structure for the electricity industry in the privatised market. As work proceeded, it was revealed that the nuclear industry, anxious to expand its market share, had hidden its real economics. The cost of de-commissioning nuclear reactors was unknown, since none had yet been dismantled. So some very unrealistic guesses emerged. Then we had to face the dilemma of costing the disposal of spent nuclear fuel. All sorts of figures emerged, mostly guesses, since to date nobody had found a way of doing it that would satisfy not just environmental lobbies, but politicians with responsibility for the safety of the nation.

Our Energy Select Committee tried to offer advice, after fact-finding visits abroad, particularly to Sweden, to see how a most safety and environmentally concerned society were doing it. Very deep underground storage in the most suitable geological conditions was their answer and our recommendation. But it would be the most costly method. However, how does one judge the financial cost and balance it against a cheaper, but less permanent and secure disposal? These were and are complex but critical issues. Their difficult and costly solution undermined the Government's plans to privatise nuclear electricity.

A botched up solution was proposed. The CEGB, our monopoly generator industry including our nuclear plants, was to be split into two companies – a big National Power, so large it could absorb the less desirable nuclear plants, and a smaller PowerGen. The twelve regional distribution companies were to be privatised separately, as was the National Grid.

But when something near the true costs and liabilities of the nuclear industry were exposed, this solution was blown apart. The City's advisers, who had to prepare the prospectuses and invite investors to subscribe, told Cecil Parkinson it was "no go." With Margaret Thatcher anxious to get the industry off the Government's books, it was decided to exclude the oldest nuclear reactors, our first generation of Magnox, from the National Power portfolio. These were now the least efficient and would be the first needing to be shut down and dismantled.

Even this did not satisfy investors, and it was clear that fear of open-ended liabilities and financial risks that were just not calculable, made an offer for sale almost impossible. By 1989 Margaret Thatcher lost patience and John Wakeham was called in to replace Cecil Parkinson as Energy Secretary and sort out the mess. By this time some of us who had studied the industry, realised that the whole of our nuclear industry had to be isolated and, at least for the time being, stay in Government hands. That was John Wakeham's solution. Unfortunately he did not at the same time redress the imbalance of one big and one much smaller generating company. It distorted the structure of the whole industry.

The proposed framework went ahead, flawed as it was. Meanwhile I had become highly critical about the plan to privatise the regional distributors as separate businesses. I was convinced this would prevent true competition. The alternative pattern of a vertically structured industry would work better. My preferred solution was to split the CEGB up into more than two companies, but to allow them also to own a portfolio of regional distributors. That way we would have a handful of competing businesses, not just generating but also selling; an integrated group of competing utilities.

What particularly appealed to me in this structure was that integrated companies with retail outlets would be eager to develop co-generation – producing combined heat and power, the sale of useful heat, as a valuable by-product from electricity generation. This pattern is what has allowed most other European countries to develop heat grids, with electricity utilities more localised and responsive to customers' needs, which are not just power but also heating. A privately owned utility, anxious to maximise profits, would see, I believed, the commercial advantage of selling heat as well as power.

A second important reason why I criticised the Government's privatisation structure, was that I believed integrated utilities, competing with each other, would be more interested in experimenting and investing in renewable energy. This would start the long overdue development in the UK of power stations burning waste as a fuel. Solar power, wind power, tidal and wave power would be, I was convinced, more likely to take off. The previous monopoly CEGB was not interested. Private utilities could see profitable outlets.

My outline for the electricity industry was not followed. Yet now it has happened by default. The industry removed from State stranglehold, has had to restructure itself. Today's industry bears no relation to the flawed position in which the Government left the electricity industry. I was to play an important role in establishing a more sensible and viable structure when I was appointed as Chairman of the Major Energy Users' Council.

The mess we made of electricity privatisation and the failure to invest in nuclear power are two striking examples of what happens when a Government lacks an energy policy. There are others. We should have used our North Sea Gas more efficiently. We were well behind our competitors in providing incentives for more efficient, less wasteful use of energy. Other European nations have not made their citizens suffer from fuel poverty.

We still have not invested in the enormous potential around our coast – the waves and tides. Most of our combustible rubbish is still dumped in landfill sites. Only recently has Government adopted a policy I advocated thirty years ago, to tax combustible landfill and use the proceeds to reward the investment into power stations using waste as fuel. We are a long way behind many of our European neighbours in heating our buildings from the steam that is produced from electricity production. Instead we still prefer to throw it away into the atmosphere in enormous cooling towers from our power stations.

Britain is built on coal, yet we have all but closed down our coal industry, rather than invest in the technology that exists to burn it more cleanly. Only in recent years have we seen incentives to invest in renewable energy. We could have done much more by now.

The cause of all these failures I attribute to a reluctance to admit that Britain needs an energy policy. We have even had Conservative Energy Secretaries who have claimed they did not believe in an Energy Policy, such as Nigel Lawson. That is why our industry suffers from higher costs than our competitors. That is why millions of our lower income citizens cannot afford to heat their homes adequately. That is why we now have to import nuclear electricity from France; oil, gas and coal from all over the world. That is why we have lost strategic security, since far too much of our energy now has to come from politically unstable sources.

If we do not need an energy policy, why do we need a defence policy, an economic policy, a taxation policy, an education, health and law and order policy? What is misunderstood, even by Conservatives who should know better, is the difference between a policy and a plan. Socialists try to plan and control. Private enterprise business and industry has to follow a policy, for research, production, marketing and investment for future growth – or go under.

Governments also need a strategy, such as providing the right market signals. An energy policy is one that uses fiscal carrot and stick, to promote investment, provide as much security and self-sufficiency as possible and achieve higher levels of efficiency in the provision and use of our energy. Without policies we cannot ensure that our economic welfare is not handicapped by higher energy costs than our competitors. And what about Global Warming? Does not energy strategy have a part to play? I would not invest in any business that rejects the need for a strategic aim. It is the failure of Governments to guide our energy provision and use that has landed us in the mess we have today. Privatising our state industry was a good start. But just as the rest of our private sector needs and accepts Government guidance – a policy – so does our supply and consumption of energy.

Chapter Thirty
Around the World

Parliamentary life includes many opportunities for official trips abroad. The disrespectful media call them "junkets", which is certainly what some of them are. However, most if not quite all, do have a serious purpose. The majority of foreign visits which I enjoyed were undertaken as fact finding tours, mostly concerned with my energy interests. The other trips are mainly aimed at allowing M.Ps to improve their understanding of other countries. Such visits also help to counter our prejudices, that if "it was not invented here it cannot be worth seeing."

The Inter-Parliamentary Union (IPU) exists to foster the relationship between democratically elected Members of Parliament over the whole world. The Commonwealth Parliamentary Union (CPU) does the same, but with the countries of the Commonwealth. Frequently, Members would be asked to host delegations from other Parliaments hoping for return visits to their countries. More often I found myself entertaining than visiting. Canadians, Australians, Japanese and many others were shown around Parliament and given lunch. Sometimes we made good friendships which endured outside the Houses of Parliament. It was through the IPU that I first became involved with entertaining the Romanians at Westminster.

Party Whips enjoy their responsibility to influence who goes and where. Absence of leave from the Westminster hothouse is granted by the whips. Most invitations from overseas governments or parliaments expect all-party delegations, so such visits remind members that there are occasions when they need to get together and temporarily call a truce to party politics. It is an important tradition that, when representing your country abroad, you show a united front and avoid party squabbling. Some hotheads find that difficult.

Whips from all parties use overseas visits as disciplinary tools. They employ and apply sticks and carrots. A "goodie" can be rewarded by being offered a particularly desired jaunt. Caribbean islands are favoured. However, some less attractive locations are used as a "punishment", perhaps to keep a vocal Member away from the House.

Shortly after my first rebellion in the voting lobby on a matter of principle which did not coincide with the party line, I was "invited" to join a three week delegation to Namibia. It would have been difficult to send me further away. But it was less of a punishment and more of a fascinating experience, particularly as it took in De Beers' diamond coast.

This was in the late 1970s, before the revolution that transformed South Africa from an apartheid society, strictly ruled on the principle of white supremacy, into a progressive multi-racial state.

The visit started from Johannesburg where we saw some of the less pleasant and repugnant gulf between two standards of living and totally separated societies. Observing the transformation today, it seems nothing less than a miracle that it all happened relatively peacefully.

Namibia was then a South African protectorate and did not achieve independence as a republic until 1990. Formerly the German protectorate of South West Africa, I still found relics everywhere of German society and influence, including German speaking communities in Windhoek.

Along the Atlantic Ocean coast, in one of the World's harshest deserts, is De Beers' concession, a coastal strip of diamond mining. Some of the World's most precious stones have been found on or near the surface, brought in previous geological ages by rivers coming from far inland Africa, to the sea.

A tour of the area was one of the highlights of our visit. Security was tighter than in a prison. Many miles of high impenetrable electrified fencing surrounds the extremely long concession area, from the Skeleton Coast in the north to Lukeritz in the south. As diamonds can literally be found lying on the sand, all employees are screened on exit from the enclosed working area. No vehicles are allowed in or out, as diamonds found by workers could easily be concealed. All employees were x-rayed on leaving so that any stones swallowed could be detected.

Not even British M.Ps on a delegation were trusted. De Beers were not taking any chances with Honourable Members. We were subjected to the same tight x-ray screening. De Beers have succeeded in protecting their world domination of the diamond market and the world price, only by such draconian measures. The outer perimeter, along and around a hundred miles of fencing, is patrolled and monitored, as smuggling by employees, in collusion with helpers outside the fencing, is a perpetual risk.

Not all newly mined diamonds are stored in the safes and vaults of De Beers, despite all these precautions. But without them, the world price of the precious stones would quickly collapse, as not even De Beers' vast purchasing power could hold up an oversupplied market due to uncontrolled and illicit extraction.

Official visits are not just first-class travel, five-star hotels and more banquets than are good for you. They also involve serious discussions, exchange of views and exhausting fact-finding visits to sites with the host country's M.Ps. They also often commit you to help host a return visit to the UK.

Another of my more interesting visits was to Bulgaria, while it was still entrapped in the dark ages behind the Iron Curtain. I sought advice from sources I believed knew something about living conditions there, because I wanted to bring some useful presents for our hosts and for Bulgarians who serviced our stay in the hotels and guest houses. It was suggested to me that, amongst the many commodities in short supply, cosmetics, particularly lipsticks, were available only on the black market. As Hilary owned a small chemist shop in Tring at the time, she packed me up a box containing about a couple of dozen different shades of lipstick.

Our luggage was opened up on the Bulgarian border. Not even M.Ps were trusted not to import such dangerous contraband. The officials raised eyebrows on inspecting my baggage. When I handed out a few lipsticks there were no further questions. However, my fellow M.Ps enjoyed teasing afterwards.

I always like to explore on my first time visits to foreign parts on foot. I found that the restricted itinerary of official visits did not include enough time for wandering and seeing the places and people. Much to the apprehension of our Communist hosts, I went for a stroll on my own whenever I could, followed, of course, always "for my own safety" by some sinister looking dark suited heavyweight official security thug. I also kept a notebook with brief comments on what I saw and heard throughout the visit. My notebook was "mislaid" one evening and mysteriously turned up the next day. I had apparently "dropped it", or so I was told. Back in the UK I reported this strange experience. A Foreign Office official was not surprised. He claimed that the Bulgarians believed that every Parliamentary delegation included one MI5 agent, "Your hosts obviously believed it was you!"

In Sophia, outside our official well-protected residence, I was stopped after dark by several young men, asking me if I had hard currency, dollars or sterling, offering to give me Bulgarian currency in return at a huge 30% premium over the official exchange rate. I resisted having been briefed that this was illegal, but hinted that I had a suitcase full of lipsticks. I was disappointed that my cosmetics currency did not interest them. However, one boy pleaded with me "Please may I have your jeans?" I never did find anyone who wanted lipstick and returned with a load back to the UK, but without my well worn jeans.

Sofia was a pitiful sight in the late 1970s. Hardly a building gave one the impression of a capital city. Shops were depleted, especially food shops. Walking around I would see one after another of empty, drab, food store windows. Then suddenly one would come to a queue, perhaps up to one hundred metres long. As a former journalist and by nature, I was inquisitive. I found someone who spoke English and asked what they were all queuing for, as the line lengthened by the minute. She did not know, but did not want to waste time and lose her place, going to the front to find out, "It must be something good, fresh supplies just come in, mustn't it?" I walked on to the shop to see. A truck load of potatoes had arrived and unloaded its precious produce from a co-operative farm.

The next day our itinerary took us out to the countryside with a visit to a co-operative farm. This was a selected "show-case" farm; even so, it looked a shambles. Masses of tomatoes some starting to rot and other vegetables were lying about. I asked why they were not being picked and packed and sent to the towns into the empty shops. They were waiting for transport I was told. Along the sides of the roads in the countryside, we could see plenty of produce, but it did not seem to be going anywhere. So efficient was the state ownership of the "means of production and distribution" that people could starve amid plenty. A powerful argument for privatisation.

At the weekend, I saw perhaps a hundred small cars coming back in the evenings to Sophia. None of them would have ever passed a British safety test inspection. Each was crammed with a family coming back into town after a tour of scavenging in the countryside. Each packed with produce brought from the outlying co-operatives and the few private farms still allowed to exist. So if you were one of the few privileged families with a car, you could go and collect. If not, you went without or shared with friends. The chaotic failure to market even basic necessities convinced me, if I needed convincing, that the Communist system could not long survive. Bulgaria had the potential not only to feed its people on more than potatoes, but also to provide a surplus, which has been proved since the collapse of Communism.

There were other foreign visits during my time in Parliament, each opening up a different view of the world and completing my education. Tanzania was particularly fascinating. We travelled the thirty-six hour railway journey from Dar el Salaam to the Rift Valley lakes. The railway was built by the Chinese and was aimed to impress a nation rich in natural resources and so strengthen the Chinese economic and political ties. The scenery was impressive and the places full of colour. We were presented with various local fruits, which unlike those that make it to our European markets were properly ripe and delicious. We had a programme of visits which included one to a drinks factory. Gin, Vodka, and Rum were produced and we followed the whole operation. Afterwards each member of our small delegation was presented with a bottle of each.

My trophies, along with ripe pineapples, were brought all the way back home, for, I hoped a ceremonial tasting with family and friends. Each bottle was labelled appropriately. We opened each in turn. They were not only too powerful to drink more than a small spoonful at a time; we found it impossible to taste any difference between them. We solved the problem of what to do with the quantities of liquor, by using it to flambé our Christmas pudding. It lasted for several years, creating sensational flames as a highlight to the Christmas feast.

There were other less adventurous visits to America, Canada and the Middle East, but which all added to my knowledge and which I put to use in Parliament. As a fluent German speaker and with a good knowledge of French, I was also selected for important delegations to France, Switzerland and Germany, often helping colleagues with more modest language skills.

There were other visits abroad which were not officially parliamentary ones. Various political or interest groups would sponsor fact finding visits to inform parliamentarians of different issues. These would be privately arranged, although of course the Foreign Office would be aware of them and would arrange for some sort of embassy or consulate contacts. On the whole they were more satisfactory than the official visits as one could decide on what one wanted to see, rather than be shuffled around on an itinerary chosen by one's hosts.

One most memorable experience was a visit to Jordan, Palestine and Israel under the auspices of the Bow Group. The visit took place in the spring of 1992, well before the building of the separation walls, when travel around the country was much easier. As a German Jewish refugee, I was of course an avid follower of the situation in Israel and was a member of the powerful Anglo-Israeli Parliamentary Group. I was on the Israeli Embassy's "invitation list" and enjoyed their hospitality at the various Conservative Party Conference venues. I was therefore most keen to go and see for myself what went on in this "brave little country."

The group included wives, often excluded from the official Parliamentary delegations, and our visit was arranged to include a fair bit of sightseeing along the way. We started off in Jordan, with a stop in Amman. For the first time ever I met and heard from some Palestinians. Having always regarded them as less educated, less cultured and detached from our Western way of life, I was surprised and impressed by the meeting which we had with several of their leaders. We met members of the Palestinian delegation to the Middle East peace process, including Hanan Ashrawi. Looking back, I now remember the shock I felt with the realisation that she so closely resembled my own sister and that the Palestinians were not the outlandish underdeveloped Arab tribe we had been taught to expect, but were intelligent and educated "cousins" to the Jewish Israelis. For the first time we began to hear the other side of the story to the one I had grown up with.

Our time in Jordan was not all serious discussion. We went to see Petra, that extraordinary place with its timeless atmosphere. We approached as all visitors do now, through the Siq a narrow natural gorge. The available transport was either camel or horse. I decided to walk. My wife, having rashly admitted that she could ride, was despatched on a horse, bareback. I caught up with her later at the famous treasury. This is not the place to describe Petra, so many guidebooks do that, but it was an incredible sight and I am determined to go back and see it again. At that time there were still one or two families living in the caves, and one of our guides, the owner of Hilary's horse, was born there and showed us his old home cut high in the rose coloured cliffs.

The following day we were taken north of Amman to the site of Jerash, one of the Roman Decapolis, or ten towns, forming the eastern frontier of the Roman Empire. Unlike most former Roman towns that had been destroyed in battles and built on over the centuries, Jerash was hit by earthquakes and the site was abandoned. As a result most of the ruined town survives, if precariously, with its temples and theatres, market places and houses. Again I vowed to come back again with more time to spare. It was on the edge of Jerash that we found a Lebanese restaurant and first discovered real excellent Lebanese cooking.

After our brief sightseeing tours and fully briefed by the Palestinian peace process delegates, we set off for Jerusalem. We went by coach from Amman to the Allenby Bridge over the River Jordan, which even in 1992 was reduced to a slow flowing brook due to the water extraction up stream.

It was at the checkpoint after crossing the rickety bridge over the river that we first encountered the Israelis. There were two entrances into the customs area, the one for visitors like us and the other, at the far side of the compound, for the Palestinians living in the West Bank who had travelled to Jordan to visit relatives and were now returning. Our entry point was relatively civilised, in that our suitcases were unloaded from our coach and we took them through the customs area on trolleys. The Palestinians' baggage was unloaded from the roof of their coach by enthusiastic baggage handlers, who threw them down on the ground with as much force as possible, before throwing them again onto the conveyor belt which disappeared into the building.

I saw several smashed bags on the ground with their contents scattered in the dust. There was only one conclusion to be drawn in my mind. The whole procedure was a deliberate exercise in humiliation, a psychological game to declare who was the boss. It was not simply a justifiable security search. The Palestinian passengers, mostly women and children were herded into their building at gunpoint. We saw all this. We were told, but of course had no way of verifying it, that they were subjected inside to humiliating body searches. From what we saw outside I could well believe this.

After an interminable wait we were passed into the customs area where our baggage was opened and searched and everyone with a camera had to take a picture of the roof of the building, to ensure that the camera was genuine. I had brought with me some oranges from our hotel in Amman. Although they were probably Israeli in the first place, they were grabbed off me and thrown into a waste bin, as probably "diseased and dangerous". I was having none of this and insisted on reclaiming them and passing them round our group to be eaten there and then in front of the officials.

We had already gone through some fairly humiliating body searches, with one of the wives having been virtually undressed to her underwear. She pointed out later that they concentrated on the fair haired blue eyed Aryan types for their most embarrassing searches. I was rather annoyed and disgusted by this time and marched off leaving poor Hilary to deal with the luggage. She grabbed my passport and leant over to the customs official and told him that they had upset her husband dreadfully. She showed them in my passport where I was born, in Berlin, and explained that I was a German Jewish refugee. She rather "egged" the story by saying how much I had been dying to see Jerusalem and how their attitude had completely spoiled it for me.

The whole atmosphere changed immediately. The fact that most of our number were Members of Parliament from another country counted for little. But suddenly, as a holocaust survivor, I was important. The rest of our group were hurried through the customs check quickly. The senior man in charge of the post arrived down and took me on one side, apologised for any difficulties I might have had and wished me well for my trip to Israel. He completely ignored my wife and the rest of our party. It seemed a British Parliamentary delegation were "non people".

We continued on towards Jerusalem making a short stop on the way at a small Palestinian refugee camp. I was appalled at the conditions in which they had lived for years. Just within sight of the village where they had originated and been ejected from, was a settlement of mud brick houses with a watch tower flying the Jewish flag at the entrance. Here we found some of the children spoke good English and they took us around, showing us at one place, where a house had been bulldozed down. We met the family that had lived there, now obliged to live with others. Evidently the fourteen year old son had sabotaged the telephone wires to the camp guard box and in retaliation the whole family had been made homeless.

We made our way towards Jerusalem and the American Colony Hotel. This amazing place, built as a sort of respite area for a group of American Christians in the 1800s, is still a sort of neutral ground where Jews and Arabs and others can meet and feel comfortable. The visitors' book has some fascinating names of past guests. Lawrence of Arabia came there after his epic crossing of the desert, and Graham Greene and Winston Churchill stayed there. The following day was Palm Sunday and Hilary had been looking forward to the monks' annual procession from the Mount of Olives into Jerusalem with palms. However, we were told that the Israeli authorities had cancelled it as there were "too many Christians" in Jerusalem because the Orthodox and Western Easters had coincided. Hilary mused what would the reaction be in Britain if a Muslim or Catholic religious festival had been banned by the Government, or synagogues compulsorily closed.

It was with a shock we realised that in the course of a day, we had completely changed our views. We had got up in the morning, sympathetic to the Palestinians but definitely pro-Israeli; we went to bed that night, without doubt, pro Palestinian and shocked at what we had seen and experienced.

Our sightseeing tours included a trip to the Dead Sea, the climb up Masada and most memorably a tour of the Old Town of Jerusalem conducted by an Armenian Christian professor, who was born there. He knew everybody and took us around parts that no tourists usually see. Even in 1992 we could observe the gradual encroachment of Israeli building around the hills of Jerusalem and the buying up of the older buildings, such as the former home of the Knights of St John of Jerusalem, by the Jewish Orthodox sects. We were taken to the temple mount and the Al Aqsa mosque.

We also visited Bethlehem and were shown around the Manger Church by the mayor. Again we went where normal tourists never go, into the vast caves under the church, which were used for storage and for animals at the time of Christ. Away from the rather gaudy decorated chapel that is purported to be Christ's birthplace, we saw the plain caves beside it, which seemed much more authentic.

Our visit had a much more serious purpose and the sightseeing was only relief from this. In Jerusalem we visited hospitals and were shocked by the number of Palestinian children we saw there suffering from injuries, most of them acquired when they were at school in the playgrounds, from bullets fired over the walls. There certainly appeared to be a policy to shoot to maim, judging from the number of blind children and those with missing limbs.

The climax of our journey was our visit to Gaza. At that time much less controlled than today, but nevertheless a disturbing experience. The juxtaposition of the houses in the Jewish settlements, with their swimming pools and green lawns, liberally watered, to the Palestinian houses, where the water, at the time, trickled from the taps a sort of brackish brown, having been drawn from where the sea leached in, was a stark contrast. Even here, however, we met with highly intelligent and well educated people, trying their best to lead civilised lives. We went on the beach and met some of the children. Talking to them, we found that they all had marks of rubber bullets somewhere on them, usually acquired when they shouted back at the Israeli soldiers or the Settlers. They all spoke excellent English, thanks to the schooling provided by UNESCO. But what sort of future waited for them. Even then the restrictions on travel by the Israelis were beginning to bite, and if they left Gaza or the West Bank, even for medics taking examinations, they could not return for years. There seemed to be deliberate policy of removing any intellectuals from the area.

No doubt some of these punishments resulted from boys throwing stones at their Israeli occupying masters. But one could not help believing Gaza had, even then in 1992, been transformed into a prison. My question to the attaché at the Jerusalem consulate, who had recently come from South Africa, was "which would you prefer to be, a Black in South Africa in the apartheid era or a Palestinian in Gaza?" His immediate answer was "Oh without doubt, a Black in South Africa!"

I came away from this visit profoundly shocked and very troubled as to the future. When I see what has happened since it was with good reason. I had been for so long an Israeli sympathiser, not simply because of my Jewish genes, but because I understood the long history of the conflict between Jews and Arabs, required the acceptance of a Jewish State and an independent Palestinian Nation within the 1967 boundaries. I was not only concerned with the plight of the Palestinians, but also of the attitude towards them that was being inculcated into the young Israelis during their compulsory military service. I feared for them too. Having come from Nazi Germany I could see only too well how this racial divide might play out.

I was invited later to talk to the pensioners at the Golders Green Synagogue. Ostensibly it was about my life in Parliament and how I had achieved so much as a refugee. I could not resist, however, telling them about my trip to Israel and Palestine, and warning them of obvious troubles to come if the Palestinians were not properly accommodated in their own state and the Israelis continued to build on Palestinian land. I was not well received. When I described the situation as even more unacceptable than the former South African apartheid regime I did not actually have anything thrown at me, but it was obvious from the questions and the aggressive noises that I was regarded as a traitor. Hilary and I escaped from the place, but not before we were taken on one side by a group of Jews from the audience, who said, "well done, you are quite right of course, but – indicating the rest of the audience - they are not, and probably never will be, ready to hear it!"

Chapter Thirty-One
Decline and Fall

Margaret Thatcher had many eminent qualities that made her our best leader since Winston Churchill's wartime premiership. However, some of us believed she lacked a robust enough sense of humour, so helpful for a politician to survive in the Westminster jungle.

Those of us with her during her eleven years as our Prime Minister have recollections. One of mine was the occasion when I had a private dinner with her in the Members' dining room. She did not often have a free evening. When there was such an occasion, she would ask her loyal, congenial Parliamentary aide, Ian Gow, to invite three or four of her backbenchers to join her for dinner.

Before he was tragically murdered by the IRA, Ian knew how to organise such a meeting on her behalf with skill. He was a popular link between the backbenchers and a leader pressured by Prime Ministerial duties. An elaborate procedure was devised on such evenings to make the whole arrangement appear spontaneous, rather than carefully organised.

On one such occasion, Ian sought me out in the afternoon in the Chamber to ask me if I was free that evening. When he explained what was planned, I made sure any alternative plans were put on hold. I was asked to be in the Members' dining room by 7.30pm and to be seated at a table for four. Two other Conservatives M.Ps were due to join me, but I had to make absolutely sure that the fourth place remained unoccupied. In no circumstances would the usual informal custom be observed on this occasion, that any fellow Conservative, walking into the dining room could seat themselves at a vacant place on any table where the company appeared congenial. Normally, such informality would ensure that any vacant place would be occupied a few minutes after our planned arrival.

Margaret Thatcher would have been briefed which table to walk to and ask if she could join us. I discovered that my other dinner guests, recruited by her aide, were new Conservative M.Ps, still rather overwhelmed when Margaret sat down with us. Their shyness, untypical of Members, was reflected by an embarrassing silence after the usual greetings had been made. It was left up to me to open up the conversation.

I thought it would be easier to break the ice with some light hearted banter, rather than the more serious matters that were bound to come up later. It was at this point I must have lost my presence of mind. I opened up the conversation in front of my silent colleagues by addressing our guest of honour, "Margaret, did you see this week's marvellously funny episode of 'Splitting Image'?"

I could not have frozen the atmosphere more if I had tried. The TV's most popular satire in the 1980s, 'Spitting Image', consisted of viscously cruel caricatures of politicians and prominent people. Their portrayal of Margaret was beyond the decent standards of humour, but we loved it. Unfortunately, she had not forgotten their recent brilliant sketch, portraying her cabinet as a row of cabbages. I should have anticipated that Margaret did not enjoy their sketches of herself and her husband Denis, which were well over the top. While my colleagues found it difficult to suppress their mirth, Margaret gave me the worst scowl I can have ever received. With a grim face, without saying a word she turned away ignoring me and proceeded to speak to the other two table guests for the rest of the meal. How not to impress your Prime Minister and mark yourself out for promotion, I thought.

There was another occasion I witnessed, which has been widely reported because it happened in the packed Chamber when Margaret was answering Prime Minister's Questions. This incident, curiously, can be interpreted both ways. It either showed that she had more of a sense of humour than any of us realised, or that she was completely oblivious that she had made a really funny remark.

The Question she had to answer from a Labour Member, was critical of her staunchest ally, William Whitelaw. He had been Chief Tory Whip, Leader of the House, Secretary of State for Ireland, Employment and Home Secretary under

Margaret's leadership. A most distinguished career caused us to regard him as Margaret's Deputy Prime Minister. Some were rude enough to tease him with the name 'Thatcher's Poodle'. But then Parliament is an unforgiving, cruel place.

In response to the aggressive attack on her loyal colleague, she stood up and said "Every Prime Minister needs a Willie!" The Chamber erupted in loud mirth. She turned round, stern faced, to look at her hysterically amused, backbenchers, apparently wondering what the laughter was about. Perhaps she knew? We never discovered if she was teasing us or had no idea what had so amused the House.

I cannot think of any colleagues who enjoyed observing the decline and fall of our greatest post-war leader. Not even those anxious to replace her were happy to witness the end-game. Much has been said and written about it. I had an observant backbenchers' view. When Margaret lost her Chancellor of the Exchequer, Nigel Lawson, in October 1989, he spelt out his reasons in a devastating resignation speech. The thrust of his anger was that Margaret preferred to listen to her select group of outside advisors, like Sir Alan Walters, rather than to her Chancellor. So he claimed.

It was the first serious crack in her control of the Cabinet, but there had been earlier tremors. In particular, when Michael Heseltine stormed out of the Cabinet meeting, resigning over the Westland helicopter affair, in December 1985. His anger was not so much that he, as the Minister responsible, did not get his way; he walked out because he was not happy about the lack of open discussion in the Cabinet of such an important strategic matter, and the manner in which decisions were taken in a less than democratic process. It exposed the divide in the Conservative Party, whether to support American domination of our defence industry or go into a European helicopter partnership.

There were certainly increasing rumbles in the Parliamentary Party, indicating the feeling that her backbenchers were being ignored, treated as voting fodder and not much more, to be dragooned by the Whips regardless of individual opinions. Advice from backbenchers was sidelined, even when it was well informed and an earlier, more open forum for the exchange of views and consultation, was forgotten. Another view held by her Parliamentary troops was that there were too many 'yes men' in her cabinet and too few prepared to argue their case. Backbenchers and many in the Cabinet saw decisions taken by an inner cabal.

Discontent and grumbles about leadership and decision taking in Government came to a most dramatic head in November 1990, when Geoffrey Howe, her former Chancellor and Foreign Secretary resigned and delivered his bombshell of a speech to Parliament. His analogy of trying to play cricket when the team captain had broken his bat, was a killer. His judgement was undermined, he claimed, by a dysfunctional Cabinet. Having become Leader of the House and deputy leader to Margaret Thatcher, he could no longer stay in his position, as a supporter of Britain's role in Europe, while Margaret became increasingly hostile and belligerent particularly in her opposition to us joining the new monetary union. As a former Chancellor, Geoffrey regarded this as damaging to Britain's interests.

His relationship with Margaret had become increasingly strained. By all accounts she treated him with less and less of the respect to which he was entitled and far less than his ability and intelligence deserved. Other Cabinet members were also unhappy that Margaret was becoming increasingly isolated, developing a 'bunker' mentality, with only a small inner circle advising her, rather than allowing all other Cabinet ministers to contribute.

I observed Geoffrey's resignation speech, which was without doubt the catalyst that led to her downfall. Knowing it was coming that afternoon, the Chamber was packed. Members were crushed together, almost sitting on each others' laps. Considering the size and width of too many M.Ps' bottoms, this was not a pretty sight or a comfortable position. I escaped the crush by finding a place on the side benches, at the furthest end of the Chamber, opposite The Speaker. From there, I could see the faces of the Members on our benches as well as those of the Opposition.

The House has an instinctive sixth sense. A critical moment in political history can be signalled in advance. Resignation speeches are always heard in silence, out of respect. But what could not be hidden, and my position gave me a direct view, was the rows of glum faces on our side. If I had occupied my usual position, behind the front bench, I would only have seen rows of backs. This time I saw the facial expressions, and the few nods of agreement, as Geoffrey explained with sadness and obvious distress, his reasons for abandoning ship. The moment he sat down to approving murmurs of respect all round, I realised that Margaret was finished.

It had been some months earlier that Hilary and I had been able to entertain Geoffrey and his wife, Elspeth, for lunch on the terrace of our old converted stone bergerie in Provence. They came out for holidays to our French hill top village of Montauroux, staying at a nearby villa which belonged to Sir Bernard Audley, whose public relations firm conducted private opinion polls for the Conservative Party. Mark Thatcher also had stayed there, as I understand Margaret did herself on one occasion.

Some years before, we had been in the village market with some friends, when Hilary noticed an obvious Englishman wearing sun glasses, in a bright pink shirt, shorts and sandals with a mass of curly hair, at one of the stalls. "Oh" she said "that man looks just like Geoffrey Howe" – "Nonsense" I said, as he disappeared into the crowd, "All Englishmen on holiday look like Geoffrey Howe!" We thought no more of it, or of the appearance of the Mark Thatcher look-alike that motored rather fast through the village. It was a year or two later, when Geoffrey was Foreign Secretary, that the phone rang. "Hello, Geoffrey Howe here, I understand we are neighbours!" Evidently, as Foreign Secretary, he had been met officially off the plane in Nice by the Honorary Vice Consul, Ronnie Challoner, an old friend of ours. Hearing where Geoffrey was staying, he had told him that we were in the same village.

We were amused at times, seeing and meeting Geoffrey about in our village, when the local population was apparently completely unaware that they had the British Foreign Secretary next to them, queuing in the bank to change money or in the market. I cannot imagine a senior French Minister doing the same.

Even at this time in our conversations, when we were invited round for lunch, it was obvious that he was uneasy about the direction in which the Government was going. Although always discreet, one detected undertones of concern. I quite understood Elspeth's anger later about the treatment which Geoffrey had received in Margaret's Cabinet. I was, however, quite convinced that the joke going the rounds at Westminster and the media was quite untrue. The gossips were saying that Geoffrey's resignation speech was the best that Elspeth had ever written. What nonsense. He was more than capable of writing his own and did, to stupendous effect. I admit to being biased as one of his supporters. I believe he would have made a good Prime Minister despite his slightly low-key style.

For those who had to observe it, Margaret's downfall had the air of an unfolding Greek tragedy. After her triumphant defeat of the Argentines and the liberation of the Falklands in 1982, she was a heroine, swamped with the upsurge of patriotic, flag-waving fervour, not seen since VE Day in 1944. She had been swept back to power in the 1983 election with most of us and new seats won, revelling in her glory. The nation was prospering. So what went wrong? Nothing that could not have been foreseen and avoided.

The economy was booming, Arthur Scargill had been humiliated, the Labour Opposition was demoralised and the nation's finances were recovering from the previous Labour Government's waste, extravagance and incompetent overspending. The tax burden was being reduced and the State Sector was being cut as our nationalised industries were being privatised. As in my dreams and hopes, we were creating a real capital owning democracy, not just with home ownership but also participation as owners in our flourishing economy.

What went wrong has often happened to entrenched leaders all over the World, when they start to believe they know it all and can do it all, in some sort of bunker with a throne increasingly isolated and surrounded by those unwilling to challenge proposed policy. So, despite good advice, the Poll Tax was enforced in an unworkable form and the Cabinet became too presidential. A psychosis of invincibility and infallibility took over in Number 10. In her speeches the 'I' started becoming the royal 'we'. One by one, her best ministers, whose advice and guidance might have saved her, were removed or walked out in despair. She gradually lost the confidence of many of her cabinet and the British system of collegiate Government was breaking down.

It was not only the Poll Tax, which was just one example of how a presidential style led to ill thought through policy. Many in the Party, of which I was one, believed we were not re-investing more of the fruits of our economic recovery. I likened it to a 'company doctor' rescuing a near bankrupt GB plc. But having started to balance the books, a good manager would also start looking ahead to modernise and expand the business. Margaret was reluctant, as was the Treasury, to believe that Britain was no longer near bankruptcy.

In my view, we had reached a recovery by the mid 1980s, when we should have increased investment in our infrastructure. Why no modern high-speed rail network? Why refuse to support a new London Airport offshore in the Thames estuary? Why a refusal to invest in the Channel Tunnel or make a massive improvement in our inadequate education system? Why not new nuclear power plant, tidal barrages, less wasted energy?

I regarded it a wasted opportunity when we should all have been making Britain more competitive. If we had done more then, our economy would not be so weak today. Every business has to share its success, its profits, between shareholders, ie tax cuts and investment in future projects. We cut taxes, but refused to fund the improvement to the infrastructure that was the State's responsibility. Others in our Party thought likewise.

A large section of the Party was also upset when Margaret became more divisive on European issues. She seemed to regard our membership of the European Community as some sort of punishment, an evil we had to live with, an enemy we had to fight. Others in our Party, myself included, regarded our membership as the great opportunity, deserving not just our reluctant support, but an enthusiastic commitment to offer leadership.

I recall the mood of the House when Margaret returned from a European summit in an angry frame of mind. The media likened her handling of delicate negotiations, as "waving her handbag" at our partners. Shouting in the Chamber about her refusal to agree to even the slightest further moves towards "federalism", with her ranting "No, No, No," pleasing the anti-Europeans in our Party, but seriously worrying and antagonising those who believed our future was in Europe. How could we ever get our way on any compromise discussion, by raving at other leaders? She found it difficult to accept that any partnership required compromise. Nobody gets all their own way, but everybody should get some. Britain's stance ensured we got none.

When Margaret announced in a media interview in 1990 that she intended to go "on and on," it was the spark that set off a simmering Party to find someone to challenge her. The rest is history. If only she had, instead, given notice of her intention to stand down before the next election, she would have avoided her embarrassing defeat and would have "gone out" on a wave of goodwill.

It was around this time I announced to my constituency officers that I would not be going "on and on." I would not be standing at the next election, due in 1992. They would have two years to find a candidate. I could not be sure if there were more of my constituency management committee who were pleased than those that regretted my announcement. But I got the clear impression from the voters and the local media, when they heard of the decision, that they were surprised and disappointed.

However, I was 60 and would be 62 by the next election. The thought of carrying on for a further four or five years did not appeal to me. It is a strenuous and stressful life and I saw too many of my colleagues who should have given up years ago. The thought of perhaps having to be carried through the Division Lobbies in a wheelchair, did not strike me as a satisfying way to struggle on. Besides, although I had a good majority, my Erewash constituency was not a safe Conservative seat and needed constant work to hold it.

I was very much involved in the energy scene, as chairman of the Utility Buyers' Forum, which took up more of my time and Hilary's, as she produced a monthly newssheet. She was also heavily committed as a county councillor and chairman of governors. She was still working full time as my secretary and was also looking forward to some time for us to enjoy more relaxation together. Our new life, during our recesses, in France, was also beckoning. Why not have more time, while we were still active and fit enough, to enjoy a leisurely retirement?

Of course in reality there was little for me to stay on for. I was by-passed for any ministerial appointment and would certainly not be chosen now. That was never my main ambition, but perhaps a hope in my early years. Later I discovered I could achieve as much, if not more, than many junior ministers. Their lives were more eventful than that of a senior backbencher, but ministers have little power unless they move up into the Cabinet. Their job is full of frustration, finding it often too difficult to persuade senior ministerial colleagues to support initiatives. They are tied in by the system, requiring rigid team work. There is no opportunity to speak out of line or on any subject not in their departmental responsibility.

Another disappointment for me was that the Energy Select Committee, through which I had made my principle contribution to Parliament, was abolished, when the Department of Energy was incorporated into the Department of Trade and Industry. No doubt the Government welcomed the opportunity to "write us out" of the political records. Our reports were often outspokenly critical, particularly on the sort of issues I have described earlier. My own contributions to the Committee had been influential. Even many of the topics to be investigated came from my suggestions being accepted by other members.

We always combined our criticism with constructive and alternative policy suggestions, but most of our recommendations were ahead of the consensus view. The idea of an energy policy, involving less reliance on imports, more progress with renewable and nuclear and above all cutting the waste of energy in the way we produce and use it, although regarded as mainstream today, were ahead of their time in the 1980s. No wonder ministers and some of the Civil service advisors found us an embarrassment. But as Parliament took so little interest, our departure was little noticed. So much for the contribution I and my colleagues tried to make on such vital matters affecting our future.

It is some satisfaction for me to see many of my themes for an energy strategy have now moved to the top of the political agenda, even if today they are ploughing the same ground that we did years earlier. I have no doubt that before much longer most of our committee's reports will be recognised, acknowledged and implemented.

Chapter Thirty-Two
Standing Down

The House of Commons has not been described as the best club in London without reason. There is a great deal of camaraderie between the Parties. The benches in the Chamber face each other in a confrontational way and the verbal fighting is bitter and sincere at times. But anger is confined to policy differences and is rarely personalised. Much of the vitriolic argument is contrived rather than genuine.

Once out of the Chamber, with its constant exposure to the television cameras and observant press in the gallery, the atmosphere is quite different. There are many all-party committees, such as the investigating Select Committees, whose members from all parties work together and try hard to achieve consensus on issues which the opposing sides in the debating chamber can never admit to reaching. Select Committee members know that their reports have more impact and carry more weight if they reach unambiguous conclusions and recommendations.

There are also at least a hundred and fifty all party groups where like-minded members meet and work for a common objective. These groups cover very specialist subjects, act to lobby Government and brief themselves from outside interests. Such groups cover every possible subject of concern to the public at large, where a voice in Parliament is desirable. There are groups for every sport and every nation in the World.

Although I was not a member of the Parliamentary Squash group, a story from them came my way. In the maze of cellars under the Houses of Parliament, where Guy Fawkes was discovered "just in time", are showers and changing rooms. A left-wing ex-miner, Labour M.P. played squash regularly with an ex-Eton Tory Member. The Tory is reputed to have said after one strenuous squash session, "Isn't it amazing, we can shout at each other angrily across the Commons' Chamber, but we can still be friends and enjoy a game and have a shower afterwards?" "Yes" came the reply from the Labour man, "the only difference between us is that I would not risk bending down to pick up the soap!"

After twenty two years, it was with a little sadness that I approached my pre-determined retirement. I was preparing myself for my escape for when Parliament would be dissolved at the forthcoming election. We believed that this would not be before 1992. John Major, having been recruited at the last minute when Margaret resigned, to challenge Michael Heseltine, needed as long as possible to rebuild voter confidence after the traumatic events surrounding Margaret's dismissal. Major, after all was barely known in the Conservative Party and was certainly not a vote winner in the Country.

The last months before the General Election were rather like the last weeks of the last term at a school you loved. There were lots of emotional goodbyes between those of my Conservative colleagues also standing down. We were gathered on the famous House of Commons terrace, alongside the river, for a grand souvenir photo. Our late leader was in the centre surrounded by all of her departing, long serving veterans.

It was time, I believed, to move on. I looked forward to enjoying the rest of my life with Hilary and our children and friends. Although Hilary was still involved as a County Councillor for Hertfordshire, we had the prospect of spending more time in our second home in the Var, rather than the odd week snatched away from Parliamentary and Constituency duties. Most of our away time in France had been during the school or college holidays and Parliamentary recesses. We looked forward to seeing the place without the tourist crowds, and to joining in with the local social life, both ex-pat and French.

However, before removing myself from the public arena altogether I felt I had the responsibility to undertake an important task. I had to help restructure our unsatisfying privatisation of the electricity industry. British industry, business and large energy users were profoundly unhappy at the flawed privatisation of the electricity industry. The structure selected by the Government was artificial and did not provide the competitive market promised.

I was introduced by Lord Ezra, former chairman of British Coal, to the Major Energy Users' Council and was appointed as chairman, to head a lobby to correct the errors. The MEUC was a sort of CBI of Britain's largest energy users. Members included a wide range of corporate intensive energy users such as cement, chemicals, steel and railways, as well as our leading multiple retailers and services like Boots, Marks and Spencer, Tesco, the banking sector and many others with a large number of retail outlets, leading to a combined significant consumption of energy. Water companies were also members. The Water industry is the UK's largest energy user. Local Government authorities were also hit by large energy costs.

The directors or senior managers of these organisations, responsible for energy provision would represent their companies at regular meetings, to discuss and deliberate on strategies to re-structure the electricity industry. Much of our work was to persuade the regulatory body to force more competition. The MEUC also had an important educational side. Presentations from leading consultants and from those energy managers with proven purchasing skills would show other members how to get better bargains from the utilities. Energy utilities were invited to tell customers what they had to offer and answer critical questions.

We needed some form of contact point between the widely distributed and very varied organisations for which we were acting as a lobby. Hilary, in her role as my secretary, was sent in search of suitable publishing software, which was less common at that time. She is fortunately a quick learner and The Major Energy User, a monthly newsletter, was started under my editorship, which outlined progress. Energy companies were invited to contribute articles outlining how they hoped to improve their service to large customers. Meetings were also organised at the premises and HQs of our energy utilities, with briefings from them to our members. These site visits proved a valuable opportunity for personal contacts between providers and their customers. We had continuous contact with the regulatory bodies.

We organised large conferences in different regions, where members could gain advice from speakers selected for their special expertise. The presence of the media helped our organisation gain a platform to expose our complaints publicly. One of my principal contributions was as the organisation's spokesman in the media, with frequent requests from radio and TV, business and news programmes, gaining plenty of coverage in the business sections of our leading newspapers. The Major Energy User, which was distributed to all the member organisations, also began to gain a circulation amongst other influential voices in the energy world. We were quoted on occasions in the regular media and made progress towards the provision of more competition from utilities.

Andrew Bainbridge, who founded the forum, was a shrewd public relations director, running his own business skilfully. He was not only the exclusive shareholder owner of the MEUC, but also its executive director. With my public profile the organisation became recognised as an influential voice, achieving some success in correcting the flawed structure of the electricity industry. We had the full support of the Regulator.

A landmark occasion occurred when the MEUC was summoned to appear before the Energy Select Committee. As I was still an M.P. and a senior member of the Committee, I found myself with a dual role, either questioning my MEUC colleagues or answering questions from my committee colleagues. There was clearly a prospective conflict of interest. It was at my request that the Committee was enquiring into the lack of competition in electricity supply and the MEUC was the key witness. My only solution was to sit back quietly with the other Select Committee M.Ps, and having, as chairman of the MEUC declared my dual role publicly, not taken any part in the questioning. I had however, helped to brief the MEUC team and the Select Committee beforehand.

There were other occasions when we were very much in the public arena. The Monopolies Commission summoned MEUC as witness to their enquiry into energy pricing. On that occasion there was no conflict, and I was able to lead the team with answers fully prepared for the Commission's questions. The finances of the MEUC were run as a private business by Andrew Bainbridge, the owner. Corporate members paid an annual subscription. Not even I as the titular chairman was able to see a balance sheet or profit and loss account. As the organisation became successful and gained recognition and publicity, this structure began to worry me and many of our important multinational corporate members. The feeling grew that although MEUC appeared to be a well run, increasingly effective and influential lobby, it was assumed to be a non-profit making institution along the lines of the CBI or TUC.

Those of us concerned in the running of the MEUC, our technical director and the organising committee, felt we were deceiving the outside world and that our credibility would be undermined as an important national body if it was seen to be our founder's private business. Along with me, our group wanted to restructure the whole organisation with a proper constitution. Sadly Andrew Bainbridge would not consider selling out or any other form of reorganisation which would protect his legitimate entitlement yet would reform MEUC as a properly structured institution.

In spite of many attempts to reach a solution, matters came to a head. The larger members, unhappy about the pretence that they were subscribing to a non-profit making, independent organisation, demanded a change to something which had a genuine respectable public face, not just a private consultancy. We could make no progress and I was asked if I would head up a break-away group with identical objectives and operations, but democratically structured, with a non-profit making constitution. Using the undoubted expertise and skills of the technical directors, Bob Spears and Richard Wills, we called ourselves the Utility Buyers Forum, which was immediately successful thanks to the committed group of corporate directors. My deputy chairman , Michael Warrander, the energy director for Diaglo, the multinational drinks group which includes Distillers and much else, was particularly supportive. Our monthly newssheet continued, under the different name.

It was an unhappy and unnecessary split with us becoming competing rivals. But having tried so hard for a compromise and failed, we believed it was the only honest way to proceed.

Having worked energetically over some years, even after I had left Parliament, to build up the high reputation and the membership of the UBF, I decided it was time to retire. In reality, we succeeded in getting genuine competition, a restructured electricity industry, which bears no comparison today to the original privatised version. The need for our continued lobbying was becoming less necessary. With our persuasion the regulatory bodies had eased the way for market forces to do the rest.

The transformation was radical. Although much of our electricity production and supply has now been taken over by French and German utilities, competition exists as vertical integration has combined power producers with retailers. The Grid is open to all. Private generators of electricity, such as wind generators, now have access to sell directly to the Grid or to third parties, at fair market prices.

By the time I had escaped from Parliament, at the 1992 General Election, I had played an important part in correcting the errors in our privatisation of the energy utilities. After Parliament I continued to Chair the organisation until satisfied that we had corrected the flaws in our privatisation structure. It was time to start to take a back seat and to downsize ourselves and spend more time in Provence.

While standing down in 1992 offered us a relatively early retirement, still young enough to enjoy a more relaxed life, there was a penalty. My Parliamentary pension after twenty two years was hardly lavish. Members retiring or those who lost their seats at the 2010 Election, would be horrified if they knew how much more modest was our retirement income in 1992. It did not worry me because our lifestyle does not depend on extravagance. Nor do Hilary and I judge our quality of life on our income. We now live in a community where wealth is not and does not need to be ostentatious. We do not judge or establish social strata according to our income. What a contrast to modern Britain!

Chapter Thirty-Three
France

My love affair with France, thankfully shared by Hilary, started during my student years. As a Geographer, our course included "field studies". One for example, was based in France in the Lyon-Grenoble region. For a Human Geography Honours degree, as opposed to a Physical Geography one studying the landscape and geology, we were concerned about the impact of the environment, such as the climate, the Alps, the Rhône River and the Massif Central, on the evolution of industry, agriculture and the history of urban and rural habitation.

It was my first proper visit to France. Although I had of course seen the Alps before with my skiing trips with my father to Davos, with the tidy and orderly Swiss scene, I had never experienced the sort of culture that France presented in the 1950s. In Grenoble at six in the morning the markets were already under way with their local produce of fresh fruits and vegetables. I was faced by the mile of charcuterie and cheese stalls, which stretched through the centre of Grenoble, with the local mountain cheeses and other 'terroir' foods. It was impossible of course to try every one, but I made the attempt. I have a passion for cheese and after the austerity of Britain, with our factory produced cheeses after the war, Grenoble was a sort of food heaven. Today the city is unrecognisable from its 1950s rural agricultural market hub.

We now see an elegant modern regional capital, a science and technology nucleus. The rows of elegant town houses, quintessentially French, speak of a former, more leisurely time. The torrential Isere tears its powerful way through Grenoble, pouring its huge volumes of melted Alpine snow down to the

Rhone at Lyons. My favourite way of using my spare time, other than cheese sampling, was to take the cable car up to the hills above the town and walk on into the surrounding countryside.

Outside Grenoble rural France after the war was also still backward. Life appeared to resemble the sort of picture one had in Britain from the school French primers. I had not really believed that people still washed their clothes in the 'fontaine' and certainly never imagined that ploughing continued to employ oxen. I was also amazed that in 1950 hotels that provided more than seatless 'hole in the ground' toilets, were the exception. I have no doubt that life was extremely hard for these people, but it was also very picturesque and attractive to the outsider. The bustling agricultural economy was then the back bone of France. Thank goodness it still remains important.

Today, with the motorways, the TGVs, tunnels, airports, the high-tech industries, science parks and all the trappings of an ultra modern society, it is difficult to find the old Grenoble which so attracted me, under the surface, as we drive through on our way to the South of France. The transformation of France from a relatively backward rural economy, into today's advanced technological economy, deserves my admiration.

Later, I learnt to appreciate Paris, spending many days wandering through the streets, with their fascinating, contrasting arrondisements and of course the 'Left Bank', Montmatre, the museums and art galleries. The extraordinary vitality of les Halles and the particular smell of the mixture of herbs, vegetables, flowers, the garlic and the gaulloises cigarettes, permeated the air. However, all this and even the Louvre, although magnificent, was not my favourite. It was the Rodin Museum that I had to visit and revisit.

My most unusual and memorable experience in Paris, was with Hilary at the start of our honeymoon. Arthur, my new father-in-law, had evidently been brought up as a strict Baptist and knew nothing about alcohol, portrayed as "the abomination of the devil", until adulthood. After a defining experience with a codfish on a Belgian fishmonger's slab, which he felt he had to punch on the nose because it was "looking at him", after he had drunk some 'caraway flavoured' drink, Arthur determined to educate himself about alcohol. As a result he became an expert in wines and insisted on making sure that his children were brought up to appreciate their subtle differences and characteristics.

Arthur became a member of the 'Conseil des Echansons' of Paris, a very select group that indulged in elaborate and exclusive wine tastings, whose seal of approval was widely sought by the wine producers. I was never told if my grandfather, a wine merchant in the Rhineland, belonged to any similar group. One of Arthur's greatest friends and fellow Conseil member was Monsieur Ravet, a French wine merchant, who offered us a Sunday lunch at an exclusive restaurant in the Bois de Boulogne. Before the lunch, we were taken on a tour of his premises and taken down into the large cellars underneath. In the far corner we were shown the way into his special "cave", which had remained bricked up all through the German occupation of Paris. For five years all his best wines were secreted away and never found by the occupiers and had now rejoined his stock. Only special guests were offered a bottle to sample at his table and we were included.

Having chosen our wines, we then proceeded to the restaurant, where I had my first experience of the French Sunday lunch. We started at noon and finally rose from the table just before six in the evening. With each course, appetiser, fish course, main dish, 'trou Normand', cheese and dessert, we had a different fine wine from Ravet's cellar. It was an amazing meal and I can still, after nearly fifty years remember the flavours. I did however, have one disappointment. For my main course I ordered 'cassoulet', expecting a casserole of stew or something similar. I received, of course, the French classic dish of beans and fat pork served in its own cooking pot, enough for about four people. Ever since my boy-scout days and National Service, I detest bake beans and I do not like fatty meat, but looking longingly at Hilary's choice of 'pintade' with ceps, I swallowed my pride and did my best to swallow my meal. I am ashamed to say that in the same circumstances today I would have insisted on her making a swap. I realised then I had much to learn about French cuisine. My academic French exam qualifications were not enough to save me.

Much more of France filled and enriched our lives later, when we explored the different corners. Our honeymoon, a slow dawdle through France into Italy in one of those Septembers when the summer seems never to have ended, included days enjoying the chateaux on the Loire, moving south through the Burgundy villages, where the signposts read like an expensive restaurant wine list. Then down the Rhone to Provence and the Riviera, where Hilary, although born and bred in England of English parents, decided she had found her real home. We passed through Antibes, accidently missing the old town which was to become later such an integral part of our lives, to reach Italy; then down towards Florence, Sienna and Rome. Eventually we made our way to Pompei and Herculaneum before returning via Venice and visiting my German relatives en route in Konigstein im Taunus near Frankfurt.

We had some excitements along the way. Our suitcase containing my wedding suit and Hilary's "going away" outfit was stolen from our car in Cannes. We wondered what the thieves made of my grey topper and 'tails'.

It was in Rome that our complete lack of Italian came into play. We failed to work out the Italian classification of their hotels, which seemed to be the reverse of the French or English system, and decided to find a small auberge type of establishment, in the older part of Rome. Using a dictionary, we found a place with a notice 'rooms to let' and I went in to book us in. "How long for?" the proprietress asked. She seemed slightly surprised when I said two or three days, and then, even though the place seemed empty of other guests, took us up an ancient staircase to the fifth floor of the mediaeval building. The room was amazing. It was an attic room, with sloping ceilings but it had a large terrace along one side which backed directly on to the Roman Forum. How romantic we thought.

We left our bags and went to explore the area and find our dinner. Even in the 1960s the traffic in Rome was terrifying. Crossing the road was a real hazard as the cars seemed to aim themselves at any hapless pedestrian. The phrase "the quick and the dead" seemed to sum it up. By the time we had found a tempting restaurant and came to return to our hotel the place had come alive and the streets had filled up with people out for the evening. The transformation in our hotel was complete. We barely recognised the building we had checked into earlier. The large reception area with its sofas running along the walls was suffused with a warm red glow. The proprietress was behind her reception desk at the far end and the sofas were draped with attractive young ladies, rather skimpily dressed.

We were greeted with welcoming smiles as we scurried past and up the steep staircase to our attic – the 'Boheme Room'? At last we understood why we were on the top floor, out of the way. However, we had not yet experienced all that our 'hotel' had to offer. The room was lit up with coloured light as the sound of operatic music came from outside. We were the backdrop for the son et lumiere performance on the Roman Forum. Flames licked up the walls as

Rome burned and we had the sounds of battle and singing. It was rather like being on the set of a grand opera like Aida. We did not get much sleep with the comings and goings, the sounds of footsteps on the echoing tiled stairs, and the lights and the noise from the Forum, but then who does on their honeymoon, especially if they choose to check into a brothel?

Later, there were many camping holidays as our family enlarged, with particularly happy explorations of Normandy and Brittany. It was not until 1974 that we decided to buy somewhere in France to escape for the holidays. The problem with holidaying in Britain was that one was always interrupted by a constituent with some form of problem and you were always at the end of a telephone. Nowadays with the mobile phone, the concept of really having a break away from it all, seems impossible, but then the best solution was to be abroad reachable only in real emergencies.

We set off every summer for the South of France, exploring the coastline and what were then miles of unspoilt beaches. We came again to Antibes, but this time found our way into the old town and immediately decided this was where we wanted to be. The heart of the old town, the ancient Greek and Roman citadel with the chateau which Picasso had used as a studio, had mostly been restored. However, the surrounding area of narrow streets and tall 'back to back' stone houses was virtually a slum. Many of the houses were tenements, often sharing one 'hole in the ground' lavatory. We found a run-down stone house, number 2 rue des Pecheurs, and set to work to restore it.

Our Antibes house was near to the traditional market, the ramparts and the maritime archaeological museum. A narrow cobbled street, barely wide enough for a very small car to squeeze through, separated us from the equally squalid three to four floored houses opposite. We were only a few yards from the sea, over the town walls.

The best part of the three storey house was the flat roof, a higher attic floor having been removed at sometime. It, like most of the neighbouring flat roofs and balconies, had been used by the previous occupants for drying the washing. The concept of creating an outdoor living space was quite alien. Our marvellous local builder constructed for us a tiled terrace with walled beds and replaced the scruffy low access doorway with a small glass fronted room facing on to our new roof garden. I set out to create my first Mediterranean garden with oleanders, plumbago, rosemary, lavender, Cannae and even an orange tree.

We would sit out in our garden, where we even had a small view of the sea at the end of our road.

Although we could bar prying eyes from the houses around, we could not shut out the aromas of all the neighbours' cooking in preparation for the evening meals, nor the endless chatter every evening in the narrow street below, where the local women would congregate on their kitchen chairs and gossip. They would fall silent as we passed and then resume again as soon as we had entered our house. There was one other house in our road which was English owned as well, and I think we were the only two houses there at the time which had proper bathrooms with 'sit down loos'!

Fortunately, there were not too many people with telephones at the time, as when a phone rang it was impossible, when sitting on the roof, to work out where the sound came from as they were all the same standard French phones. One was permanently rushing downstairs to grab the phone, only to find it was ringing in the house opposite. But unfortunately, all round our French peasant neighbours had TVs, which they kept blaring away in the hot evenings through the open windows. Most of the residents of rue des Pecheurs were tenants of Italian origin. They spoke a heavily accented Provencal French which was difficult to understand.

This was still very much a French artisan land. Around us were small workshops with mattress makers, carpenters, potters, glass blowers, furniture makers and many other craftsmen. Our children would spend hours watching from the street as craftsmen worked making objects that in England were mass produced. The ground floors and many of the cellars were used as workshops. Ours were filled in with rubble and we emptied one side out, when we restored the house, to create a bedroom. We found we had a former stable with a stone manger and iron rings in the walls to secure the animals. Amongst the rubble we found the pieces of a large ancient pot which Hilary managed to put together. We later saw its double in a museum dated from the 12th Century.

A year or two later we decided to excavate the much larger cellar which was at the other side of the house so that we could create another larger bedroom, semi-underground, in the coolest and quietist part of the house. At the time we had Hilary's brother, Philip and his wife Jill, staying with us. They had three sons, Timothy, Julian and Rupert who along with my own older children, Judith and Bruno, were persuaded to help. I hacked out and filled builders' buckets and for a tempting pocket money payment of several centimes per load, they carried them away.

Finding suitable places to dispose of rubble was not easy in the old town. They started by tipping buckets over the ramparts on to the beach. Sunbathers soon complained and chased them off. So the enterprising work gang, determined to earn their promised pay, started tipping in the nearby public gardens. The flower beds and under the palm trees were soon covered with little mole hills. Not knowing about their enterprise, I thought all was going well, until a stern looking French lady in a black uniform, knocked noisily on our door, speaking in a loud voice so that the whole neighbourhood could hear. She represented something like the Antibes Green Spaces Protection Society and had followed the boys back to their base. By this time my daughter Judith had left the team, rather wisely scenting trouble.

Excavation slowed down, as I had to move much of the remaining rubble away from the town in the boot of my car. The job was finally finished by our builder, who was amazed that we had even tried to do the excavation ourselves. The cellar we found had been a winery and had a beautifully tiled press, the sort where you toss in the grapes and strip to leap in after them to crush them with your feet. On the lower level we found the head of a Roman column which had obviously been used to wedge under a barrel, and beneath the clay floor we found some small pieces of pottery, which the archaeological museum identified as Greek.

All that remained to complete our new bedroom was a bed. The odd awkward entrance with the narrow doorway and steps, made the provision of a standard bed from a store impossible. The only answer was to get the local furniture factory to make us one to order, with the mattress maker to complete the bed with a new lambs-wool mattress. The bed arrived in bits and was carried round by a string of the workshop employees, whistling as they came. The bed was put together, the huge double mattress completed the affair and we spent our first night in our new room. Later we got the mattress maker to split the large mattress into two smaller ones, as it was impossibly heavy to turn over. We still have the bed head in our spare bedroom and use the mattresses.

Our little house in Vielle Antibes became our hide-away for parts of the Parliamentary recesses, when we could decently not be seen in the constituency for a week or two. The run up to Christmas in the constituency was a hectic affair, with the visits to the various institutions and hospitals. We would have Christmas at home at Norcott with the family, a grand party for friends on Boxing Day and then pack into the car to celebrate the New Year in France. When we first started to drive down for the New Year there were no motorways and we had to cross London to the Dover road, to take the ferry across the Channel. We would spend a night in an hotel with the children on the way. It was a crushed and uncomfortable journey. Today the whole trip can be done in a day from door to door on motorway standard roads, using the Channel Tunnel or we can take a quick flight from Luton to Nice.

In the summer, we would come down separately. I would enjoy the drive, gradually unwinding, while Hilary would set off with the children with our VW Camper van and take in various sights on the way. We would all meet up in Antibes and I would be ready to hear about their adventures, fishing in the Loire, visiting the cave paintings or exploring the Rhone Glacier on their way down.

In spite of all our efforts to persuade our children to learn to speak French, they would always identify the other English children on the beach within ten minutes of arriving. Hilary would send them out to buy things at the small local shop nearby and to practice their French. She was impressed by the way they managed so quickly to buy what they wanted. It was some time later she discovered that one of the assistants came from the north of England and was thrilled to be able to speak English to them. Even when we bought a French TV, Julius would turn off the sound and lip-read the American actors, dubbed into French. He became quite good at it. However, eventually something rubbed off on them and all four of them today speak excellent French.

In the 1970s there was no satellite TV or mobile phone. The London newspapers were only printed in London and shipped overnight to continental holiday spots. One could just about pick up the BBC World Service. But living abroad was then still like isolation from the home country. Following the Test Match cricket was almost impossible, although when we introduced ourselves to the only other English-owned house in the road; we found John listening to the Test Match on his roof terrace with the aid of his home-made aerial which consisted of a length of cable ending in a metal coat hanger. Even so, the reception was not very good!

The British newspapers arrived in Antibes about midday. There would always be a small cluster of Brits hanging about the newsagent by the port entrance to the old town area. Tables outside a restaurant and cafe opposite provided a relaxed way to wait for the van's arrival, over a glass of chilled Provencal wine. Many a day we would see Graham Greene sitting at an adjoining table at 'Chez Felix' also waiting patiently.

Graham Greene had become something of a recluse, as far as the English were concerned, although he was well known by the local French and took a very full part in the local life. He lived in an apartment facing the harbour, in a 1930s block of flats, lined with balconies, which were more like small terraces, overlooking the sea. Although fairly spacious, they were by no means luxurious and Graham lived a modest life there.

Hilary's father had of course been a classmate at Berkhamsted School with Graham, but unfortunately Arthur died before we had bought our French house. We would often speculate how much Arthur, as a confirmed Francophile, would have enjoyed the life in Antibes, the cafes and the local French characters, and of course meeting his former school friend again.

Arthur would tell us about his life at Berkhamsted School as a scholarship boy, describing the way in which the "free scholars" were regarded as lesser beings. One master in particular would pick on the scholars and on one occasion made them all stand up in class, while telling the other boys that these pupils were free-loading on them as their parents paid no fees and that they were to avoid them and make sure that they did not slack or put a foot out of place. After this occasion, Graham Greene, the headmaster's son and obviously shocked, went out of his way to make a friend of my father-in-law, asking his opinion and sharing conversations and valuing his abilities. As Arthur used to say wryly, he was top in the class in English above Graham Greene, but who had ever heard of him.

We would see Graham from time to time in the different Antibes restaurants where we shared the same taste in food, particularly our favourite fish restaurant. In Antibes he could move about freely and largely unrecognised. In spite of his very striking appearance, the English visitors were not aware of who he was. He was obviously very contented with his French life. If the French inheritance laws had been different, he might possibly have stayed there until the end of his life as a French resident instead of finally cancelling his "carte de séjour" and moving to Switzerland.

It was however, when Hilary became a governor at Berkhamsted School that she came to know him better. It was well recorded that Graham Greene did not have particularly good relations with the school in the early days, given his reaction to the sort of situation that Hilary's father described; it is not surprising that he avoided any contact there. Yet, he has always made a point of sending a signed copy of each of his books to the school library and as time went on and attitudes changed, he became more accessible. Contact was reopened, but by this time Graham was getting older and he was not persuaded to come back and visit the school officially although I believe he did visit the town of Berkhamsted.

Hilary's brother, Philip, was also a "scholarship boy", but in his case he was lauded by the school and held up as an example to others. How much things had changed. Perhaps if the school had tried earlier, Graham would have softened his attitude sooner. Anyone reading his autobiography "A Sort of Life" must be aware of how much his school days hurt. As it was, contact by the school had been re-established and Hilary got to know him, visiting him for tea and taking him books about Berkhamsted life, with old photos and talking about her father, whom Graham remembered well and regretted not being able to meet again. He was full of memories of life in Berkhamsted, outside the school. Hilary's interest in local history inspired him to describe his early experiences. It was evident that he loved the place and the people, but not the atmosphere in the school.

Where was I when all this was happening? Unfortunately, this all coincided with the House of Commons at its busiest. No 'pairing' allowed and certainly no time for trips down to the South of France for tea. By the time I did have some leisure, he had moved himself to Switzerland to avoid the French Napoleonic Laws to protect his intellectual estate.

Several people from the school were concerned that there was no recognition of Graham Greene at Berkhamsted, either in the school or the town. An annual festival has now been established, around the time of Graham's birthday, which has become an international event. With lectures, including from his biographer, Norman Sherry, rare footage of Graham Greene and the films of his books being shown in the local cinema, it is a very scholarly and fascinating occasion. The school has also now a blue plaque on the old 16th century school building, where Graham was born and brought up.

There was another coincidence arising from having a home in Antibes.

Our Honorary Consul, based at his apartment in Nice, was Col Ronnie Challoner. Our paths had crossed earlier, as I have already recorded when his public relations business in London handled Westinghouse's Nuclear Power plant promotion.

We had become good friends and when we found we were now neighbours in France, we often met up as families, mostly at his most attractive, very ancient stone house in the picturesque hilltop village of Le Broc, up the Var valley, north of Nice. Although he had his large apartment in Nice, he had bought the ruined house in Le Broc, which was part of the old village's fortified ramparts and had converted it into a charming house on many different levels. Our children loved it. Ronnie's wife Brett was Italian and a splendid cook. She was also a fanatical Conservative working tirelessly for the cause and returned to Kensington, where they had lived before moving to France, to help in every election. I am afraid she put me to shame as I withdrew from active involvement in the political scene, when I left Parliament. She sadly died last year but we always recall our introduction to some real Italian cuisine. Ronnie Challoner has also recently died. In his last years he had moved into Graham Greene's former home in Antibes. He would show us proudly the table where Graham Greene did his last writing, which had been left behind when he went to Switzerland. After Ronnie retired from his post as Honorary Consul, his daughter Pauline, who worked as a solicitor in France, took the job over.

The purchase of our house in Antibes involved a quaint procedure. It was long before Parliamentary expenses existed to have helped pay for it. The Harold Wilson Government had imposed exchange controls. Apart from the miserly amount which we were allowed to take abroad each year for holidays, to purchase property it was necessary to change sterling into a dollar-related premium currency. So the going cost was around 25% more than the Sterling price. That was bad enough, but at the seller's end there was another handicap – French capital gains tax at penal rates.

So, many similar property transactions involved a large undeclared cash payment. The French seller would insist on an 'official' price, much lower than we had to pay. They liked doing business with foreigners as the money was not visible to the French authorities. So we had to arrive at the Notaire with a suitcase full of notes. After the formal signing of the legal documentation the

Notaire would tactfully find a reason to leave the room while the cash was counted. Only when he returned and was made aware that both parties were 'happy' with the arrangement, would he put his signature to the change of title.

As Parliamentary duties and the children's schooling, only allowed us short infrequent escapes to France, and as we needed extra French currency to pay bills, we decided to rent the house out for a few weeks a year. After some time struggling with finding people to help clean and prepare the house, we decided to employ a local agent.

We had held a fund raising "auction of promises" in the constituency, offering our house as one of the lots. A family party of our local conservatives had made a successful bid for two weeks in our villa in the South of France and duly set off. When they arrived, Hilary received a call from them. The house reeked of cats and was full of fleas. The agent had evidently been round to the house at some time and had left one of the windows open in the cellar bedroom to 'air' the place. Antibes was overpopulated with feral cats. The beds were ruined as obviously the cats had given birth on them. It was horrendous.

My constituents spoke no French and the agent was not much help, beyond finding them an hotel for the night. Fortunately, we had some good friends who had a large "villa" on the Cap d'Antibes, Gladys and Bill. Gladys was an American and Bill had gone to the States many years ago from Britain and had been financially very successful. They had moved to France where they had brought up their family. In spite of having lived in France for years, and having daughters at University in France neither spoke much French and what they did was always with an incredible American accent. My children were fascinated by them and always liked to get them talking about places just to hear them pronounce the town Nice, like the English word 'nice', nearby Digne as 'dig nee' and Grenoble as 'Grenables'.

Gladys and Bill very kindly took my constituents in and saved my damaged reputation. It did have one plus. Our constituents were not likely to go round Derbyshire suggesting their M.P. had a "Grand Villa" in the South of France. That would have damaged our status far more than a few smelly cats.

The House had to be fumigated and the mattresses destroyed. The agency tried to wriggle out of their responsibilities for the damage. We did not use any agencies after this. As we had already got lettings for the House, Hilary made sure it was scrupulously cleaned to start with and we reduced the rent and explained that as we had no cleaner, could they make sure it was well cleaned when they left. Surprisingly, this worked. We never had any more problems and when we returned ourselves the place was immaculate.

Often we would lend to friends and one such occasion, when they were in occupation resulted in an interesting, informative experience. The occupants were expecting us on the Saturday and we were driving down separately, Hilary in the VW camper with the children and me by car. We arranged to meet on the Friday night by the Port in Antibes, but with few autoroutes it was too late when we arrived to find an hotel.

As the children were by this time comfortably tucked up asleep in the van, Hilary and I decided to prepare our car for a night's sleep in the marina. We had bedding from the van and with a foam mattress and some sheets and pillows, all that was required on a hot summer night, we settled down to sleep on the quayside. Hilary had wisely draped the windows with towels to preserve our privacy and we slept easily after the long drive.

However, too much of a nightcap awoke me at 3am. I needed to relieve myself. I got out of the car completely starkers and walked the five yards or so to the edge of the quay, for a 'piddle'. I returned to the car and climbed back into bed. Within minutes, the door on Hilary's side of the car was wrenched open and a young man looked down at her in amazement. He retreated shutting the door saying "pardon, pardon". We discovered the next day that we had parked in the heart of the Antibes' 'gay' district!

It was in my early years on the Riviera that I developed a fascination with the casinos. One occasion I had a week of recess without any constituency engagements, but as our children were at school and Hilary was occupied with various Council commitments, I decided to go down alone to the house, driving my new car, with a pile of historical books and biographies, borrowed from the excellent House of Commons library. I needed a few days to chill out.

The casino in Juan les Pins was fun but the Nice Casino, until it was wrecked by the mafia, was much more splendid. Having learnt over the years to resist temptation, I would never go in with more cash than I was prepared to lose. No cheque book or credit card, just perhaps up to £50 in notes. I was not one of the casino s big rollers. I would leave when I had lost or doubled my stake. I did do better than I should statistically as, on the whole, I won more often than I lost. Playing mostly the fifty-fifty odds, I patiently risked little and usually came out winning. Nobody could accuse me of playing the James Bond role, but I enjoyed watching the many addicts and their sometimes enormous winnings or losses.

On the last evening of this particular week alone, I packed my car ready to start the drive home. Before beginning the long drive through the night, back to Calais, I decided to call in at the Nice casino first for a last flutter. As usual I left my wallet and cheque book hidden in the car, to resist temptation, and parked the car in a nearby street.

I played and, unusually, I lost my stake and returned to find my car for the long journey back. The car had gone. I checked the surrounding area just to make sure I had not made a mistake, but the car was nowhere to be seen. With no cash, identity card or any belongings, not even my passport, I stood in the middle of Nice at 1am wondering what to do next. Would a hotel take me in, how would I pay or get home?

I found the police station. I asked them to phone the British Consulate who might vouch for me. There was no response. This was before the days when Ronnie was an Honorary Consul in Nice and I knew no-one there. The police probably did not believe that I was a British M.P., but they did find me a comfortable cell with a bunk bed and a blanket for the night.

In the morning we tried again to establish some identity. The Consulate confirmed that I was genuine. I was taken to the home of the local British Airways manager and given breakfast. He took my story on trust and organised a ticket for me on the airline. I managed to phone Hilary and explain what had happened and asked her to arrange to meet me at Heathrow with some form of identity, so that I could be admitted into the United Kingdom without a passport or any other means of proving who I was.

Hilary, rather brightly brought along the Times book of the House of Commons from the previous election, which had a photograph of me. She brought her own passport and then to prove she was indeed married to me, our marriage certificate. She went straight to the immigration area and after having proved who she was, she had to remain behind glass and identify me as I came through. It was the fastest I have come through an airport as Hilary pointed me out and we left together immediately. I have often wondered whether all stranded tourists receive the same VIP treatment. It would be nice to think so, but I have my doubts.

The sequel to this tale came some weeks later when we had a call from the police at Nice. They had 'found' my car. They could not have looked very hard for it as it was parked just round the corner from the police station, very dirty, having been left there for some weeks. They had been alerted to it by a woman who lived nearby concerned to see what had obviously been a new car, getting more and more neglected. There were several bits missing from the car, including the windscreen wipers and the back seat. My passport and wallet were gone, but so also was some of my luggage and some of the books which I had taken with me to read. Somewhere in the South of France is Gladstone's biography, prominently stamped 'House of Commons Library', probably quite a valuable book.

The Commons had returned from its recess by this time, so Hilary was despatched to Nice to organise the return of the car. I had forgotten that before I had set off I had bought several choice cheeses which were in my luggage, Chaource, Camembert and Brie. They had certainly matured in the super sun-heated car over the weeks it had been standing. The flies were fat and the stench was appalling.

Hilary had to wait while a local garage sorted out the car and put back some of the essential missing parts. We discovered why the thieves had taken the back seat, as it had still been in its plastic wrapping. It took weeks for the replacement to arrive after the car had come back to Britain. Eventually, Hilary was able to leave and drive home. The smell of cheese still lingered, but faintly. My casino visits were curtailed.

We had many happy times in Antibes, particularly as we had opportunities to enjoy the company of our four growing children. The times were precious to me, between such a high-pressured life. Our holiday breaks included walking tours of the surrounding regions of Provence and skiing in the nearby resorts.

However, as the years slipped by, the old romantic town we loved became more and more taken over by the tourist industry. Some of our favourite restaurants changed management and catered for visitors willing to pay too much for too little. Boutique shops replaced the traditional local artisans. The marina became enormous with a deep water port for the larger cruise ships and filled with the yachts of wealthy owners with their guests. The streets were all paved with pretty cobbles and at one time they even started to play piped music in the old town. However, this was stopped by a mass protest of the occupants. The old provencal Italian tenants had disappeared, no doubt to purpose built modern accommodation outside, while the old houses were all refurbished and became chic pieds a terre for the rich and famous.

The final falling out of love with our summers in Antibes was the fact that our car was repeatedly broken into. It was difficult to find anywhere to park and impossible to drive round the town. Out of season it still had its charms, but in July and August it became a monster, no longer the Antibes of our memories. Like so much of the Riviera, it was overcrowded, noisy and polluted. It was a hub for Europe's hippies and penniless students, sleeping on the beach, scrounging for food and cash to pay for drugs and drink. Fortunately, the authorities have cleaned the town and beach up today, but in the mid 1980s the picture was very different.

We decided to look for somewhere inland, for the quieter long stays we anticipated with retirement in mind. I wanted to fulfil an ambition of mine of constructing a Mediterranean garden, growing fruits, vegetables and flowers around some picturesque ancient house.

We toured the estate agents and scoured the property pages in the local paper, 'Nice Matin' and spent days visiting the outlying villages within an hour of the coast. Many of them were familiar from our numerous explorations. We found various properties but none of them had quite what we were looking for. One village kept coming up with a name which we did not recognise, Montauroux. We decided to find it.

Chapter Thirty-Four
Montauroux

Montauroux is one of the picturesque hilltop villages, just over the border of the Alpes Maritimes, in the Department of the Var. Twenty miles inland, north of Frejus, the village is perched on the northern edge of the Lac St Cassien, well known to any fishing addict for its amazing variety and size of freshwater fish particularly carp. It is also a haven for bird watchers with a large nature reserve and fish breeding area. We have watched the fish in the lake leaping, and they are indeed enormous.

The area has a magnificent micro-climate. Inland the pre-Alp slopes keep the dreaded north-westerly Mistral out of the sunny basin and we are protected from winter's easterly winds by the Esterel – a low range of hills between the village and coast below Cannes. Citrus and Bougainvillea, both sensitive to frost, thrive on the southerly facing slopes of the terraces, running down from the ancient village. On the less sheltered slopes are very old former olive groves.

But what most brings strangers to Montauroux is its scenery. We were stunned when we first came here with the expansive views, both across the Esterel to glimpse the sea and back towards the mountains, where the villages of Mons and St Cezaire seem to grow out of the rocks. How could one not fall in love with such a quiet and unspoilt Shangri-la, after the bustle and overcrowded, noisy and polluted Riviera? Yet it is only half an hour from Cannes and forty minutes from Nice Airport.

It was the summer of 1986 and we were already thinking about our life after Parliament. A holiday home in the quaint heart of Antibes was not where we wanted to spend more of our retirement and for the longer term; we decided to look for a place with some land. We were used to the rural quiet of the garden at Norcott, sitting out on the large lawn under our great arching lime tree. The house in Antibes had the added annoyance of having only one door to access it, leading straight in from the narrow street outside. Whoever and whatever came in and out was open to the inspection of the whole road. We wanted some privacy as well as peace and quiet. I also had an ambition, as a keen gardener, to accept the challenge of creating a Mediterranean garden.

We made an appointment with the only estate agent we could find in the area, nowadays there must be a dozen. Claud Chartroule was very friendly and we found, married to Joan a former British Olympic swimmer. We set out our price range, which after the high prices on the coast seemed to give plenty of scope, and we specified that we wanted something with character, an old stone building, secluded and with views. We did not want a modern villa on a "domaine" and it had to have some substantial land, but not be too far from the village. He had found eight properties to show us.

At that time the hilltop villages were only just beginning to be sought by foreigners or by the French working on the coast, anxious to enjoy a more rural life within easy commuting distance. There were plenty of older farm houses, needing restoration and modernisation and prices away from the Côte d'Azur flesh pots, were still reasonable. We had made our decision just in time, before demand and prices started to soar in what has become a prime international market.

We set off with Claud. The first of our eight viewings was a small stone 'bastide', the oldest building at the far end of a stony unmade-up lane, with fantastic and unspoilt views towards the Esterel lying between us and the coast. The old house was set in five acres of terraces on the slopes of a secluded valley with plenty of Mediterranean oaks, trees which had seeded themselves between what had been an olive grove. The boundary was the bed of a small stream, dry in the summer but turned into a torrent of waterfalls after the winter and spring rains.

The house was a small, fortified shepherd's hut, with two main rooms, the old bergerie downstairs with the metal rings on the walls to tether the sheep and goats and upstairs a place for the shepherd to sleep with the hay. The building had been very modestly converted for living in with the addition of bathroom and a small further bedroom downstairs. It had potential for enlargement without spoiling it.

With its massive beams, stone walls and large fireplace it was like a fairytale cottage. I looked at Hilary, she nodded to me. We did not say a word; we knew that this had to be it. The place was owned by a French couple, living in Nice. It was a tragic story. Until illness prevented him he had been an air traffic controller at Nice Airport and was suffering from cancer which was not responding to treatment, and he could no longer look after the place properly.

Claud told us that the house had only been on the market for two weeks and had been viewed by some German prospective house hunters, who were scheduled to return in September with an offer. Apart from that there were no other offers or buyers in prospect. He told us the asking price and without hesitation, I accepted. Claud was surprised. He immediately blustered "But what about the other seven places on the list to see?" Hilary said "But this is exactly what we are looking for. If I go to buy a hat and find the right one, I don't try on all the others in the shop!"

We became very good friends and he told us later how amazed he was. Never in his long estate agent career, had a client agreed the asking price instantly, without first going away and thinking about it and then putting in a lower bid. Nor could he recall anyone making such an instant decision. We also heard, after our offer was naturally accepted, that Claud had told friends, who later became mutual ones, how 'stupid' he thought we were, buying this tiny remote house, two miles from the village, without even bidding less than the asking price. I replied "But Claud, you told us some Germans were about to put their towels on the beach!"

The French owners had an amazing collection of antique Provencal furniture, chests of drawers, cupboards, tables, beds, chairs, artefacts and historic farming tools, ornamentally filling the house. Yokes for oxen, earthenware pots, pitchforks made from olive wood, wooden collars for the sheep to carry their bells, spits for roasting meat on the open fire which was the shepherd's 'kitchen' and much else.

The owners met us at the house. With his health deteriorating Monsieur Sayous offered us everything at a bargain price. Again we did not haggle. He told us after the transaction was completed, how much they had loved their week-end home, which they had restored themselves from a ruin and how sad they were to lose it. However, they had been thrilled to find us, seeing how much we loved it immediately and would look after it. It was so sad, we felt like crying.

Monsieur Sayous lived for over a year after we had bought their retreat. He never managed to come and see us again although we invited him. His wife did however, telephone us from time to time and Hilary would describe what was happening, whether the wild orchids on the terraces were blooming, the cherry blossom or the broom were flowering, to be relayed on to him. After he died we heard that his wife, Geraldine had committed suicide. A very sad tale.

We moved ourselves in soon afterwards, bringing up some things from Antibes to make ourselves comfortable. For some time we kept both French houses, renting out the Antibes house for holiday lets and to students from the University Science park at Sophia Antipolis. However, we eventually decided that keeping two places going at such a distance, when Parliamentary duties meant we could not spend much time supervising them, was too much of a strain, and by 1990 we had sold the house in Rue des Pecheurs to some Swedes.

Sadly, soon after we had moved ourselves into the old stone house in Montauroux, my mother-in-law, Ena, died of a heart attack. She was in her eighties and seemed to be full of energy still and she was very badly missed by us, especially our children. When Hilary and her brother Philip sold her cottage and had to empty it quickly, many of the oddments ended up coming down to France which perpetuated her memory. We spent what time we could in France, but it was still only during the holiday periods from the children's schools and universities and when Parliament let me get away.

We quickly put down roots, which was not difficult. Our lane had a very friendly community. The French made us really welcome. We soon learnt that, contrary to the myth that the French are formal and remote, they were quite the opposite, if you meet them half way by making it clear that you wish to join their community. Too many of the British with holiday homes or even domiciled in the South of France, live within their own set. Too few even try to grasp the language or join with the local life. No wonder they are shunned by the French residents. For us it was quite different. We found the French hospitable and welcoming, and very informal, within their established rules of etiquette. So you call on neighbours unannounced and uninvited, exchange garden produce, stay for a coffee or glass of chilled rosé, but not between noon and three pm, nor after six thirty unless invited. The rest of the day is open house.

On the other side of our lane we had an English couple living permanently. Pam Marks was a professional artist, an excellent water colourist, painting under the name of Pamela Kerr. Her husband Harry was a former guardsman and an excellent saxophonist. They took it upon themselves to make sure we were introduced to everyone in the area and in a short time we seemed to have as many friends as we had back in Britain. We have many of Pam's landscapes on our walls in both France and England and still, after over twenty years, we find them in houses all over the area although Pamela is long gone.

Thanks to Pamela and Harry Marks and Claud and Joan Chartroule's efforts to introduce us to the life in Provence, we were soon joining in lunches and dinners, hosted by our neighbours, so getting to meet an ever widening group of all nationalities. Inviting the French back for a formal meal was a little daunting at first, but we discovered how to impress and have our hospitality appreciated. Again contrary to the accepted contention, we found the French love British cuisine. They rarely have the opportunity to discover it properly. Overpriced fast food outlets in London are as much as many have experienced. Hilary prides herself in English home cooking and we would always bring Stilton and real farmhouse Cheddar from England. In later years, once we were able to be in France long enough to establish a proper vegetable garden, we could offer my own organic salads and vegetables. Hilary makes a mean steak and kidney pie, a combination that is unknown in French cuisine, as they eat steak and kidney, but never put them together in the one dish. Crumble was also unknown to the French, although now it appears in packet form on the supermarket shelf. Fruit crumble with proper custard 'crème anglaise' as they call it, is a favourite with the French, but their real love is for Christmas pudding, which seems surprisingly to have no equivalent in France. The ritual flambé, when I must admit to being a bit free with the brandy, always produces exclamations of admiration.

Our confidence to entertain French guests has grown over the years, so that we now even dare to invite back Jean-Pierre and Ghislane Phily, who run our favourite farm restaurant, where the authentic Provencal menu, made from home grown produce, is known for miles around. Ghislane once confessed to us that she is directly descended from the man who shot Lord Nelson, but she is nevertheless a great anglophile and speaks excellent English. In return for our invitations they invite us to their private party to commemorate the

Beaujolais Nouveau arrival. This is not widely celebrated in the heart of the Provence wine region, but is so by our restaurant friends because Jean-Pierre comes from the Beaujolais country.

Even after I had stood down from Parliament, we were not able to be in France for long periods. Hilary was a County Councillor for Hertfordshire, chairing a committee and I was still very involved with the work of the Utility Buyers' Forum, where we were producing a monthly newsletter. At least without the constituency work, Hilary and I were more flexible and we tried to get away for at least two weeks, four or five times a year, with the whole month of August. My confidence in subscribing as a founder shareholder in Eurotunnel began to pay off when we could travel through at £1 per time. We made our journeys down to the South and back, part of our holidays, exploring parts of France on our way and finding small hotels and restaurants. Our main criteria were not the quality of the bedroom but the standard of the food and we enjoyed many delicious meals.

From our early days in Antibes, we would listen to the local English language radio station, Riviera Radio, based in Monte Carlo. At the time it broadcast a mix of local news, the BBC World Service, useful information on living in France and of course, music. Our children liked the music, we preferred the news. Unfortunately, it was bought out later and now has very little proper news content and is mostly music. My life was enlivened when I was asked to broadcast once a week, giving a report of the British political scene.

The preparation of a light-hearted but informative 'Week in Westminster' was quite hard work, and I spent several hours preparing my fifteen minute soliloquy – a much less serious version of Alastair Cooke's "Letter from America" broadcasts.

I continued the ordeal even after I retired from Parliament in 1992, until eventually the whole format of Riviera Radio changed with its new owners. It made me a minor celebrity in the area, from Monaco to St Tropez. They only offered a token fee, but we did get to know many more people and enjoyed plenty of hospitality. Even some of my parliamentary colleagues contacted me after a stay in the South of France. "We heard your broadcast in Nice" Sir Michael Spicer once said to me. "Yes" I replied "but you would not have done it. They pay peanuts."

By the year 2000 our U.K. commitments were much less and we began to spend longer periods in France. A serious injury allowed me to experience the French health service. I had been starting to clear some of the trees from our lower terraces and strolling around I missed my footing and tripped over one of the steep dry-stone walls and crashed badly on my back. Trying to get up was too painful.

A distance below the house, I knew that nobody would hear me or find me and that Hilary would not start looking for me until I failed to come in for lunch, so I had to make my way up the steep terraces. I managed to turn over and crawled, slowly and painfully on all fours and got to the house. I laid myself flat on my back on the floor on some cushions, not wanting to move another muscle.

When Hilary returned from shopping in the village, she found me in a white faced condition, by this time unable to move. She could not move me on her own and sought help from our neighbours. She returned bringing with her Leon, one of our French neighbours who was a vet with a practice in Paris fortunately on holiday, and his son. He had brought his "vets' bag" with him and duly examined me and tested my reflexes. He advised us to go to hospital and we duly rang the pompiers, the French paramedics.

I was wheeled into the accident section at Grasse hospital and given a thorough examination, cardiogram, x-ray, blood tests and all. My back was clearly damaged, the question was how seriously? Against my protests – I have a fear of hospitals – the doctor insisted on keeping me in. Hilary pointed out that as I could not move and as she had no intention of taking me back home, I would have to stay. It was time for the evening meal, so with the true French concern for food, I was parked in a side ward and presented with my four course dinner – onion tart starter, boeuf wellington, some cheese and a glazed pear to finish.

I was delivered to a room with two beds, which seems to be the standard arrangement in French hospitals, with its own washroom and toilet, and put to bed with a drip to revive me. In spite of my meal, I was feeling pretty awful. Next morning the senior doctor came round and examined me. I was still prone. He was followed by the chef's assistant to get my choices for lunch – three courses and dinner +four+. When the meals arrived they were accompanied by a menu sheet on which was printed in French the Chef wishes you bon appétit. Such sentiments would be met with derision in a

British hospital. Anxious friends enquired if I had survived the night. I had obviously under-estimated my prospects of recovery, presumably to win sympathy. My Member of Parliament, Richard Page even offered to visit. As a fanatical half owner of a race horse, he must have been used to catastrophes, I believed I was about to become one.

Richard had overlapped my period at Westminster and was a minister in the Department of Trade and Industry under John Major, with special responsibility for promoting the Government's support programme for renewable energy. The Pages had stayed at our house in Antibes and after visiting us in Montauroux, they too had fallen in love with the area and had a villa built near us.

I told Richard, please do come and visit if I survive the third day. But no flowers, please. Bring wine, well disguised, as Grasse hospital is an alcohol free zone, which was doing nothing to help my recovery. He and his wife Madeleine spent some time carefully cleaning out an orange juice carton and filling it with the forbidden Côte de Provence.

When the doctor came to see me on the third morning, I asked how long I would be in bed, motionless on my back and when could I go home? The reply was as soon as I could get out of bed. So I moved and felt no pain. I sat up, still no pain. I got out of bed and managed to walk. It seemed like a miracle, except of course the doctor guessed I was no longer crippled. He knew from the x-rays the spasms in my vertebrae would have eased by day three. My next glass of Provence wine came from a bottle, not an orange carton.

I recall this experience because it confirmed my view that Britain's marvellous Health Service leaves a lot to be desired. The treatment I had in France was speedy and efficient and the service was three-star. For years afterwards Hilary has caused a laugh among friends by explaining that when I have an accident, she calls in the vet.

There was another consequence of this accident. We had been due to set off on our long drive home the following weekend, but in no way was I fit to drive or to sit for long periods in the car. As we had rented the house out, we asked a friend, Maria if she could accommodate us. We knew she had a spare bedroom on the ground floor, which would be suitable. We duly moved in at the end of the week and found ourselves overlooking her French neighbour's garden.

Danielle and Francois had a pair of Irish Terriers, and gazing at us through the fence were five adorable and comical puppies. It was love at first sight. We negotiated via Maria and soon found ourselves the prospective owners of Rocker, one of the five puppies. The French have a system of naming dogs and cats, rather as we used to do with cars, with a letter for the year of birth. So all five puppies had names beginning with R. We set in train the procedures for Rocker's rabies injection and blood tests and returned to England to nurse my back.

The six months wait before we could bring our new member into the family, was hard. But after five months we came to the August break when we were able to have him with us in Montauroux and then to go through the lengthy rigmarole of the checks at the Eurotunnel dog pound, run by our Ministry of Agriculture in France, before finally bringing Rocker home to England. This was in the days before each dog had a neat passport and we had to produce a sheaf of papers and fill in a lengthy form each time.

Our old Bearded Collie had died and he had been suffering from back problems, so I had not had much walking recently. All this changed with Rocker who had the Irish Terrier's energy and passion for walks and chasing scents. He also had the Irish Terrier's disregard for anything that resembled obedience training, although he was slightly more obedient if addressed in French. We found ourselves shouting "Viens ici!" in the English woods at Ashridge, much to the bemusement of fellow dog walkers. He would also do "Assis" if you held a suitable treat out for long enough.

The new animal passports were issued and at last all the paperwork was simplified. For three years we went through the Tunnel with the dog on our many regular trips down to Montauroux. He became a seasoned traveller and we discovered that France is very dog-friendly. Arriving on a hot day at a restaurant, the first item brought to the table, without being asked, is the bowl of water for the dog. All French dogs know exactly what to do in restaurants. After the people settle into their chairs; the dog goes and lies quietly under the table. There may be several dogs in a particular restaurant at a time, but none are visible. This does not apply to the "handbag dog" which seems to be quite a different species. They are privileged to travel free on the TGV while other real dogs are graded according to size, at one half or one quarter the child's fare. Rocker was a one quarter fare size.

Three years after we had been travelling back and forth through the Tunnel, we were suddenly brought up short at the dog immigration centre by an eagle-eyed, gauleiter, who pointed out an error in Rocker's passport and would not let him in to Britain. We argued for hours that he had been coming in and out for years and that he could not have rabies. But the rules evidently could not be broken. I had to return with the dog to the South of France, while Hilary was put on the ferry, without the car, burdened with as much luggage as she could manage to get herself across the Channel and up from Dover by rail.

Evidently the vet had done the taking of blood for the rabies test, before he had implanted the identity chip, or puce. Although Rocker was identified by a tattoo number in his ear, which had been noted when his blood was taken and was also on the papers for his microchip, this was not enough for our authorities to prove it was all the same dog. He had to have another blood sample taken to prove he was still resistant to rabies. We accepted this and with the proof of his test we tried to enter the UK again, but the British rules then insisted that even with a very high resistance shown, he would have to wait another six months in quarantine after a blood test, just in case he might develop rabies. Hilary took another ferry alone to the UK, but this time she hired a car from Dover.

I remained in France with Rocker and this was really the point at which I felt that I had left England and that France was to become my home. Sulkily I thought, if they don't want our dog they can't have us. But I have not regretted it yet.

Chapter Thirty-Five
Provence Ever After

My early years at Mediterranean gardening were fraught with a series of disasters. Living on the edge of the village, with wild woodland over our boundaries, my vegetable terraces, already suffering from drought, were invaded by a herd of wild boar. These are not pets. An adult sanglier will weigh as much as an overweight human. They leave no stone unturned and the result resembles an onslaught by bulldozers. The whole of my potagier was ransacked.

There was some consolation. Our valley contains some really dense undergrowth, so far not cleared for villa construction. We are favoured with a geological fault running through the valley rendering it unsuitable for building. As well as providing perfect cover for the nightingales, it is one of the remaining refuges for the sangliers. A local builder, Richard Laugier, who helped us enlarge our bastide, happened to be the president of the local boar hunt, a most prestigious position in this part of the world, some say second only to the mayor. To capture the sangliers, you need a team moving in from all sides of the valley, with dogs wearing bells around their necks, rooting through the undergrowth, flushing out the boars and baying. Our side of the valley is an essential point to cut off their escape.

One winter the hunt shot thirty, and that represented only a traditionally necessary culling. In return for allowing the hunt to close in from our side of the valley, we are included in the "share-out" and presented with one or two haunches. That was enough for our enormous New Year's Eve party, suitably marinated in the powerful red Provence wine and slowly cooked in a Provencal daube. Few of our friends turn down our invitations, as our wild boar daube is so much fuller of flavour than the farmed version. We are not exactly breaking the dictat of the European Union's food police, who have prohibited the sale of wild boar for fear of a health risk. The meat is rendered perfectly safe by being kept for some time in large freezers to kill off the worrying parasites. There is a black market and we earned our share, and did not buy it. Several local restaurants mysteriously have wild boar on the menu at certain times of the year, in the much tastier version.

My gardening efforts were also handicapped because the previous French owners of our terraces had not been optimistic enough to try and grow anything except grass for sheep and olive trees. For more than twenty five years I have been struggling to make the ground fertile and rich enough for tomatoes, courgettes, French beans and the rest, to say nothing of the flower beds I have tried to surround the house.

When we were still only managing to sneak the odd week in France, I spent hours hauling up sacks of leaf compost from underneath the oak trees in our valley, interspersed with hacking down the undergrowth, letting light once more on to our olive terraces. This activity was an excellent antidote to the sedentary life in Parliament and I am sure was excellent for my health, but it made for very slow progress with my gardening. Also the acute lack of water led to the loss of plants, in spite of our rigged up watering system. Hilary provoked amusement one year, when alarmed at the amount of time I was spending dragging up leaf mould from the woods, she presented me with a lorry load of well manured topsoil for my birthday present. Was she trying to tell me something? I was happy enough. Far better than another pair of socks.

The situation improved however, in more recent years, when we found a regular source of improver for the soil. I have imported at least two hundred large sacks of horse manure a year. One of our friends, Julia Lady Arbuthnot, liveries horses on her nearby farm. She calls me in despair every few weeks, begging me to remove enough so that she can open and shut the stable doors. I have now been collecting the stuff year after year, but I cannot understand why it has improved my soil so little. Hilary's view is that it might be because I keep expanding the area of cultivation. At least I have been able to tease Julia "I must be the only retired M.P. who shovels out stables. It's that miserly pension of ours!" "You should have stayed on a few years longer" she replies.

More recently retired colleagues seem to be doing much better in the pension and garden improvement stakes.

It is not only horse manure that we recycle from Julia's farm. Some years ago her much loved billy goat died. It was midwinter and her estate is a few miles inland and a bit of a frost pocket. She called me for help, would I hack out a grave. I replied persuading her that my terraces were frost free, and I had a very large compost heap. Billy could rest in peace there.

She agreed to bring Billy to our place, getting the help of a couple of lusty lads to carry him into her van and from our gate down to the "burial" place. Meanwhile Hilary and I had prepared for an appropriate funeral ceremony. Calling in a handful of our friends at short notice, we stood round the compost heap, the centre of which I had removed to make a substantial hole which was adorned with French and British flags. The mourners were each given a bucket of compost. Billy was reverently placed in the hollow and covered with the buckets full of soil.

For the last rites we had constructed a pedestal from where Hilary read solemnly from a book entitled "How to look after goats" – which did not however have a chapter on disposing of them. A bottle of champagne was then opened and we all drank our sorrows away. Poor Julia did not know whether to laugh or cry.

We soon learnt to admire Julia's amazing story of overcoming misfortune. She had come out to France after being widowed and bought a small farm, which she was carefully restoring. She was a member of a Lloyds Underwriting Syndicate, which risked open-ended liability as had Stock Exchange Membership for me. Her syndicate met a catastrophe and she found a large part of her investments vanished. Somehow she managed by sheer hard work to make her way and restore her fortune by running a guest house, catering for parties with her excellent cooking, servicing people's villas and continuing to breed the Staffordshire Bull Terriers for which she has gained an international reputation, winning prizes all round Europe. I regularly collect the manure from her stables, where she has horses at livery. I think it amuses her to have a former M.P. collecting the 'horse-shit', while I claim that the 'titled muck' produces excellent vegetables.

The most rewarding aspect of our retirement life in Provence has been our reconnection with our children. Now, also with our grandchildren, they visit us regularly and we spend special times together in a way I had to sacrifice during my time in Parliament. There were never enough opportunities to relax and enjoy each other's company. I often wonder if we would have had so many visits in recent years, if we were not living in such a delightful part of the world. What child cannot enjoy holidays here, skiing, swimming and so much else, even if it means having to put up with one's parents and grandparents?

Perhaps we have provided some compensation for our partial neglect to live together more as a family over the years. Each of our children has been given legally by us a quarter share of our French property, under the French law. Our children now own the roof and walls, while we retain the "usufruits" or "fruits of use" of the interior. Only the devious French could have come up with such a clever inheritance arrangement. We cannot sell the property, nor can our children evict us! It is not just our family that visit. Having embarked on building extensions over the years, we have added on a third and a fourth bedroom for guests. It sometimes feels as if we are running a hotel. However, when guests emerge from our past, where our only contact with them for decades has been the traditional exchange of Christmas cards, their surprise visits revive nostalgic, pleasurable memories.

I do not need to be reminded that the French know how to enjoy themselves. What strikes me though, is how pathetic it is that we, with our glorious history, cannot agree to declare a real national day, which can be widely celebrated as if we actually mean it, not just as an excuse for a day off.

Feasted everywhere and with enthusiasm, is Bastille Day, July 14th. The first year I really celebrated this, was when my youngest son, Julius, had been doing a holiday job working for the local farmers. When the two of us were invited by a French farming family, we realised we had really gained acceptance and "gone native". Our host's son met Julius and I in the village at noon, correctly fearing we would never find the party place, some miles away. The celebrations were as near a traditional peasant's party as I would ever experience. The delicious rough Provencal buffet lunch lasted until 4pm, with dancing in the farm courtyard. We seemed to be privileged as the only non-French invited. I wondered when it was time to go home, but the local wine continued to flow, as the conversation, joking, singing and laughter grew more raucous.

At five in the afternoon I decided it was time for a strategic withdrawal, while still on my two feet. Our hosts sounded offended. The party we were told, had only just started. I discovered they were right. Around seven in the evening reinforcements started to turn up. More farming friends arrived and other locals swelled the party, presumably having had to do a day's work locally first, even though it was a public holiday. By nine in the evening my stamina was beginning to weaken, but the scene was livening up. Lots of chains of coloured lights, a really magnificent "paysan" supper, some loud and jolly music and energetic dancing moved things forward. It was midnight before I escaped. I was assured by my son later that it all went on many more hours.

Soon after we had made our first extension to our house in Montauroux, we started to entertain guests and to invite the locals in for the inevitable aperitif. On the first occasion when we invited our French neighbours for drinks at the usual 'happy hour' on a Sunday evening, we learnt an important lesson. We had some old friends of ours staying with us and we had asked our French neighbours, who rented the house next door, to join us for drinks before we had our evening meal.

Many hours had passed since we had enjoyed our usual light salad lunch and Hilary and Shirley had prepared a large dinner for the four of us, which was in the oven. The visitors arrived and we provided drinks and nibbles. The party went well but the French guests showed no sign of leaving. When finally we got to 9 o'clock, we gave in to hunger and invited them to stay for a meal, which by this time was a trifle overdone. So in this way we learned about the French Sundays in Provence. If you invite French guests on a Sunday evening at drinks time, they expect to stay on, and do not think about leaving until after nine o'clock. On Sunday the main meal of the day is lunch, lasting from 12 noon until at least four in the afternoon and often until five or six. The evening meal is light, what is called an "aperitif dinatoire", with drinks and upmarket nibbles, the local dried sausage, homemade quiche or pâtés. Now we do Sunday lunch like the best of them, never less than four courses and rarely get up from the table before four o'clock, or we invite guests for drinks and expect them to stay until late.

Every French village has its festivals. The summer season is particularly crowded with events – concerts, dances, markets of all descriptions and sporting activities. We particularly enjoy our village "Aioli", celebrating St Bartholomew's feast day on the 24th of August. The village square is filled with long trestle tables and the local fete committee organises a fantastic community lunch.

The meal is traditional Provencal fare. After far too much pastis and "nibbles",comes a starter of a slice of pissaladier – a sort of olive pizza – or a slice of melon with ham, the main course is boiled salt cod, surrounded by generous portions of plain cooked vegetables. Baked potatoes, carrots, beetroot and french beans with a hard- boiled egg are accompanied with a large dish for each person of the aioli. Aioli for the uninitiated is a garlic mayonnaise, made by pounding fresh cloves of garlic, egg yolks and the local olive oil together. It took me some years to enjoy the strong garlic flavour, but Hilary relished it immediately.

Litre bottles of the local wine, from our Cote de Provence appellation region, are spaced liberally along the tables and refilled regularly. Tasty french bread, cheese and apple tart, plus a digestif, conclude the meal, when those that are able, take part in the dancing. Before all assemble at the tables, everyone mixing in, Monsieur le Maire invites us all to suitable aperitifs from a lengthy self service bar. It's his freebie, but we pay, not only in the local rates but also by having to suffer a long speech first. As the village festival is non-profit making, we pay all of €18 a head, everything included, as much wine as you like and second or even some manage third helpings of the food.

At our first village Aioli in 1987 we met our Norwegian friends. A regal looking couple, he in a suit and she wearing a vast flowery Ascot hat, were strolling along between the tables. We were all already seated except for them. They stood out, stopping at almost every place for a few words, as they seemed to know everybody. I said to Hilary "That must be the Mayoress". When they stopped, not having met us before, they introduced themselves. Each summer they stayed at their nearby villa, built like a Norwegian chalet, with their family for a few weeks. They spent most of August in Provence attending the many celebrations in the surrounding villages. They seemed incapable of missing out on any festival over a wide range of our area. We admired their enthusiasm and stamina. We joined up at many future village celebrations. It was after they became great friends that I explained why the English always laughed when they introduced themselves. Ingmar's English was excellent, having escaped from Norway and fought with the British navy during the war; his formal introduction of "I am Ingmar and this is my wife, she is Randy" was irresistible.

The village aioli is not the only part of the St Bartholomew festivities. Montauroux village was the site of the last battle of the wars of religion and where Henry IV's Constable of France, the Duc d'Epernon, defeated the Duke of Savoy. It was by all accounts a bloody battle which finished with the Duc d'Epernon hanging several of the opposition from the town battlements, the Duke of Savoy having escaped to Piedmont. The battlements were dismantled, apart from a few walls around an ancient chapel, so that unlike neighbouring villages, Montauroux does not have any fortifications.

We do, however, have a uniquely blood thirsty ceremony, which I am sure would not be approved of in Britain. Dressed in mediaeval costume, a band of men beating drums and followed by villagers with candle lanterns, go round the village into various houses looking for the Duc d'Epernon. When he is found he is dragged to the main square and hoisted up on a rope and burned suspended over a large bonfire, while the children hold hands and dance around. They do usually substitute an effigy for the burning. The whole affair is followed by a firework display, put on by the pompiers, who one year managed to set fire to a roof!

It is a slightly muddled up historical event, which I think came about at the Revolution as we end up singing the Marseillaise very heartily. The St Bartholomew's day mass in the church is always in Latin with parts sung in the Old Provencal dialect and followed by a strange dance around burning olive branches outside, with the Bravadeurs, the former militia, banging off ancient guns to the surprise of the local pigeons, not all of which survive.

Every spring on a Sunday, the flocks of sheep that have wintered on the valley pastures, join up for a ceremonial march of over sixty miles inland to the Pre-Alp summer pastures. The trail starts on the land of our local shepherd, M. Timeulian, where all the sheep are sheared and branded. Certain sheep, the leaders of the flock which have done the trip many times, are partially sheared leaving great pompoms of wool on their backs, which will be visible to the following sheep. Called the 'floucas' they also have large bells hung on wooden collars round their necks. After they are prepared they seem to realise their importance and sit apart quietly chewing cud.

We have a mini-festival, with sheep dogs working and lamb kebabs, before the transhumance starts on its first stage up into the centre of the village, with between one and a half to two thousand sheep, several dogs, a couple of donkeys and the shepherds all on foot. In the village they are helped along with a prayer from the village priest and a glass of wine from the Mayor, before setting off for their first stop for the night at "Caesar's camp", five or six kilometres up the road climbing towards Mons. The very small lambs are carried separately, some on the shepherds' shoulders and some in a small van the only concession to modern living, to be reunited with their mothers each night. Every evening, at a prearranged village on the way up to the mountain pastures there is a welcoming ceremony.

The transhumance is a very ancient tradition, probably dating from when the wild herds came down from the high pastures to get shelter in the valleys, and men domesticated and followed them. The shepherds say that the sheep which do this climb on the hoof are much stronger and fitter and have less problem lambing than those that are ferried around in the vast cattle trucks, with less time to adjust to the changes in altitude. The shepherds are certainly fitter.

The sheep return, around the time of the harvest festival. But there are of course many fewer of them as only the basic flock returns, the lambs having been sold in markets around in the pre-alps, famed for their meat. Such village festivities, going back into distant history make me realise how much we have lost in Britain, the price for becoming a more urban society and sacrificing so much of the real quality of life. The French too have become much more urbanised, enjoying a much higher standard of living than their peasant parents and grandparents. But they have become so without losing their quality of life or forgetting their roots.

Chapter Thirty-Six
Turning Native

Our area is splendid rambling country. With our Irish Terrier, we go for five to six hour ; 'randonées' around or above the lake, 'Lac St Cassien', down to the mini gorge in the woods beside us, with its Roman bridge and up to the other hill top villages. Other times we ramble through the woods, the dog following scents of wild boar and other exciting trails. In the autumn, after the rains have started again and broken the summer drought, the woods are full of edible mushrooms.

I recall one occasion, before I became confident enough to identify the 'eaters' from the poisonous variety, I was filling my basket with, what I believed were, beautiful ceps. But I was not sure that my collection contained those most sought after and tasty mushrooms. Coming towards me were an elderly couple, obviously French country people, carrying their covered basket. Who better to reassure me? I stopped as they came level with me and showed them my harvest. In my best French I asked them if my finds were good. She looked as I picked each one out and shook her head. One after the other I threw them on the ground, until my basket was empty. I thanked them for saving me from poisoning myself and murmured "quel domage" and walked on rather despondently. As the dog had not caught up with me, I turned round. I saw the wretched couple on their knees picking up each and every one of my mushrooms and placing them carefully in their basket.

November, December and January is olive harvest time. Most villages have a mill, the older ones with enormous heavy grinding wheels to crush the olives and presses to extract all the oil from them. The most desirable mill in our area is the one in the hill top village of Speracedes on the way to Grasse, which uses a centrifuge, getting a great yield of high quality oil. It also has a small unit beside it which converts the unwanted pith and stones into small bricks to burn in the local wood stoves.

Locals watch the weather carefully, rather like the wine growers. The main threat is from strong winds, as the olives quickly deteriorate once they have dropped from the tree. We join up with our neighbours, having managed to book a slot in the Speracedes mill's crowded diary, so that we can have enough olives for our own pressing and can control the quality. Giving ourselves about a week, we then start the competition to pick as many olives as possible before our appointment. We pick into large plastic boxes which measure two 'douvres', an ancient measure of roughly twelve kilos. In a good year we will pick more than 150 kilos from our terraces, which will be around seventy five hours work and will produce just over thirty litres of top quality oil, enough to last us a good two years in the kitchen, and allow us to supply our children and friends with a 'special' bottle.

The large perfect olives are hand-picked for eating. They have to be cured first by washing them with fresh water daily for ten days, and then soaked in a brine solution for about two months. Our area seems to produce very good flavoured olives and oil, although we go about the business in a very amateurish way and do not prune our trees to maximise production. Allowing for the labour and the payment to the mill, I have never deluded myself that we produce the most expensive olive oil in Provence.

It took us a long time to join the British Association of the Var. We were reluctant to admit that we had almost become domiciled and even longer to agree to join a 'Brits only clique'. However, as so many of our friends were from a wide range of countries and we had become integrated with our French neighbours, there seemed no threat of us becoming exclusively part of the British set.

We have found the organisation is widening our circle with the most interesting collection of exiles, from all walks of life. We now play our part in sponsoring one of their regular 'get-togethers', a country lunch. They do a very good job helping to give support to those in need, particularly with illness or bereavement, but also helping with translations, advice on such matters as registering cars and changes in the French law.

I must admit to being a very poor church goer. I leave that to Hilary, who is a regular attendee. A curiosity of Montauroux village is that this small place of some 5,000 population, in the middle of Provence, happens to have a thriving Anglican chapel attached to a house run by Jean and Cecile who belong to an Anglican order, the Community of the Glorious Ascension. On the first and third Sundays of the month they hold a service, such as you might find in any Parish Church. Their congregation is usually around twenty five to thirty people, which changes according to who happens to be around, so there are probably around fifty to sixty people associated with it.

Hilary first found Prasada one Easter when Cecile and Jean who run the large old house as a guest house, invited her to join the services in their chapel. Soon, although I do not come to the service, I was warmly welcomed to the 'bring and share' lunch afterwards. I walk down with our dog to join in. Unlike church services in Britain, there are no coffee and biscuits afterwards, only glasses of kir or champagne if it is somebody's birthday. The lunch is usually a delicious many course affair, with a wide selection of homemade dishes brought by the congregation. There is copious wine and fascinating conversation with most interesting people. We have retired diplomats, civil servants, journalists and several younger people working in the area. There are a number of clergy, who have retired to the sunshine, plus the clergy families who come for holidays at Prasada where the prices are very modest. I now have many priests and bishops among my acquaintances. We have expanded our list of friends enormously since finding Jean and Cecile.

We also see our children regularly, except our eldest Judith. To see her and our grandchildren we had to go to Australia as they have moved their life to the Gold Coast near Brisbane. They are making a successful fresh start following an acrimonious divorce.

Jessica, our artist, runs an expanding business with her husband Simon, "Festive Road". Organising and building carnival floats and figures, they stage events for local authorities and schools. They are building up an impressive reputation, winning recognition in various carnivals over the country. Jessica has been working with several local authorities helping to frame their promotional plans. The company specialises in making giant figures which glide along, leaving them with a problem of what to do with them afterwards. I believe she is still looking for a home for a giant shoe, which led the procession for Northampton's carnival. We have had to turn down the offer.

She has used her professional artistic talent to help make our parties in France such memorable events, both with the decorations and her undoubted talent for film making. Her variations on the "Big Brother House" and the M&S advertisements, - "this is not just . . . . etc." putting her parents into all sorts of embarrassing situations, have amused our guests.

Julius too has helped us build a reputation for providing entertainment at our festivities. He and his musician friends from Brighton, not only liven up our parties, they provide professionally organised shows. Julius is our technical boffin. When he is not keeping our computers going, he records and publishes several professional artists and works with different commercial clubs in Brighton. He has always written and composed songs, but in recent years this has become more professional. He also sings regularly with a choir.

Our eldest son, Bruno, is a fanatical cricketer. He plays for the M.C.C. – The Mountsorrell Cricket Club based in Melbourne in Derbyshire where Bruno, his wife Joanne and son Louis live, was at one time part of my constituency. He works in Nottingham running the public relations, business strategies side of Experian, the leading marketing and credit rating consultancy. Always eager to find an excuse to combine holidays with cricket, he cleverly decided to bring his cricketers to the South of France.

We were aware that there was at least one cricket ground in our area, we were however amazed to discover how many teams and other pitches there were. We were also surprised to discover that Ted Dexter, the celebrated cricketer was living in our commune. Bruno and his friend Phil Stanhope have organised an annual tour in Provence for the 'No Hope XI' over the Easter break. Hilary and I act as hosts, with rather basic accommodation and have assembled a supporters club. In recent times they have played against the Riviera Cricket Club, Entrecasteaux CC and the Mediterranean CC, with mixed results due no doubt to the difficulty in resisting the evening entertainment provided. I have acted as twelfth man and have had to revive my failing fielding skills, although they do not risk putting me in to bat. It would be pretentious to suggest that we have introduced cricket to the French. Although I understand there is the odd Frenchman now playing we did not see them, the opposing teams are British and Commonwealth exiles. But who knows?

Clearly, I could not claim that cricket once again became part of my life. But skiing did. While in Parliament my choice of enjoying the slopes was limited to a few days during the Christmas recess, competing against the Swiss Parliament. The days were the shortest in the year. The weather was the least friendly. Several seasons we were submerged in days of continuous blizzard at minus ten degrees centigrade, when only the bravest ventured out of the cosy, overheated mountain restaurants for very long.

After my retirement, it was easy to pick later weeks towards Easter, with still excellent snow and warm sun. What was even more exciting was to discover that our French home was less than an hour's drive to some reasonable runs and only two hours from international standard resorts. So we could go at short notice when the weather was fine and between school holidays, when the slopes were less crowded and safer.

Sometimes we even decided just to go for a full day's skiing, although mostly we book one of the many charming small hotels for a couple of nights. There is another bonus, the French treat us 'oldies' with more respect than we deserve. All the resorts offer discounts on the ski lift passes. Off-peak times are even free for the over 75s. They call us l'âge d'or, and I have certainly made the most of it every winter and hope to for a year or two yet. That is unless I have any more serious accidents.

Some years ago I was going up on one of those horrid 'dinner plate' lifts, which can castrate you if you are careless. It was the steepest lift in the resort and very icy. Ahead of me was my daughter Judith. She is an excellent skier, but lost concentration and allowed her skis to skid on the ice. They criss-crossed so she had to let go. Before I could pass by safely, she came tumbling down the slope, knocked me off the lift and we both started rolling down, crashing into one after the other of those coming up behind us.

Modern plastic style shiny ski-wear, does not grip well on iced up snow. The slope was steep. Before the lift stopped, a pile of bodies had rolled down to the bottom. Broken skis and bones, created a scene of devastation. One of the victims happened to be a doctor. Having discovered that Judith was not resident in France and that therefore an insurance claim could not be made, as his two children had their skis broken, he insisted on taking Judith to the nearest bank till to draw out enough cash to pay for the damage. On the journey back to the resort, he noticed at last that Judith had been injured. She had been keeping a very stoical silence, but there was blood trickling down into his car.

He took her to the first aid centre, where each resort has a full medical kit and gave her a thorough examination. Very carefully he stitched up the two large gashes in her legs and gave her a sedative. She was due to fly back to England that evening and she left with instructions to go immediately to a hospital for a check up. Meanwhile, I had broken my arm, without realising it, thinking it was only a bruise. The pain increased over the next few days, possibly because I insisted on finishing the gardening I had started, before I too left for the UK.

The story gets even more bizarre. Fortunately a friend was able to help drive my car back to the UK; this was before I became resident in France. When I got back, Hilary who had already seen the state Judith was in, with barely a gap between her bruises, marched me off to the local hospital, in spite of my protests that I was fine. The x-ray showed otherwise. I had broken my arm and was put into a plaster cast.

My wise daughter decided to check her household insurance. In France household insurance, which is compulsory, covers third party accidents. Because the accident happened in France, it appeared that Judith's insurance covered any claims. It was agreed that I would make a claim against her for the costs and damage of the whole exercise. I was not surprised that the insurance company was suspicious enough to pay me a visit, inspect my arm and my x-rays. They agreed to pay up.

This experience did not keep me off the slopes for long. At Val d'Allos we have an ancient village tucked in the mountains rising up to two thousand meters. It is surrounded by a huge range of modern, fast chair lifts and cable cars taking you up to the tops of runs to two thousand six hundred metres – as good as anything in Switzerland.

We now ski with friends, including Jean-Pierre the patron of our favourite farm restaurant. Before moving here from the Beaune region, he was a 'blood wagon' sledge driver at Val d'Isere. Injured bodies on the pistes are strapped and wrapped up and skilfully skied down for hospital treatment. To qualify for this work you have to be even better than a ski instructor, but going down with Jean-Pierre is a ski-lesson well ahead of my standard. We start at the top, "Now I will go slowly" he says. Just when I feel encouraged to follow, after fifty meters he forgets his promise and 'schusses' off down leaving me standing in admiration.

I recall one occasion at Allos, when we were skiing with our friends. The weather had not been too good and the visibility was getting poorer. The six of us arrived at the topmost run. We were in a fog and snow blizzard. Hilary and Sandie decided wisely to take the cable car back down. Jean-Pierre, as usual, set off in front with his wife Ghislane following, I came next with Geoff, Sandie's husband, fortunately following me. After a very short distance the two in front had disappeared into the mist and I was left facing a white blanket. I missed the run and came over the edge of a ridge, fortunately seen by Geoff. He managed with some difficulty to haul me up from my precarious position. I could not have managed it without his help. Some days later on retracing the run in beautiful sunshine, I was horrified to discover that I had been perched at the top of a huge precipice. I still shudder at the thought of what could have happened that day. To Hilary's relief I have given up skiing in blizzards.

Another bonus from using our house as a base for such good ski resorts so near, is that we can be back at our place for our evenings. After a hard day on the pistes, the best treatment is a sauna to prevent stiffness, and a glass or two of Provence wine to ease the aches. I have a sauna fitted in our French home and I learnt early in life what a wonderful relaxer and reviver it is.

Every time I indulge, I recall my first sauna. It was such a terrifying experience; I have surprised myself that I ever dared to have another. When on a student visit to Finland, I walked round Helsinki on a freezing winter afternoon. Slushy, wet snow was falling heavily and what little daylight is available at that time of year was already fading. No wonder, I thought, the Finns survive their miserable winters in saunas.

I was given directions to the city's public baths, had my swim and proceeded, tentatively to the sauna suite. It was a treat to feel warm for the first time that day. Chatting to a Finnish addict, he told me my next stage was a massage. Nervously, I took his advice and moved myself, wrapped in a towel, to the massage parlour. No sooner had I ventured towards an enormous marble table than a huge, beefy woman grabbed hold of me and slammed me on the massage block. She was twice my size and weight. I did not stand a chance of resisting as she pulled off my protective towel and started to pummel me so hard I thought my bones were breaking. It was not hard to believe that she was getting more of a thrill than me.

It was a long time before I dared to go near any public sauna again. The opportunity to overcome my timidity came on a trip to Sweden. We had become friends with a family in Stockholm, who had a holiday chalet on the edge of one of the forest lakes surrounding the capital. Hilary and I were taken there for a weekend and I was given the opportunity to see at first hand if the Swedes really do jump from their saunas directly into the adjoining freezing lake, as is rumoured.

The pinewood sauna chalet was beautifully equipped, lacking only the usual shower facility. Our host did not need one. He confirmed my worst fears. Boiling hot from 80 Centigrade, he ran stark naked out of the hut and down a track along a jetty, straight into the freezing water. I was expected to follow and would have been shamed not to do so. It was not my idea of an enjoyable experience and I feared such reckless activity would precipitate a heart attack. Hilary rather smugly claims that it was not nearly as traumatic as the icy cold tub she was induced to try by one of the Members of the German Bundestag, at a ladies only session in the sauna, during one of our Parliamentary visits.

It was on a visit to Cyprus that I experienced an oriental Turkish bath, for the first and last time. Very close to the horrid, misnamed, 'green line' wall, dividing the Greek side of Nicosia from the Turkish side was an ancient bath house. With its domes, it looked more like a Muslim mosque. I was told western tourists do not go in there. Such a challenge was too hard to resist and I ventured in. It was a memorable experience.

Squatting all over the place on a cavernous underground heated tiled floor, were groups of very Arab looking men. There was no separate steam room; the whole place was a hot house. However, the temperature seemed only a little higher than a normal hot day in the Middle East. I was surprised how long it took to work up any perspiration, which is the purpose of a Turkish bath.

Many of the other occupants were either playing gambling games in little groups sitting on the floor, others seemed to be picnicking, having brought baskets of food and drink. The lower temperature than I was expecting, was explained by the traditional behaviour. Instead of a concentrated half hour in a Western sauna or Turkish bath, the pattern here seemed to be more or less a full day's occupation. Having a day off, appeared to be spent leisurely socialising in the city baths.

I survived, having been the subject of many expressions of surprise, as if I were intruding on a private party. But I was relieved that I was not subjected to any improper approaches. That is more than I can claim from other experiences in less discrete establishments in New York, London and Paris. I was met on my final exit from the baths, by a very worried Hilary. She had spent some time looking around the shops and exploring Nicosia, only to find that I had still not emerged. Sitting herself down outside to wait, she said was most uncomfortable, as it was obviously not the place for a respectable Western woman to be seen, haunting the Turkish baths. By the time I came out she was on the point of sending for the police in case I had been kidnapped.

But back to Montauroux and France. I have often asked myself why has it been easier and more pleasant to put down roots and feel at ease in a foreign country, than we expected? There are plenty of stories about disillusioned exiles, with some even returning home. In our experience such unhappy emigrants were never prepared to commit themselves to make the necessary adjustments. Transforming at a later stage, one's original holiday second home into a principal retirement residence, involves a decision and commitment to move on.

It requires determination to learn the new language, adjust to a different way of life, meet its citizens half-way and avoid living in a cliquish British ghetto abroad. That has not been difficult for us, as we did not fall into the mistake of a sudden disruptive choice. We moved ourselves slowly in stages over several years. It allowed us to acclimatise ourselves into a new social environment. I sum it up, on reflection, with a simple explanation. We, like many others, have looked for and discovered a way of life that we were no longer able to find or enjoy in today's Britain.

Chapter Thirty-Seven
Back to my Roots

Over the years, I have returned to Germany many times, mostly to Frankfurt and the Rhineland. After the war my mother and her sister Tillo, who had always been very close, resumed their normal contact. My elderly grandmother, Oma, who had always had a soft spot for me, was able to meet Hilary and my two elder children, whom she spoiled. My aunt Tillo, who had had a fourth child, Ulrike, much later, was most welcoming and we would stay with her and my grandmother on our way to and from our regular skiing holidays in Davos.

However, although I still had a good rapport with my cousin Hannelore, who was the nearest in age to me, I never felt at ease with either of her brothers, Gunther and August. They were polite but distant. Their lengthy indoctrination growing up in Nazi Germany had obviously had its effect and it was only in much later life that I came to be at ease in August's company. This certainly came about with his change in attitude towards me when he heard I had been awarded the Verdienst Kreutz.

Neither of my cousins, several years my senior, would ever discuss the past with me. We talked about our present lives and the future. But there seemed to be a hang-up about referring to their wartime life. My explanation is that there existed a deeply engrained guilt complex. They must have realised how misguided they were to become brainwashed by Nazism and wanted to forget their involvement and the money they must have made from converting their factory to military hardware production.

August's son Ronald came to live with us at Norcott while I was still stockbroking and he worked for two years with me as an assistant, before returning to Germany speaking excellent English and almost Anglicized. He has built up a successful interior design company in Munich. We have regular contact with him in the South of France and he never concealed to us his disjointed relationship with his father.

Hannelore was married to a heart specialist, with a daughter Andrea, the same age as my eldest daughter, Judith. After she was widowed, she took up sculpture. She and my youngest daughter Jessica, also a sculptor, had a combined exhibition in Munich, 'Kindred Roots', illustrating the coming together of the family after the wreckage of war. One of the pieces Jessica showed was a life-sized representation of my sister Margie as a refugee. 'Effie' as the piece was called is now part of the Open University's course on Art and War, featured next to Picasso's Guernica. Andrea's children and Jessica's two boys now know each other, like any normal family. As if the disruption of conflict had never happened.

I did not return to Berlin until after I had been elected to Parliament. Some Germans in Berlin told me they could never forgive the British and American forces for deliberately slowing their advance into the capital, despite feeble resistance from what was left of the German army. A sick and exhausted Roosevelt felt obliged to meet Stalin's demand for a symbolic meeting of all the Allies in Berlin. Churchill wished to press on before the Red Army reached Berlin, but was out manoeuvred. He correctly predicted and feared the Iron Curtain.

It was in 1985 and I was on a ten day Parliamentary visit to the German Democratic Republic (GDR). It did not take me long to see the consequences of that fateful conclusion to the defeat of Hitler. One could understand why so many East Germans felt betrayed. Having suffered a decade of Nazi oppression and witnessing the destruction of Berlin, they were not liberated but subjected to forty years of imprisonment by a brutal regime.

It still amazes me that the East German authorities were so eager to invite British Parliamentarians to see their good works. I was selected as one of the six to accept an invitation to see the GDR 'paradise'. Was it pride at what little reconstruction they had achieved and how living standards had been modestly raised by the Communist regime? Or was it naivety, not realising how blatantly obvious was the contrast with the West for all to see, particularly to someone like myself who knew Germany so well.

It was still several years before the head of state, Eric Honecker, had to accept failure in the shape of the rising flood of humanity demanding freedom. When we were there, the Wall was still intact and reinforced, with the population locked behind it – those that had not escaped, been shot trying to escape or who had not been 'exchanged' for cash with West Germany. We had welcomed one young East German to our home, seventeen year old Thomas Mann, who had been in prison for writing derogatory remarks about the GDR. He had been 'bought' from jail by West Germany and came to improve his English with us. He spent a week at Westminster School with my eldest son, Bruno. The contrast with his previous life must have been amazing.

The disparity between the two sides of the Wall was striking. We were shown modern new high-rise housing, but I managed to explore the many slums remaining all around. We were shown new department stores, but not many other shops had anything much to sell. The Wall, we were told, was to protect East German citizens from being corrupted and exploited by capitalist gangsters. East Germans told me they would not mind a share of the gangsters' prosperity.

It was not only the drabness of the buildings that shocked me, with the pot holes from the bullet and shell fire still devastating their facades four decades after the ceasefire; it was also the dowdy attire. East Berliners could see the other side of the Wall was bustling with prosperous shoppers, spoiled for choice. Traffic jams caused by too many new brightly coloured BMWs, Mercedes and Volkswagens contrasted the almost empty East Berlin streets, with just a few 'brabbies' polluting the air as they spluttered and rattled around.

Observant visitors detected, as I did, a tense, uneasy and stressed atmosphere. East Berlin seemed to be crowded with sinister-looking large-jawed dark-suited types looking like retired heavyweight boxers. I could identify the regular Stasi, as could every East German, so feeble was their disguise, perhaps intentionally. However, it was not only the large number of secret police observing everybody everywhere, they were obvious to spot. What really created the atmosphere of fear were the many informers. They were easily camouflaged as citizens, but sneaking on each other, brother betraying brother and son reporting father as a dangerous dissident. It was the palpable undercurrent of anxiety and distrust that undermined the harmonious society.

We were taken up the Fernsehturm (television tower) built at Alexanderplatz in the 1960s as a symbol of the GDR's triumphant reconstruction of war torn Berlin. A rotating restaurant, at the top of the popular observation tower, was crowded. It was a poignant experience for me to observe the many young couples filling every table in the evening, ordering coffee and patiently sitting there for hours. When every half hour, the restaurant rotated to overlook the West, elated conversation and gasps of excitement were heard, as the youngsters longingly observed the bright lights in the part of the city they had never been allowed to enter. Then once again the dull, gloomy East reappeared.

These were the young generation that finally, bravely challenged the armed police and border guards with direct action in the streets, breaking through the check-points and finally tearing down the Wall. Observing them, and later talking to some of the students, it was ominously clear to me that they would eventually take risks with their lives and fight for freedom.

It was notable how nervous the authorities were already in the mid eighties, as opposition became more vocal and challenging. Our hosts asked us what we would particularly like to see during our stay in Berlin. I had two requests, to visit the University and spend an evening in a popular 'Bier Stube'. The first request was conveniently overlooked. I asked the next day what arrangements were in hand. Still no clear reply. After another enquiry, I was told that the University was in recess, but they could arrange for me to tour the campus, even though all the students would be on vacation. I did not believe this and my suspicions were confirmed when the visit was arranged on a Sunday morning! Two or three professors were recruited to show me around, but I was hardly surprised that there were no students for me to meet. Eventually we entered a lecture room, where a small handful of students awaited us. Needless to say they were loyal Marxists, entrusted to cope safely with my inquisitive questioning.

Not willing to be so easily diverted from talking to students about life in the GDR, I looked forward to my other request – a drink in one of the many bars which were still open for business in East Berlin. This surely would allow me to meet up with some of the young Berliners. But it was not without difficulties. Our hosts had carefully planned the event. A large table had been reserved for our visit and only our guide hosts sat with us. I could see several secret police types placed around at the nearby tables. Clearly my 'socialising' experience was to be confined to our table, without any students.

It would have required a blatantly obvious move of insurrection for me to leave our group and move myself, uninvited, to another table where I could see a group of young people enjoying a boisterous conversation. Much to the discomfort of our minders, I did just that. Suddenly the group I joined became hushed. I introduced myself and asked if they felt free and safe enough to talk to me. Two of them consented, the others were clearly too fearful, recognising the place was stuffed with Stasi. After a few minutes of some frank exchanges, they all relaxed enough, let their hair down and told me what they thought about their lives and prospects of a less restrictive political regime. They all seemed to have contacts in the West and expressed the hope that we in the west would continue our efforts to bring about a reunited Germany. I learnt a great deal about their captive existence. They were University students and I hope that my contact had not brought them into danger.

Our special residence, reserved for guests of the GDR, was luxurious and well guarded by the police. Presumably they were not there only to ensure our safety, but to observe any of our delegation venturing out to explore parts of Berlin. As the only native German speaker of our group, I spent all my free time doing just that. I have no doubt my wanderings were well followed.

Near the residence was a public park with large areas of allotment style private gardens adjacent. Continental garden plots are much more elaborate than in Britain. With the large number of flats and few houses with gardens attached, they are more like week-end hideaways, with small summer houses and facilities for spending a day in deck chairs picnicking. This was how Berliners spent much of their spare time in leisurely relaxation, as well as gardening and growing vegetables. I invited myself to chat with several such families. For many it was their only way to escape from the drabness of their lives. No doubt those who spoke to me were suitably interviewed afterwards.

I could not predict that four years after my visit, the whole edifice would collapse in an historic night of Wagnerian drama, when mass passive resistance became a triumphant celebration of freedom over captivity. But I could see that it would, sooner or later.

There were other depressing experiences. We were taken to the GDR Parliament, the Volkskammer. A specially-selected group showed us round. We had a little debate, when we were educated about their democratic system. I had the courage to ask why none of our group of host parliamentarians represented an opposition party. There is no opposition, I was firmly told. So there was no need for more than one party, added the spokesman. So why do you have General Elections, was my next and last, cheeky question. I do not recall hearing a reply. We moved on, but I could not resist thinking how much easier our life as British politicians would be if the same 'harmonious' system were accepted.

My next visit to my place of birth could not have been more of a contrast. It was three years after the Wall had been torn down and East Berlin was, correctly, described as the biggest building site in the world.

We were accepting the generous gesture of the City of Berlin's elders, offered to all refugees who had started their school years in Berlin before the war. As some sort of token of reconciliation and perhaps compensation for the past, such pre-war children were invited back, with their spouses, for a week's hospitality, all expenses paid. Hilary and I joined up with our friends, Wilfrid and Shirley Rodwell; she was British but Wilfrid, a year or two older than me, was a Berliner. We were splendidly accommodated in the East Berlin Hilton, given theatre and concert tickets, guided tours and even some pocket money. Most of the week was leisure time for us to explore.

Berlin is a fascinating mixture of architecture, a sort of architects dream and more buildings were going up around us. However, we could still find parts in the old East Berlin which resembled the film sets of the 1930s alongside the 'brutalist' architecture of Honecker's communist regime. We spent hours just wandering around, finding disused underground stations, riding on the U-Bahn, which used to be my 'treat' as a child and generally looking in amazement at the activity all around us.

Even after three years of frantic reconstruction, much of today's rebuilt Berlin was still then a building site. We found the remains of Potsdamerplatz; just a circle of roads and a few buildings selling souvenirs next to the vast empty swathe which had been the Wall and its death strip. There was a circus installed on the sandy strip and beyond we were directed to the remains of the Führer's bunker, a sandy hump. We climbed to the top, but did not remain long, observed as we were by several unsavoury looking young men, who appeared to be guarding their hero's last known resting place.

I had an interesting experience which underlined for me the essence of the difference between East and West. We were in Alexanderplatz by the Red

'Rotehaus', the old Berlin Town Hall in the former Eastern part. There were some stalls selling fruit and vegetables, and as I am known not to be able to go very long without my daily dose of apples, we queued up to buy some. Unfortunately, when I got to the head of the queue, the electronic weighing machine on the stall stopped working. Sorry, I was told, she could not serve me without the apples being weighed. I offered to pay well over the odds for my five apples, but she was adamant, she could not take responsibility for doing a 'deal' with me. I went without my apples. I could not imagine any other western market stall where the trader would not have accepted my generous offer, but this was the attitude of mind which had been instilled into a whole population and was so ingrained after so many years.

One of my outstanding memories was the Sunday morning's enormous 'flea market', a mile long straddling the East West divide. Many of the stalls were run by East Berliners selling their less essential possessions, to raise Deutschmarks. Most of the buyers seemed to be West Berliners or foreigners like ourselves.

It was pathetic to see the piles of antique silver, glass and porcelain as well as 'bric-a-brac' kept throughout the Communist occupation, but now needing to be sacrificed. I procured a pair of shoes for five marks. They were the finest shoes I have ever possessed, handmade in best leather, they would have cost two or three hundred pounds in Bond Street or Knightsbridge. We also bought a fine set of hand blown wine glasses, and from a small stall on the edge of the market, we acquired a Russian soldier's cap. The Russians had been left in limbo when the Wall fell, and had been reduced to selling their uniforms to get money to live on.

We exhausted ourselves revelling in the sight of the rebirth of a reunited, free Berlin. I was not the only tourist returning "home", who picked up a piece of the Wall from amongst the debris, one of my treasures. I was not the only refugee from Berlin, returning to celebrate what looked like becoming a new and happier era. I recalled what Eric Honecker had boasted, "The Wall will last a hundred years" and recalled too an earlier boast that the "Third Reich will last a thousand years." Like the Berliners, I was joyful to have outlived both nightmares.

Chapter Thirty-Eight
On the Couch

It was not easy to find friends frank enough to say what they truly think of what I have written about my life.

Stacey Bouvier did. An avid reader, she begged me to let her see my story. Her reaction was how did I find the courage to expose so much of my private life to the outside world? My reply was to suggest that no biography is honest unless it reveals the more private side of your life and personality.

A totally different reaction came from Robyn and Michael Weigall. They are well respected for their work transferring contemporary historical writing into radio and TV documentaries. Praising my effort as a 'page turner', I was shocked to be asked "but what are you hiding?" "Nothing consciously" I replied.

It was clear I was about to be psychoanalysed. Robyn's perceptive 'sixth sense' was not prepared to accept my answer. "Freud would have got you on the couch and probed you in a penetrating manner, right back to the beginnings!" was her next stab.

I gave it considerable thought through a restless night. If Robyn believed I was hiding something, I needed to face up to it, as it was subconscious. The answer began to emerge once I decided to unearth it. I could do it without Freud's help. The key question I did not seem to want to think about, was why did my political career grind to a premature halt, when many friends and family thought I was destined for higher achievement?

It would be easy to answer that it started from the unjust and damaging accusation of improper behaviour made by an undemocratic, secretive group of ageing grandees, members of the Stock Exchange Council. Their false and unfair charge was spread by the media, and tainted my career from the start, as a 'bit of a dishonest rogue'. Without a proper right of defence, the widely read biography of M.Ps published by Andrew Roth referred to me mischievously as one who 'cuts corners'. Private Eye also published a false and nasty piece.

While that relatively minor squabble with the Stock Exchange Council, grossly and inaccurately exaggerated, did indeed damage my prospects, it cannot be excused as a full explanation. After all, many well known highly successful people in public life have overcome unjust punishment. Jeffrey Archer comes to mind as a contemporary example.

A reply to Robyn's piercing question required a deeper and more penetrating analysis. I was not really ambitious enough. There was always more in my life I believed, than the sort of fanatical ruthless drive that is required by those who reach the top or their full potential. I rather regarded the election to Parliament as sufficient fulfilment in itself, rather than just a first step, as many of my more ambitious colleagues looked on it.

That may still not be the full answer. I have to dig deeper into my earlier upbringing. I never learnt the rules of the 'Old Boys' Network', nor ever participated, except at the fringes. This is where my public school educated associates scored. I never accepted that talent was not always as important as 'who you know' and who likes you. I was brought up to believe that people would automatically recognise your ability, intelligence and qualifications. I assumed one should not need too much self-promotion, lifts up from old school mates, club friends and Masonic contacts. I had some of these and indeed mixed with many of the most senior politicians, as these writings have recorded. But I have never learned the art of asking for help or expecting it. Indeed, I mistook friendly socialising with people of influence as 'boot-licking' and regarded it as undesirable pushiness. Perhaps, deep down I also had the outsider's fear of failure and possible rejection that held me back from full participation.

So we rarely entertained those who would probably have found us quite nice and suitable to join the club, if only I had given them the opportunity to know us socially. Hilary and I certainly had the opportunity to entertain informally all sorts of top politicians, those with influence and those on the way up. We had enough income to maintain a home with a fascinating history, mentioned in the memoirs of famous politicians. A marvellous base for those one wanted to impress. On reflection, we did not make sufficient of our opportunities.

To put it another way, I was handicapped with too German a characteristic. I took life too seriously and separated my working career side from my social life, instead of blending them as I learnt to do and enjoy in my later years. I believed that to do justice to my work as an M.P., it was irresponsible to think about enjoying too much of a private life. I gave up many of my regular non-political activities, such as the Masonic lodge, my cricket and tennis clubs and the City Livery and did not try hard enough to replace them with a social life in the Westminster village. If you asked some of my contemporaries in Parliament, I suspect they would suggest that I was a bit of a recluse, spending more time working in the House of Commons library than enjoying too many jolly hours in the Members' dining rooms and bars.

Plenty of my contemporaries reached the highest achievement without a privileged background. They more than compensated for such disadvantages with a single-minded determination, a resolute ambition to overcome such handicaps. My problem was that I did not fall into either category. I had some privileges and some ambition, but perhaps not enough of either or both. Nor perhaps did I go out of my way enough to help others. Mutual back-scratching has never been my style and I have always been very wary of those who self-promote themselves as distasteful.

Because I regarded my work as an M.P. more important than socialising, I found it difficult to integrate with those who did not. And finally, I have always believed that one is recognised for one's ability in the end and naively assumed that in life one gets one's deserts according to what one contributes. I know now that this is untrue. It is an illusion, a self-deception and I failed to discover it early enough. Perhaps Robyn and Michael will regard this as honest an answer I can give, to what I was 'hiding'.

Appendix

Extracts of proceedings in Parliament from 'Hansard'

Maiden Speech - Rolls Royce   23rd November 1970

It cannot be often that a new Member is given the opportunity to intervene for the first time in a debate of such importance on a subject so directly affecting his own constituency. South-East Derbyshire is Rolls-Royce country. Many thousands of my constituents depend for their livelihood upon the prosperity of Rolls-Royce, not only through direct employment but through sub-contracting industries and the service industries.

I am intervening in this debate because I believe that it is time someone spoke up for Rolls-Royce. I have listened patiently to a number of hon. Members opening their remarks by saying that of course they support Rolls-Royce—and then they went on to devote the rest of their address to tearing the company to pieces. In South-East Derbyshire we are justly proud of Rolls-Royce. ...... I do not regard kicking an organisation when it is down as a particularly endearing or particularly British characteristic. I urge the House to consider ceasing from this activity .... Knocking the British aero-engine industry is entirely unjust. It has a world-wide reputation for technological achievement. It has met overseas contractual obligations with honour in the face of extreme difficulties and even financial loss. That is not something to be criticised. The eventual rewards which some such commercial risk brings is well accepted in this country.

Those critics of the Government's policy should ask themselves whether they would be sitting in this House today had it not been for Rolls-Royce in 1940. We undoubtedly owe our salvation to that brilliant team, the saviours of Western civilisation in a time of great crisis. I challenge those critics to stand up in this House and say that there may never come a time when this country will again depend upon Rolls-Royce for its future survival, will never again depend upon the skills of those who now work on the thresholds of advanced aero-space technology.

... I endorse the future prosperity of this industry by supporting the BAC311 project, which is essential if we are to have an airframe industry in this country into which we can put British engines. I also endorse and congratulate the achievements of the Tristar RB211 development. .... an incalculable symbol of Britain's inventive genius.

On School Meals 10th June 1971 *Mr. Rost* : Does not my right hon. Friend feel that it would be appropriate to remind the Opposition and the country that it is not the State's responsibility to feed children, that her resources in the education service should be concentrated on improving educational facilities, and that if parents are not prepared to ensure that their children are properly fed, they are not fit to be parents and should not have children?

Mrs. Thatcher (Minister for Education) : I believe that most mothers in this country are fully capable of looking after the nutritional requirements of their children.

Mr. Swain: The hon. Member for Derbyshire, South-East (Mr. Rost) wants to go into his constituency and say that on the public platform. His constituents would lynch him.

Extracts from his first speech (March 10th 1972) on national fuel policy, CHP,energy issues, including energy conservation. (Comments - *Eric Varley*: "The most tolerant and liberal speech since he came into the House" - *Joseph Harper*. "Best speech from the Government side.")

Peter Rost ..... I am interested in the one field of technology which has now become a practicality, whereby one can generate electricity on site in a far more economical way than has hitherto been possible through total energy installations. ..... this development, which is already extremely successful in other areas of the world...

The point about total energy on-site generation is that it is not just an installation which provides electricity in the way that one has an auxiliary supply in this building ..... A total energy installation provides all the different energy requirements of a building or an industrial complex (lighting, power, heating, refrigeration, air conditioning, process steam, hydraulic power and whatever else is needed) all supplied on plant from one input fuel with an overall efficiency which can be up to 80% compared with 35% through the grid system. This is why I believe that we must in future think more along the lines of converting our energy more efficiently because it has become a practicality....It is not only more economical for the consumer, but it reduces pollution and conserves ... hydrocarbon resources with which we have been endowed.

Parliamentary Questions and points:

16th February 1984 – Is my right hon. Friend aware that the only action taken by Derbyshire county council has been to set up a so-called nuclear-free zone? Are not my constituents in towns like Ilkeston and Long Eaton right to be concerned at this disgraceful dereliction of the responsibility of a local authority to prepare for even simple emergencies, nuclear or non-nuclear?

13th March 1984 – Will the Prime Minister today send a message to Mr. Arthur Scargill reminding him that, although he may be a Marxist, we live in a democracy where those who do not wish to join a suicidal strike should be given the opportunity to say so through the ballot box, rather than be coerced, intimidated and bullied by mobs of flying pickets?

22nd October 1984 – As pits are being geologically damaged beyond repair, and markets lost, is it not clear that the NUM leadership is implementing its own pit closure programme and butchering the industry by causing the loss of thousands of jobs which might not otherwise have been lost?

From the Front Bench 28th of July 1974 – I declare an interest which is well known to the House. I am the director of two small companies giving advice on energy issues. But I have a much more important interest to declare, more relevant to the subject of energy conservation. It is that I am a member of the human race and have four small children.

Eng 141